06/18

D1524498

100 Greatest American and British Animated Films

OTHER ROWMAN & LITTLEFIELD BOOKS BY THOMAS S. HISCHAK

Boy Loses Girl: Broadway's Librettists
The Disney Song Encyclopedia, with Mark A. Robinson
The Encyclopedia of Film Composers
Enter the Players: New York Actors in the Twentieth Century
Enter the Playmakers: Directors and Choreographers on the New York Stage
The Jerome Kern Encyclopedia
1939: Hollywood's Greatest Year
Noel, Tallulah, Cole and Me: A Memoir of Broadway's Golden Age by John C. Wilson,
   co-edited with Jack Macauley
The Off Broadway Musical Since 1919: The Greenwich Village Follies to The Toxic
   Avenger
The 100 Greatest American Plays
Theatre as Human Action
Through the Screen Door: What Happened to the Broadway Musical When It Went to
   Hollywood

100 Greatest American and British Animated Films

Thomas S. Hischak

ROWMAN & LITTLEFIELD
Lanham • Boulder • New York • London

Published by Rowman & Littlefield
An imprint of The Rowman & Littlefield Publishing Group, Inc.
4501 Forbes Boulevard, Suite 200, Lanham, Maryland 20706
www.rowman.com

Unit A, Whitacre Mews, 26-34 Stannary Street, London SE11 4AB

British Library Cataloguing in Publication Information Available

Library of Congress Cataloging-in-Publication Data Available

ISBN 9781538105689 (hardback : alk. paper) | ISBN 9781538105696 (electronic)

∞™ The paper used in this publication meets the minimum requirements of
American National Standard for Information Sciences—Permanence of Paper
for Printed Library Materials, ANSI/NISO Z39.48-1992.

Printed in the United States of America

For Mark and Karen,
very animated, very dear

Contents

Preface

All movies are a trick of the eye. A motion picture is a series of images projected at a speed that creates the illusion of movement. And what genre tricks the eye as thoroughly as the animated film? At the same time that movie pioneers were experimenting with photographs that move, other artists were figuring out how to make drawings move. Animation is as old as the movies themselves. The first successful animated shorts were made in France at the turn of the twentieth century. Just as live-action movies quickly became more sophisticated, so too did animated films. Although the first American feature-length "cartoon" did not come about until 1937 with *Snow White and the Seven Dwarfs*, the art of animation was very impressive in the 1920s and 1930s. Extending a movie short to feature length brought to animated films a higher level of creativity. The animated features were not only longer, they were able to develop character and plot in ways a cartoon short never could. The arrival of the animated feature is the beginning of a new cinematic art form.

This book is about one hundred of the greatest feature films in American and British animation. The term "greatest" implies more than just success or popularity. These one hundred films were selected because they are important in one way or another. Some are historically significant because they mark some kind of advance in the art form. *Tron* (1982), for example, may lack a strong plot and memorable characters, but it was very innovative in its early use of the computer. Other films on the list are included because they introduced subject matter not previously seen. Movies as different as *Pocahontas* (1995) and *Fritz the Cat* (1972) fall into this category. Some films, such as *The Land before Time* (1988) and *Toy Story* (1995), introduced to the screen beloved characters that were seen in subsequent movies. Several entries boast superior music and/or songs, as with *The Jungle Book* (1967) and *Yellow Submarine* (1968). But most of the one hundred selected films are simply so well made that they are considered classics. Choosing which films from the hundreds of British and American features that have been made over the past eighty years was not a rewarding task, and the reader is bound to find a favorite film missing from the list. The most we can hope for is that these one hundred movies accurately represent the very best of American and British animation.

By definition, an animated film is one in which motion is created by the artist and not the actor. Hand-drawn and computer-generated films are the most common, but also on the list are stop-motion movies such as *The Nightmare before Christmas* (1993) and *Chicken Run* (2000). Films employing puppets or other actor-activated motion, such as the various Muppet movies, are not included. Features that utilize live-action as well as animation are considered if there is substantial animation. *Song of the South* (1946) and *Who Framed Roger Rabbit* (1988) have plenty of animation while *Mary Poppins* (1964) and *Pink Floyd: The Wall* (1982) do not. Animated movies made for television or directly for video are not included; only films that were initially shown in theaters are on the list. Sequels to animated features are discussed in the entry for the original movie. Finally, all of the selected movies are feature length. We consider an animated film running an hour or more to be long enough to qualify as a feature.

It is the goal of this book to explore animated films the reader may already be familiar with and to introduce movies that are not so widely known. We hope to include new information and commentary about even the most popular animated features. In every case, we aim to celebrate the magic of the art of animation and the wondrous things that can happen with a trick of the eye.

Acknowledgments

I wish to thank Cathy Hischak for watching dozens of animated films with me and for her proofreading of the manuscript. At Rowman & Littlefield, I wish to acknowledge the fine work by my editor, Stephen Ryan, and managing editor, Jessica McCleary.

Chronological List of Animated Films

Snow White and the Seven Dwarfs (Disney, 1937)
Gulliver's Travels (Paramount/Fleischer, 1939)
Pinocchio (Disney, 1940)
Fantasia (Disney, 1940)
Mr. Bug Goes to Town (Paramount/Fleischer, 1941)
Dumbo (Disney, 1941)
Bambi (Disney, 1942)
The Three Caballeros (Disney, 1945)
Make Mine Music (Disney, 1946)
Song of the South (Disney, 1946)
Fun and Fancy Free (Disney, 1947)
Melody Time (Disney, 1948)
The Adventures of Ichabod and Mr. Toad (Disney, 1949)
Cinderella (Disney, 1950)
Alice in Wonderland (Disney, 1951)
Peter Pan (Disney, 1953)
Animal Farm (Halas & Batchelor, 1954)
Lady and the Tramp (Disney, 1955)
Sleeping Beauty (Disney, 1959)
One Hundred and One Dalmatians (Disney, 1961)
The Sword in the Stone (Disney, 1963)
The Jungle Book (Disney, 1967)
Yellow Submarine (Apple/King Features, 1968)
A Boy Named Charlie Brown (Cinema Center Films, 1969)
The Aristocats (Disney, 1970)
Fritz the Cat (Black Ink/Fritz Productions, 1972)
Charlotte's Web (Paramount/Hanna-Barbera, 1973)
Robin Hood (Disney, 1973)
Wizards (20th Century Fox, 1977)
The Many Adventures of Winnie the Pooh (Disney, 1977)
The Rescuers (Disney, 1977)
Watership Down (Warner Brothers/Nepenthe, 1978)
Tron (Disney, 1982)
The Secret of NIMH (Aurora/Don Bluth Productions, 1982)
The Last Unicorn (Rankin/Bass, 1982)
An American Tail (Universal, 1986)

The Great Mouse Detective (Disney, 1986)
The Brave Little Toaster (Disney / Hyperion 1987)
The Land before Time (Universal, 1988)
Oliver & Company (Disney, 1988)
Who Framed Roger Rabbit (Disney, 1988)
The Little Mermaid (Disney, 1989)
Beauty and the Beast (Disney, 1991)
Aladdin (Disney, 1992)
The Nightmare before Christmas (Disney, 1993)
The Lion King (Disney, 1994)
A Goofy Movie (Disney, 1995)
Toy Story (Pixar / Disney, 1995)
Pocahontas (Disney, 1995)
The Hunchback of Notre Dame (Disney, 1996)
James and the Giant Peach (Disney / Skellington Productions 1996)
Anastasia (20th Century-Fox, 1997)
Hercules (Disney, 1997)
Antz (DreamWorks, 1998)
A Bug's Life (Pixar / Disney, 1998)
Mulan (Disney, 1998)
South Park: Bigger, Longer & Uncut (Comedy Central Films, 1999)
Tarzan (Disney, 1999)
Chicken Run (DreamWorks, 2000)
Dinosaur (Disney, 2000)
The Emperor's New Groove (Disney, 2000)
The Road to El Dorado (DreamWorks, 2000)
Monsters, Inc. (Pixar / Disney, 2001)
Shrek (DreamWorks, 2001)
Ice Age (20th Century Fox, 2002)
Lilo & Stitch (Disney, 2002)
Finding Nemo (Pixar / Disney, 2003)
Home on the Range (Disney, 2004)
The Incredibles (Pixar / Disney, 2004)
Corpse Bride (Warner Brothers, 2005)
Wallace & Gromit: The Curse of the Were-Rabbit (Aardman / DreamWorks, 2005)
Madagascar (DreamWorks, 2005)
Cars (Pixar / Disney, 2006)
Happy Feet (Warner Brothers, 2006)
Ratatouille (Pixar / Disney, 2007)
Meet the Robinsons (Disney, 2007)
Bolt (Disney, 2008)
WALL-E (Pixar / Disney, 2008)
Kung Fu Panda (DreamWorks, 2008)
Coraline (Focus Features, 2009)
Fantastic Mr. Fox (20th Century Fox, 2009)
The Princess and the Frog (Disney, 2009)
Up (Pixar / Disney, 2009)

Tangled (Disney, 2010)
Despicable Me (Illumination/Universal, 2010)
How to Train Your Dragon (DreamWorks, 2010)
Rango (Paramount, 2011)
Rio (20th Century Fox, 2011)
Frankenweenie (Disney, 2012)
ParaNorman (Focus/Laika, 2012)
Frozen (Disney, 2013)
The Boxtrolls (Laika, 2014)
Big Hero Six (Marvel/Disney, 2014)
The Lego Movie (Warner Brothers, 2014)
Inside Out (Pixar/Disney, 2015)
Anomalisa (Snoot Entertainment, 2015)
Shaun the Sheep Movie (StudioCanal/Aardman, 2015)
Kubo and the Two Strings (Laika, 2016)
Zootopia (Disney, 2016)
Moana (Disney, 2016)

A

THE ADVENTURES OF ICHABOD AND MR. TOAD
1949
(USA: Walt Disney Productions)

Directed by James Algar, Jack Kinney, Clyde Geronimi
Written by Erdman Penner, Winston Hibler, Joe Renaldi, Ted Sears, Harry Reeves, and Homer Brightman, based on Washington Irving's story "The Legend of Sleepy Hollow" and Kenneth Grahame's novel *The Wind in the Willows*
Produced by Walt Disney
Score by Oliver Wallace
Songs by Gene de Paul, Frank Churchill, Charles Wolcott, Don Raye, Larry Morey, and Ray Gilbert
Specs: Color (Technicolor); 68 minutes; traditional animation

---

A "package" film from the Disney studio that serves as a kind of double feature, this pair of animated adventures offers superior animation, voices, and music that still pleases.

The Wind in the Willows is set in 1908 England, where the reckless but fun-loving Mr. Toad enjoys life to the fullest. He lives at the manor house known as Toad Hall and spends much of his time scampering about the countryside in a horse and buggy. His friend Angus MacBadger volunteers to act as Toad's bookkeeper and explains to Toad that the family fortune has been spent and bankruptcy is unavoidable. But Toad doesn't listen and, when he sees the new-fangled contraption called a motorcar, he steals one and his countryside jaunts are more dangerous than ever. When charged with theft and brought to trial, Toad is found guilty and sentenced to prison. Toad Hall is taken over by weasels, so Toad's horse, Cyril Proudbottom, helps him escape from prison and they chase the weasels away. Toad is pardoned, but as soon as he is free he takes hold of an airplane and his reckless adventures continue.

The Legend of Sleepy Hollow is set in 1790 in the village of Tarrytown, New York, where the new schoolmaster, the lean and superstitious Ichabod Crane, thinks he is quite a ladies' man. When he turns his attentions to the lovely Katrina van Tassel, the brawny he-man Brom Bones gets jealous and decides to ridicule Ichabod. At a Halloween party, Brom tells the schoolmaster about the Headless Horseman

The haughty schoolmaster Ichabod Crane's encounter with the so-called Headless Horseman appears to frighten the horse as much as his rider. *Walt Disney Pictures / Photofest. © Walt Disney Pictures*

that haunts the town each October 31st looking for his head. On his way home that night, the nervous Ichabod encounters the crazed horseman (Brom in disguise), who chases him and even hurls his pumpkin head at the fleeing Ichabod. The next morning the villagers find a smashed pumpkin and no Ichabod. The schoolmaster has fled the town and Brom marries Katrina.

The 1940s were tough times for the Disney studio with so many employees involved with the Second World War and overseas markets limited by the international hostilities. The studio produced many training films for the government and some propaganda cartoons during the war years but had difficulty making

Voice Cast

Bing Crosby	Narrator and all voices in *Ichabod Crane*
Basil Rathbone	Narrator of *Mr. Toad*
Eric Blore	Mr. Toad
J. Pat O'Malley	Cyril Proudbottom
Campbell Grant	Angus MacBadger
Colin Campbell	Moley
Claud Allister	Ratty
John McLeish	Prosecutor

feature-length movies. So Walt Disney resorted to "package films" or anthology programs. *The Adventures of Ichabod and Mr. Toad* was the last of this kind of movie and, although the production budget and resources were restrictive, the double bill turned out to be first-rate. The screen rights for Kenneth Grahame's 1908 children's book *The Wind in the Willows* were purchased by Disney in 1938 with the intention of making a feature-length film from the British tale. A script and a song were completed, but the project was put on hold when the United States entered World War II. When the studio returned to *The Wind in the Willows* in 1945, it was decided that the story would not support a full-length movie, so a "featurette" version was begun with the idea of combining it with *Mickey and the Beanstalk*. But by 1947 the beanstalk tale was added to *Fun and Fancy Free* and production began on an animated version of Washington Irving's 1820 tale *The Legend of Sleepy Hollow*. The double bill, now titled *The Adventures of Ichabod and Mr. Toad*, was the work of many different artists, few of whom worked on both sections of the movie. There is no theme connecting the two parts aside from the idea of the main characters having an adventure. The animation, characterization, background art, and music are very individual for each one, yet the combination of the two distinct halves is very satisfying.

Songs

"Ichabod" (de Paul/Raye)
"Katrina" (de Paul/Raye)
"The Headless Horseman" (de Paul/Raye)
"Merrily on Our Way (to Nowhere in Particular)" (Churchill/Wolcott/Morey/Gilbert)

The Wind in the Willows starts slowly and casually with a very prim, British demeanor as Basil Rathbone narrates the story. Once Mr. Toad comes on the scene, the movie turns raucous and physical. The animation of Toad and his horse, Cyril Proudbottom, as they ride through (and destroy) the countryside is wild and frantic. Both characters and their carriage defy gravity and other laws of physics as they bounce along like a thrill ride at a theme park. The background art is sunny and colorful as the British landscape is rendered in a romantic yet childlike fashion. Later scenes at Toad Hall and the courtroom are similarly bright and playful as if the world was seen through Toad's adventurous point of view. The animation in *The Legend of Sleepy Hollow* is also very physical but in a more restrained manner until the famous chase scene with the Headless Horseman. The palette for the Irving tale is autumnal (the climactic scene takes place on Halloween) and the Catskills landscape is more severe and dramatic than the rolling hills of *The Wind in the Willows*. The animators had a great deal of fun creating and moving the tall, thin Ichabod, who has a wide variety of movements. When the artists found out that the character was to be voiced by singer Bing Crosby, they enlarged Ichabod's ears to resemble the popular star. The scene in which the Headless Horseman appears and then chases Ichabod is filled with dynamic movement and wonderful art that uses shadows and silhouettes effectively. Although Ichabod remains a comic character, the scene is one of the most terrifying in the Disney canon.

> MR. TOAD: A motorcar! Gad . . . what have I been missing?
>
> MOLEY: Ratty! It isn't! He hasn't!
>
> RATTY: It is and he has it: a new mania. Motor mania!

The voice work in both sections of the movie is splendid, as is the music. British character actor Eric Blore's Toad is a funny combination of stuffy British nasal tones with gleeful abandon. American character actor J. Pat O'Malley has fun with a lower-class British dialect as the horse Cyril. Claude Allister is a gentlemanly Ratty and Campbell Grant is a feisty Scottish badger. Oliver Wallace's soundtrack score for the Grahame story is carefree and light. The segment's only song, "Merrily on Our Way (to Nowhere in Particular)," a kind of rapid drinking song in the British manner, is a tuneful romp that seems to bound ahead as fast as Toad and Cyril. Crosby not only serves as the narrator for the Irving story but also voices Ichabod and Brom. Much of the text is sung, and Crosby's smooth and enticing voice dictates the tone of the piece. "Ichabod" is an easy-going narrative ballad about the silly schoolmaster, "Katrina" is a warm love ballad, and "The Headless Horseman," which explains the legend, is more urgent and even frightening. All of the songs in the Sleepy Hollow story have a slightly swinging Big Band sound, whereas the Grahame piece has more conventional movie scoring. Wallace also scored the background music for the Irving tale and it is sometimes fervent and dynamic, particularly during the big chase scene.

Award

Golden Globe Award: Best Cinematography—Color

Disney released the *Adventures of Ichabod and Mr. Toad* in 1949 and it met with favorable reviews and healthy box office. The studio never rereleased the movie in theaters but both sections were broadcast on Disney television shows several times beginning in 1955. Each story was put on VHS in 1990 and then sold as a DVD collection in 2009. Parts of the film have also shown up on Disney TV specials and made-for-video anthologies.

See also *Melody Time, Make Mine Music,* and *Fun and Fancy Free.*

Did You Know . . . ?

The weasels in *The Wind in the Willows* segment were the inspiration for the Toon Patrol characters in *Who Framed Roger Rabbit* four decades later.

ALADDIN

1992
(USA: Walt Disney Pictures)

Produced and directed by Ron Clements and John Musker
Written by Ron Clements, John Musker, Ted Elliott, and Terry Rossio
Score by Alan Menken
Songs by Alan Menken (music), Howard Ashman, and Tim Rice (lyrics)
Specs: Color (Technicolor); 90 minutes; traditional animation with some computer effects

A fast-paced Arabian Nights farce from Disney's renaissance period, Aladdin *is one of the funniest of all animated films. The exotic nature of the tale is downplayed and the comic elements predominate, particularly in the characters.*

The "street rat" Aladdin lives by his wits in the city of Agrabah with the help of his monkey sidekick Abu. The Princess Jasmine, on the other hand, lives a life of luxury in the palace as the daughter of the Sultan but yearns to see the real world. When she goes out into the city incognito, Jasmine is helped by Aladdin, who doesn't know her true identity. The palace guards find her and bring her home while the conniving vizier Jafar has Aladdin thrown into prison. Jafar has long wished to enter the Cave of Wonders filled with treasure and, most importantly, a magic lamp with great powers. When he and his parrot sidekick Iago learn that Aladdin is the prophesied "diamond in the rough" who is needed to enter the sacred cave, the boy is allowed to escape prison and go to the cave. Jafar fails to get the lamp from Aladdin, who is trapped in the Cave of Wonders with Abu. Out of the lamp comes an exuberant Genie who is able to turn Aladdin into the wealthy Prince Ali and woo Jasmine. But Jafar discovers his true identity and steals the lamp, turning the sultan and his daughter into slaves. Aladdin outwits Jafar by convincing him that a genie is the most powerful force imaginable. Jafar uses his last wish to become a genie and is immediately a prisoner inside the lamp. Aladdin gives his Genie his freedom and gets to wed Jasmine.

Voice Cast

Scott Weinger	Aladdin (speaking)
Brad Kane	Aladdin (singing)
Linda Larkin	Jasmine (speaking)
Lea Salonga	Jasmine (singing)
Robin Williams	Genie/Peddler
Jonathan Freeman	Jafar
Gilbert Gottfried	Iago
Douglas Seale	Sulton
Frank Welker	Abu

Although Aladdin possesses the magic lamp, his relationship with the Genie seems to be that of bosom friends rather than master and slave. *Buena Vista Pictures / Photofest. © Buena Vista Pictures*

The original story of Aladdin and the magic lamp was told in the Arab folklore collection known as the *Arabian Nights*. There have been countless adaptations over the years, and much of the Disney version is original and frequently departs from the familiar tale. Before he died from complications from AIDS, Howard Ashman wrote a screenplay and, with composer Alan Menken, a handful of songs for a very hip and modern version of *Aladdin*. The script went through several re-writes and characters were dropped and added before a screenplay was finalized. The hero Aladdin went from a thirteen-year-old kid with a mother to an eighteen-year-old adventurer. Jasmine was changed from a spoiled brat to a determined and self-sufficient woman. The Genie, conceived as a swinging jazz singer along the lines of Cab Calloway, was completely changed when Robin Williams was cast and he improvised a stand-up comic approach to the character. The parrot Iago began as a stuffy British assistant, but when voiced by Gilbert Gottfried, the sidekick was loud and obnoxious. The look of the movie was suggested by the Middle East and featured flowing lines in both the characters and the settings. The animation of the Genie was taken from the work of cartoonist Al Hirschfeld, the simple but expressive lines moving and changing as quickly as Williams's rapid-fire delivery. Jafar, on the other hand, was depicted with severe lines and sharp angles to contrast with the constantly moving Genie. Perhaps the most challenging animation was that for the Magic Carpet, which exhibited personality without words or appendages to express itself. The animators used the computer for some of the special effects in the film, such as the way the Cave of Wonders appeared and disappeared. But most of *Aladdin* was traditionally animated and resulted in one of Disney's most physical and frenetic movies.

Songs

"A Whole New World" (Menken/Rice)
"Arabian Nights" (Menken/Ashman)
"Friend Like Me" (Menken/Ashman)
"Prince Ali" (Menken/Ashman)
"One Jump Ahead" (Menken/Rice)

Aladdin was cast with comedy in mind, and the voices are as lively and silly as the animation. Aladdin and Jasmine are spoken and sung with a Broadway style, and the four performers—Scott Weinger, Brad Kane, Linda Larkin, and Lea Salonga—give the most conventional performances in the film. The movie is dominated by Williams's vocals as the Genie, arguably the most hilarious performance to be found in any animated film. The Golden Globe committee was so impressed that they gave a special award to Williams. Jonathan Freeman's Jafar is very menacing yet in a comic vein. He is supported by Gottfried's vociferous vocals as Iago. All of the voices, even those for Aladdin and Jasmine, have a satirical tone to them, keeping *Aladdin* in a vivacious mode filled with different sounds. The film was directed by Ron Clements and John Musker, who had begun the Disney renaissance with their production of *The Little Mermaid* (1989). Yet the farcical *Aladdin* is in a very different vein than that earlier film.

ALADDIN: You're a prisoner?

GENIE: It's all part and parcel, the whole genie gig. (grows to gigantic size) Phenomenal cosmic powers! (shrinks down inside the lamp) Itty bitty living space!

Alan Menken provided the pseudo-exotic music for the soundtrack score, conjuring up the lyrical sounds of the Middle East. Yet the songs he wrote with lyricists Howard Ashman and Tim Rice are firmly in the Broadway style. The opening number "Arabian Nights" flows like a desert chant but there is plenty of showbiz razzle-dazzle in the Genie's "Friend Like Me." "Prince Ali" is a merry march while "One Jump Ahead" is a jazzy number in which the words come as fast as Aladdin's movements. The hit ballad "A Whole New World" is both romantic and vocally expansive as it soars much like the Magic Carpet during the song. Although *Aladdin* is a farce, it is interesting that the songs do not hinder the action or dampen the pace.

Coming on the heels of *Beauty and the Beast* (1991), *Aladdin* might have been a disappointment to some moviegoers. But the two animated musicals are so different in temperament that one does not compare them. The reviews were almost all raves with unanimous plaudits for Williams's performance. *Aladdin* cost $28 million, but it ended up being the top-grossing film of 1992 and earned over $500 million worldwide on its first release. The two direct-to-video sequels—*The Return of Jafar* (1994) and *Aladdin and the King of Thieves* (1996)—were also successful. *Aladdin* was released on home video in 1993 and a special edition came out in

Awards

Academy Awards: Best Song ("A Whole New World"), Best Score, and Best Sound. Oscar nominations for Best Song ("Friend Like Me") and Best Sound Effects Editing.
Golden Globe Awards: Best Score, Best Song ("A Whole New World"), and a Special Award to Robin Williams. Golden Globe nominations for Best Picture—Comedy or Musical and Best Song ("Friend Like Me" and "Prince Ali").
British Academy of Film & Television Arts (BAFTA) Award nominations: Best Score and Best Special Effects.

2004 followed by the Blu-ray Disc in 2013. A stage version of *Aladdin* opened on Broadway in 2014 and was an immediate hit. A few songs Ashman had written with Menken but were dropped from the film were used in the stage version, and Chad Beguelin provided the lyrics for some new numbers. Rather than try to replicate Robin Williams's performance, the Genie was played by an African American with a Fats Waller kind of persona, much as Ashman had originally intended. The original *Aladdin* has joined the ranks of the most beloved Disney animated movies, one of the few comedies to have that distinction. Chuck Jones, legendary creator of Warner Brothers' Looney Tunes cartoons, said the film "juggles a 90s impudence with the old Disney swank and heart" and declared it "the funniest feature ever made." Many agree with him.

Did You Know . . . ?

Most of the Genie's dialogue was ad-libbed by Robin Williams in the recording studio. The producers had over sixteen hours of Williams's comedics to use. Because of the considerable amount of improvisation in the final product, *Aladdin* could not be nominated for the Best Screenplay Oscar.

ALICE IN WONDERLAND

1951
(USA: Walt Disney Productions)

Directed by Clyde Geronimi, Wilfred Jackson, and Hamilton Luske
Written by Winston Hibler, Bill Peet, Ted Sears, Joe Rinaldi, Erdman Penner, Milt Banta, Dick Kelsey, Joe Grant, Dick Huemer, Del Connell, Tom Oreb, John Walbridge, and Willian Cottrell, based on Lewis Carroll's *Alice's Adventures in Wonderland* and *Through the Looking Glass*
Produced by Walt Disney
Score by Oliver Wallace
Songs by Sammy Fain, Gene de Paul, Bob Hilliard, Jerry Livingston, Oliver Wallace, Al Hoffman, Mack David, Don Raye, Ted Sears, and Lewis Carroll
Specs: Color (Technicolor); 75 minutes; traditional animation

In many ways an atypical Disney animated film, Alice in Wonderland *lacks a traditional heroine and storyline but is filled with memorable characters and animated moments that make it highly accessible to audiences today.*

The Victorian youth Alice falls asleep in a garden while her sister is giving her a history lesson and is awakened by the White Rabbit scurrying past and declaring he is late. Alice follows the rabbit into a rabbit hole and falls through a deep tunnel before landing in a room with one small door, which the White Rabbit goes through. The Doorknob advises Alice to drink from a potion that shrinks her to a size that allows her to enter Wonderland. Her adventures there include joining a caucus race with a Dodo and other creatures, growing so large she fills a whole house, questioning the Caterpillar and the Cheshire Cat, partaking of a tea party hosted by the Mad Hatter, and angering the Queen of Hearts during a game of croquet. Brought to trial, Alice is revisited by various characters she has met in Wonderland, who serve as witnesses. Alice flees the courtroom and is chased by all the residents of Wonderland until she realizes that it is all a dream and all she need do is wake up. So she does and returns to the real world, where it is time for tea.

Lewis Carroll's *Alice's Adventures in Wonderland* and *Through the Looking Glass* have seen many stage and screen adaptations since their publication in the 1860s.

Filmdom's craziest tea party includes the March Hare (left) and the Mad Hatter while Alice retains a sense of sanity as they celebrate their un-birthdays. *RKO Radio Pictures / Photofest.* © *RKO Radio Pictures*

Voice Cast

Kathryn Beaumont	Alice
Ed Wynn	Mad Hatter
Jerry Colonna	March Hare
Sterling Holloway	Cheshire Cat
Richard Haydn	Caterpillar
Bill Thompson	White Rabbit
Verna Felton	Queen of Hearts
J. Pat O'Malley	Walrus/Carpenter
James MacDonald	Dormouse
Dink Trout	King of Hearts
Joseph Kearns	Doorknob
Doris Lloyd	Rose

Walt Disney had produced a series of "Alice" cartoons in the 1920s with a live-action Alice (Virginia Davis) playing opposite animated characters. Plans for an animated feature based on the books went back to the 1930s, but production for this film did not begin until the mid-1940s. Because the two books are episodic and have no linear plot line, the studio's many writers struggled with the script. Alice's curiosity holds the movie together. She pursues the White Rabbit down the rabbit hole and throughout Wonderland, giving her a reason for encountering the famous Carroll characters. The writers created a grand race as the climax of the film with Alice pursued by everyone she had met in Wonderland. Characters and episodes from both Alice books were used and only one new character was introduced: the Doorknob, who instructs Alice on how to change her size. Alice is not like any other Disney heroine. True to the books, she is a forthright young girl who is not afraid of any of the creatures she meets in Wonderland. Alice can be sarcastic or haughty and, consequently, not a heroine that all audiences warm

Songs

"A Very Merry Un-birthday (The Un-birthday Song)" (David/Hoffman/Livingston)
"I'm Late" (Hilliard/Fain)
"Alice in Wonderland" (Hilliard/Fain)
"All in a Golden Afternoon" (Hilliard/Fain)
"'Twas Brillig" (Raye/de Paul)
"March of the Cards" (Hilliard/Fain)
"Painting the Roses Red" (Hilliard/Fain)
"Very Good Advice" (Hilliard/Fain)
"The Caucus Race" (Hilliard/Fain)
"The Walrus and the Carpenter" (Hilliard/Fain)
"In a World of My Own" (Hilliard/Fain)
"We'll Smoke the Blighter Out" (Wallace/Sears)
"A E I O U" (Wallace/Sears)
"Old Father William" (Wallace/Sears)

up to quickly. The colorful residents of Wonderland, on the other hand, are lively and fun. Animation is the ideal medium for Carroll's world and this film version makes the most of it.

Lewis Carroll's sense of satire and the highly Victorian look of John Tenniel's illustrations for the original books may have been lost in this animated version of the Alice stories, but the movie has a distinctive look of its own. The background art is colorful and exaggerated. The animation of the characters is creative and sometimes deliciously surreal at times. The Cheshire Cat's disappearing body parts, the movement of the smoke from the Caterpillar's hookah, and the optical illusions created by the cards are among the many memorable animated sequences in *Alice in Wonderland*. Breaking away from tradition, Walt Disney enlisted some famous performers to do the voices and then had the animators use physical characteristics from the actors. The popular comics Ed Wynn and Jerry Colonna, for example, can easily be recognized as the Mad Hatter and the March Hare. Some of the studio's favorite voice actors are heard in the movie, including Sterling Holloway (Cheshire Cat), Verna Felton (Queen of Hearts), Bill Thompson (White Rabbit), and J. Pat O'Malley (Walrus and the Carpenter). Kathryn Beaumont voiced Alice with a clear, no-nonsense tone and her performance holds the movie together. Much of *Alice in Wonderland* is unconventional, which has led some film historians to call it ahead of its time.

> ALICE: I'm sorry I interrupted your birthday party.
>
> MARCH HARE: Birthday? My dear child, this is NOT a birthday party.
>
> MAD HATTER: Of course not. This is an un-birthday party.

Alice in Wonderland has more songs than any other Disney feature but many of them are short and they rarely stopped or slowed down the action. A few numbers used Carroll's poetry, as in "The Walrus and the Carpenter," "'Twas Brillig," and "Old Father William." The most catchy number in the score is the silly "A Very Merry Un-birthday" sung at the tea party, but also memorable are the operetta-like "All in a Golden Afternoon," the frantic "I'm Late," the march "Painting the Roses Red," and the lyrical title song. This last number later became a favorite of jazz musicians. Several songwriters contributed to the songs for *Alice in Wonderland* but the score is consistently daffy throughout. Since there is no love story (another nontraditional aspect of the film), there is no love song and the only quiet and wistful number is Alice's "In a World of My Own." In some ways, Carroll's sense of wry satire is best captured in the movie's songs.

The film met with mixed notices when it was released in 1951. Some critics felt the British classic had been Americanized and the Carroll satire softened. Others praised the animation and the way Wonderland and its characters came to

Award

Academy Award nomination: Best Score.

life. The movie did disappointing business, particularly in comparison with its blockbuster predecessor *Cinderella* (1950). Because of its lukewarm reception and box office, Walt Disney did not rerelease *Alice in Wonderland* in theaters during his lifetime. Instead in 1954 it became the first Disney film to be shown on television, though it was edited from seventy-five minutes to one hour to fit into the weekly *Disneyland* spot. Television audiences liked it but it wasn't until the theatrical re-releases in the late 1960s that the movie became a beloved classic. For a time *Alice in Wonderland* was a cult favorite with the drug culture, getting a reputation as a favorite "head" film with surreal aspects that were viewed as psychedelic. The studio had to pull the movie from college and independent theaters to combat this association with drugs. By the time *Alice in Wonderland* was rereleased in 1974 and 1981, it was again considered a family favorite. It was one of the first Disney films to be available on VHS (1981), then later on DVD (2000) and Blu-ray (2011). Walt Disney, who was himself disappointed in the way *Alice in Wonderland* turned out, never lived to see the movie join the ranks of Disney favorites.

Did You Know . . . ?

The renowned British author Aldous Huxley worked on early versions of the script for *Alice in Wonderland*, but Walt Disney thought his writing too sophisticated and highbrow and none of it was used in the movie.

AN AMERICAN TAIL

1986
(USA: Universal Pictures)

Directed by Don Bluth
Written by Judy Freudberg and Tony Geiss
Produced by Steven Spielberg, Kathleen Kennedy, Gary Goldman, Deborah Jelin,
    David Kirschner, Frank Marshall, Kate Barker, John Pomeroy, and Don Bluth
Score by James Horner
Songs by James Horner, Barry Mann (music), and Cynthia Weil (lyrics)
Specs: Color; 80 minutes; traditional animation

The experience of Jewish immigrants in New York City at the end of the nineteenth century was re-created from the point of view of mice in this family-friendly adventure from animator-director Don Bluth.

After a pogrom in 1885 destroys a Russian Jewish village, the Mousekewitz family of mice emigrates to America believing there are no cats in the New World. On the steamship crossing the Atlantic, the young son Fievel is washed overboard and his Papa, Mama, and sister Tanya think he is dead. But Fievel survives inside a bottle and is washed up in New York City just as his family disembarks the ship. The French pigeon Henri, in town for the erection of the Statue of Liberty,

The Mousekewitz family may be mice, but their experience in emigrating from Europe to America echoes the plight of thousands of human immigrants at the turn of the century. *Universal Pictures / Photofest. © Universal Pictures*

encourages and helps Fievel, but the young mouse is soon in the clutches of the confidence dealer Warren T. Rat (who is really a cat in disguise) and is forced to work in a sweat shop. Fievel escapes and has encounters with the tough but friendly Italian mouse Tony Toponi; the corrupt Irish politician Honest John; the pretty Bridget, who is rousing the mice to move against the cats; the rich Gussie Mausheimer, who leads a crusade to get rid of the cats; and even a goofy vegetarian cat, Tiger. Fievel suggests the mice construct a giant mouse to scare the cats onto the pier just as a boat is leaving for Hong Kong. The plan works and Fievel is eventually reunited with his family.

David Kirschner came up with the idea for *An American Tail* and it interested both producer Steven Spielberg and director Don Bluth, as well as Universal Pictures, which hadn't released an animated feature since 1965. Although the screenplay was original, it included many familiar elements from immigration stories, this time retold from the viewpoint of Jewish mice. The film included many animal characters (mostly mice and cats) but humans were glimpsed throughout the movie, from the immigrants on board ship to the "greenhorns" working in sweat shops. Since the immigrant mice came from all over Europe, the voice cast had to provide a variety of dialects. Most enjoyable were Christopher Plummer's French pigeon Henri, Madeline Kahn's lisping German Gussie, John Finnegan's New Yorkese Warren T. Rat, and Dom DeLuise's very American

Voice Cast

Phillip Glasser	Fievel Mousekewitz
Erica Yohn	Mama Mousekewitz
Nehemiah Persoff	Papa Mousekewitz
Amy Green	Tanya Mousekewitz (speaking)
Alitzah	Tanya Mousekewitz (singing)
Betsy Cathcart	Tanya Mousekewitz (singing)
Dom DeLuise	Tiger
Christopher Plummer	Henri
John Finnegan	Warren T. Rat
Pat Musick	Tony Toponi
Madeline Kahn	Gussie Mausheimer
Cathianne Blore	Bridget
Neil Ross	Honest John
Will Ryan	Digit
Hal Smith	Moe

Tiger. The voices of the Mousekewitz family were less exaggerated in an effort to avoid Jewish stereotypes. Paul Glasser's vocals for Fievel were not ethnic and, like the character, very naive and even stupid at times. There is plenty of action in *An American Tail* but the film quiets down for some tender moments, most memorably for the children's lullaby "Somewhere Out There." It is not a particularly clever screenplay but it works efficiently and offers many opportunities to illustrate the immigrant experience.

Songs

"Somewhere Out There"
"Never Say Never"
"There Are No Cats in America"
"A Duo"

The character animation in *An American Tale* is not very subtle, the movements and facial expressions more basic than revealing. The animators also try to express Fievel's naïveté by having his tongue dandling, a look that makes him appear less than bright. There is better animation with the movie's tougher and funnier characters. The background art is very accomplished, recreating the New York of the 1880s but always from a rodent point of view. The household objects that become the homes and businesses of the mice are often rendered with accurate and witty detail, such as the intricate views of the hold of the ship and the street of mice vendors. *An American Tail* offers a poetic view of New York with some stunning cityscapes during different times of day and night. Adding to this romantic treatment is an excellent soundtrack score by James Horner. The music varies greatly throughout, including majestic and inspiring sections, dramatic music for the many action scenes, stirring choral passages, and period tunes. Although there are four songs (lyrics by Cynthia Weil and Barry Mann) sung by characters in the film, *An American Tail* doesn't feel like a musical. The rousing folk dance "There Are No Cats in America," the predictable buddy song "A Duo," and the repetitive "Never Say Never" do not add much to the movie but the plaintive "Somewhere Out There" succeeds nicely and enjoyed a popularity not usual for animated films at the time.

HENRI: You want to find your family. And you will.

FIEVEL: But how? They're so far away, and it's so big. I'll never find them.

HENRI: Excuse moi, pardon, did you say never? So young, and you've already lost hope! This is America, the place to find hope. If you give up now, you will never find them. So never say never.

An American Tail was fraught with production problems, including Universal's interference that caused scenes to be redone and an animation process that was much slower than anticipated. The first cut of the movie was so long that songs and whole scenes had to be dropped, leaving some unclear gaps in the storyline. Although the budget ballooned up to $9 million, *An American Tail* was a box office smash when it opened in 1986, earning $47 million in America and another $40 million internationally. Reviews were mixed, but the public was enthusiastic, allowing the film to out-gross that year's Disney feature, *The Great Mouse Detective*, by more than $20 million. The 1987 release of the home video version was also a success, as well as the DVD in 2004 and Blu-ray in 2014.

Awards

Academy Award nomination: Best Song ("Somewhere Out There").
Golden Globe nomination: Best Song ("Somewhere Out There").

Bluth was not involved with the 1991 sequel *Fievel Goes West*, which Spielberg produced for Universal. The Mousekewitz family decides to immigrate to the Wild West and again Fievel is separated from his family for most of the film. Dom DeLuise returned to voice Tiger, the only non-family character to appear in the sequel. The reviews were not very favorable but the film still grossed $40 million. In 1992 there was a television cartoon series titled *Fievel's American Tails* and there were two made-for-video sequels: *An American Tail: The Treasure of Manhattan Island* (1998) and *An American Tail: The Mystery of the Night Monster* (2000).

Did You Know . . . ?

The hero was named after producer Steven Spielberg's grandfather Fievel.

ANASTASIA

1997
(USA: Fox Animation Studios)

Directed by Don Bluth and Gary Goldman
Written by Noni White, Susan Gauthier, Bruce Graham, and Bob Tzudiker
Produced by Maureen Donley, Don Bluth, and Gary Goldman
Score by David Newman
Songs by Stephen Flaherty (music) and Lynn Ahrens (lyrics)
Specs: Color (Technicolor); 94 minutes; traditional animation

One of the most accomplished efforts to make a Disney-like animated musical in the 1990s, this part-history, part-legend movie with an unlikely subject matter offered Broadway-quality voices and songs. It is a notable achievement when one considers that Anastasia *was the first animated feature musical in the long history of 20th Century Fox.*

During a ball given by Czar Nicholas II, the banished sorcerer Rasputin appears and puts a curse on the Romanov family. The Russian Revolution breaks out, troops storm the palace, and only the Dowager Empress Marie and her grand-daughter Anastasia escape, thanks to the help of the young servant boy Dimitri. Rasputin pursues them but he drowns in the icy river. Marie boards a train to Paris but the young Anya falls while trying to catch the train and hits her head, causing amnesia. Ten years later, rumors circulate throughout St. Petersburg that the Grand Duchess Anastasia was not killed with the rest of the Royal Family and is alive somewhere. Marie offers a large reward to anyone who can find her. Dimitri, now an adult, and his cohort Vladimir find the young Anya, who has left an orphanage looking for her family even though she has no memory of the past. With Dimitri's knowledge of the royal palace, he and Vladimir teach the orphan Anya all she needs to know to fool Marie into thinking she is the lost Anastasia. They head to Paris, and on their trail is the resurrected Rasputin,

Voice Cast

Meg Ryan	Anastasia (speaking)
Liz Callaway	Anastasia (singing)
John Cusack	Dimitri (speaking)
Jonathan Dokuchitz	Dimitri (singing)
Christopher Lloyd	Rasputin (speaking)
Jim Cummings	Rasputin (singing)
Kelsey Grammer	Vladimir
Hank Azaria	Bartok
Angela Lansbury	Dowager Empress
Bernadette Peters	Sophie
Andrea Martin	Phlegmenkoff

The heroine in this fanciful version of Russian history may be a combination of fact, fiction, and legend, but she is still a strong and engaging character. *20th Century Fox Film Corporation / Photofest.* © *20th Century Fox Film Corporation*

who now has demonic powers and, with his bat stooge, Bartok, is out to destroy the remaining Romanov. In Paris, Marie's cousin Sophie quizzes Anya and is convinced that she is the true Anastasia. When presented to Maria, Anya knows things that Dimitri never taught her. Realizing she is the real grand duchess and that he has fallen in love with her, Dimitri refuses the reward money and departs. Anya pursues him, disintegrates Rasputin by destroying the reliquary of his ashes, and is reunited with Dimitri.

The legend of the missing Romanov princess Anastasia had been the subject of books, plays, and films, but the mystery was pretty much solved in 1994 when DNA tests proved that the so-called survivor, Anna Anderson, was not a blood relative of the Romanovs. All the same, 20th Century Fox went ahead with a very fictionalized version of the story, building an animation studio in Arizona and hiring the Broadway songwriters Stephen Flaherty (music) and Lynn Ahrens (lyrics) and a top-notch cast of performers. The screenplay caused many difficulties, as directors Don Bluth and Gary Goldman wanted to include the Russian Revolution and the demonic Rasputin and still come up with a family musical film. History was stretched and reworked, the long-dead Rasputin was brought back to life, and the princess Anastasia not only survived but found romance along the way. One had to forget a lot of facts to enjoy *Anastasia*, but as a romantic fairy tale it was very effective. Anya was a likable heroine, the con-men Dimitri and Vladimir end up being very enjoyable, and the evil Rasputin is a villain in the grand manner. There were many Disney-like touches, such as Rasputin's sidekick, Bartok, and Anya's puppy, Pooka, but the tale was still a bit too severe for young children. Regardless, the craftsmanship in *Anastasia* is of a high order, from the ingenious animation to the atmospheric recreations of St. Petersburg and Paris. The animators had the most fun with Rasputin, having body parts fall off as he fussed and fumed as only a resurrected corpse could. The background art is expert, and the animation has a polish that often rivals Disney. Much of this can be credited to the veteran animator Bluth.

Songs

"Once Upon a December"
"Journey to the Past"
"A Rumor in St. Petersburg"
"In the Dark of the Night"
"Learn to Do It"
"Paris Holds the Key (to Your Heart)"
"At the Beginning"

The songs by Flaherty and Ahrens were also Disney quality. The evocative lullaby "Once Upon a December" was key to the plot and was repeated effectively in the storyline. The warm character song "Journey to the Past" for Anya soared with emotion, the creepy conjuring number "In the Dark of the Night" solidified the character of Rasputin, and the rousing "Paris Holds the Key (to Your Heart)" was a first-class showstopper. Fox hired movie talent (Meg Ryan, John Cusack, and Christopher Lloyd) for the speaking voices and recording talents (Liz Callaway, Jonathan Dokuchitz, and Jim Cummings) for the singing. Broadway favorites Angela Lansbury, Kelsey Grammer, Bernadette Peters, and Hank Azaria did both speaking and singing for Marie, Vladimir, Sophie, and Bartok. David Newman's soundtrack score is also commendable. In addition to using melodies from the songs in the scoring, he composed some original themes that were the most Russian-sounding passages in the movie.

VLADIMIR: She certainly has a mind of her own.

DIMITRI: Yeah. I hate that in a woman.

So much time and money had been invested in *Anastasia* that Fox spent some $50 million on marketing the movie with ads, television spots, merchandise, and tie-ins with companies such as Burger King and Sea World. The Disney studio was threatened by word of mouth on *Anastasia* and refused to let Fox advertise it on ABC-TV, which Disney owned. The rivalry extended to the release dates as well. Disney rereleased *The Little Mermaid* during the Christmas season that Fox had scheduled for *Anastasia*. So Fox moved the general release to several months later. While many critics carped about the sugar-coating of history in the film, *Anastasia* received mostly positive reviews and was compared favorably with the current crop of Disney movies. International reviews of the film were also supportive, though in Russia and Greece the Orthodox Church condemned *Anastasia* for its romanticized treatment of Anya, who had been canonized as a martyr in 1981. Domestic and international box office for *Anastasia* totaled nearly $140 million, a record high for a Bluth feature and a surprisingly good start for Fox Animation Studios.

Awards

Academy Award nominations: Best Score and Best Song ("Journey to the Past").
Golden Globe nominations: Best Song ("Once Upon a December" and "Journey to the Past").

There was a direct-to-video spin-off, *Bartok the Magnificent*, in 1999, and even an *Anastasia on Ice* in the late 1990s. The merchandising of the movie was on a Disney scale and the home video sales in 1998 were in the millions. The DVD version came out in 2006 and the Blu-ray in 2011. A musical stage version of *Anastasia* was produced regionally in 2016 and opened on Broadway in 2017. Many changes were made in the script (Rasputin was totally eliminated) and there were new songs by Ahrens and Flaherty. The production was panned by the theater critics but *Anastasia* was a box office hit all the same.

Anastasia was one of the first non-Disney animated features to become a blockbuster with a lucrative franchise. Its success encouraged other studios to pursue the field of feature animation, thereby changing the history of the genre in America.

Did You Know . . . ?

Although the film shows Rasputin dying by falling through the ice while chasing Anastasia and her grandmother, the real Rasputin was murdered by Russian officials and his body was dumped into the Malaya Nevka River by chopping a hole in the ice.

ANIMAL FARM

1954
(UK: Halas & Batchelor/British Pathé)

Produced and directed by John Halas and Joy Batchelor
Written by Lothar Wolff, Borden Mace, Philip Stapp, Joseph Bryan III, John Halas, and Joy Batchelor, based on the book by George Orwell
Score by Matyas Seiber
Specs: Color (Technicolor); 72 minutes; traditional animation

Based on George Orwell's allegorical novel of the Stalinist era in the USSR, although this was a British production, the CIA provided the funding as part of the American cultural offensive during the Cold War.

When Manor Farm falls onto hard times and farmer Jones turns to drink, the animals are either neglected or abused. The aged prize boar, Old Major, calls a meeting of all the animals and urges them to rise up and take over the farm. Before he dies, Old Major teaches the animals a song of freedom that becomes the anthem of the revolution. The animals drive out Jones and succeed in taking over the farm. They work the farm themselves, governed by a set of rules that states "all animals are equal." The pigs, considered the smartest in the animal society, take command and the farm prospers. The leader, Snowball, has plans for a windmill to provide power to the farm but the ambitious pig Napoleon drives Snowball away, declares to the other animals that he was a traitor, and becomes the sole leader of the farm. Under Napoleon, the animals work harder than ever, but their lives get worse; the pigs begin living in comfort in the farm house like humans, and they alter the farm's motto to "all animals are equal, but some animals are more equal than others." Conditions worsen for the laboring animals until they converge on the pigs and a new revolution is begun.

This Soviet-style poster honoring the pig Napoleon illustrates the leader's maxim that "All animals are equal, but some animals are more equal than others." *Louis De Rochemont Associates / Photofest. © Louis De Rochemont Associates*

Voice Cast

Maurice Denham	All Animals
Gordon Heath	Narrator

George Orwell's novel was subtitled a "fairy story" when it was published in Britain in 1945. Although the Cold War was just beginning, Orwell's satirical fable had obvious parallels to the Russian Revolution of 1917 and the birth of Communism. Russia had been England's ally in World War II, but Orwell saw Stalin's empire as a threat to democratic nations. Orwell had difficulty finding a publisher for his controversial novel and even the British Ministry of Information discouraged its publication, fearing it might harm British-Soviet relations. Once the book was finally published, it met with mixed reactions. Interest in the book grew in both Britain and the States and by the 1950s *Animal Farm* was considered a modern classic of political satire. The American documentary producer Louis de Rochemont wanted to make an animated adaptation of the book with English directors John Halas and Joy Batchelor but had trouble raising funds for what would be the first British animated feature film to be shown in a theater for the public. The American CIA (Central Intelligence Agency) thought the book excellent pro-democracy propaganda during the Cold War and provided over half of the money for the film version. Halas and Batchelor spent three years making *Animal Farm*, and it was well received on both sides of the Atlantic when it was released in 1954.

SNOWBALL: No animal shall drink alcohol. No animal shall sleep in a bed. Four legs good, two legs bad. (the chickens squawk)

SQUEALER: Wings count as legs. (the chickens show approval)

SHEEP: Four legs good, two legs bad! Four legs good, two legs bad!

The screenplay for the movie follows Orwell's book rather closely until the very end. The novel ends on an enigmatic note as the worker animals watch the pigs as they dress and act like humans and one cannot tell the difference between Jones and Napoleon. The film goes further and suggests that Napoleon and his cronies will soon be ousted, a kind of wish fulfillment that the democratic nations had about Stalin. Other than that, the animated adaptation is very accurate to Orwell and pulls no punches in showing the story's most disturbing scenes. Napoleon's killer dogs attack supporters of Snowball and the sign on the barn that once read "no animals shall kill another animal" is amended with the words "without cause" in red paint. When the faithful workhorse Boxer is wounded and needs recovery, Napoleon sells him to a glue factory in a horrifying scene that, like most of the movie, is not for children.

Award

British Academy of Film & Television Arts (BAFTA) Award nomination: Best Animated Film.

While *Animal Farm* cannot match the technical and poetic quality of the Disney films in the 1950s, the movie is very impressive at times. The animation of the animals and humans is very polished, but the background art is disappointing. At times the farm is pictured as dark and oppressive, even resembling a Soviet gulag, but the landscapes outside the farm are not very interesting and lack atmosphere. On the other hand, the animators were very successful in the way shadows were used so effectively in both interior and exterior scenes. The score by Hungarian-born composer Matyas Seiber is very accomplished. There is a socialist anthem that has no words, only the squawks and howls of the animals, but is very Soviet in feeling. The soundtrack score is lively and only gets oppressive when needed. Yet never does the music sound lighthearted or frivolous. The narration voiced by Gordon Heath is sometimes unnecessary, since the movie is very visual. What dialogue there is Maurice Denham does expertly, voicing all the different animals with a somber subtext. *Animal Farm* may not look very polished today, but it is still powerful filmmaking. The story and the characters are well served by the film, and watching it now the propagandist approach is not overbearing. One might say that the movie's ending foreshadows the fall of Soviet Communism in the early 1990s. Yet the message of the film applies to all forms of totalitarianism and, like Orwell's book, remains a biting and cautionary tale.

Did You Know . . . ?

Animal Farm was the first animated feature film to be made and shown in Britain. Directors Halas and Batchelor had made the animated feature *Handling Ships* in 1945 but it was made for military personnel and not shown to the public.

ANOMALISA

2015
(USA: Snoot Entertainment)

Directed by Duke Johnson and Charlie Kaufman
Written by Charlie Kaufman, based on his 2005 play
Produced by David Fuchs, Adrian Versteegh, Kassandra Mitchell, etc.
Score by Carter Burwell
Song "None of Them Are You" by Carter Burwell (music), and Charlie Kaufman
   (lyrics)
Specs: Color; 90 minutes; stop-motion animation

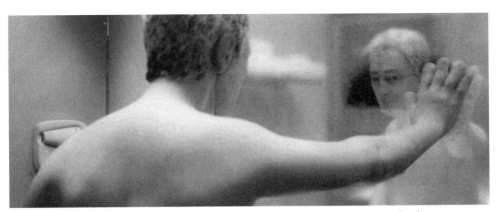

All the characters in the film wear some kind of mask although the antihero, Michael Stone, cannot even see through his mask when he gazes at himself in the bathroom mirror. *Paramount Pictures / Photofest. © Paramount Pictures*

The edgy writer-director-producer Charlie Kaufman presents a numbing but intriguing view of modern society in this stop-motion movie that is adult in subject matter as well as in presentation.

Michael Stone, an expert on consumer service with a popular book on the subject, flies to Cincinnati to address a conference on customer service but he has no enthusiasm for his job, his family, or anything else. Every person Michael encounters—a fellow passenger, the taxi driver, hotel clerk, bellboy, etc.—has the same bland face and the same bland voice. When he talks to his wife and son on the phone, they also sound the same, as does an old girlfriend he looks up and has a drink with in the Fregoli Hotel bar. But when Michael meets the awkward Lisa, also in the hotel to attend the conference, she has a distinctly feminine voice and he is captivated by her. They make love that night but by the next morning even Lisa's voice is starting to sound like all the others. During his speech at the conference, Michael has a mental breakdown. He then returns home, where he continues his lifeless life with indistinguishable family and friends.

The premise behind *Anomalisa* is the "Fregoli delusion," which psychologists describe as the belief that everyone one knows is the same person but in different disguises. Charlie Kaufman used this idea for his play *Anomalisa*, which was produced in Los Angeles in 2005. The stage version was so stylized that Kaufman did not think it would make a very effective live-action movie. Yet the concept of an animated version of the play intrigued him, and he and codirector Duke Johnson raised the money through Kickstarter.com to make a stop-motion film

Voice Cast

David Thewlis	Michael Stone
Jennifer Jason Leigh	Lisa Hesselman
Tom Noonan	Everyone else

using the voices of the same stage actors. The robotic movement of the characters and the nearly expressionless gestures on their generic faces supported the minimalist ideas in the story. The puppets had creases in their faces that suggested robots with human masks. At one point in the film, Michael loses part of his face and the mechanics underneath are exposed. There is even something mechanical about the sex scene between Michael and Lisa, surely the most graphic portrayal of lovemaking in an animated movie. The settings are realistic down to the tiniest details, yet there is a sterile sameness to all the locations. Not just the characters but the very places they inhabit are drained of life. This absolute malaise in *Anomalisa* makes for a very slow-moving movie, but the artistry of the piece helps the viewer get involved in the story and even the characters. This is not a film for mainstream audiences, but for the adventurous moviegoer it is provocative and surprisingly haunting.

> MICHAEL: I think you're extraordinary.
>
> LISA: Why?
>
> MICHAEL: I don't know yet. It's just obvious to me that you are.

Charlie Kaufman, known for such beguiling live-action films as *Being John Malkovich* (1999) and *Adaptation* (2002), is a writer and director who is interested in the themes of identity and psychology. He uses the medium of film in unreal, often surreal, ways. *Anomalisa*, his first animated movie, is similarly stylized. The stop-motion technique is seemingly realistic yet the flavor of the movie is dreamlike. It has more dialogue than many animated movies, much of the film being two-person conversations that seem mundane and even nonsensical. Yet the scenes slowly build until there is drama, though rarely broad dramatics. It certainly helps that the three voice actors are first rate. British actor David Thewlis voices Michael with a weariness and quiet disgust. But when he hears Lisa's voice for the first time, he comes to life. Jennifer Jason Leigh's Lisa is vocally very ordinary, yet to Michael her feminine sounds are like music. Tom Noonan provides the voices for all the other characters, both male and female, without any attempt to distinguish one from the other. This is so well done that when the audience first hears Lisa's voice, we are as surprised as Michael is. Adding to the weird tone of *Anomalisa* is Carter Burwell's musical score. He uses mostly percussion instruments to create a minimalist sound to go with the cold and lonely world portrayed on the screen. Burwell also wrote the music to Kaufman's lyrics for the song "None of Them Are You," a Leonard Cohen–like dirge sung by Noonan on the soundtrack.

Awards

Academy Award nomination: Best Animated Feature.
Golden Globe nomination: Best Picture—Animated.

Production on *Anomalisa* was slow and expensive and the movie ended up costing $8 million. After premiering at various film festivals and getting largely enthusiastic notices, *Anomalisa* was given a wider distribution by Paramount in 2015. Again the reviews were mostly laudatory, but it was a difficult movie to sell to the public. All the same, within a year the film grossed over $5 million, an impressive sum for a very offbeat and challenging piece of filmmaking. None of Kaufman's movies have been mainstream blockbusters, but they are admired and cheered by many looking for a cinematic adventure. *Anomalisa* is precisely that.

Did You Know . . . ?

Although *Anomalisa* was rated R, it was still nominated for an Academy Award for Best Animated Feature, the first time such an adult movie was nominated in that category.

ANTZ

1988
(USA: DreamWorks Animation)

Directed by Tim Johnson and Eric Darnell
Written by Todd Alcott, Chris Weitz, and Paul Weitz
Produced by Penny Finkelman, Sandra Rabins, Carl Rosendahl, Aron Warner, Patty Wooton, and Brad Lewis
Score by Harry Gregson-Williams and John Powell
Song standards by various artists
Specs: Color (Technicolor); 83 minutes; computer animation

DreamWorks' first animated feature film, Antz *is an early computer-generated movie that has a very polished look and sound, as well as some dark themes and images.*

The ant Z is one of the millions of workers in a colony ruled by the Queen but actually run by the greedy General Mandible. Z meets the Princess Bala when she goes slumming in a workers' nightspot. He is so infatuated with her that the next day he changes places with his pal, the warrior ant Weaver, in order to catch a glimpse of the princess during a military review. Before he knows it, Z is marching into a suicidal battle against the more powerful termite colony. He is protected for a time by the powerful warrior ant Barbatus, but by the time the bloody attack is done, all the termites and the ants are killed except Z. He is declared a hero when he returns to the colony and is reunited with Bala, who doesn't share his affections for her. Z mistakenly kidnaps her and the two fall through a garbage chute to the outside world, where they discover the wondrous land of Insectopia, filled with all kinds of bugs and food. Mandible has Bala captured by his flying henchman, Colonel Cutter, and returned to the colony. There she learns that the tunnel that is near completion is going to surface at a lake, thereby drowning the whole colony

The Princess Bala (right) is superior to the worker ant Z (left) in the social order of the colony, but in his own clumsy way Z becomes a hero and wins her hand. *DreamWorks / Photofest.* © *DreamWorks*

and allowing Mandible to start a new one with Bala as his queen. Z returns to the colony and helps the ants survive the flooding by building a tower with their bodies and safely reaching the surface. Cutter turns on Mandible and drowns him and Z and Bala are reunited.

DreamWorks cofounder Jeffrey Katzenberg recalled a movie idea from years earlier when he worked at the Disney studio. The idea of a worker ant who changes a nightmarish "brave new world" was developed by Katzenberg unaware that Pixar/Disney was also working on an animated feature about ants to be titled *Bugs*. By the time John Lasseter at Pixar found out about *Antz*, production was so far along that he decided to proceed as scheduled. So both ant films contin-

Voice Cast

Woody Allen	Z
Sharon Stone	Princess Bala
Gene Hackman	General Mandible
Anne Bancroft	Queen
Christopher Walken	Colonel Cutter
Dan Aykroyd	Chip
Sylvester Stallone	Weaver
Jennifer Lopez	Azteca
John Mahoney	Grebs
Danny Glover	Barbatus
Jane Curtin	Muffy
Paul Mazursky	Psychologist

ued production and the rivalry between DreamWorks and Pixar/Disney heated up. When the release date for *A Bug's Life*, as it was retitled, was announced, Katzenberg rushed production and released *Antz* a few months earlier. While there were many similarities in the plots of the two movies, they were very different in look and tone. The Pixar film has a bright and sunny look with mostly comic characters. *Antz* is darker, not only in its below-ground setting but in its themes about war and totalitarianism. In fact, there is very little for children to enjoy in the DreamWorks film. Its depiction of the battle between the ants and termites is graphic and not glorious at all. The way Mandible schemes to destroy millions of ants so he can control a new colony is also very disturbing. His persona and the images of millions of warrior ants marching in formation recall the worst days of the 1930s and 1940s. There is humor in *Antz*, but it is a nervous, uncomfortable kind of levity as personified in Woody Allen's comic-neurotic performance as Z. Allen wrote many of his lines, including Z's wry commentary that recalls some of the best Allen films. His vocals help turn *Antz* from an apocalyptic nightmare into a sly and pointed movie about human behavior as filtered through an ant colony.

> Z: I think everything must go back to the fact that I had a very anxious childhood. My mother never had time for me. You know, when you're—when you're the middle child in a family of five million, you don't get any attention. I mean, how is that possible?

While Allen's performance dominates the film, there are several other expert vocal artists in *Antz*. Gene Hackman's General Mandible is a humorless villain, all the more terrifying because he sounds like the Fascist dictators of the past. Christopher Walken's Cutter is more ambivalent, changing his philosophy as the plot progresses. Sharon Stone is a spunky Princess Bala and Anne Bancroft is a caring Queen. The most enjoyable vocals come from Z's friends: the dense but loyal Weaver voiced by Sylvester Stallone, the sexy, no-nonsense Azteca by Jennifer Lopez, the stalwart soldier Barbatus by Danny Glover, and the WASP wasps Chip and Muffy voiced by Dan Aykroyd and Jane Curtin. Added to these vocals are a handful of popular songs sung by various artists, from Doris Day's rendition of "High Hopes" to Neil Finn's recording of "I Can See Clearly Now." The soundtrack music by John Powell and Harry Gregson-Williams can sometimes be as flippant as these interpolated tunes, but other sections of the score are deadly serious, particularly during the battle scenes.

Award

British Academy of Film & Television Arts (BAFTA) Award nomination: Best Special Effects.

Ironically, the rivalry between *Antz* and *A Bug's Life* had little bearing on the box office. Both were well reviewed and were very popular. Opening first, *Antz* had something of an advantage. It earned over $17 million during its first weekend. The cost of the film is not public knowledge, but sources say DreamWorks spent between $40 million and $60 million. Regardless, its international gross was over $171 million. (The final earnings for *A Bug's Life* was around $363 million.) The VHS edition of *Antz* was released in 1999, the same year a DVD version was also available.

See also *A Bug's Life*.

Did You Know . . . ?

Woody Allen had never voiced an animated feature before and was reluctant to do so. He ended up providing some of the dialogue for his character Z, but some of his lines had to be cut in order to maintain a PG rating.

THE ARISTOCATS

1970
(USA: Walt Disney Productions)

Directed by Wolfgang Reitherman
Written by Larry Clemmons, Ralph Wright, Ken Anderson, Vance Gerry, Frank Thomas, Julius Svenden, and Eric Cleworth
Produced by Winston Hibler and Wolfgang Reitherman
Score by George Bruns
Songs by Richard M. and Robert B. Sherman, Terry Gilkyson, Floyd Huddleston, and Al Rinker
Specs: Color (Technicolor); 78 minutes; traditional animation

---

A charming Disney feature that might be described as the feline version of One Hundred and One Dalmatians *(1961),* The Aristocrats *has some memorable characters and songs as well as a masterful artistic look.*

The retired opera singer Madame lives in a palatial Paris house in 1910 with her beloved cat, Duchess, and her three kittens, Berlioz, Toulouse, and Marie. Madame calls in her lawyer, Georges, and rewrites her will, all her estate going to the cats and, upon their death, to her butler Edgar. Overhearing the conversation, Edgar gets resentful and greedy and that night he drugs the four felines, puts them in a basket, and drives them out into the countryside on his motorbike. There he dumps them but is attacked by the local hounds Napoleon and Lafayette, barely escaping with his life. When the cats awake the next morning, they are lost and confused, but the confident alley cat Thomas O'Malley, who immediately takes a shine to Duchess, promises to guide them back to Paris. After a series of adventures, the foursome arrive in Paris and are put up in the house of Scat Cat. Instead of getting any rest, the weary travelers are greeted by Scat Cat and his musician friends and they jam together all night long. Duchess and her kittens find Madame's house, but Edgar sees them and packs them in a trunk being mailed to Timbuktu. With the help of Thomas and the household mouse Roquefort, the

Performing the jumping number "Ev'rybody Wants to Be a Cat," the hep cat musician friends of Scat Cat enjoy themselves as they destroy a Parisian townhouse. *Walt Disney Pictures / Photofest.* © *Walt Disney Pictures*

cats escape the trunk and put Edgar in it. Once he is shipped off to Timbuktu, the felines are happily reunited with Madame.

Inspired by the true story of a wealthy Parisian who left all her fortune to her cats, Walt Disney asked Harry Tytle and Tom McGowan in 1962 to use the idea to write a two-episode, live-action program for his television series *Walt Disney's*

Voice Cast

Eva Gabor	Duchess (speaking)
Robie Lester	Duchess (singing)
Phil Harris	Thomas O'Malley
Liz English	Marie
Gary Dubin	Toulouse
Dean Clark	Berlioz
Roddy Maude-Roxby	Edgar
Hermione Baddeley	Madame
Scatman Crothers	Scat Cat
Sterling Holloway	Roquefort
Pat Buttram	Napoleon
George Lindsay	Lafayette
Monica Evans	Abigail
Carole Shelley	Amelia
Charles Lane	Georges

Wonderful World of Color. The more the project progressed, the more Disney thought it ought to be an animated feature. *The Aristocats* ended up being the last movie that Disney initiated and approved before his death in 1966. Early versions of the story were set in New York City and involved a maid and a butler who try to get rid of the cats destined to inherit a fortune. When Tom Rowe, an American writer living in Paris, was brought into the project, the location of the tale was moved to France and a sole butler was made the villain. The rich and colorful world of Paris became more important as the project developed and the background art returned to the splashes of color with ink details that had distinguished the look of *One Hundred and One Dalmatians*. As with that film, the animators sought to make the animal characters as accurate as possible. The movements of cats were studied in particular and the artists managed to distinguish each feline character with individual physical traits ranging from the regal and statuesque Duchess to the wild and chaotic Scat Cat. While some consider the story in *The Aristocats* less than gripping, the movie is an artistic and animation delight.

Songs

"The Aristocats" (Shermans)
"Thomas O'Malley Cat" (Gilkyson)
"She Never Felt Alone" (Shermans)
"Ev'rybody Wants to Be a Cat" (Huddleston/Rinker)
"Scales and Arpeggios" (Shermans)

The Aristocats calls for a large and varied voice cast, and the vocals in the movie are superb. Eva Gabor's soft Hungarian-accented voice gives Duchess a very regal and exotic flavor while Phil Harris's raspy American voice provides the right contrast for Thomas O'Malley. The accents in *The Aristocats* are all over the map. The hounds Lafayette (George Lindsay) and Napoleon (Pat Buttram) are rural American, the geese Abigail (Monica Evans) and Amelia (Carole Shelley) are very British, the accordion-playing cat Peppo (Vito Scoti) is Italian, the bass player Billy Boss (Thurl Ravenscroft) is Russian, and so on. The songs by the Sherman brothers and Terry Gilkyson are equally diverse. The title song, sung with warmth by Maurice Chevalier over the opening credits, is a pleasing French sidewalk cafe ditty, "Scales and Arpeggios" is a classically flavored minuet, and "Thomas O'Malley

THOMAS O'MALLEY: Why, your eyes are like sapphires sparkling so bright. They make the morning radiant and light.

MARIE: How romantic.

BERLIOZ: Sissy stuff.

DUCHESS: Oh, c'est très jolie, monsieur. Very poetic. But it is not quite Shakespeare.

THOMAS: 'Course not. That's pure O'Malley, baby. Right off the cuff. Yeah. I got a million of 'em.

Cat" is a smoothly swinging jazz piece. Floyd Huddleston and Al Rinker wrote the most vivacious song in the film, the contagious and raucous jazz number "Ev'rybody Wants to Be a Cat." George Bruns composed the soundtrack score that is heavily French at times and simply fun and exciting at other times. *The Aristocats* sounds terrific and doesn't seem to date.

During the difficult years after Walt Disney's death, *The Aristocats* was a much needed hit. The film cost around $4 million to make and earned over $10 million in the States alone. After the rerelease in 1980, the VHS edition in 1990, the DVD version in 2000, and the Blu-ray edition in 2012, it is estimated that the movie has grossed over $55 million. The critics varied in their opinions of *The Aristocats* when it was released in 1970. Some reviews thought it a pale copy of *One Hundred and One Dalmatians* and *The Jungle Book* in plot, characters, and music. Others lauded the film as pleasing and entertaining with superior art and animation. Many critics felt that the fumbling Edgar was a weak and ineffective villain. Some of the other characters have endeared themselves to moviegoers over the decades. *The Aristocats* has secured its place as a beloved Disney film if not one of the studio's major achievements.

See also *One Hundred and One Dalmatians*.

Did You Know . . . ?

Songwriters Richard M. and Robert B. Sherman wanted the famous French entertainer Maurice Chevalier to sing the title song and for jazz legend Louis Armstrong to sing "Ev'rybody Wants to Be a Cat" but both performers had retired. Armstrong was willing but was too ill to record so that jazz song was done by Scatman Crothers. The brothers persuaded Chevalier to come out of retirement to record "The Aristocats." It was his last credit before his death in 1972.

B

BAMBI

1942
(USA: Walt Disney Productions)

Directed by Bill Roberts, Paul Satterfield, Sam Armstrong, Graham Heid, James Algar, David Hand, and Norman Wright
Written by Perce Pearce and Larry Morey, based on Feliz Salten's book *Bambi, a Life in the Woods*
Produced by Walt Disney
Score by Frank Churchill and Edward Plumb
Songs by Frank Churchill (music) and Larry Morey (lyrics)
Specs: Color (Technicolor); 70 minutes; traditional animation

---

Pastoral animation reaches a kind of high point in Bambi, *a film that celebrates nature even as it somberly portrays the cycle of life and death. Without a human character in sight, this movie remains one of the most engaging and effective of all Disney efforts.*

The fawn Bambi is born in the spring, the son of the Great Prince of the Forest who protects the animals when hunters enter the woods. The young Bambi befriends the rabbit Thumper, the skunk Flower, and the female fawn Faline. The three youngsters discover the natural wonders of summer and then winter. But when hunters come on the scene, Bambi's mother is shot and dies. The Great Prince informs Bambi that he is his father and that one day Bambi will take over his position of guardian of the forest. Bambi and his friends grow up to adulthood, Bambi falling in love with Faline and Flower and Thumper also finding mates. Some hunters neglect to put out their campfire, resulting in a major forest fire, and Bambi and the Great Prince have to lead all the animals to safety on a riverbank. The next spring, the forest starts to come back to life and Faline gives birth to twins. Bambi is now the Great Prince and dedicates himself to protecting the animal community as the cycle of nature continues on.

The Hungarian-born author Felix Salten's *Bambi, a Life in the Woods* was published in Austria in 1923 and became a bestseller in 1928 when translated and published in English. MGM bought the screen rights with the intention of making a live-action movie adaptation but the project had so many difficulties that the studio sold the rights to Walt Disney in 1937. The Disney artists also encountered

The rabbit Thumper and the fawn Bambi first meet as children and remain lifelong friends over the years, to the delight of movie audiences everywhere. *Walt Disney Pictures / Photofest.* © *Walt Disney Pictures*

problems trying to tell a sometimes-grim tale in the format of a family movie. The large number of animal characters in the book had to be cut down to a handful, and the decision was made not to show any humans, making Man more mysterious and evil. One of the screenplay's merits was the creation of Thumper, the rabbit who has endeared himself to audiences for generations. The book's most

Voice Cast

Bobby Stewart	Baby Bambi
Donnie Dunagan	Young Bambi
Hardie Albright	Adolescent Bambi
John Sutherland	Adult Bambi
Paula Winslowe	Bambi's Mother
Will Wright	Friend Owl
Stan Alexander	Young Flower
Tim Davis	Adolescent Flower
Sterling Holloway	Adult Flower
Peter Behn	Young Thumper
Tim Davis	Adult Thumper
Sam Edwards	Adult Thumper
Cammie King Conlon	Young Faline
Ann Gillis	Adult Faline
Fred Shields	Great Prince of the Forest

challenging scene was the death of Bambi's mother. Early versions of the script showed the doe getting shot while jumping over a log. Another approach was to show Bambi discovering his dead mother in a pool of blood. It was finally decided that the sound of a gunshot and the reporting of her death by the Great Prince was more effective and less grim. All the same, the death of Bambi's mother remains one of the most powerful and upsetting moments in the Disney canon.

Songs

"Love Is a Song"
"Little April Shower"
"Looking for Romance (I Bring You a Song)"
"Let's Sing a Gay Little Spring Song"
"Twitterpated"
"Thumper Song"

The animation of the woodland creatures in *Bambi* is far more sophisticated and accurate than the animals seen in *Snow White and the Seven Dwarfs* five years earlier. The artists studied real animals at the Los Angeles Zoo and some species were temporarily housed in the Disney studio during production, resulting in a poetic yet lifelike ballet of different kinds of movement. The distinction between the ways the young animals moved as opposed to the adults is noticeable and effective. There is also a playful tone to some of the animation, most memorably the sequence when Bambi, Thumper, and other animal youngsters discover an icy pond. Although the setting for Salten's book was a forest in Austria, Disney moved the locale to the woods of Maine and Vermont and had his background artists tour the region making sketches and notes. A major production problem was having the animal characters disappear in the detailed background settings. Disney hired the Chinese artist Tyrus Wong to oversee the background art because of his talent for mixing impressionism and realism. In many of the scenes, the area with the characters present is sharper and more realistic while the edges of the setting are softer and less real, thereby helping the moviegoer to focus on what is essential. The re-creation of nature during the different seasons is one of *Bambi's* many artistic triumphs. The entire story takes place in one forest, yet the variety the artists found within the setting is masterful. *Bambi* also used the multi-plane camera effectively throughout the film, allowing the audience to move through the forest, discovering new vistas with each turn.

Frank Churchill and Edward Plumb wrote the soundtrack score for *Bambi* and captured the different moods of the film beautifully. From the serene sounds of a

YOUNG BAMBI: What happened, Mother? Why did we all run?

BAMBI'S MOTHER: Man was in the forest.

quiet forest to the violent sounds of a forest fire, the score is a symphony of nature. Churchill and Larry Morey wrote the six songs in the movie, most of them short and not intrusive to the storytelling. The lyrical "Love Is a Song," sung on the soundtrack by a chorus, is used in the opening and closing of the film, as well as in a few scenes between. A chorus also sings the plucky little ditty "Little April Show," in which the notes and the lyric are patterned after the tempo of raindrops during Bambi's first experience with rain. The love song for Bambi and Faline is "Looking for Romance," a dreamy number that was later recorded successfully by various artists. Perhaps the most ingenious use of song and movement is found in "Let's Sing a Gay Little Spring Song." Spring is welcomed by this chipper number that accompanies the bustle of animals in the new season.

Awards

Academy Award nominations: Best Score, Best Song ("Love Is a Song"), and Best Sound Recording.
Special Golden Globe Award to producer Walt Disney.

Because both *Pinocchio* (1940) and *Fantasia* (1940) had cost much more than they earned at the box office, the budget and time restraints on *Bambi* were severe. During production an entire sequence running about twelve minutes was abandoned because the studio was running out of time and money. When the movie was released in 1942, it could not be sold to most European countries because of World War Two. *Bambi* ended up making just under its $1.7 million budget but was a major hit when rereleased in 1947, 1957, 1966, 1975, 1982, and 1988. The home video version came out in 1989, the DVD in 2007, and Blu-ray in 2011. A sequel, *Bambi II*, arrived in 2006 as a direct-to-video movie though it was later shown in theaters in several foreign countries.

As popular and beloved as *Bambi* is today, controversy still surrounds the film. Some hunters and sportsmen consider the movie insulting and anti-American, turning Man into a villain. Some critics in 1942 thought *Bambi* too harsh and disturbing for young children, and many still maintain that opinion today. Other reviewers stated that they missed the fantasy and magic of the previous Disney features. *Bambi* is totally realistic in story, though the animals are humanized, making death in the forest more upsetting. The fact that the film still rouses strong emotions is part of its timeless artistry.

Did You Know . . . ?

Late in life, Walt Disney stated that *Bambi* was his personal favorite of all his films.

BEAUTY AND THE BEAST

1991
(USA: Walt Disney Pictures)

Directed by Gary Trousdale and Kirk Wise
Written by Linda Woolverton, based on the story by Jeanne-Marie Leprince de Beau-
    mont
Produced by Howard Ashman, Don Hahn, and Sarah McArthur
Score by Alan Menken
Songs by Alan Menken (music) and Howard Ashman (lyrics)
Specs: Color (Technicolor); 84 minutes; traditional and some computer animation

*There is something special about this animated film, the second entry in the so-called
Disney renaissance. It tells a well-known tale but tells it with such charm and romance
that it's easy to understand why the Academy of Motion Pictures Arts and Sciences broke
precedent and nominated it as one of the Best Pictures of the year.*

In a French provincial village, the young Belle is considered odd because she
likes to read books and does not fawn over the muscular huntsman Gaston like
all the other unmarried girls. Also an outcast of sorts is her father, Maurice, a
crackpot inventor who, on his way to a country fair to show off his latest contraption, gets lost in the forest and stumbles onto a gloomy castle. It is inhabited
by a prince turned into a bitter and fearsome Beast by an enchantress because of

Belle is a unique Disney heroine in that she is not looking for a prince and is more interested in
books and a life of some personal merit. *Walt Disney Pictures / Photofest. © Walt Disney Pictures*

Voice Cast

Paige O'Hara	Belle
Robby Benson	Beast
Richard White	Gaston
Angela Lansbury	Mrs. Potts
Jerry Orbach	Lumiere
David Ogden Stiers	Cogsworth
Rex Everhart	Maurice
Jesse Corti	Lefou
Bradley Pierce	Chip
Tony Jay	Monsieur D'Arque
Jo Anne Worley	Wardrobe

his selfishness, and he is waited on by his staff, who have all been turned into enchanted objects. Maurice is held prisoner in the castle, and when Belle comes looking for him, she makes a bargain with the Beast: if he will let her father go, she will remain and be his prisoner. The Beast agrees, and he tries to act civil toward Belle, but his excitable anger gets in the way. With the help of the enchanted candlestick, Lumiere; the clock, Cogsworth; the teapot, Mrs. Potts; and others in the castle, Belle feels less threatened and even starts to have feelings for the Beast. He lets her go to tend to her sick father, only to have Gaston and the villagers, who have heard about the Beast from Maurice, attack the castle. The enchanted objects drive the horde away, but the Beast is mortally wounded by Gaston before the hunter falls to his death. Before the Beast dies, Belle tells him that she loves him, which removes the curse placed on the Beast. He is transformed back into a prince and lives to marry Belle.

Jeanne-Marie Leprince de Beaumont's 1740 tale *La Belle et la Bête* has seen many variations and adaptations over the years. In the original, Beauty has several brothers and sisters who try to keep her from returning to the Beast after she has promised him she would. When the magic mirror shows that the Beast is dying of heartbreak, she returns to his castle for a happy ending. In many adaptations of the story, Beauty has two mean-spirited sisters who are jealous of her riches at the castle. The Disney version gives Beauty a name (Belle, which means *beautiful* in French), gets rid of the sisters, and provides the boastful Gaston as the antagonist. He starts out as a laughable buffoon, but by the end of the movie he is definitely the villain. The father, Maurice, is in the original tale, but in this version he is an oddball inventor who is an outcast just as Belle is in their little French town. The enchanted objects are also an invention of this film. (In the original, Beauty is waited upon by invisible servants.) They give Belle someone to talk with before she and the Beast are on speaking terms. The objects also provide exposition about the past. *Beauty and the Beast* is a well-plotted movie in which the action is always justified. Maurice is something of a joke in the town, so it makes sense that no one believes him at first when he tells them about the Beast. Maurice is later used by Gaston to get back at Belle and to hunt the Beast. The end of the film stays close to the original tale as the Beast is transformed back into a prince.

Among the delights of the movie are the several distinct characters. The Beast is understandably gruff at first, but Belle starts to feel differently about him after he saves her from some forest wolves. Belle is not just a beauty but also a smart woman who loves to read and does not wish to marry just any man. She is headstrong and not a helpless female. Mrs. Potts is the mother figure in the film and adds a warm touch to the story. Among the enchanted objects, the fussy Cogsworth and Lumiere with his joie de vivre are the most interesting. The villain Gaston is given a comic sidekick, the foolish Le Fou, and Mrs. Potts has a teacup son, Chip, all of them helping to fill out the story with a menagerie of delicious characters. Linda Woolverton is the sole author of the screenplay, a rarity in animation, and her script can take credit for much of the success of *Beauty and the Beast*.

Songs

"Belle"
"Be Our Guest"
"Beauty and the Beast"
"Gaston"
"Something There"
"The Mob Song (Kill the Beast)"

Few Disney films are as beautifully rendered as this one. It has a fairy-tale look but with a feeling of a Gothic mystery. The Beast's castle is obviously gloomy but one detects an elegance that has been hidden away. When the Beast is transformed at the end of the movie, so too is the castle. The background art throughout is exceptional. From the bright primary colors of the village to the haunted corridors of the castle, the decor is detailed and accurate even as the sets are whimsical. Computer animation was already being used in short subjects by Pixar and some of that technology was used in the final stages of making *Beauty and the Beast*. The justly famous ballroom scene with the camera seeming to sweep around the dancing Belle and the Beast was only possible with the new technology. Yet the scene is far from technical looking and has a keen sense of majesty. The success of that scene alone prompted Disney to invest more in computer animation for the future. The hand-drawn animation is also very impressive. From the enticing opening in which the multi-plane camera moves though the woods and approaches the castle to the finale in which the castle and its servants break away from the spell, *Beauty and the Beast* is filled with superior animation. Perhaps the most dazzling of the many effects in the movie is the scene in which the Beast is transformed back into a prince. The way the moviegoer sees hands, feet, and other details before showing the prince's face is an animation triumph.

The directors, Gary Trousdale and Kirk Wise, selected an experienced Broadway cast for the speaking and singing vocals. Paige O'Hara had been in a handful of New York stage shows since 1983 but was little known to the public. Her interpretation of Belle is that of a clear-headed individual but with a definite soft side. Robby Benson had enjoyed a successful career on television, films, and some Broadway credits but he was not physically or vocally very beast-like. The sound engineers were able to give his voice a gruff and deeper sound yet one detects a sensitivity underneath. Broadway musical veterans Jerry Orbach (Lumiere), Angela Lansbury (Mrs. Potts), David Ogden Stiers (Cogsworth), and others provided a rich tapestry of sounds that help make *Beauty and the Beast* so effective. Also, all of the performers did their own singing, doing justice to the excellent songs.

> GASTON: If I didn't know better, I'd think you had *feelings* for this monster.
>
> BELLE: He's no monster, Gaston, *you* are!

Alan Menken's soundtrack score borrows from some French composers, in particular Camille Saint-Saëns and Erik Satie. The opening theme is a delectable homage to those French masters and does much to set up the mood of the movie. The songs Menken wrote with Howard Ashman are in the Broadway mold yet are also very French. The title song is a lovely, flowing ballad that also has a touch of mystery in it besides being very romantic. "Be Our Guest" has French can-can music and is delivered by Lumiere like a flashy nightclub number in a Paris cabaret. The rollicking "Gaston" is a vigorous drinking song that sounds very European. "Something There" is like a sprightly French dance, although the lyrics make it more of a revealing character song. "Kill the Beast" is a repetitive march led by Gaston to rouse the townspeople to action. Perhaps the most theatrical number is the opening song, "Belle," in which the heroine, several major characters, and the villagers themselves are introduced. It has pleasing music that sweeps along like a village dance. "Human Again" is a number written for the film but originally cut in the released version. It was later used in the Broadway adaptation of *Beauty and the Beast* and then later was put back in the DVD version of the movie. The number is a fast waltz and also sounds very French.

Awards

Academy Awards: Best Score and Best Song ("Beauty and the Beast"). Oscar nominations: Best Picture, Best Sound, and Best Song ("Be Our Guest" and "Belle").

·Golden Globe Awards: Best Picture—Comedy or Musical, Best Score, and Best Song ("Beauty and the Beast"). Golden Globe nomination: Best Song ("Be Our Guest").

British Academy of Film & Television Arts (BAFTA) Award nominations: Best Score and Best Special Effects.

Beauty and the Beast received the most rapturous reviews of any animated movie in years, even surpassing the plaudits earned by *The Little Mermaid* two years before. Its box office success was also overwhelming, quickly breaking the record for an animated film by earning $100 million domestically and, during its first release, over $400 million internationally. The movie was reissued in 2002 in an IMAX format (with the song "Human Again" restored) and a sing-along version was in theaters in 2010. The home video of *Beauty and the Beast* was released in 1992 and two direct-to-video spinoffs were also made: *Belle's Enchanted Christmas*

(1997) and *Belle's Magical World* (1998). Disney Theatricals made its Broadway debut with the 1994 stage version of *Beauty and the Beast*. Because Howard Ashman had died, British lyricist Tim Rice provided the lyrics for Menken's new songs. Critics were wary of Disney on Broadway and the show met with mixed notices, but it was very popular with theatergoers, running fourteen years in New York. The stage version was also a hit on tour and later became a favorite musical for community and school groups. *Beauty and the Beast* came full circle in 2017 when Disney released the live-action film version based on the animated original and the Broadway adaptation.

   Beauty and the Beast ranks with the Disney classics of old and shows no signs of dating or losing its effectiveness. With so many variations of the film available for viewing, the original animated version remains the most satisfying and a high point in feature animation.

Did You Know . . . ?

The animators for the character of Gaston took their inspiration from the brawny Brom Bones from *The Legend of Sleepy Hollow* sequence from *The Adventures of Ichabod and Mr. Toad* (1949).

BIG HERO 6

2014
(USA: Marvel Entertainment/Disney)

Produced by John Lasseter, Roy Conli, Kristina Reed, and Brad Simonsen
Directed by Don Hall and Chris Williams
Written by Jordan Roberts, Robert L. Baird, and Daniel Gerson, based on characters
   created by Man of Action (Steven T. Seagle, Duncan Rouleau, Joe Kelly, and Joe
   Casey)
Score by Henry Jackson
Specs: Color; 102 minutes; computer animation

Marvel Comics and Disney combined to make this sci-fi adventure filled with superheroes, villains, nonstop action, and plenty of clever gadgets.

Teenager Hiro Hamada is a whiz at gadgetry and enjoys entering his robotic fighters in illegal matches in the back alleys of the futuristic city of San Fransokyo. His older brother Tadashi is also an inventor and has just completed developing Baymax, an inflatable robot who tends to the health of humans. Hiro is so impressed with Tadashi's lab at the Institute, its head Professor Callaghan, and the "nerd" inventors who work there, that he wants to enroll there. To gain admittance, Hiro creates a microbot, a tiny robot that, when combined with thousands of other microbots, can form any object that the operator can imagine. The demonstration

The cinema has seen all kinds of robots over the decades, but the idea of a soft rather than metal robot was something new, especially in a comic book–inspired action film. *Walt Disney Pictures / Photofest.* © *Walt Disney Pictures*

of the microbots impresses everyone, including the manufacturer Alistair Krei, who wants to buy the invention. But Hiro decides to attend the Institute instead. That night, a fire breaks out in the lab and Tadashi and Callaghan are believed killed and the various experiments are destroyed, including Hiro's microbots. Hiro is too depressed to attend the Institute and is comforted by Baymax. The robot notices that Hiro's lone surviving microbot is very active and leads them to a warehouse where there are millions of other microbots being manufactured.

Voice Cast

Ryan Potter	Hiro
Scott Adsit	Baymax
Daniel Henney	Tadashi
T. J. Miller	Fred
Jamie Chung	Go Go
Damon Wayans Jr.	Wasabi
Genesis Rodriguez	Honey Lemon
James Cromwell	Robert Callaghan
Alan Tudyk	Alistair Krei
Maya Rudolph	Cass
Abraham Benrubi	General
Katie Lowes	Abigail
Paul Riggs	Yama

Hiro and Baymax are attacked by a masked man who is controlling the microbots, but the two manage to escape. Hiro reprograms Baymax into a flying and fighting robot and recruits Tadashi's friends from the lab to become superheroes. Together they pursue the masked man. They are convinced he is Krei and that he started the fire and stole the microbots. But it turns out Callaghan survived the fire using the microbots and is now using them to get revenge on Krei because Callaghan's daughter Abigail died during one of Krei's mismanaged experiments. The superheroes stop Callaghan, find Abigail still alive, and turn Baymax back into the health care robot he was intended to be.

The Disney company bought Marvel Entertainment in 2009 and soon several ideas for an animated feature based on one of the Marvel comics were considered. The lesser-known comic book *Big Hero 6* had the characters and thrills the company was looking for and production began in 2012. While the film was made by Disney artists and computer animators, personnel from Marvel Entertainment served as advisors and consultants. The finished movie resembles Marvel products in its action and superhero characters but is very Disney-like in its relationship between Hiro and his brother as well as Hiro and Baymax. The Disney artists visited robotic labs and hit upon the look for Baymax when they saw an inflatable robot made of vinyl at the Carnegie Mellon University's Robotics Institute. The idea of a "soft" robot fit in nicely with the concept that Baymax was a gentle and helpful machine. The setting of the story was envisioned as a futuristic city with aspects of Asia and the West. Visual elements from both San Francisco and Tokyo were used in creating the look of the movie's urban setting, hence the new name San Fransokyo. New software programs were created by the Disney engineers to handle the film's many characters, settings, and special effects. The final price tag for *Big Hero 6* was a whopping $165 million.

GO GO: There are no red lights during car chases!

While the look of *Big Hero 6* is distinctive with its Asian and Western buildings, it is the mechanics in the film that most impress. The microbots are like tiny building blocks that almost instantly link together to form all kinds of shapes and designs. This is very effective when Hiro demonstrates his invention for the Institute, but the microbots take on a different kind of power when used for evil. All the inventions at the lab are ingenious; later in the movie they become super-powered gadgets when outfitted to battle the masked man. With so much hardware on the screen, the simple white form of Baymax stands out and offers a different point of view when it comes to technology. The warm and reassuring voice of Scott Adsit used for Baymax adds much to the character, a welcome sound amid all the noise in the comic book tale. Ryan Potter sounds a bit too mature for the fourteen-year-old Hiro but Daniel Henney is very effective as Tadashi. Alan Tudyk and James Cromwell are ideally sinister as Krei and Callaghan, but the voices for the nerd inventors are more interesting, supplied by such actors as Damon Wayans Jr., Jamie Chung, T. J. Miller, and Genesis Rodriguez. The musical score by Henry Jackson is as frantic and propulsive as the action on screen, but there are some tender moments as well, mostly associated with the relationship between the Hamada brothers. While *Big Hero 6* may often resemble a rapid video game more than a Disney movie, the film has some strong storytelling and engaging characters that help it function as more than a comic book.

Awards

Academy Award: Best Animated Feature.
Golden Globe Award: Best Animated Feature.
British Academy of Film & Television Arts (BAFTA) Award: Best Animated Feature.

Big Hero 6 premiered in Tokyo in 2014 then was given a wide release in the States later that year. The film was greeted with positive reviews and won several awards. The domestic box office was a hefty $222 million but it made twice that much overseas. Also successful were the DVD and Blu-ray editions in 2015. A video game based on the movie was released in 2014. A television series and a feature film sequel are in the works.

Did You Know . . . ?

The animators came up with the slow and careful moves for Baymax by filming a baby as it moved about with a full diaper.

BOLT

2008
(USA: Walt Disney Pictures)

Directed by Byron Howard and Chris Williams
Written by Dan Fogelman and Chris Williams
Produced by John Lasseter, Clark Spencer, and Makul Wigert
Score by John Powell. Song "I Thought I Lost You" by Miley Cyrus and Jeffrey Steele
Specs: Color; 96 minutes; computer animation

A clever premise, some delightful characters, and a strong plot line make Bolt *a highly enjoyable Disney entry. The setting and the sense of humor are very modern, but there is still plenty of heart in the film.*

The canine hero of the hit television action series *Bolt* is played by a dog who has been raised on the set and believes he has super powers. In each episode, Bolt battles the evil Doctor Calico and rescues the young girl Penny from danger. Bolt believes the series is real and is unaware that there are actors, writers, a director, and

The three travelers in this "road picture" are an unlikely but sportive trio: the optimistic dog Bolt, the reluctant feline Mittens, and the overenthusiastic hamster Rhino. *Walt Disney Pictures / Photofest.* © *Walt Disney Pictures*

other staff. When Bolt mistakenly believes Penny has been kidnapped by Calico, he jumps into action but gets trapped in a box being shipped from California to the East. In New York City he tries to use his super powers but they seem to have disappeared. Bolt meets the street-wise cat Mittens and convinces her to help him travel back West to California. On the journey they meet up with the hyperactive hamster Rhino, who has seen Bolt on TV and is anxious to go on adventures with him. When the threesome finally make it to the studio in LA, a replacement dog has been found and Bolt realizes that the series is not real and that he is just an ordinary dog. While filming an action scene in the studio, the replacement dog panics and knocks over some torches, setting the studio on fire. Penny is trapped inside but Bolt, reverting to his heroic character, manages to rescue her. Fed up with talent agents and directors and the world of show biz, Penny quits the series and moves to the countryside, where she and her mother adopt Bolt, Mittens, and Rhino as family pets.

Voice Cast

John Travolta	Bolt
Miley Cyrus	Penny
Susie Essman	Mittens
Mark Walton	Rhino
Malcolm McDowell	Dr. Calico
James Lipton	Director
Greg Germann	Agent
Nick Swardson	Blake
J. P. Manoux	Tom
Dan Fogelman	Billy
Kari Wahlgren	Mindy

Disney animator Chris Sanders first came up with the plot premise for *Bolt*, although most of the details were different from the finished product. When Pixar pioneer John Lasseter joined the Disney studio, he turned the project over to directors Byron Howard and Chris Williams, who made many changes in the characters, settings, and plot details. While the idea of a dog on television believing he was that character remained, Lasseter wanted the film to be a journey of discovery for Bolt as he travels the country and sees the real world. Williams and Dan Fogelman wrote the clever screenplay that allowed for incisive character development in between the action and comedy scenes. While Bolt is a starry-eyed superhero with an eager sensibility, Mittens is a sarcastic, even bitter, cat who has known neglect, hunger, and survival. Rhino is the funniest character in the movie, a star worshipper and TV addict who is thrilled to be on a real adventure. The minor characters, right down to the Manhattan and Los Angeles pigeons, are satirical as the film makes fun of show business. *Bolt* was also the first Disney movie to use the relatively new neo-photorealistic rendering (NPR) process, which has a more painterly look rather than a photographic one. *Bolt* was also the first Disney film made in both 2-D and 3-D; previous 3-D features had been made in 2-D then later remade as 3-D. The look of *Bolt* is vibrant and detailed. The movie has more locations than most animated films and each one is rendered with a somewhat poetic look. (The artists used paintings by Edward Hopper as their inspiration.) The animation of both humans and animals is also slightly romanticized. The most challenging (and fascinating) animation in *Bolt* is the movement of the hamster Rhino, who remains in a plastic bubble for much of the story. The animators used Lasseter's pet chinchilla in a similar bubble to study the variety of ways to create movement for the funny hamster.

> MITTENS: You came all the way back here . . . for me?
> BOLT: Yeah.
> MITTENS: But how'd you . . . ? I mean . . . You don't have superpowers!
> BOLT: I know.
> MITTENS: Really?
> BOLT: Yeah.
> MITTENS: Wow. Crazy day for ya, huh?

The studio recruited some famous film and television stars for the voices for *Bolt*. John Travolta captures both the optimistic enthusiasm and the crushing realization of the truth that the title character goes through. Miley Cyrus is convincing as the young girl Penny, Malcolm McDowell is a grandly stereotypic villain as Calico, and Greg Germann is appropriately sleazy as Penny's agent. But the standout performances are given by Mark Walton as the out-of-control Rhino and Susie Essman's sardonic Mittens. John Powell's soundtrack score is sometimes flashy, as expected for the action scenes, but also has its tender moments. Some of the "travel" music is expansive and fun, as when the animal trio ride along in a house trailer and Bolt experiences the heavenly feeling of the breeze against his face. The pop ballad "I Thought I Lost You" by Miley Cyrus and Jeffrey Steele was sung by Cyrus and Travolta on the soundtrack but was not worked into the story.

Awards

Academy Award nomination: Best Animated Feature.
Golden Globe nominations: Best Animated Film and Best Song ("I Thought I Lost You").

Bolt met with favorable but not rave reviews when released in 2008 but has since risen in the estimation of critics and audiences. Box office for the first release started modestly then grew, bringing in over $114 million just in domestic sales. The film ended up making over $300 million by 2011. The Blu-ray edition (2009) of *Bolt* was available before the DVD was released later that same year. *Bolt* also inspired a popular video game and the 2009 animated short *Super Rhino*.

Did You Know . . . ?

Although the film was computer generated, the Disney artists still drew sketches for the animation and, after filming was complete, they added brushstrokes to the images to soften the computerized look.

THE BOXTROLLS

2014
(USA: Laika Entertainment)

Directed by Graham Annable and Anthony Stacchi.
Written by Irena Brignull and Adam Pava, based on Alan Snow's book *Here Be Monsters!*
Produced by David Bleiman Ichioka, Matthew Fried, and Travis Knight
Score by Dario Marianelli
Songs by Dario Marianelli, Eric Idle, Malvina Reynolds, Jessie Donaldson, and Ritchie Young
Specs: Color; 96 minutes; stop-motion animation

An imaginative stop-motion film with a distinctive look, The Boxtrolls *is a slightly bizarre fantasy with some very real social implications.*

The Victorian town of Cheesebridge is lorded over by Sir Charles Portley-Rind and the other upper-class White Hats who eat cheese in the Tasting Room. The Red Hat commoner Archibald Snatcher is desperate to enter high society (even though he is severely allergic to cheese), so he starts rumors that a baby has been kidnapped by the boxtrolls, creatures who live under the town and wear boxes for clothes. In truth, the boxtrolls are harmless creatures and Snatcher gave the baby to them in order to start a panic. Snatcher vows to destroy all the boxtrolls if he is

Named for the box he wears, the human youth Eggs feels very at home with the odd but likable Boxtrolls, who live beneath the surface of the Victorian city of Cheesebridge. *Focus Features / Photofest. © Focus Features*

given a White Hat when the job is done, and Portley-Rind reluctantly agrees. The baby grows up to be the boy called Eggs because he wears an eggs box. With the help of Portley-Rind's young daughter Winnie, Eggs fights to convince the townspeople that the boxtrolls are not evil and that Snatcher is behind all the panic. Eggs urges the boxtrolls to abandon their boxes and let Snatcher think that they are all dead when the boxes are flattened by a deadly machine. When Snatcher announces that all the boxtrolls are destroyed and he is given a White Hat, he greedily consumes the gourmet cheese and, because of his allergy, explodes into pieces. The townspeople realize the boxtrolls are not the enemies and the happy creatures decide to live in the open air with the humans.

Voice Cast

Isaac Hempstead Wright	Eggs
Elle Fanning	Winnie Portley-Rind
Ben Kingsley	Archibald Snatcher
Jared Harris	Lord Portley-Rind
Nick Frost	Mr. Trout
Richard Ayoade	Mr. Pickles
Dee Bradley Baker	Fish
Steve Blum	Shoe
Nika Futterman	Oil Can
Tracy Morgan	Mr. Gristle
Pat Fraley	Fragile
Fred Tatasciore	Clocks
Toni Collette	Lady Cynthia Portley-Rind

The fantasy novel *Here Be Monsters!* by British author Alan Snow is a massive work about five different species of creatures who live underground. Codirector Anthony Stacchi and the artistic staff at Laika Entertainment had quite a challenge editing down the book, and the early drafts were confusing and ineffective. Stacchi then decided to make the film about only one species, the boxtrolls, and the screenplay finally came together. Although the story is completely set in the hilltop city of Cheesebridge, there are dozens of different locations and a large cast of characters. Another difficulty was how to handle the nonhuman language of the boxtrolls. The actor Dee Bradley Baker, who voiced the primary boxtroll character Fish, was mostly responsible for coming up with the funny and expressive gibberish that the underground creatures spoke. Although the final shooting script was full of action, it also allowed the audience to distinguish several individual characters besides the leading roles. Snatcher's henchmen, Portley-Rind's fellow aristocrats, and a handful of boxtrolls were clearly defined and delightfully individual. *The Boxtrolls* ended up having a solid story with estimable character development throughout.

Songs

"The Boxtrolls Song" (Idle)
"Little Boxes" (Reynolds)
"Quattro Sabatinos" (Marianelli)
"Some Kids" (Donaldson/Young)

The visuals in *The Boxtrolls* are superior on all accounts. Cheesebridge is portrayed as a cockeyed British city perched on a cone-like hill with steep winding streets and crooked houses. The humans are exaggerated Victorians with sometimes-grotesque facial features and elaborate costumes. Madame Frou Frou, Snatcher's female disguise, is a hilarious caricature of a cabaret performer whose ogre-like shape is more hideous than the so-called monsters under the city. The boxtrolls are less gruesome, their bald heads and various boxes giving them a more comical persona. Their movements are a cross between human motions and animal ones. The fact that the boxtrolls and their boxes are very individual helps humanize the creatures. Even with their gurgling language, these underground characters are endearing and accessible to moviegoers.

WINNIE: A Boxtroll? Oh . . . really? Then let's see you fit into your box!

EGGS: Err . . . I can't right now.

WINNIE: Ummhmm.

EGGS: I'm long boned.

The outstanding vocal performance in the film is Ben Kingsley's outrageous theatrics as Archibald Snatcher. Hitting every note on the vocal scale, Kingsley growls, swoons, purrs, and shouts with abandon as the villain. He then finds even more vocal qualities as Madame Frou Frou (though her singing is done by an uncredited singer). Also playful are Jared Harris as the pretentious Portley-Rind and Snatcher's three stooges, voiced by Nick Frost, Tracy Morgan, and Richard Ayoade. Isaac Hempstead Wright has the right amount of innocence and spunk as Eggs, while Elle Fanning fluctuates between saucy and sweet as Winnie. Dario Marianelli's soundtrack score is sometimes urgent and fierce, other times lyrical and mysterious. The music for the boxtrolls and their underground world is sweeping and circus-like while the themes behind the Cheesebridge scenes are elegant and silly, as during the fun fair and the ball at the Portley-Rind mansion. There are also a handful of cockeyed songs by various songwriters, most memorably the carnival-like "The Boxtrolls Song" and the mock operatic quartet "Quattro Sabatinos." *The Boxtrolls* is a satiric film well supported by its daffy vocals and agile music.

Awards

Academy Award nomination: Best Animated Feature.
Golden Globe nomination: Best Animated Feature.
British Academy of Film & Television Arts (BAFTA) Award nomination: Best Animated Feature.

The final cost of the movie was about $60 million but when it was released in 2014, it earned an impressive $108 million worldwide. The reviews were nearly all very favorable and audiences responded well during the early weeks of its nationwide release. *The Boxtrolls* also did surprisingly well overseas, particularly in the English-speaking nations of Britain, Ireland, and Australia. The 2015 release of the DVD and Blu-ray editions was also surprisingly successful for a movie that was not aimed at young children. *The Boxtrolls* is considered by many to be the most ingenious stop-action product by Laika Entertainment. It is not as dark as *Coraline* (2009) nor as family friendly as *ParaNorman* (2012); rather, it is a very individual animated movie. The idea of a villain creating widespread prejudice against a social group is not unknown in animated movies, but rarely have such ideas been so potent as presented in an entertaining way.

Did You Know . . . ?

The studio had to make over 20,000 boxes and other props for the stop-motion film.

A BOY NAMED CHARLIE BROWN

1969
(USA: Cinema Center Films)

Directed by Bill Melendez
Written by Charles M. Schulz
Produced by Bill Melendez, Lee Mendelson, and Charles M. Schulz
Score by Vince Guaraldi
Songs by Rod McKuen
Specs: Color (Technicolor); 86 minutes; traditional animation

The comic strip everyman Charlie Brown made it to the big screen in this, the first (and arguably the best) animated feature based on Charles Schulz's characters.

Charlie Brown is more perplexed and depressed than ever after once again failing to get his kite in the air, losing a baseball game, and having his faults pointed out by the amateur psychiatrist Lucy. She jokingly suggests that Charlie compete in the school's spelling bee and he sees it as a way to show himself as a winner. He wins the bee because the words he is given, such as "failure" and "insecure," are

In the comic-strip world of Charles Schulz, Charlie Brown and Lucy may be in two-dimensional profile, but everything essential is told in those few well-placed lines. *National General Pictures / Photofest. © National General Pictures*

Voice Cast

Peter Robbins	Charlie Brown
Pamelyn Ferdin	Lucy Van Pelt
Glenn Gilger	Linus Van Pelt
Andy Pforsich	Schroeder
Sally Dryer	Patty
Erin Sullivan	Sally
Christopher DeFaria	Pig Pen
Lynda Mendelson	Frieda
Ann Altieri	Violet
Bill Melendez	Snoopy

ones he is very familiar with. Winning the bee gives Charlie confidence and a bit of happiness until he learns that he must move on to the regional spelling bee in the big city. As Charlie boards the bus, Linus gives him his blue security blanket for good luck. The pressure of not letting down his school forces Charlie to cram for the bee to the point he is dazed and exhausted. Linus suffers such anxiety over not having his blanket that he and Snoopy take the bus to the city to join Charlie. After a long search, the blanket is found and Linus is relieved. At the spelling bee, Charlie makes it to the final round but loses when he misspells "beagle." Charlie is so depressed when he returns home that he wants to hide from the world. But when he does venture out the next day, he realizes that the world moves on and his failure does not destroy or even alter his everyday life.

Charles M. Schulz's popular comic strip *Peanuts* began in 1950 and by the 1960s was the most beloved, quoted, and read strip in America. The characters first appeared on television in the thirty-minute animated special *A Charlie Brown Christmas* in 1965, and it has remained a favorite holiday attraction ever since. After other small-screen specials, Schulz agreed to a feature film version and co-produced and wrote *A Boy Named Charlie Brown*. Like the shorts, the look of the movie resembles that of the comic strip. The characters are simply drawn only in full-front and profile. The backgrounds are also simple and two-dimensional. Movement is not at all realistic. The characters usually move with only the feet animated. Facial expressions are limited to a few lines yet are very expressive in a cartoonish way. Also, the characters move in front of the background, casting no shadow and rarely blend into the scenery. This approach to animating the comic strip had worked so well on television that there were few changes when translated to the big screen.

Songs

"A Boy Named Charlie Brown"
"Champion Charlie Brown"
"Failure Face"
"I before E" (John Scott Trotter)

A Boy Named Charlie Brown is not just a long TV special shown in the theater. The storyline, though hardly complex, was involved enough to sustain a feature-length movie. Also, director Bill Melendez (who had done the earlier television shorts) took advantage of the big screen to explore new ways to present the *Peanuts* gang. Influenced by the pop art movement of the 1960s, Melendez sometimes used bold colors and quick cutting for some sequences, as in the playing of the National Anthem before the baseball game. Rapid flashes of stars and stripes changing colors were set to the march music. For two sequences when Snoopy imagines himself as a skating champ and an ace pilot, the backgrounds become surreal and the movement is intricate and dazzling. Melendez also uses split screen effectively in some of the narrative scenes, allowing for two or more images—something not possible on the small TV screens of the 1960s. Perhaps the most cinematic sequence in the film is when Linus plays Beethoven's *Pathetique* Sonata and his imagination conjures up vibrant images of Beethoven, music notes, cities where the composer lived, and classical and religious art. The beautifully designed and rendered section might be described as psychedelic, while others see the influence of pop artist Andy Warhol.

> LINUS: Well, I can understand how you feel. You worked hard, studying for the spelling bee, and I suppose you feel you let everyone down, and you made a fool of yourself and everything. But did you notice something, Charlie Brown?
>
> CHARLIE BROWN: What's that?
>
> LINUS: The world didn't come to an end.

Jazz musician and composer Vince Guaraldi scored the *Peanuts* television specials and some of the music was reused in *A Boy Named Charlie Brown*. He also wrote some new themes for the movie. John Scott Trotter arranged the music and wrote one of the songs, the rhythmic "I before E" about spelling. The soundtrack score is in the jazz mode and some of the numbers have found wide recognition outside of the movie. Rod McKuen wrote the three songs, which are catchy but perhaps too simplistic. "Failure Face" is a taunting number for Lucy and the girls to sing about Charlie, "Champion Charlie Brown" is a happy march, and the title number a wistful ballad. The songs do not slow the movie down, but they do not add much either. It is the jazzy soundtrack score that gives the film a lift.

Award

Academy Award nomination: Best Score.

A Boy Named Charlie Brown received positive press and the public reaction was enthusiastic. Cinema Center Films was nervous that the public would not pay to see what was free on television and in the newspapers. But the movie went on to earn $12 million and encouraged other features starring the *Peanuts* characters. The film was released on home video in 1985, on DVD in 2006, and Blu-ray in 2016. In an era dominated by Disney animation, *A Boy Named Charlie Brown* was a pleasing alternative.

Did You Know . . . ?

The voice actor Peter Robbins's cry of "Aaaugh!," first heard in this film, was used for screams for several different characters in the *Peanuts* movies and TV specials for the next thirty years.

THE BRAVE LITTLE TOASTER

1987
(USA: Hyperion Pictures/Disney)

Directed by Jerry Rees
Written by Joe Ranft and Jerry Rees, based on the book by Thomas M. Disch
Produced by Willard Carroll, Peter Locke, Donald Kushner, James Wang, Thomas L. Wilhite, and Cleve Reinhard
Score by David Newman
Songs by Van Dyke Parks and standards by various artists
Specs: Color; 90 minutes; traditional animation

A very atypical Disney product, The Brave Little Toaster *has a look and sound that offers an original world in which inanimate objects come to life and engage our attention and emotions.*

A family summer cottage in the mountains has been left unoccupied for years but inside the furniture and a handful of appliances remain. The old-fashioned Toaster, the desk lamp Lampy, the electric blanket Blanky, the talkative Radio, and the upright vacuum cleaner Kirby fondly recall their young "Master" (a boy named Rob) and patiently wait for him to return someday despite the taunting of the sour window Air Conditioner. When a For Sale sign is posted in front of the cottage, the five appliances set off to find their Master in the big city. Using a car battery to power the vacuum cleaner, Kirby pulls the other four appliances, who ride in a wheeled office chair. The troop encounters rigorous terrain, scary nights, a devouring mud pit, and a junk dealer who wants to dismantle them for parts before arriving at the Master's apartment. Ironically, the college-age Rob and his girlfriend Chris have gone to the cottage to collect the appliances for his dorm room. The newer and more modern appliances in the apartment are threatened by the arrival of Rob's old favorites and toss them all into the dumpster. Disappointed that his childhood "friends" are gone, Rob returns to the city, where he decides to buy some used appliances to bring to college. He and Chris go to the junkyard Ernie's Disposal, where the Toaster and his friends have been dumped. They and Rob are almost destroyed in a crushing machine but the brave Toaster jumps into the gears of the machine and disables it. Rob and his old friends are reunited and he repairs Toaster before setting off for college with the appliances.

Thomas M. Disch's children's book *The Brave Little Toaster* first appeared in magazine format in 1980 and two years later the Disney studio bought the rights. Animator John Lasseter thought the story was ideal for his concept of a totally

The four household appliances—Radio, Lampy, Toaster, and Vacuum Cleaner—decide to leave the safety of their mountain cabin and set out on a quest to find their master. *Walt Disney Pictures / Photofest. © Walt Disney Pictures*

computerized animated film. He presented a proposal to the studio executives on how it could be done and what it would cost. The Disney producers not only turned down the idea, the studio dismissed Lasseter and he went on to found Pixar and direct *Toy Story* (1995), the first computer feature. Disney passed the project on to the new Hyperion Pictures, an independent company with strong ties to Disney. With a budget under $3 million, *The Brave Little Toaster* had to cut many corners and relegated a lot of the animation labor to Wang Film Productions in Taiwan. Director Jerry Rees and coproducer Joe Ranft adapted the book into a workable screenplay, moving the suspenseful junkyard scene to the end of the film and adding Toaster's self-sacrificing feat of stopping the crusher. Like the book, *The Brave Little Toaster* has a dark subtext and brings appliances to life

Voice Cast

Deanna Oliver	Toaster
Jon Lovitz	Radio
Timothy Stack	Lampy
Timothy E. Day	Blanky
Thurl Ravenscroft	Kirby
Phil Hartman	Air Conditioner
Wayne Kaatz	Rob (The Master)
Collette Savage	Chris

only to put them in danger. Although the story takes place in the present, there is a very retro feeling to the movie. The old appliances represent the past and Rob's wanting to bring them with him to college adds a nostalgic aspect to the film. Each of the appliances has a distinct character. Toaster and Blanky are both childlike and naive at times but Toaster is the assertive appliance while Blanky is fearful and needy. Kirby the vacuum cleaner is a pessimist, Lampy is dense and clueless, and Radio is sarcastic. The personality conflicts keep the characters lively. The challenge for the animators was to give inanimate objects movement and expression. Making objects behave like people went back to silent cartoons but rarely were such objects the main characters in the tale. The appliances have eyes and a mouth cleverly added to the object. Only Radio is faceless though he uses his short antenna just like an appendage. The most ingenious animation is for Lampy and Blanky. The latter object forms dozens of shapes and forms, from a bed to a tent. Lampy's long neck allows him to take various positions and he has the most expressive eyes and mouth. The characters and the background art are very traditional and even primitive at times. The movie has the look of 1960s television cartoons with a simple color palette, flat drawing, and uncomplicated backgrounds. *The Brave Little Toaster* does not have the polished and multi-textured quality of Disney films of the time. Some of this was due to the limited budget, but some of it is a conscious effort to achieve that retro look.

Songs

"City of Light"
"Worthless"
"Cutting Edge"
"It's a B-Movie"

The Brave Little Toaster may not look rich and polished but it certainly sounds like it. The voice cast includes some splendid vocals, most memorably those by Jon Lovitz. The television comic ad-libbed much of his non-stop chatter as the Radio and turned the character into a funny annoyance. Lovitz even uses an old-fashioned radio announcer voice and broadcasts his nonsensical talk with a wry grin. Tim Stack's Lampy is also slightly annoying with his fretting and questioning. The deep-voiced actor Thurl Ravenscroft voices Kirby with an authoritative thunder while Phil Hartman has fun doing a Jack Nicholson impersonation as the Air Conditioner. Hartman also does a wicked Peter Lorre impersonation as the hanging lamp in the junk shop. The young and little-known David Newman composed the excellent soundtrack score. In addition to different musical themes for each of the major characters, Newman provides some expansive passages for the journey that the appliances make. The music ranges from exuberant symphonic sections to some dissident and reflective themes denoting danger and fear. The four original songs in *The Brave Little Toaster* are by Van Dyke Parks and they slyly comment on the story and characters' temperament. The cheerful travel song "City of Light" as the appliances begin their journey is contrasted with the rocking dirge "Worthless" sung by the battered cars in the junkyard. The tattered

RADIO: Things could be worse, you know.

LAMPY: How?

RADIO: How what?

LAMPY: How could they be worse?

RADIO: They couldn't; I lied.

appliances in the junk shop frighten Toaster and his friends with "It's a B-Movie," a song that echoes the horror movies of the 1930s. Happily, the songs do not stop the action; rather, they emphasize the state of affairs.

After being shown at various film festivals, *The Brave Little Toaster* was given a very limited release by Disney in 1987, then the next year was shown on the Disney Channel. Not wishing for the inexpensive little film to compete with Disney's big-budget releases, the studio did not distribute the movie overseas, so it took quite a while for *The Brave Little Toaster* to find an audience and to eventually pay back its investment. This is particularly odd, as the movie received mostly favorable reviews. It was the 1991 VHS version and the 2003 DVD edition that finally made the film popular. This led to two sequels: *The Brave Little Toaster to the Rescue* (1997) and *The Brave Little Toaster Goes to Mars* (1998), both of which were made-for-video movies. Today *The Brave Little Toaster* enjoys a kind of cult status with adults, as many first saw it as kids and find it as nostalgic as it is dark and unconventional.

See also *Toy Story*.

Did You Know . . . ?

Because Jon Lovitz had to go to New York City to work on the television show *Saturday Night Live*, he did all his dialogue for Radio in one long recording session by himself, sometimes ad-libbing and other times racing through his lines.

A BUG'S LIFE

1998
(USA: Pixar Animation Studio/Disney)

Directed by John Lasseter and Andrew Stanton
Written by Andrew Stanton, Don McEnery, and Bob Shaw
Produced by Darla K. Anderson and Kevin Reher
Score by Randy Newman
Song "The Time of Your Life" by Randy Newman
Specs: Color (Technicolor); 95 minutes; computer animation

The second feature film from Pixar, A Bug's Life *boasted a larger cast of characters and a wider scope than its predecessor* Toy Story *(1995). It also contained more sophisticated computer animation, which allowed for some dazzling visuals.*

An ant colony ruled by the Queen and her daughter, Princess Atta, is tormented by a gang of grasshoppers, led by the sinister Hopper, who arrive every year to collect the grain from the colony. The inventor ant Flik comes up with a grain harvester to improve production, but it only succeeds in dumping all the grain into a stream. When Hopper and his gang arrive to collect and find no grain, he demands twice the amount the next year. Flik believes the ants should fight back and goes to the big city to recruit warrior bugs to help save the colony. Instead he comes across a troupe of circus performers run by P. T. Flea. Thinking they are warriors, Flik convinces the circus performers to abandon the circus and return to the colony with him. Flik then has a plan to defeat the grasshoppers. He and the ants construct a giant airplane shaped like a bird to scare off Hopper and his thugs. The plan nearly works until P. T. accidentally sets fire to the flying contraption and Hopper sees it is a fake. When the grasshoppers make a second attack, a real bird swoops down on them. Believing it to be another fake, Hopper confronts the bird, only to be eaten by the bird's chicks. Flik is a hero and weds Atta who becomes queen of the colony.

A Bug's Life is a variation on the ancient Aesop fable "The Ant and the Grasshopper," in which the grasshopper frolicked all summer while the ant labored. In the screenplay by Andrew Stanton, Bob Shaw, and Donald McEnery, the grasshoppers are mafia-like thugs who force the ant colony to turn over the fruits of their labors to them. Pixar founder John Lasseter made Stanton codirector on the complicated project that would make more demands on the studio than *Toy Story*. In early versions of the script, it was the circus performers who decided to defend

VOICE CAST

Dave Foley	Flik
Julia Louis-Dreyfus	Atta
Kevin Spacey	Hopper
Hayden Panettiere	Dot
Richard Kind	Molt
Phyllis Diller	Queen
David Hyde Pierce	Slim
Denis Leary	Francis
Joe Ranft	Heimlich
Madeline Kahn	Gypsy Moth
John Ratzenberger	P. T. Flea
Jonathan Harris	Manny
Michael McShane	Tuck & Roll
Bonnie Hunt	Rosie
Braf Garrett	Dim
Roddy McDowall	Mr. Soil

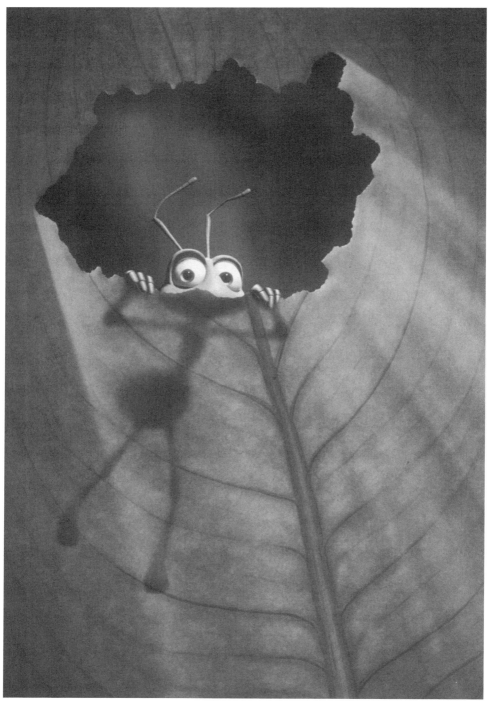

The technical advances made in computer animation in this film are many, including the ability to look through translucent objects, such as a leaf, as Flik demonstrates here. *Walt Disney Pictures / Photofest.* © *Walt Disney Pictures*

the colony against the grasshoppers. Later the character of Flik was created and the plotting changed considerably. *A Bug's Life* involves a wide variety of bugs once Flik goes to the city, and the animators struggled with ways to humanize insects that had rarely been used in animation before. The challenge was solved by the wacky circus troupe that included a walking stick, ladybug, praying mantis, pill bugs, gypsy moth, black widow spider, rhinoceros beetle, caterpillar, and a flea. These performing bugs ended up being the comic highlight of the movie. It helped that the voice actors for these circus misfits were so talented. The studio hired mostly television sitcom actors for *A Bug's Life*, such as Dave Foley (Flik), Julia Louis-Dreyfus (Atta), David Hyde Pierce (Slim), Richard Kind (Molt), Brad Garrett (Dim), and John Ratzenberger (P. T. Flea). Dramatic actor Kevin Spacey got to show off his comic villainy as Hopper and Roddy McDowall, in his last film assignment, was the stage-struck Mr. Soil.

HOPPER: Where do you get the gall to do this to me?

FLIK: You were . . . you were gonna squish the queen. (all the ants gasp)

DOT: It's true.

HOPPER: I hate it when someone gives away the ending.

Both the characters and the settings in *A Bug's Life* involved a great deal of innovation as well as trial and error. The shiny surface of some insects, the wing movement of others, and the necessity to move many ants at the same time were all very challenging. Yet the results are often thrilling. The variety in the animation is a technological breakthrough for the movies. The background art is also unique. The Pixar artists created a movie camera on little wheels that they pushed through different settings to get a bug's-eye view of the world. The city settings are particularly clever with trash items turned into buildings in a cityscape. Similarly, the tall grass acted as a kind of canopy in the yard where the ant colony lived. The variations in the different grasses and flowers gave the film an unusual and even exotic look. Randy Newman composed the bucolic soundtrack score that often flowed like an Aaron Copland nature symphony. There is a cockeyed theme for P. T. Flea's circus, raucous music for the big city, a western-like theme for the working ant colony, and an oppressive battle march for the grasshoppers. Newman also wrote the song "The Time of Your Life," a funky blues number, which he sang on the soundtrack.

Awards

Academy Award nomination: Best Score.

Golden Globe nomination: Best Score.

British Academy of Film & Television Arts (BAFTA) Award nomination: Best Special Visual Effects.

The 1998 release of *A Bug's Life* came at a time of great rivalry with DreamWorks. The new company announced that its first animated feature would be *Antz*, an adventure tale set in an ant colony. Accusations were made that DreamWorks had inside knowledge of Pixar's ant movie in production. These were met by statements from DreamWorks that the story had been in development long before *A Bug's Life* began. Pixar announced a spring opening for its film, so DreamWorks rushed production in order to complete *Antz* and release it the previous fall. This further strained relations between the two studios. Ironically, the movie-going public didn't think two ant movies were too much and both films were box office hits. *A Bug's Life* met with enthusiastic reviews praising the technological strides made in the movie but also the engaging characters and story. The expensive movie cost $120 million but went on to earn over $360 million domestically and internationally. The VHS and DVD editions came out in 1999, a special edition was released in 2003, and the Blu-ray disc went on sale in 2009.

See also *Antz*.

Did You Know . . . ?

A Bug's Life was the first animated feature film to show outtakes at the end of the movie. In live-action features, outtakes are footage of the mistakes actors make on the set. Since there are no physical actors in animation, the outtakes had to be written, designed, and filmed as new material.

C

All kinds of motor vehicles make up the cast of this Pixar film that is about much more than just race cars and auto racing.

The Piston Cup championship car race ends in a three-way tie with seasoned auto Strip Weathers (known as the King), the sneaky Chick Hicks, and the newcomer Lightning McQueen as the finalists. A rematch is planned for the Los Angeles International Speedway in a week. While McQueen is being shipped to California in the big rig Mack, the rookie falls off the truck and ends up in the sleepy town of Radiator Springs with his trusty sidekick, the rusty tow truck Mater. The town once prospered until the new interstate bypassed it. McQueen damages the town's main drag, so he is arrested and brought to court. The local judge, the aged Doc Hudson, turns out to be the famous Hudson Hornet, who won many championship races in the distant past until a crash forced him to retire. The local lawyer, the Porsche 911 Sally Carrera, gets McQueen out of jail by having him do community service repairing the road. McQueen is soon liking small-town life and Sally as well. But when the road is finished and the media find out McQueen's whereabouts, he has to move on to Los Angeles. During the big race, McQueen is losing until Doc, Sally, and others from Radiator Springs show up and encourage him. But McQueen realizes that celebrity and life in the fast lane is not for him. He purposely lets Chick Hicks win the race and returns to Radiator Springs, where he will help put the town back on the map.

The kinship between the self-centered racing car Lightning McQueen and the humble tow truck Mater is honest and sincere, giving the movie heart. *Buena Vista Pictures / Photofest.* © *Buena Vista Pictures*

The original 1998 plot premise for *Cars* was about a yellow electric car amid gas-guzzling bigger autos. The project was put on hold until 2000, when producer-animator John Lasseter took a cross-country road trip with his family, part of it on the historic back road Route 66. Inspired by the beautiful landscape and the forgotten towns along the once-busy route, Lasseter and other writers reworked the original script into the plot for *Cars*. Long a fan of all kinds of cars, Lasseter envisioned a new way of portraying anthropomorphic autos in an animated movie. Usually the two headlights served as eyes and the front bumper as a kind of mouth. Lasseter instead put the eyes on the windshield, making it look like the car was the driver as well as the automobile. Efforts were made to distinguish the way the different kinds of cars moved. Basically all four-wheel vehicles move forward in the same way. Only the speed is variable. But in *Cars* the racing autos were

Voice Cast

Owen Wilson	Lightning McQueen
Paul Newman	Doc Hudson
Larry the Cable Guy	Mater
Bonnie Hunt	Sally Carrera
Tony Shalhoub	Luigi
Cheech Marin	Ramone
Guido Quaroni	Guido
Jenifer Lewis	Flo
Paul Dooley	Sarge
George Carlin	Fillmore
Michael Keaton	Chick Hicks
Michael Wallis	Sheriff
Katherine Helmond	Lizzie
Richard Petty	The King
John Ratzenberger	Mack

more tightly strung and the bodies more flexible than those of the trucks, in which weight controlled movement. Characterization is very difficult with autos because there are no arm or leg appendages to create emotion and physical reaction. The eyes and eyebrows on the windshield had to do all the character animation. There are more named characters in *Cars* than in any other Pixar movie so it was important to visually distinguish each vehicle. Diverse voices were also crucial in keeping each of the characters unique, and *Cars* boasts a superlative voice cast. Comic actor Owen Wilson gives McQueen a slick, cocky, and urban voice, while Larry the Cable Guy makes Mater rural, slow, and even philosophical. Paul Newman gives a splendid performance voicing the elderly curmudgeon Doc Hudson. Other outstanding voice work includes the Italian Fiat Luigi (Tony Shalhoub), the smart but pert Porsche Sally Carrera (Bonnie Hunt), the gruff and precise jeep Sarge (Paul Dooley), the Hispanic Chevy Ramone (Cheech Marin), and the aging hippy Volkswagen bus Fillmore (George Carlin). Even some very small roles are memorable, such as brothers Tom and Ray Magliozzi, the radio commentators of *Car Talk*, as the Dodge autos Rusty and Dusty. There are voice cameos from famous entertainers, such as Jay Leno, Tom Hanks, and Billy Crystal, as well as those of celebrated race car drivers, as with Mario Andretti and Richard Petty.

> SALLY: Forty years ago, that interstate down there didn't exist.
>
> LIGHTNING: Really?
>
> SALLY: Yeah. Back then, cars came across the country a whole different way.
>
> LIGHTNING: How do you mean?
>
> SALLY: Well, the road didn't cut through the land like that interstate. It moved with the land, it rose, it fell, it curved. Cars didn't drive on it to make great time. They drove on it to have a great time.

Cars begins with a race, so the movie starts on a high-speed level with lots of flashing lights and swirling images. The shiny chrome and the metallic body paint of the cars are flashy and impressive. But once the story moves to the secluded town of Radiator Springs, the color palate changes, as does the pace of the film. Here the vehicles are covered with dust, move slowly, and suggest a weathered way of life. The desert landscape is rendered beautifully with flat pastels rather than the bright colors of the racing world. On second viewing of *Cars*, the moviegoer starts to see the shapes of cars in the lazy clouds and in the long shadows. *Cars* is about two very different worlds but united in the way mechanized objects become engaging characters. Randy Newman's score helps distinguish these two environments. The racing scenes are filled with robust passages that slip into heavy metal rock at times. The music for Radiator Springs has soft and mellow themes, mostly in the country-western mode. There are also some gentle sections in the score that are close to Mexican ballads, played on acoustic guitar. Also heard in the movie are some song standards, such as Bobbie Troup's jazz favorite "Route 66," and Newman's original heartfelt ballad "Our Town," sung on the soundtrack by James Taylor.

Awards

Academy Award nominations: Best Animated Feature and Best Song ("Our Town").
Golden Globe Award: Best Animated Film.
British Academy of Film & Television Arts (BAFTA) Award nomination: Best Animated Feature.

The final cost for *Cars* was around $120 million, but the critical and popular reception was so great that it earned half of that the first weekend. The reviews not only praised the technical achievements of the film but also applauded the way in which the nonhuman characters engaged one's emotions. By the end of its first release, *Cars* had earned over $462 million internationally. Such success meant a sequel was in demand. *Cars 2* (2011) follows McQueen and Mater when they go to Europe and Japan for international racing competitions. Generally the critics thought the sequel was lacking in plot and premise, but it managed to earn $562 million internationally. In *Cars 3* (2017), the aging McQueen gets help from the young technician Cruz Ramirez (Cristela Alonzo) to reenter the racing world taken over by a new generation of racing cars. Reviews for the movie were much more approving than those for *Cars 2*, though both films were box office hits.

Did You Know . . . ?

Paul Newman, who voiced Doc Hudson, had also been a race car driver and racing enthusiast. He considered his performance in *Cars* to be one of his best. It was also his last film; he died of lung cancer two years later.

CHARLOTTE'S WEB

1973
(USA: Hanna-Barbera Productions / Paramount)

Directed by Charles Nichols and Iwao Takamoto
Written by Earl Mamner Jr., based on E. B. White's book
Produced by William Hanna, Joseph Barbera, and Edgar Bronfman
Score by Irwin Kostal
Songs by Richard M. and Robert B. Sherman
Specs: Color (Technicolor); 94 minutes; traditional animation

The prolific television producing team of Hanna-Barbera made eight feature cartoons, and most agree that Charlotte's Web *is the best of them, a charming and touching movie musical that has not dated.*

The runt of a litter of piglets is saved by the farmer's daughter Fern and raised as a pet with the name Wilbur. But when Wilbur is sold to the Zuckerman farm and

The pig Wilbur may be depressed about his upcoming doom, but the maternal and ingenious spider Charlotte uses her wits and manages to save his life. *Paramount Pictures / Photofest.* © *Paramount Pictures*

learns that he is to be slaughtered to make bacon, he is saved by the ingenious spider Charlotte, who writes the words "some pig" with her web over Wilbur's sty. Zuckerman and the neighbors are amazed, and Wilbur is temporarily spared. After Charlotte weaves other words, Wilbur becomes famous and is featured at the county fair. Charlotte and the sly rat Templeton accompany Wilbur to the fair, where Charlotte spins other words, making Wilbur a celebrity. After laying many

Voice Cast

Debbie Reynolds	Charlotte
Henry Gibson	Wilbur
Paul Lynde	Templeton
Pamelyn Ferdin	Fern Arable
Agnes Moorehead	Goose
Dave Madden	Ram
Martha Scott	Mrs. Arable
Danny Bonaduce	Avery Arable
John Stephenson	Farmer Arable
Bob Holt	Homer Zuckerman
Joan Gerber	Mrs. Zuckerman
Herb Vigran	Lurvy
Don Messick	Jeffrey
Rex Allen	Narrator

eggs in an egg sac, Charlotte weakens and dies, happy to know she has saved Wilbur's life. Wilber convinces Templeton to get the egg sac and bring it back to the Zuckerman farm. The next spring Charlotte's many eggs hatch and three of the baby spiders become Wilbur's new friends.

E. B. White's *Charlotte's Web* was first published in 1952 and quickly found an international audience. (In 2000, it was declared the best-selling American children's book of all time.) Walt Disney tried to secure the screen rights to *Charlotte's Web*, but White refused, not wishing to see his book turned into an optimistic and cheery Disney product. Surprisingly, White did sell the rights to Hanna-Barbera, who were mostly known for making Saturday morning kids' cartoons. Animation producers William Hanna and Joseph Barbera took a bold step in leaving Yogi Bear and their other television characters behind and making an animated feature of a children's classic. Because every detail in the book was known by generations of readers, Hanna and Barbera made sure the screenplay was faithful to the book. The studio consulted with White, who insisted on certain sections of the story being included in the film, in particular Charlotte's death. The book had to be condensed to make room for the nine songs in the movie, but the spirit of the original was retained. Hanna-Barbera enlisted some name stars to do the voicing and singing. When Debbie Reynolds heard about the project, she contacted the studio and offered to voice Charlotte for free because she so loved the book. Paul Lynde turned Templeton into a hilariously self-centered rat and Henry Gibson brought a cockeyed kind of innocence to the voice of Wilbur. Also memorable was Agnes Moorehead's haughty Goose. All in all, the voice cast is excellent and for many viewers the sound of these actors became identified with the characters.

Songs

"Chin Up"
"I Can Talk"
"There Must Be Something More"
"We've Got Lots in Common"
"Mother Earth and Father Time"
"A Veritable Smorgasbord"
"Zuckerman's Famous Pig"
"Deep in the Dark"
"Charlotte's Web"

The look of *Charlotte's Web* is richer and more detailed than the studio's television art. The background settings have a rustic charm without getting too realistic. A different look is used during the evening when Charlotte spins out her first words. Without actually seeing Charlotte, an impressionistic view of moonlight and trees and bits of webbing become a kind of dance. The character animation, on the other hand, is often lacking. The human characters seem stiff and unexpressive. The animals are animated better but lack variety. None of the barnyard characters move with any accuracy to the actual animal but are often playfully rendered. There is little opportunity for movement with a spider but Wilbur, on the other hand, is a very physical character and has much more interesting movement.

The Disney songwriters Richard M. and Robert B. Sherman were recruited to score *Charlotte's Web* and hopefully come up with some tuneful hits. None of the songs became famous, yet it is a delightful score all the same. The title number is haunting and even a bit solemn, as a male chorus sings about Charlotte spinning all night to save Wilbur. Reynolds sang the film's other ballad, "Mother Earth and Father Time," about the change of seasons and the idea of birth, death, and rebirth in nature. There are two merry marches: the optimistic "Chin Up" with a sprightly lyric, and "Zuckerman's Famous Pig," sung by a barbershop quartet. "There Must Be Something More" is a plaintive song of affection. The comic highlight of the *Charlotte's Web* score is the daffy list song "A Veritable Smorgasbord," in which the Goose and Templeton sing about all the delectable garbage worth eating at the fair.

WILBUR: I think you're beautiful.

CHARLOTTE: Well, I am pretty. Nearly all spiders are good looking. I'm not as flashy as some, but I'll do.

The movie met with mixed notices, as expected with a musical cartoon version of a children's classic. Some critics and audiences felt that White's book was trivialized. White himself was not happy with the movie, particularly how the story was interrupted by the songs. Others complained that the animation was of television quality rather than feature film. *Charlotte's Web* suffered in comparison to the more polished Disney products of the time, and its initial release was only moderately successful. When the film was shown on television it started to gain more acceptance, and by the time it was issued on home video *Charlotte's Web* was finally a hit. Later critics applauded the film for showing the darker and more sobering side of the book. Today *Charlotte's Web* is a much appreciated animated favorite. In 2003, a direct-to-video sequel was released, *Charlotte's Web 2: Wilbur's Great Adventure*. Missing White's charm and humor, the movie was generally dismissed as a mistake.

Did You Know . . . ?

True to the book, the film includes Charlotte's death. The movie received a G rating by not showing the dead spider.

CHICKEN RUN

2000
(UK: Aardman Animations/DreamWorks)

Produced and directed by Nick Park and Peter Lord
Written by Karey Kirkpatrick, Mark Burton, John O'Farrell, Nick Park, and Peter
   Lord
Score by Harry Gregson-Williams and John Powell
Specs: Color (Technicolor); 84 minutes; stop-motion animation

---

Nick Park's stop-motion cartoons featuring the cheese-loving Wallace and his sardonic dog Gromit had found an audience on both sides of the Atlantic, but for his first feature-length movie, Park created a whole new set of characters and came up with the delightful satire Chicken Run.

The chickens at the egg farm run by the nasty Mrs. Tweedy and the dense Mr. Tweedy are encouraged by the radical hen Ginger to escape and live free, but her efforts to get away fail. The American rooster Rocky from the circus arrives and boasts of his ability to fly. Ginger doesn't like the cocky rooster but believes he can save them all by teaching the hens how to fly. When Mrs. Tweedy invests in a complicated machine that turns live chickens into pot pies, the pressure is on to escape. Rocky admits he cannot fly and leaves the farm. Hearing the old cockerel Fowler brag about his days in the Royal Air Force, Ginger gets an idea and organizes the hens to build an airplane out of tools purchased from the black marketeer rats Nick and Fletcher. Ginger expects Fowler to pilot the plane but he admits he never was a pilot, just an RAF mascot. But Rocky returns and mans the cockpit. With the hens providing the peddle power, the clumsy plane manages to outwit the Tweedys and fly off to a bird sanctuary where all the fowls can live happily away from danger.

The British firm of Aardman Animation had presented Park's Wallace and Gromit stop-motion cartoons and other shorts, but *Chicken Run* was the com-

---

Voice Cast

Julia Sawalha	Ginger
Mel Gibson	Rocky
Miranda Richardson	Mrs. Tweedy
Tony Haygarth	Mr. Tweedy
Lynn Ferguson	Mac
Jane Horrocks	Babs
Imelda Staunton	Bunty
Benjamin Whitrow	Fowler
Phil Daniels	Fletcher
Timothy Spall	Nick

The rooster Rocky (center with kerchief) tries to assure the hens (foreground, left to right) Bunty, Babs, and Ginger that his escape plan will work, but they seem dubious. *DreamWorks / Photofest.* © *DreamWorks*

pany's first feature film. They received funding from the American studio DreamWorks, which had been trying to sign Park up for its animation division for some years. Park worked on the script with three writers and codirector Peter Lord, turning the simple idea of a spoof of POW movies into a full-length comedy. The Tweedys' egg farm was designed to look like a German prison camp, and the characters consisted of various types seen in war movies. The fact that the prisoners were chickens offered numerous comic possibilities and a half dozen of the hens were given specific character traits as often happens in war films. The movie most referenced was *The Great Escape* (1963) and the heroine of *Chicken Run* shared personality traits with the character Steve McQueen played in that film. The boastful Rhode Island Red named Rocky paralleled the cocky American who often showed up in British war movies. The script is mostly farcical, but there is a somber subtext, especially when it is clear that Mrs. Tweedy plans to kill all of the chickens because she can make more money out of chicken pot pies than from eggs.

The design of the characters closely resembles the figures seen in Park's Wallace and Gromit shorts. None of the hens have feathers but instead are made of plasticine or silicon, giving them a tough plastic texture. Exaggerated eyes, noses, and mouths were applied not only to the human characters but to the fowls as well. The fact that Ginger and the other hens are not physically very accurate to actual chickens helps remove some of the uncomfortable aspects of the story. Yet the hens have such likable human qualities that the moviegoer gets attached to them in an odd way. Similarly, the human Tweedys are so grotesquely rendered that one sees them as straightforward villains to be laughed at more than feared. The plotting of *Chicken Run* is episodic until the "great escape" is planned, then the story proceeds quickly and efficiently. It helps that the dialogue is particularly funny and the British voice actors are expert.

   Production of *Chicken Run* was slow and expensive. Over two dozen different settings had to be created with exacting detail, and the character figures themselves were made with the flexibility to render all kinds of physical movements as well as several facial expressions. Many of the chickens were made in two sizes, one for close-ups and then another on a smaller scale for crowd scenes. The stop-motion process was particularly complicated because of the frequent movement of the camera, especially in the flying sequences. When Ginger and Rocky are caught inside the pie-making machine, the coordination of the characters' movements and the moving gears and treadmills posed all kinds of problems, but the scene ended up being exciting even as it was silly. The airplane that the hens construct is similarly complicated because the wings are not stationery but move like the wings of a bird. Of course little in *Chicken Run* is very realistic, but bringing a somewhat-surreal world to life is no less difficult.

> GINGER: So laying eggs all your life and then getting plucked, stuffed, and roasted is good enough for you, is it?
>
> BABS: It's a livin'.

   Aardman gathered a voice cast filled with top British actors from stage and screen. Julia Sawalha has a spunkiness in voicing Ginger that comes close to parody. Mel Gibson is properly swarthy (and American) as Rocky, and there are fine comic performances from such performers as Miranda Richardson (Mrs. Tweedy), Timothy Spall (Nick), Jane Horrocks (Babs), Imelda Staunton (Bunty), and Benjamin Whitrow (Fowler). Much of the enjoyment of *Chicken Run* can be attributed to the strong vocals. Because every character, including the villains, is comic, the movie is not slowed down by expositional characters or romantic sequences. The relationship between Rocky and Ginger is curt and sarcastic rather than tender, even though it serves as the film's muted romance. (Until the end of the film, Ginger and Rocky's attempts to kiss each other are always interrupted.) Although the premise of *Chicken Run* is about killing off chickens, there is very little violence. Even the Tweedys are punished without being disposed of.

Awards

Golden Globe nomination: Best Motion Picture—Comedy or Musical.
British Academy of Film & Television Arts (BAFTA) Award nominations: Best British Film and Best Special Effects.

The score by John Powell and Harry Gregson-Williams is a variety of spoofs of different movie genres. The main title is a pompous march with light-headed fifes, flutes, and kazoos. There are a military theme, circus music, inspirational sections, and downright silly music. The rats Nick and Fletcher have their own cockeyed theme, and Rocky is backed by American patriotic music. Two songs are heard on the soundtrack: Ellis Hall sings "Flip, Flop and Fly" by Charles Calhoun and Lou Willie Turner, and Dion performs "The Wanderer" by Ernest Peter Maresca. In all, it is a superior soundtrack that supports the offbeat humor of the tale.

Chicken Run was a surprise success in both Great Britain and the States. Critical and popular approval helped the movie find an audience far beyond fans of Park's shorts. It went on to become the highest-grossing stop-motion film to date. The production cost $45 million, but by the time it was released internationally it had brought in over $106 million. *Chicken Run* broadened the appeal for stop-motion comedy, drawing on an audience wider than those who had patronized the darker films in the genre, such as *The Nightmare before Christmas* (1993). It is also a movie that offers new details and jokes on subsequent viewing.

See also *Shaun the Sheep Movie* and *Wallace and Gromit: The Curse of the Were-Rabbit*.

Did You Know . . . ?

The producers of *Chicken Run* made strong efforts to get their film nominated in the Best Picture category for the Academy Awards. They failed, but there was enough positive reaction from Academy members that the next year a new category was added: Best Animated Feature.

CINDERELLA

1950
(USA: Walt Disney Productions)

Directed by Clyde Geronimi, Wilfred Jackson, and Hamilton Luske
Written by Bill Peet, Homer Brightman, Erdman Penner, Winston Hibler, Harry
  Reeves, Ken Anderson, Ted Sears, Joe Rinaldi, and Maurice Rapf, based on the
  story by Charles Perrault
Produced by Walt Disney
Score by Paul J. Smith and Oliver Wallace
Songs by Jerry Livingston, Mack David, and Al Hoffman
Specs: Color (Technicolor); 74 minutes; traditional animation

---

Of the many princess characters the Disney studio has presented over the years, perhaps the one young girls still most identify with is Cinderella as she is portrayed in this animated classic.

When Cinderella's father died, she was reduced to a servant by her cold-hearted stepmother, Lady Tremaine, and forced to wait on her spoiled stepsisters Drizella

Poor and neglected Cinderella certainly has a more promising future once she meets Prince Charming at the palace ball. *RKO Radio Pictures / Photofest.* © *RKO Radio Pictures*

and Anastasia. In order for the unmarried Prince to meet the eligible maidens in the kingdom, a ball at the royal palace is announced. The mice in the household make a ball gown for Cinderella, but the jealous stepsisters rip it to shreds. Cinderella's Fairy Godmother conjures up a new gown, as well as a coach, horses, and footmen, to take her to the ball, but the magic will last only until midnight. The Prince meets and falls in love with Cinderella at the ball, but at midnight she runs off leaving only a glass slipper. A search of the kingdom for the maiden whose foot fits the slipper brings a courtier to the Tremaine house but Lady Tremaine, suspecting that Cinderella is the girl they are looking for, locks her in the attic. Once

Voice Cast

Ilene Woods	Cinderella
William Phipps	Prince Charming (speaking)
Mike Douglas	Prince Charming (singing)
Eleanor Audley	Lady Tremaine
Verna Felton	Fairy Godmother
Rhoda Williams	Drizella
Lucille Bliss	Anastasia
James MacDonald	Jaq and Gus
Luis Van Rooten	King and Grand Duke
Betty Lou Gerson	Narrator

again the mice come to Cinderella's aid, stealing the key and freeing Cinderella to provide the matching glass slipper and be united with the Prince.

After a busy but unprofitable 1940s for Disney, the studio returned to the fairy-tale format with *Cinderella* and finally had a major hit. *Pinocchio* (1940), *Fantasia* (1940), and *Bambi* (1942) did not make a profit on their initial releases, and the less-expensive anthology films such as *The Three Caballeros* (1945), *Make Mine Music* (1946), and *Melody Time* (1948), saw disappointing profits. The studio was some $4 million in debt when Disney began production of *Cinderella*. To save on costs, much of the action was filmed with actors and these were used as the models for the animators. Disney needed to have some hit songs to help promote the movie so he hired reputable Tin Pan Alley songwriters for the score. The script went through many versions before the storyline was solidified, and casting was problematic until the right actors were found. Despite its difficult birth, *Cinderella* turned out to be one of the studio's best romantic fantasies and a major box office hit.

Songs

"A Dream Is a Wish Your Heart Makes"
"Bibbidi-Bobbidi-Boo"
"So This Is Love"
"The Work Song"
"Sing, Sweet Nightingale"
"Cinderella"

The familiar Charles Perrault fairy tale was given added touches of humor and romance in this animated version. In addition to the expected characters, such as the wicked stepmother Lady Tremaine, the vain stepsisters Drizella and Anastasia, and the warm Fairy Godmother, the screenplay by Ken Anderson and others added such delightful supporting characters as the villainous cat Lucifer and a gang of friendly mice led by Jacques and Gus. The character of Prince Charming gets very little screen time and he is not terribly interesting, but at least he is not as wooden as the Prince in *Snow White and the Seven Dwarfs* (1937). Cinderella herself is portrayed as patient and dreamy without being insipid or frightened. The plotting is tight and full of suspense, yet there is time in the movie for comic relief and wonderful songs. Of the many satisfying versions of Cinderella over the years, Disney's is perhaps the most fanciful. The look of the film is soft and poetic. The castle, seen today at the Magic Kingdom in Walt Disney World, is actually less realistic and even suggested rather than rendered with too many details. The Tremaine household is less subdued, and some places within, such as Lady Tremaine's bedroom, are practically frightening. The animation of the human and animal characters is compelling throughout. The cat Lucifer, who never speaks, is filled with venom and slyness, while the chattering mice are playful and engaging. The movement of the humans is more realistic than in some Disney movies, but the stepsisters are delightfully exaggerated. *Cinderella* is filled with memorable animation sequences, such as the way Cinderella's torn dress is turned into a ball gown by the Fairy Godmother, one of the most iconic of all Disney moments. Even more impressive is the scene in which Cinderella is scrubbing the floor and the soap bubbles that are rising into the air reflect her face in various angles. The voice cast is first rate, from Betty Lou Gerson's warm narration to James MacDonald's squeaky vocals for the mice Jaq and Gus. Ilene Woods does Cinderella's speaking and singing with sincere innocence, while Eleanor Audley's Lady Tremaine is icy cold with every word. One of the reasons given for the overall high quality of *Cinderella* is that it was the first time the legendary animators known as the Nine Old Men worked together on a Disney film.

CINDERELLA: I can't believe. Not anymore. There's nothing left to believe in. Nothing.

FAIRY GODMOTHER: Nothing, my dear? Oh, now you don't really mean that.

CINDERELLA: Oh, but I do . . .

FAIRY GODMOTHER: Nonsense, child. If you'd lost all your faith, I couldn't be here. And here I am.

Both the comedy and the romance in *Cinderella* are supported by the fine soundtrack score by Paul J. Smith and Oliver Wallace. Some of the music they built on came from songwriters Jerry Livingston, Mack David, and Al Hoffman. Disney was hoping for some hit songs, and they provided two: the wistful "A Dream Is a Wish Your Heart Makes" for Cinderella and the catchy "Bibbidi-Bobbidi-Boo" for the Fairy Godmother. Both received many recording by various artists. The other romantic number is "So This Is Love" for Cinderella and the Prince, a song that seems to float in the air. "The Work Song," sung by the mice as they make Cinderella's dress, is another catchy ditty that once heard is not forgotten. Perhaps the most interesting song in the score is "Sing, Sweet Nightingale," which sounds like an operetta nightmare when performed by the stepsisters but becomes a flowing ballad when Cinderella sings it. All in all, it is one of the most accomplished of Disney scores.

Awards

Academy Award nominations: Best Song ("Bibbidi-Bobbidi-Boo"), Best Score, and Best Sound Recording.

Cinderella saved the Disney studio from bankruptcy. It not only brought the studio out of the red but turned the company into a formidable enterprise once again. For the first time since *Dumbo* in 1941, a Disney movie opened to runaway box office. This success was repeated when *Cinderella* was rereleased in 1957, 1965, 1973, 1981, and 1987. It was first available for home video in 1988, then in 2005 *Cinderella* broke sales records with the DVD version. The Blu-ray edition was released in 2012. There have been two direct-to-video sequels, *Cinderella II: Dreams Come True* (2002) and *Cinderella III: A Twist in Time* (2007). The studio released a live-action version of *Cinderella* in 2015, which varied the tale a little and did not have any songs. To say that the original *Cinderella* is timeless is an understatement. It seems as fresh and beguiling today as when it was first released.

Did You Know . . . ?

This was not Walt Disney's first animated version of *Cinderella*. As part of the Laugh-o-Gram series of cartoons in the 1920s, Disney presented a short adaptation of the tale in 1922. For nearly three decades he considered a full-length version of the story.

CORALINE

2009
(USA: Focus Features/Laika Entertainment)

Directed and written by Henry Selick, based on the book by Neil Gaiman
Produced by Michael Zoumas, Henry Selick, Alex Heineman, Claire Jennings, Mary Sandell, and Bill Mechanic
Score by Bruno Coulais
Songs by Henry Selick, Bruno Coulais, Kent Melton, and They Might Be Giants
Specs: Color/black and white; 100 minutes; stop-motion and computer animation

---

A dark Alice in Wonderland *for the new century,* Coraline *both haunts and dazzles its audience, which, hopefully, doesn't have young children in attendance.*

Eleven-year-old Coraline Jones moves with her parents into an apartment in an old Victorian house in the hills of Oregon. Also in residence are the retired actresses Misses Spink and Forcible and the past-his-prime Russian acrobat Boris Bobinsky. The neighbor boy Wybie Lovat finds a doll in his grandmother's attic and gives it to Coraline because it looks a lot like her even though its eyes are buttons. Coraline, neglected by her busy parents, follows a mouse to a secret door, which leads to a fantasy world where her Other Mother and Other Father are caring and fun loving even though they also have buttons for eyes. By the time Coraline learns that the fantasy world is a trap and that the Other Mother wants to replace Coraline's eyes with buttons, the girl has lost her real parents who are imprisoned by the evil Other Mother. With the help of a talking Cat and the Other Wybie, Coraline rescues her parents and destroys the Other Mother.

Soon after Neil Gaiman's book *Coraline* was released in 2002, writer-director Henry Selick and the author were contracted to make a film of the dark children's story. Selick's screenplay made minor changes in the plot and added the character of Wybie. Selick then enlisted the Japanese artist Tadahiro Uesugi to come up with designs for the movie's real world and fantasy world. The character models were created with exaggerated features so that they were recognizable

Coraline (far right) finds that her Other Father and Other Mother give her all the love and attention she lacks from her real parents, but it turns out to be too good to be true. *Focus Features / Photofest.* © *Focus Features*

in both worlds, just as there were two distinct but recognizable versions of each of the film's many interior and exterior settings. Also very intricate were the many costumes, which ranged from the everyday (Coraline and her parents) to the outrageous (the Misses Spink and Forcible). *Coraline* was filmed in a large warehouse in Hillsboro, Oregon, and took over a year for cinematography and the computerized special effects. Adding to the complexity of the production was the decision to have scenes in color dissolve into black and white and then disintegrate into dust. Other special effects were time consuming, as was filming the movie for 3-D showings. The result is an ambitious animated film that is hypnotic in its visuals and overwhelming in its sinister feel. There is a dark pallor over the scenes in the real world but the fantasy world is bright and colorful. The character animation is flamboyant for many of the characters, which gives the movie a satiric tone. Yet the humor in *Coraline* is so bizarre that one does not

Voice Cast

Dakota Fanning	Coraline Jones
Keith David	Cat
Teri Hatcher	Mel Jones/Other Mother
John Hodgman	Charlie Jones/Other Father
Jennifer Saunders	Miss Spink/Other Spink
Dawn French	Miss Forcible/Other Forcible
Robert Bailey Jr.	Wybie Lovat
Ian McShane	Sergei Bobinsky/Other Bobinsky

laugh very easily. The film is so effective that it is often oppressive. Even more so than Selick's *The Nightmare before Christmas* (1993), *Coraline* gets closer to the nerve and ends up being more frightening.

Songs

"Dreaming" (Coulais)
"Nellie Jean" (Melton)
"Other Father Song" (They Might Be Giants)
"Sirens of the Sea" (Selick)

Some of the voice cast are able to match the movie's exuberant visuals with outlandish vocals. British comic actresses Jennifer Saunders and Dawn French are deliciously overblown as the aging thespians, and Ian McShane's Bobinsky is also very exuberant. More reserved vocals are provided by Dakota Fanning as Coraline and Keith David as the Cat. But the most accomplished vocal performance is given by Teri Hatcher, who captures the three versions of the mother: bored and distracted, warm and oozing with affection, and dripping with evil.

CORALINE: How can you walk away from something and then come towards it?

CAT: Walk around the world.

CORALINE: Small world.

French composer Bruno Coulais wrote the marvelous soundtrack score for *Coraline*, and it sets the tone for the movie's many moods. Sometimes a children's chorus is heard singing in a gibberish language; other times the music is propulsive and urgent. Throughout the film there is unsettling underscoring that seems as ephemeral as the fog that envelops some of the scenes. There are also a handful of songs that are as odd and unsettling as the visuals. The group They Might Be Giants wrote ten songs for the film; it was later felt that they distracted from the somber tone of the movie, so all the musical numbers were cut except the oddball "Other Father's Song." The similarly offbeat "Sirens of the Sea," sung by the two actresses, and the eerie children's chorus "Dreaming" were composed by Coulais. *Coraline* boasts one of the finest scores in contemporary animated cinema.

Awards

Academy Award nomination: Best Animated Feature.
Golden Globe Award nomination: Best Feature Film.
British Academy of Film & Television Arts (BAFTA) Award: Best Feature Film. BAFTA nomination: Best Animated Film.

Coraline was greeted with almost unanimously enthusiastic reviews when it was released in 2009, though many critics pointed out that the film was too disturbing for young children. After a surprisingly strong opening weekend, the movie gained even more support over the next few weeks and by the end of the year had earned over $75 million domestically. Internationally, *Coraline* grossed over $124 million, an impressive number when one considers the movie was made for just under $17 million. Also very successful were the DVD and Blu-ray editions, which were released late in 2009. That same year, an award-winning video game of *Coraline* was released with success.

See also *The Boxtrolls*.

Did You Know . . . ?

After Jennifer Saunders recorded the dialogue for Miss Forcible and Dawn French voiced Miss Spink, director Selick was not happy with the result and had the two actresses switch roles and rerecord all their scenes. The second recording was used, but Miss Spink still resembles French and Forcible looks a lot like Saunders.

CORPSE BRIDE

2005
(USA/UK: Laika Entertainment/Warner Brothers)

Directed by Tim Burton and Mike Johnson
Written by John August, Caroline Thompson, and Pamela Pettler
Produced by Joe Ranft, Jeffrey Auerbach, Tim Burton, Allison Abbate, Derek Frey, and Tracy Shaw
Score by Danny Elfman
Songs by Danny Elfman and John August
Specs: Color; 77 minutes; stop-motion animation

A fanciful stop-motion film from the creative mind of Tim Burton, Corpse Bride *is very macabre but also very poetic and at times quite moving.*

The Victorian aristocrats Lord and Lady Everglot are broke and have arranged for their daughter Victoria to wed Victor Van Dort, the son of the prosperous but low-class fish merchant William Van Dort, in order to save their estate. Victor and Victoria do not meet until the day before the wedding but, to the surprise of each of them, they fall in love. While Victor is practicing his wedding vows in the local cemetery, the deceased Emily rises out of the grave and accepts his words as a marriage bond then drags him down to the Land of the Dead. There he learns from the singing skeleton Bonejangles that Emily was murdered on the night she tried to elope. Desperate to return to the Land of the Living and see Victoria, Victor tells Emily he wants to introduce her to his family. The sorcerer Elder

Scraps the dog and Emily the bride are dead, but the groom Victor is very much alive, making for very unique, not to say odd, wedding plans. *Warner Bros. / Photofest. © Warner Bros.*

Gutknecht arranges for the couple to temporarily go to the Land of the Living, but when Emily sees Victor trying to explain to Victoria what has happened to him, Emily gets jealous and they are immediately in the Land of the Dead again. Resigned to his fate, Victor agrees to go through a wedding ceremony and drink poison so that he too will be a corpse. But Emily moves the ceremony to the Land of the Living, where Victoria is getting married to the crass opportunist Lord Barkis Bittern. Emily recognizes Bittern as the man who murdered her and has a change of heart, giving Victor to Victoria. Bittern drinks the poison intended for Victor and dies, ending his marriage to Victoria. Victor and Victoria are wed and Emily finds peace in the Land of the Dead.

Voice Cast

Johnny Depp	Victor Van Dort
Helena Bonham Carter	Corpse Bride (Emily)
Emily Watson	Victoria Everglot
Tracey Ullman	Nell Van Dort
Paul Whitehouse	William Van Dort
Joanna Lumley	Maudeline Everglot
Albert Finney	Finis Everglot
Richard E. Grant	Barkis Bittern
Christopher Lee	Pastor Galswells
Michael Gough	Elder Gutkecht
Enn Reitel	Maggot
Jane Horrocks	Black Widow Spider
Danny Elfman	Bonejangles

Coproducer Joe Ranft suggested the idea for *Corpse Bride* to Tim Burton while they were still making *The Nightmare before Christmas* (1993), adapting an old Russian folktale but setting it in a European world. Other projects intervened, but in 2003 production began in London with Burton codirecting with Mike Johnson. Although *Corpse Bride* is stop-motion animation, some innovations were made by cinematographer Pete Kozachik, who shot the movie digitally then was able to add realistic touches and special effects with computer animation. All the same, production was slow and time consuming and *Corpse Bride* ended up costing around $40 million. The look of the film is indeed unique. The softer presentation and the careful blending of the puppets, settings, and special effects are less sensational than those in *The Nightmare before Christmas*. Instead, the movie is more subtle at times and the characters seem to breathe like live actors. The Victorian world of the Van Dorts and the Everglots is filmed in color, but all the buildings, props, costumes, and characters are in black and white. Contrary to tradition, the Land of the Dead is more colorful, although the tones of green, blue, and orange are unsettling. The characters in both lands are exaggerated in their look and movement, often grotesquely so. Yet there is more a sense of death in the somber living characters than in the colorful dead ones. The people in Victorian Europe move slowly with weight, while the deceased float about rapidly. It follows that most of the living souls are sour and unhappy, while the world below comes across as one big party. *Corpse Bride* is a visual feast and served as a major step forward for stop-motion animation.

Songs

"Remains of the Day"
"Tears to Shed"
"According to Plan"
"The Wedding Song"

American actor Johnny Depp voices Victor but most of the rest of the cast for *Corpse Bride* is British. It is an outstanding cast, the voices coming across as both sinister and funny. Helena Bonham Carter's Emily is very human sounding, her voice soft and caressing when needed. Yet there is still a deathlike tremor to her voice. More robust are delicious performances by Joanna Lumley and Albert Finney as the Everglots, Tracey Ullman and Paul Whitehouse as the Van Dorts, Richard E. Grant as the sinister Bittern, and Christopher Lee as the bombastic Pastor Galswells. Depp's Victor is hesitant but engaging, and Emily Watson is an endearing Victoria. Right down to the smallest role, the film boasts superior voice talents.

CORPSE BRIDE: I was a bride. My dreams were taken from me. But now—now I've stolen them from someone else. I love you, Victor, but you are not mine.

Danny Elfman's soundtrack score and songs, like the softer look of the movie, are much more subtle than those for *The Nightmare before Christmas*. There is also a wider variety here. The opening number, "According to Plan," has some of the freakish patterns of *The Nightmare before Christmas* music, but the rest of the score is quite unique. The Victorian era is best evoked in the Gilbert and Sullivan–like "The Wedding Song," while Bonejangles's narrative number about Emily's past, "Remains of the Day," is very slick and jazzy. Emily gets a morose but pleasing ballad, "Tears to Shed," that emphasizes her still-human persona. Elfman's soundtrack music is equally diverse. There are the expected horror-movie passages with organ and choir, raucous party music for the ever-bustling Land of the Dead, and rich symphonic sections for the magical scenes. Perhaps the most memorable pieces of music in the movie are those played on piano by the characters. Victor plays a very romantic theme on the Everglot piano, which helps Victoria fall in love with him. Later he and Emily play a duet on a coffin-like piano that links them musically and emotionally. While the music for *Corpse Bride* never found the popularity of that for *The Nightmare before Christmas*, it is arguably the more accomplished score.

Award

Academy Award nomination: Best Animated Feature.

Corpse Bride opened in the United States and Great Britain in 2005 to mostly commendatory reviews by the press. Many were surprised by how romantic the movie was considering its morbid premise. Besides being a box office hit in America and the United Kingdom, the film was also particularly successful in France and Japan. Domestic and international sales were over $117 million, followed by lucrative DVD and Blu-ray sales in 2006.

See also *The Nightmare before Christmas*.

Did You Know . . . ?

It has been calculated that 109,440 separate shots were set up and filmed over the course of one year to create the movement in *Corpse Bride*.

D

DESPICABLE ME

2010

(USA/France: Illumination Entertainment/Universal Pictures)

Directed by Pierre Coffin and Chris Renaud
Written by Cinco Paul and Ken Daurio
Produced by Nina Rappaport, Sergio Pablos, Dave Rosenbaum, John Cohen, Janet
  Healy, Christopher Meledrini, and Robert Taylor
Score by Heitor Pereira and Pharrell Williams
Songs by Pharrell Williams with song standards by various artists
Specs: Color; 95 minutes; computer animation

The villain is the hero in this breezy animated adventure, which was popular for itself and for introducing the lovable critters known as the Minions.

After spending his whole life trying to be an archvillain, Gru is frustrated and bitter when the ancient Pyramid at Giza is stolen by the younger villain Vector. Gru vows to top this feat by stealing the moon. His colleague, Dr. Nefario, plans to build a spaceship using the dozens of Minion creatures at hand, but Gru needs money from evil banker Mr. Perkins, who is also Vector's father. Gru sees three orphan girls—Margo, Edith, and Agnes—who are selling cookies door to door and adopts them from Miss Hattie's orphanage so that he can get to the reducing machine inside Vector's house. The girls sell Vector some robot cookies, which allows Gru to steal the reducing machine. He then plans to travel to the moon and shrink it to a size in which he can carry it away. Gru is an awful "father" to the three girls, but they slowly start to melt his heart, giving him the love he never got from his mother. The launch is successful and Gru is able to shrink the moon, but when Vector kidnaps the girls and demands the moon, Gru gives it to him. Vector double-crosses Gru and tries to escape with the moon and the girls, but Dr. Nefario and the Minions help Gru rescue the trio of orphans. The moon enlarges itself to its full size and returns to its orbit and Gru is reunited with Margo, Edith, and Agnes.

The film began as a project at the French animation studio MacGuff and was titled *Evil Me.* The studio was acquired by the new company Illumination Enter-

Audiences took their time warming up to the despicable villain Gru (center) but had no trouble liking his trusty and silly Minions at first sight. *Universal Pictures / Photofest. © Universal Pictures*

tainment and its first animated feature was the Universal-backed film *Despicable Me*. The computer-generated movie was made in France with both American and French artists but the voice cast came from the States. Television comic Steve Carell provided the voice for Gru, creating an odd and funny dialect that sounded Russian, Spanish, and Transylvanian. Englishman Russell Brand voiced Dr. Nefario with a British accent, while American actor Jason Segel gave Vector a very American sound. Yet the most interesting vocals in the film are those of the Minions. Both French and American writers worked on a new language for the Minions, coming up with a gibberish vocabulary that used both English and French words. Codirectors Pierre Coffin and Chris Renaud did the vocals for most of the Minions and the funny little creatures stole the movie.

Voice Cast

Steve Carell	Gru
Miranda Cosgrove	Margo
Dana Gaier	Edith
Elsie Fisher	Agnes
Jason Segel	Vector
Russell Brand	Dr. Nefario
Julie Andrews	Gru's Mom
Will Arnett	Mr. Perkins
Kristen Wiig	Miss Hattie
Chris Renaud	Dave the Minion
Jemaine Clement	Jerry the Minion
Pierre Coffin	Other Minions
Danny McBride	Fred McDade

Songs

"Despicable Me"
"Fun, Fun, Fun"
"Prettiest Girls"
"Rocket's Song"
"Boogie Fever"
"The Way It Is (Vector's Theme)"
"My Life"

The plot for *Despicable Me* is unusual in that the main characters are villains. Gru is quickly established as a man who is cruel to both children and adults. Then his insecurity, going back to his childhood, is revealed and the audience starts to prefer him over the other villains introduced: the obnoxious Vector, the sadistic Perkins, and the bully Miss Hattie. The orphans Margo, Edith, and Agnes are cute and needy, but it turns out they have strengths of their own, and the way they wear down Gru is believable. The film is filled with chases and action sequences, but what one most remembers are the character scenes, such as Gru trying to read a bedtime story to the girls or the way the Minions rally around Gru when he feels defeated. *Despicable Me* turns sentimental as it goes along, and the filmmakers make no apologies. The villain becomes the hero, which, all things considered, is much more difficult to do than to have the hero simply destroy the villain.

GRU: Assemble the minions!

The visual look of *Despicable Me* is stylized realism in settings but very cartoon-ish in characterization. The city portrayed is bright with color except for Gru's dark homestead, which is squeezed in between two colorful homes. Even the diabolical Vector's modern house is cheerful in comparison. Gru's oddball vehicle and spaceship are also dark and industrial. Gru himself is usually dressed in black, while all the characters around him have color, including the yellow Minions in blue overalls. With his pointed nose, thin legs, and hunched back, Gru looks like an Igor character from a horror film. Yet his eyes are large and they quickly change from menacing to gentle. The jowly Dr. Nefario resembles an animal more than a human, just as Perkins has large bull-like features. Vector, with his potbelly and unflattering clothes, looks less like a villain than a sleazy lounge singer. The most intriguing characters visually are the Minions, who sport goggles over their one or two eyes. Some are bald, others have a few prickly hairs. They do not move like humans but neither are they purely mechanical. With such a look and their quirky language, it is little wonder why the Minions became so popular.

Awards

Golden Globe nomination: Best Animated Film.
British Academy of Film & Television Arts (BAFTA) nomination: Best Animated Film.

Heitor Pereira and Pharrell Williams's musical soundtrack for the movie is very diverse, utilizing symphonic sequences as well as solo instruments. The music often echoes the oddball tone of the movie, particularly in the action scenes. Williams wrote a handful of original songs that are heard on the soundtrack. The numbers range from pop-rock and disco to hip-hop and funk. Several song standards are also heard in *Despicable Me* and they are quite diverse as well. Selections range from "Copacabana" to "Swan Lake."

Universal did a great deal of marketing tie-ins for *Despicable Me*. Best Buy and the International House of Pancakes offered products related to the film and NBC-TV was filled with ads and promotions in anticipation of the opening in 2010. The reviews were mostly favorable and the movie was a box office hit from the start. Production costs were around $69 million, but the first release brought in over $540 million internationally. *Despicable Me* also launched a very successful franchise, including Minion figures and dolls, video games, books (including the one Gru reads in the film), a ride at Universal Studios Hollywood, and film shorts. The sequel *Despicable Me 2* (2013) concerned Gru trying to bring down a new villain and the prequel *Minions* (2015) told the story of how the critters ended up serving Gru. These were followed by *Despicable Me 3* (2017) and eventually *Minions 2* (2020).

Did You Know . . . ?

There are different explanations for the name of Gru. The French *grue* is a "crane" and Gru's body structure does suggest a crane. In Russia, the GRU is an acronym for the nation's military intelligence agency. Gru could also be short for "gruesome."

DINOSAUR

2000
(USA: Walt Disney Pictures)

Directed by Eric Leighton and Ralph Zondag
Written by John Harrison and Robert Nelson Jacobs
Produced by Pam Marsden and Baker Bloodworth
Score by James Newton Howard
Specs: Color (Technicolor); 82 minutes; computer animation and live-action footage

The first fully computerized animated feature by Disney, it mixes location film footage for the settings with computer-generated animal characters who move effectively through the various prehistoric environments.

The orphaned iguanodon Aladar grows up with a family of lemurs headed by the patriarch Yar. Aladar's best friends are the smart aleck Zini, the caring Plio, and the young Suri. When a meteor lands on the island and sets fire to all the trees, Aladar and the lemurs swim to the mainland looking for a new home. They encounter a dinosaur herd and hear of a fertile land called the "Nesting Grounds,"

Nature is perhaps the true antagonist in this prehistoric adventure movie, which looks so real that one is surprised to find the dinosaurs actually talking. *Buena Vista Pictures / Photofest.* © *Buena Vista Pictures*

so they join the migration headed by the stern iguanodon Kron and his second-in-command, Bruton. Also in the group are the lovely Neera, the elderly Eema, and the wise Baylene. They all nearly die of dehydration crossing a desert and then are attacked by a pack of deadly Carnotauruses who kill Kron, leaving Aladar in charge. He inspires the dinosaurs and lemurs to press on and, after killing the Carnotaurus leader, he leads them into the Nesting Grounds, where they join other dinosaurs and lemurs and begin a new life.

Voice Cast

D. B. Sweeney	Aladar
Max Casella	Zini
Hayden Panettiere	Suri
Alfre Woodard	Plio
Ossie Davis	Yar
Samuel E. Wright	Kron
Peter Siragusa	Bruton
Julianna Margulies	Neera
Joan Plowright	Baylene
Della Reese	Eema

The Disney studio had long hoped to make a movie in which the backgrounds and the animal characters were very realistic and the story was told without dialogue. In 1988 Paul Verhoeven and Phil Tippett proposed a stop-motion feature using various kinds of dinosaur models, but the movie that later emerged consisted of computerized animals that talked and live-action backgrounds taken from location shooting in South America. *Dinosaur* did not end up like Verhoeven and Tippett envisioned, but it is a visually stunning movie all the same and an important step in Disney animation. The blending of the complex and evocative settings with the characters is so well done that it is often impossible to tell where the vegetation leaves off and the animals begin. The opening scene, in which the dinosaur egg survives a stampede of dinosaurs, is done without dialogue and illustrates the kind of film that Verhoeven and Tippett had in mind. The plot was originally much darker, with all of the characters dying. The final script was much more hopeful, showing the effects of the meteor but allowing certain animals to survive. Yet there are some very serious passages in *Dinosaur* and a somber tone throughout, suggesting that the survival of all these animals can only be temporary. While the story of journeying to a new home is a familiar one, the individual characters are distinct and often unique. Aladar grows from a confused orphan to a driven leader who has a soft spot in his heart for his friends and his sweetheart, Neera. Zini is the comic character, and his wisecracking dialogue cuts through the serious, even reverent, tone of the movie. The cold and dispassionate leader Kron is contrasted by the motherly Plio and the reassuring Baylene. The deadly Carnotaurus, the villains of the film, do not have names or characters and do not speak, adding to their fierceness. The dangers the migrating herd encounters are very realistic and sometimes *Dinosaur* resembles a fabricated documentary about prehistoric extinction. It is the engaging characters that keep the movie on an empathetic level and make it entertaining.

> ALADAR: He's my grandfather—couple of generations removed.
>
> ZINI: Try a couple of species removed.

The voice cast for *Dinosaur* is very diverse, the actors coming from the theater, television, and the movies. Such distinguished African American artists as Samuel E. Wright (Kron), Alfre Woodard (Plio), Ossie Davis (Yar), and Della Reese (Eema) are joined by renowned British actress Joan Plowright as Baylene. D. B. Sweeney is very proficient as Aladar but much of the movie is stolen by Max Casella as the nimble-witted Zini. James Newton Howard composed the stirring soundtrack score for *Dinosaur* and the grandeur of the landscape is often complemented by the majestic music. There are also some African-flavored sequences with choral singing arranged and conducted by Lebo M, the same artist who created the sounds of the savanna in *The Lion King* (1994).

Dinosaur opened in 2000 to mixed notices. Almost all the critics praised the strong visuals but some found the story and the characters lacking. Comparisons were made with *The Land before Time* (1988), also about dinosaurs searching for a new home, but that Don Bluth movie was about animal children and was geared to younger audiences. The public was less critical, however, and *Dinosaur* earned over $137 million in North America and ended up grossing $349 million internationally. Since the cost of the movie was around $127 million, it was a major hit for the Disney studio. Both the VHS and DVD editions were released in 2001 and the Blu-ray version in 2006.

See also *The Land before Time.*

Did You Know . . . ?

Originally, the predatory villains in the movie were to be Tyrannosaurus dinosaurs, but because of the recent and popular *The Lost World: Jurassic Park* (1997), the creative team changed them to Carnotaurus. To make them more ferocious, the Carnotauruses were made larger than scientific studies believe they actually were.

DUMBO

1941
(USA: Walt Disney Productions)

Directed by Ben Sharpsteen, Samuel Armstrong, Norman Ferguson, Bill Roberts, Jack Kinney, Wilfred Jackson, and John Elliotte
Written by Joe Grant and Dick Huemer, based on the book by Helen Aberson and Harold Pearl
Produced by Walt Disney
Score by Frank Churchill and Oliver Wallace
Songs by Frank Churchill (music) and Ned Washington (lyrics)
Specs: Color (Technicolor); 64 minutes; traditional animation

---

One of the shortest of all Disney features, Dumbo *packs a lot of humor and warmth during its sixty-four minutes, making it an enduring favorite over the past seventy years.*

When Mr. Stork delivers a sackful of baby animals to the circus train, the elephant Mrs. Jumbo is thrilled with her new son, Jumbo Jr. Because his ears are so large, the other elephants make fun of him and call him Dumbo. Later some cruel spectators at a circus performance taunt Dumbo, and Mrs. Jumbo loses her temper and tries to attack them. Considered dangerous, she is taken from Dumbo and locked in a wagon. The enterprising Timothy Q. Mouse befriends the abandoned Dumbo and gets him into the circus act as a clown, but being laughed at by audiences only depresses Dumbo more. One of the human clowns dumps a bottle of champagne into a bucket of water and when Dumbo and Timothy drink from the bucket they get drunk and see all kinds of hallucinations. The next morning Dumbo wakes up high in a tree and cannot understand how he got there. Timothy figures out that Dumbo flew up there using his large ears as wings. His theory is supported by a quartet of crows who saw Dumbo fly. Timothy comes up with a circus act in which

Since Dumbo remained silent throughout the film, most of the talking was done by Timothy Q. Mouse, who also was filled with promotional ideas for his elephant friend. *Walt Disney Pictures / Photofest. © Walt Disney Pictures*

Dumbo flies and he is an immediate sensation. Mrs. Jumbo is released and Dumbo becomes the star of the circus.

After losing so much money on both *Pinocchio* (1940) and *Fantasia* (1940), Walt Disney needed to make a less costly movie to get the studio into the black. Also, with the war in Europe the overseas market had shrunk considerably and none of the Disney movies were selling well. Production for *Dumbo* was rushed, but

Voice Cast

Edward Brophy	Timothy Q. Mouse
Verna Felton	Mrs. Jumbo
Sterling Holloway	Mr. Stork
James Baskett	Crow
Jim Carmichael	Crow
Cliff Edwards	Crow
Nick Stewart	Crow
Verna Felton	Elephant Matriarch
Herman Bing	Ringmaster
John McLeish	Narrator

the result does not look like a rush job. The characterizations and animation are first-class and the screenplay succeeds even as it breaks many rules of feature animation. There is no villain in the script. The closest the movie comes to violence is when some boys taunt Dumbo and Mrs. Jumbo tries to attack them. There is very little action in the story and even less suspense. Whether Dumbo's belief in the "magic feather" is strong enough to let him fly is the closest the film comes to tension. Also unusual: the title character does not utter one word or sound. (Mrs. Jumbo has only one line.) Much of the talk is handled by the loquacious Timothy Q. Mouse. Most of the songs are sung by a chorus on the soundtrack and not by the characters. The original book, written by Helen Aberson and illustrated by Harold Pearl, is a short children's book with only eight pictures and very little text. The movie fills out the basic story, further developing Timothy, the female elephants, and the crows. It is a tightly structured script with no chases or dramatics. The story unfolds in a leisurely fashion, slowly growing on the audience so that by the end one gets the sense of a complete feature movie. There is no other Disney film quite like it.

Songs

"Baby Mine"
"Look Out for Mr. Stork"
"When I See an Elephant Fly"
"Pink Elephants on Parade"
"Casey Junior"
"Song of the Roustabouts"

The look of *Dumbo* is very much like a children's book with a colorful palette and simple backgrounds that are rendered in watercolor. This simpler look was utilized to save on expenses, yet the background artists and animators did not scrimp on creativity. Some scenes are very dynamic, such as the roustabouts raising the circus tent in a rainstorm or the circus train casting shadows on the landscape as it rushes past. Some characterization touches are also memorable, such as Dumbo's first out-of-focus view of the world and the way everything comes into focus when he sees his mother for the first time. Many of the film's most compelling scenes are visual rather than vocal, and the rendering of the different characters is often pure animation. The silent Dumbo is filled with curiosity and emotion. His visit to his locked-up mother as "Baby Mine" is heard on the soundtrack rates as one of the most heart-wrenching scenes in the Disney canon. The creative highlight of the movie is the justly famous "Pink Elephants on Parade," a dazzling sequence with surreal images, vibrant color contrasts, and eye-popping visuals. *Dumbo* used fewer cels and fewer artists but it is still an animation triumph.

CROW #1: Did you ever see an elephant fly?

CROW #2: Well, I've seen a horse fly.

CROW #3: Ah, I've seen a dragon fly.

CROW #4: Hee-hee. I've seen a house fly.

As short as *Dumbo* is, there is still room for seven songs by Frank Churchill and Ned Washington, and every one is a winner. The singing quartet the Sportsmen perform the jaunty "Look Out for Mr. Stork" on the soundtrack while the bundles of baby animals are delivered. They also sing the catchy ditty "Casey Junior" as the circus train bounces along through the landscape. Another singing group, the King's Men, delivers the vigorous "Song of the Roustabouts" as the big top is being raised and are heard singing the oddball march "Pink Elephants on Parade." The crows sing the ribald "When I See an Elephant Fly," a daffy number with silly lyrics and a bebop sound. The finest song in the film is the tender lullaby "Baby Mine," which is as moving as it is simple and melodic. As sung by Betty Noyles on the soundtrack, it is a song that once heard is never forgotten. The soundtrack score by Frank Churchill and Oliver Wallace is also first-rate, ranging from spirited circus music to gentle scoring behind the film's more tender moments. Musically, *Dumbo* is a delight with the quality of Disney's more expensive and complex movies.

Awards

Academy Award: Best Scoring of a Musical Picture. Oscar nomination: Best Song ("Baby Mine").

Dumbo was the studio's first major box office hit since *Snow White and the Seven Dwarfs* (1937), earning over $1.5 million on its first release. Considering the film cost around $900,000 to make and that most overseas markets would not see *Dumbo* until years later, this initial income was much needed and helped Disney get out of debt as the lean war years approached. Reviews and audience reception were both strong, and *Time* magazine planned a cover story for the December 29, 1941, issue, in which the baby elephant was named the "Mammal of the Year." But the attack on Pearl Harbor on December 7 changed all that. All the same, *Dumbo* sold very well during the first year of the American involvement in World War II, as it did during the rereleases in 1949, 1959, 1972, and 1976. *Dumbo* first appeared on home video in 1981 and there was a sixtieth anniversary edition in 2001 on DVD. The Blu-ray edition came out in 2016, the seventy-fifth anniversary of its premiere.

During the 1960s there were some criticisms of the portrayal of the crows in *Dumbo*. Some critics saw them as "Negro stereotypes" in their dress, looks, and voices. (Three of the four voice actors were African American.) Others argued that there was nothing derogatory about the crows. They are hip characters who use jive in their speech and are far from dumb or lazy, the usual racist attributes of black characters in movies at the time. *Dumbo* is a sweet tale and, as many have pointed out, these wisecracking dudes provide a kind of humor and attitude much needed in the movie.

Did You Know . . . ?

Dumbo is the only Disney animated feature in which the title hero does not speak one word. Years later, the alien Stitch in *Lilo and Stitch* (2002) spoke only gibberish but no decipherable words.

E

THE EMPEROR'S NEW GROOVE

2000
(USA: Walt Disney Pictures)

Directed by Mark Dindal
Written by David Reynolds
Produced by Don Hahn, Randy Fullmer, Patricia Hicks, and Prudence Fenton
Score by John Debney
Songs by Sting
Specs: Color (Technicolor); 78 minutes; traditional animation

---

Comic sarcasm goes hand in hand with sentiment in this very funny Disney feature that has a playfully stylized look and some outrageously farcical characters.

Kuzco, the young and self-centered emperor of the Incas in South America, is suspicious of his aged advisor, the sorceress Yzma, so he fires her. To get revenge, Yzma turns Kuzco into a llama and then makes plans to take over the empire herself. The humble peasant Pacha discovers the lost Kuzco and agrees to take him back to the palace if he will abandon his plans to destroy Pacha's village for a wealthy housing development. During the long journey to the palace, the two men argue, part, reunite, and end up friends. At a hillside eatery, Pacha overhears Yzma and her stooge Kronk plan to kill Kozco, so he warns the llama emperor.

Voice Cast

David Spade	Emperor Kuzco
Eartha Kitt	Yzma
John Goodman	Pacha
Patrick Warburton	Kronk
Wendie Malick	Chicha
Kellyann Kelso	Chaca
Eli Russell Linnetz	Tipo
Tom Jones	Theme Song Guy

The spoiled emperor Kuzko (far left) has to deal not only with the sorceress Yzma (far right) but also her thick-headed but warm-hearted sidekick Kronk (center). *Buena Vista Pictures / Photofest.* © *Buena Vista Pictures*

Back at the palace, Yzma plans to uses magic potions to take over the empire but Pacha and Kuzco steal the potions from her and Kronk abandons Yzma to help the emperor. Using the potions, Kuzco is turned back into a human, Yzma is transformed into a cat, and the Incas now have a more caring emperor.

Under the working title of *Kingdom of the Sun*, the project was begun in 1994 but went through many changes in plot, staff, and look over the next six years. The story originally centered on a young Incan emperor who trades places with a look-alike peasant and learns about the real world. But after such serious movies as *Pocahontas* (1995) and *The Hunchback of Notre Dame* (1996), the Disney studio wanted to offer the public a comedy, so this *Prince and the Pauper*–like tale was totally rewritten into a farce. Even the villainess Yzma was turned into a comic character, and her henchman became the dense and hilarious Kronk. The central character, changed from Manco to Kuzco, was reimagined as a stand-up comic. Codirector Roger Allers and other members of the team withdrew from the project, retitled *The Emperor's New Groove*, and it was directed by Mark Dindal. The singer-songwriter Sting wrote six songs for *Kingdom of the Sun*, but all but two were dropped. With a reduced budget and a closer production deadline, the making of the film was fraught with tension, and at one point the entire project was nearly canceled. Yet the resulting movie is a breezy, flippant, and thoroughly enjoyable comedy.

Songs

"My Funny Friend and Me"
"Perfect World"

Television comic actor and writer David Spade was involved with the production early on and the character of Kuzco was influenced by Spade's smart-aleck, quick-talking style of delivery. Kuzco narrates *The Emperor's New Groove*, so the tone of the whole film is set by Spade's roguish performance. In an inspired bit of casting, the seventy-three-year-old singer and actress Eartha Kitt plays Yzma, her unique voice ideal for the predatory sorceress. John Goodman as Pacha plays straight man to Spade, but Patrick Warburton steals several scenes with his cheerful and obtuse Kronk. Not since *Aladdin* (1992) and *Hercules* (1997) has the dialogue in a Disney film been so joke filled, and the top-notch cast never falters in delivering such silliness. Even the singing is satirical, as with the lounge singer Theme Song Guy sung with snide bombast by popular Welsh crooner Tom Jones.

KUZCO: Okay, I admit it. Maybe I wasn't as nice as I should have been. But, Yzma, do you really want to kill me?

YZMA: Just think of it as you're being let go, that your life's going in a different direction, that your body's part of a permanent outplacement.

KRONK: Hey, that's kinda like what he said to you when you got fired.

YZMA: I know. It's called a "cruel irony," like my dependence on you.

The Emperor's New Groove does not have a traditional Disney look. The background art is very cartoonish with simple shapes and colors fashioned into a very modern style. In fact, the movie resembles a Warner Brothers cartoon in many ways. Everything from the palace to the Andes Mountains is presented as large geometric shapes with splashy coloring. The characters are equally exaggerated, Kronk and Pacha drawn as impossibly bulky men and Yzma as ridiculously thin. Kuzco spends most of the film in the guise of a llama, yet the selfish emperor's human moves are sometimes replicated in animal form. Touches of Incan architecture, dress, and art are used throughout, but again in an oversized and satirical way. What the Disney artists did to ancient Greece in *Hercules*, they do here to the native world of South America. One might describe the look of the locale and the people as Incan Las Vegas.

Awards

Academy Award nomination: Best Song ("My Funny Friend and Me").
Golden Globe nomination: Best Song ("My Funny Friend and Me").

Because of the many production problems, the release of *The Emperor's New Groove* was pushed to the end of 2000 when DreamWorks' *The Road to El Dorado* opened. That animated feature was also set in South America, so the rivalry between the two studios was rekindled. Disney ended up spending around $100 million on *The Emperor's New Groove*, so when it grossed only $169 million, the film was considered less of a success than the studio's 1990s projects. Yet most critics applauded the movie's irreverent tone and rapid-fire comedy. Some also noted that *The Emperor's New Groove* offered more entertainment for adults than for kids. All the same, the film was turned into a successful television series and two video games. The VHS and DVD editions of the original film were released in 2001 and in 2005 there was a direct-to-video sequel titled *Kronk's New Groove* with some of the same voices back in the cast.

See also *Hercules* and *The Road to El Dorado*.

Did You Know . . . ?

Pacha's wife, Chicha, is very obviously pregnant with their third child. Chicha is the first pregnant character in a Disney animated feature.

F

FANTASIA

1940

(USA: Walt Disney Pictures)

Directed by Ben Sharpsteen, Bill Roberts, James Algar, Samuel Armstrong, Wilfred Jackson, Paul Satterfield, T. Hee, Jim Handley, Ford Beebe Jr., Norman Ferguson, and Hamilton Luske
Written by Joe Grant and Dick Huemer
Produced by Walt Disney and Ben Sharpsteen
Score by Johann Sebastian Bach, Ludwig van Beethoven, Paul Dukas, Amilcare Ponchielli, Igor Stravinsky, Modest Mussorgsky, Pyotr Tchaikovsky, and Franz Schubert
Specs: Color (Technicolor); 125 minutes; traditional animation

---

A bold experiment by the Disney studio that was generally dismissed on its first release, Fantasia *today is a widely accepted masterpiece of American animation.*

Eight classic concert pieces are illustrated and animated in various styles and moods to bring the famous music to life rather than just serve as background music. Bach's vigorous Toccata and Fugue in D Minor becomes an abstract expression of lines and music. Dukas's dramatic *The Sorcerer's Apprentice* tells a story with Mickey Mouse as an overeager wizard-in-training who steals the sorcerer's magic hat and loses control of his new powers. Tchaikovsky's fanciful *Nutcracker Suite* comes to life as a nature ballet with fairies, flowers, fish, and even dancing mushrooms. Beethoven's expansive *Pastoral* Symphony serves for mythological characters cavorting in a sunny landscape. Ponchielli's spirited *Dance of the Hours* is turned into a comic ballet featuring ostriches, crocodiles, and hippos. Stravinsky's powerful *Rite of Spring* shows the creation of the planet and primeval life, ending with the extinction of the dinosaurs. Mussorgsky's violent *Night on Bald Mountain* illustrates the battle between good and evil with devils, ghosts, and skeletons. The film concludes with Schubert's sacred hymn "Ave Maria" sung by pilgrims as dawn brings tranquility and hope.

Fantasia originated as a way to reestablish Mickey Mouse as the preeminent figure of Disney animation. In the late 1930s, Donald Duck had grown in popularity so much that he was overshadowing the mouse who began it all. Walt

In the movie's most famous sequence, the sorcerer's magic hat gives Mickey all kinds of powers but stopping an army of brooms and water buckets is not among them. *Walt Disney Productions / Photofest. © Walt Disney Productions*

Disney wanted to make an elaborate Silly Symphony cartoon set to *The Sorcerer's Apprentice* starring Mickey. But the cartoon got so complicated and expensive that the studio decided to turn the cartoon into an anthology program featuring other classical pieces of music set to animation. When Disney mentioned the idea to the world-famous conductor Leopold Stokowski, the maestro immediately wanted to conduct the soundtrack. Also hired was the Philadelphia Orchestra to record the score and music critic and author Deems Taylor as narrator for the movie. Many different classical works were considered before the studio decided on the seven selections to be heard in addition to the Dukas piece. Different artists worked on

Voice Cast

Walt Disney	Mickey Mouse

Live-Action Cast

Deems Taylor	Narrator
Leopold Stokowski	Leopold Stokowski

different pieces, so the style of each section of the film varies greatly, from pastoral lyrical to boldly abstract. Happily, the quality was consistently high in each section and many new and exciting ideas were used throughout. The Bach Toccata and Fugue was pure animation with no story or characters. Nothing quite like it had been seen in American movies before. The seemingly three-dimensional snowflakes in the *Nutcracker* sequence and the harsh expressionism in the *Bald Mountain* nightmare were similarly inventive. The complicated multi-plane camera shots during "Ave Maria" caused a great deal of problems but once solved resulted in a glowing impressionistic marvel of camera movement. As highbrow as *Fantasia* seems at times, it is also filled with humor. For example, the dancing hippos in the Ponchielli sequence were masterful moments of inspired silliness. Two of the longest pieces, Stravinsky's *Rite of Spring* and Beethoven's *Pastoral* Symphony, are not as successful as the rest of *Fantasia*. yet even those sections have some dazzling animation and background art. As for the original *Sorcerer's Apprentice* cartoon, it remains the highlight of the movie. The tale is whimsical yet a bit frightening, and the animation of inanimate objects come to life is still compelling on many levels.

Musical Selections

Toccata and Fugue in D Minor (Bach)
The Nutcracker Suite (Tchaikovsky)
The Sorcerer's Apprentice (Dukas)
Rite of Spring (Stravinsky)
Symphony No. 6 (*Pastoral*) (Beethoven)
Dance of the Hours (Ponchielli)
A Night on Bald Mountain (Mussorgsky)
"Ave Maria" (Schubert)

Since the music recording was essential to the classical sound of *Fantasia*, the studio spared no expense. It took Stokowski and the Philadelphia Orchestra seven weeks to record the music on a new stereophonic system that was dubbed Fantasound, using eight separate recording machines and heard through a series of speakers situated in different parts of the movie theater. No movie had ever sounded so vibrant as the music heard during the early days of the film's release. But setting up the complex sound system in movie houses was expensive and prohibitive, limiting the number of venues for *Fantasia* to be screened. The critics and audiences who saw the original "road show" screening of *Fantasia* were certainly impressed. Reviews were mostly raves for both the visuals and the new sound system, and it looked like "Disney's Folly" might pay off. But the public was not interested in *Fantasia* and the box office across the country and in Great Britain was disappointing. Because World War II was raging, the studio could not show the movie in most of Europe, where there was a higher appreciation of classical music. When *Fantasia* was rereleased in 1942 in a simpler mono version, it was edited down to 100 minutes and was missing all narration and the abstract Bach piece. It still failed to interest the public. A restored version in

1946 and again in 1956 found more favor, but it was not until the 1963 rerelease that *Fantasia* finally found a wide audience. Moviegoers not born when the film first appeared found it unique and innovative and *Fantasia* became an art house favorite. There were also releases in 1969, 1977, 1982, 1985, and 1990. Later in 1990, the movie was put on home video, and in 2000 it was available on DVD. It took years for *Fantasia* to become a hit, but today it is firmly placed near the top of the cinema's greatest animated films.

> MICKEY MOUSE: Mr. Stokowski! Mr. Stokowski! My congratulations, sir!
>
> LEOPOLD STOKOWSKI: (shaking hands with Mickey) Congratulations to you, Mickey!
>
> MICKEY MOUSE: Gee, thanks! He-he! Well, so long! I'll be seeing ya!

Walt Disney had envisioned *Fantasia* as a movie that would change with each new release. He planned to substitute new animation for different pieces of classical music each time the movie was rereleased. But the initial failure of *Fantasia* made such plans impractical. It was not until sixty years later that his nephew Roy Disney spearheaded a new *Fantasia*, in which *The Sorcerer's Apprentice* was reprised but the other segments were original. Titled *Fantasia 2000*, the new anthology film included Beethoven's vivacious Fifth Symphony as the music for another abstract animation segment; Ottorino Respighi's majestic *Pines of Rome* as a water ballet for whales; George Gershwin's *Rhapsody in Blue* capturing busy Depression-era New Yorkers in busy Al Hirschfeld–like line drawings; Dmitri Shostakovich's Piano Concerto No. 2 illustrating the Hans Christian Andersen tale, "The Steadfast Soldier"; a movement from Camille Saint-Saëns's *Carnival of the Animals* for a playful sequence with bouncing flamingos and a yo-yo; Edward Elgar's stately "Pomp and Circumstance" providing the music for all the animals marching onto Noah's Ark, with Donald Duck as Noah's frustrated helper; and Stravinsky's passionate *Firebird* ballet suite dramatizing a mythic parable about a sprite and an elk restoring life to a ravaged forest. James Levine conducted the Chicago Symphony and various guest stars, such as Angela Lansbury, Quincy Jones, Bette Midler, and Steve Martin, introduced each section. Once again, the styles of animation and background art were as varied as the different musical selections. The animation throughout is superb and there are no weak sections. Highlights include the surreal ballet-like movement of whales in the Respighi march; the vibrant line drawings and rapid action in the Gershwin rhapsody; and the visuals depicting life and death in nature in the Stravinsky section. *Fantasia 2000* is a testament to the Disney studio in its ability to present an animated masterwork that compares favorably with the original.

Awards

Special Academy Awards to Leopold Stokowski for his conducting and to Walt Disney, William E. Garity, and J. N. A. Hawkins for the "advancement of the use of sound."

Fantasia 2000 cost over $90 million and many at the studio called it "Roy Disney's Folly." It was first released in a limited number of IMAX theaters, so it took time before *Fantasia 2000* started to show a profit. It went into widespread release in 2000 and eventually earned back its initial investment before finding success on DVD in late 2000.

Did You Know . . . ?

The inspiration for the Sorcerer who is Mickey Mouse's boss in *The Sorcerer's Apprentice* segment was Walt Disney himself. The animators even copied Disney's stern look and raised eyebrows when he was displeased with something. The staff nicknamed the Sorcerer "Yen Sid," which is "Disney" spelled backwards.

FANTASTIC MR. FOX

2009
(USA: 20th Century-Fox)

Directed by Wes Anderson
Written by Wes Anderson and Noah Baumbach, based on the book by Roald Dahl
Produced by Arnon Milchan, Steven Rales, Allison Abbate, Scott Rudin, Wes Anderson, Jeremy Dawson, and Molly Cooper
Score by Alexandre Desplat
Specs: Color; 87 minutes; stop-motion animation

Offbeat director-writer Wes Anderson brought his quirky style of live-action movies to this animated film, which is visually and vocally delightfully different.

When Mrs. Fox finds out she's pregnant, she makes Mr. Fox give up his life of stealing fowls from farmhouses and settle down as a newspaper columnist. But Mr. Fox misses the thrill of the kill and convinces the opossum Kylie to help in a raid on the three most prosperous farms in the area. The two successfully steal chickens, smoked meats, and hard cider from the farms of Boggis, Bunce, and Bean. When Mrs. Fox finds out what her husband is doing, she is furious but eventually helps Mr. Fox when the three farmers take their revenge on the foxes and attack with bullets and bulldozers. The Foxes' son Ash and nephew Kristofferson, teenagers who do not get along, also get involved as Mr. Fox leads the various local wildlife in outwitting the three farmers and finding a new life in the sewers of the nearby town.

Roald Dahl's book is about a parent trying to protect his family, written at a time when the author was dealing with the loss of two of his children. Wes Anderson's film version maintains some of that feeling but is more interested in Mr. Fox trying to deal with his wild animal instincts. Characters were added, the plot frequently departed from the original story, and a wacky tongue-in-cheek tone was utilized,

The former chicken thief Mr. Fox (left) yearns to return to his criminal ways, but Mrs. Fox does everything she can to keep him domesticated and at home. *Fox Searchlight Pictures / Photofest.* © *Fox Searchlight Pictures*

making *Fantastic Mr. Fox* more an Anderson product than a Dahl one. The look of the animals involved puppets with real fur but very human movement and modern, sarcastic dialogue. The stop-motion process used a faster film speed than usual in order to give the movement a jerky and even primitive look. The aim was to replicate the early stop-motion television specials by Rankin and Bass. The background settings were also deliberately artificial with fields made from cloth and smoke fashioned from cotton. The entire film is rendered in autumnal colors that match the Fox family's browns and yellows. The humans were made

Voice Cast

George Clooney	Mr. Fox
Meryl Streep	Mrs. Fox
Jason Schwartzman	Ash
Wallace Wolodarsky	Kylie
Eric Chase Anderson	Kristofferson
Michael Gambon	Bean
Robin Hurlstone	Boggis
Hugo Guinness	Bunce
Bill Murray	Badger
Willem Dafoe	Rat
Owen Wilson	Skip Coach
Jarvis Cocker	Petey
Karen Duffy	Linda Otter
Helen McCrory	Mrs. Bean
Wes Anderson	Weasel

to look like papier-mâché dolls with few facial expressions. In addition to the many different locations, *Fantastic Mr. Fox* required over five hundred puppets and hundreds of props. The result is not an intricate and detailed stop-motion film like *Chicken Run* or *The Boxtrolls* but a rough-and-tumble movie that seems to poke fun at the very nature of stop-motion filmmaking.

> MRS. FOX: This story's too predictable.
>
> MR. FOX: Predictable? Really? Then, how does it end?
>
> MRS. FOX: In the end, we all die. Unless you change.

Anderson was able to assemble a first-rate cast of celebrities for the voices, some of the actors veterans of his live-action movies. George Clooney delivers Mr. Fox's lines with a hurried, unemotional tone that makes him very flippant and even superficial. Meryl Streep, on the other hand, brings a warm sincerity to Mrs. Fox. Jason Schwartzman and Eric Anderson as Ash and Kristofferson are very droll as teenagers with attitude while Wallace Wolodarsky underplays the idiotic Kylie with great effect. Bill Murray, Michael Gambon, and Willem Dafoe stand out among the large cast. All of them sound a little less canned because their vocals were recorded in various locales outside of a studio. Alexandre Desplat, another veteran of Anderson's works, composed the daffy soundtrack score, which ranged from a children's chorus to some surreal symphonics one might hear in a science fiction movie. Sprinkled throughout the film are some song standards that are used as ironic commentary. The Beach Boys' recording of "Ol' Man River" and The Wellingtons' version of "The Ballad of Davy Crockett" were among the pleasingly incoherent song interpolations.

Awards

Academy Award nominations: Best Animated Feature and Best Score.
Golden Globe nomination: Best Animated Feature.
British Academy of Film & Television Arts (BAFTA) Award nominations: Best Animated Film and Best Score.

Fantastic Mr. Fox was filmed at a studio in London and the movie had its premiere in the same city in 2009. When widely released, it met with mostly favorable reviews, several critics applauding the retro look of the film. Most commentators praised the eccentric voice performances, though some complained that Dahl's book was treated rather shabbily by the moviemakers. The public enjoyed *Fantastic Mr. Fox*, but not in large enough numbers to make the movie a runaway hit. It grossed some $46 million but it cost roughly $40 million to make; not a success by Hollywood standards. Like Anderson's live-action films, his animated effort did not appeal to mainstream audiences but was much appreciated by those who enjoyed his unorthodox filmmaking.

Did You Know . . . ?

Director Wes Anderson was not always on the set during the tedious stop-motion filming. Much of his direction was sent through his iPhone.

FINDING NEMO

2003
(USA: Pixar Animation Studios/Disney)

Directed by Andrew Stanton and Lee Unkrich
Written by Andrew Stanton, Bob Peterson, and David Reynolds
Produced by John Lasseter, Graham Alters, and Jinko Cotoh
Score by Thomas Newman
Specs: Color; 100 minutes; computer animation

One of Pixar's most beloved films, this computer-generated movie has equal doses of adventure, comedy, and heart. It is also unique for its setting in the waters near Australia and its cast of diverse sea life.

After a barracuda kills his mate, Coral, the clown fish Marlin is overly protective of the one surviving egg, which he names Nemo. He continues to worry after Nemo is born and is old enough to go to school under the protection of Mr. Ray. On a field trip, Nemo is captured by a diver, an Australian dentist who adds the little clown fish to his aquarium in his office. The only clue Marlin has regarding Nemo's whereabouts is the dentist's diving mask with a Sydney address. He sets off for the Sydney harbor, along the way meeting the blue tang Dory, who suffers from short-term memory loss and agrees to help him. The two fish encounter the three sharks Bruce, Anchor, and Chum on their journey, as well as a bunch of jellyfish and a parade of sea turtles. Nemo manages to escape from the dentist's office before the obnoxious girl Darla has a chance to kill him, and he follows the pipes into the harbor. After Nemo saves Dory's life, he is reunited with Marlin and the three return to their home in the Great Barrier Reef.

Director Andrew Stanton's childhood memories of an aquarium filled with colorful fish in his dentist's office led to the premise for *Finding Nemo*. Stanton wondered if those fish wished they could escape back to the ocean and how they would set about to accomplish such a feat. His own experiences as a protective father with a young son also contributed to the screenplay, which he wrote with Bob Peterson and David Reynolds. In some of the test footage, Stanton provided the voice for the laid-back sea turtle Crush and the staff thought his performance could not be bested, so he reprised it for the film. Just as the background artists studied the look of the Great Barrier Reef, the animators visited different aquariums to observe the look and movements of different sea creatures. All the species seen in the movie are accurately portrayed with no exaggerated features

The clown fish Marlin (far right) gets help on his mission to find his son, Nemo, from the ditzy blue tang fish Dory, the laid-back sea turtle Crush, and Crush's enthusiastic son Squirt. *Walt Disney Pictures / Photofest. © Walt Disney Pictures*

or human movement. It is the superb voice work in *Finding Nemo* that turns the creatures into empathetic characters. Comic actor Albert Brooks turns in a multilayered performance as the worried father Marlin, and child actor Alexander Gould gives young Nemo a spunky reading. Of the many aquatic characters in the movie, the showcase performance is that by comedienne Ellen DeGeneres as the wacky and lovable Dory with short-term memory loss. Most of the characters

Voice Cast

Albert Brooks	Marlin
Alexander Gould	Nemo
Ellen DeGeneres	Dory
Andrew Stanton	Crush
Nicholas Bird	Squirt
Willem Dafoe	Gill
Brad Garrett	Bloat
Allison Janney	Peach
Austin Pendleton	Gurgle
Geoffrey Rush	Nigel
Vicki Lewis	Deb & Flo
Stephen Root	Bubbles
Joe Ranft	Jacques
Elizabeth Perkins	Coral
Bob Peterson	Mr. Ray
Barry Humphries	Bruce
Eric Bana	Anchor
Bruce Spence	Chum
Bill Hunter	Dentist
Lulu Ebeling	Darla

in *Finding Nemo* are comic, yet several get the opportunity to tug the heartstrings as well. Perhaps the most interesting fish character-wise is Bruce (voiced by Barry Humphries), the great white shark who suffers an internal battle between vegetarianism and his carnivore instincts. Although there is plenty of action in the film, a large cast of characters manages to reveal individual personality traits. Similarly, the background artists were able to illustrate the very different environments in the movie, from the colorful coral reef to the city of Sydney. Thomas Newman's spirited soundtrack score contributes much to the different moods in the film. Most memorable is the theme for the sadistic child Darla, which is an homage to Bernard Herrmann's music in *Psycho* (1960).

> MARLIN: I promised I'd never let anything happen to him.
>
> DORY: Hmm. That's a funny thing to promise.
>
> MARLIN: What?
>
> DORY: Well, you can't never let anything happen to him. Then nothing would ever happen to him. Not much fun for little Harpo.

Finding Nemo was an immediate hit with both the critics and the moviegoing public. The $94 million project ended up earning ten times that amount internationally. In addition to the successful merchandising, the sale of aquariums and tropical fish soared, even though the theme of the movie was against the captivity of sea life. Even more damaging, there was such a great demand for clown fish that the species has been threatened ever since the film was released. When *Finding Nemo* was released on DVD in 2003, it broke sales records with over 40 million copies sold over the next three years.

Awards

Academy Awards: Best Animated Feature and Best Screenplay. Oscar nominations: Best Score and Best Sound Editing.
Golden Globe nomination: Best Picture—Comedy or Musical.
British Academy of Film & Television Arts (BAFTA) Award nominations: Best Feature Film and Best Screenplay.

With such impressive numbers, it is surprising that it took so much time before a sequel was made. The popularity of Dory (and DeGeneres's wonderful voice performance) pushed Stanton and the studio to feature the lovable blue tang in the sequel. *Finding Dory* (2016) continues the story of Marlin, Nemo, and Dory with some other characters returning with the same voice actors. Dory has flashes of memory of her childhood and her separation from her parents. She sets out across the Pacific to the waters off California to find her family, running into several complications along the way. The movie has even more action than the original, including a chase scene in which an octopus drives a truck. But there are some tender moments as well. *Finding Dory* was one of the most anticipated films of its time, and it did not disappoint audiences or most of the critics. It was an even bigger international hit, and the possibility of another sequel is very real.

Did You Know . . . ?

The name of the shark Bruce is a movie industry joke. The crew working on Steven Spielberg's film *Jaws* (1975) nicknamed the troublesome mechanical shark "Bruce."

FRANKENWEENIE

2012
(USA: Tim Burton Productions/Disney)

Directed by Tim Burton
Written by John August and Leonard Ripps, based on the 1984 animated short of the same title
Produced by Don Hahn, Allison Abbate, Tim Burton, Derek Frey, and Connie Nartonis Thompson
Score by Danny Elfman
Songs by various artists
Specs: Black and white; 87 minutes; stop-motion animation

An offbeat variation of Mary Shelley's Frankenstein, *this Tim Burton stop-motion fantasy manages to be both grotesque and endearing.*

The preteen Victor Frankenstein, a budding scientist and filmmaker, features his beloved bulldog, Sparky, in his homemade movies, and when the pet is killed by a car, the boy is despondent. Mr. Rzykruski, the eccentric new science teacher at school, demonstrates the use of electricity to make a dead frog move and Victor is inspired to do the same thing with Sparky. He digs up the dog's body and, harnessing electricity from a thunderstorm, manages to bring Sparky back to life. Victor's hunchbacked schoolmate Edgar E. Gore finds out that Sparky is alive and tells some of the other students, who are hoping to win the upcoming science fair. Copying Victor's experiment with electricity, Victor's rivals bring their pets back to life, but with weird and dangerous consequences. Soon the town is overrun with a giant ferocious turtle, a crazed mutation of a bat and a cat, and a gang of hyperactive sea monkeys. A major thunderstorm sends deadly volts of electricity to the local windmill and kills all the creatures but, with the help of the townspeople, Sparky is brought back to life and the outcast Victor is hailed a hero.

Tim Burton's 1984 film short *Frankenweenie* is a twenty-nine-minute sci-fi homage to *Frankenstein* and has pretty much the same plot as the later feature. Twelve years later, writer John August was asked to expand the short into a feature-length movie also to be directed by Burton. Characters were added or embellished, names were changed, and some subplots were included, the result being a sci-fi spoof with room for some heart-tugging scenes. Victor's fellow students were designed to resemble famous monsters from filmdom, such as Frankenstein, Dracula, Igor, and the Mummy. *Frankenweenie* was filled with dozens of visual and

The brilliant but misunderstood youth Victor so loves his dog Sparky that when the canine dies, Victor uses his special scientific knowledge to bring Sparky back to life. *Walt Disney Pictures / Photofest. © Walt Disney Pictures*

audio references to these old horror classics. Yet there is a sense of identification with Victor that the audience experiences in this movie that rarely occurs in sci-fi works. Over two hundred puppets were fashioned, and the many locations within the town were created in a London film studio. The stop-motion animation is unusually detailed in *Frankenweenie*, from the intricate movement of the electrified Sparky to the complex mechanics in Victor's attic laboratory. The human characters are exaggerated in look and motion just as the animals are almost surreal in their anatomically bizarre forms. Interestingly, the grotesque look of the human and animal figures does not stand in the way of the audience finding sympathy with them. The dog Sparky, in both his natural state and in his electrified transformation, can hardly be described as cute and cuddly, yet soon the moviegoers see him with the affection that Victor has for the pet. The settings are also stylized,

Voice Cast

Charlie Tahan	Victor Frankenstein
Catherine O'Hara	Mrs. Frankenstein
Martin Short	Mr. Frankenstein
Martin Landau	Mr. Rzykruski
Atticus Shaffer	Edgar E. Gore
Winona Ryder	Elsa Van Helsing
Martin Short	Mayor Burgermeister
Robert Capron	Bob
James Hiroyuki Liao	Toshiaki
Martin Short	Nassor
Conchata Ferrell	Bob's Mom

most memorably the pet cemetery filled with variously shaped monuments. The houses and other buildings in the town suggest a 1950s television sitcom world, particularly when rendered in black and white. *Frankenweenie* looks like a fusion of *The Bride of Frankenstein* and *The Donna Reed Show*.

VICTOR: Nobody likes scientists.

MR. RZYKRUSKI: They like what science gives them, but not the questions, no. Not the questions that science asks.

VICTOR: Actually, I have a question.

MR. RZYKRUSKI: That is why you are scientist.

Some actors from previous Burton movies, both live-action and animated, are heard in *Frankenweenie*. Holding the cast together is a solid and sincere performance by young Charlie Tahan as Victor. Perhaps the most vibrant voice performance is given by Martin Landau whose Mr. Rzykruski is a cross between Boris Karloff and Vincent Price. Martin Short voices three very different characters but his gruff Burgermeister is the funniest. Atticus Schaffer is also very entertaining with his vocals for Edgar that suggest an adolescent Peter Lorre. Danny Elfman provided the soundtrack score, which is also an homage to the Hollywood horror classics. The music is eerie and often bombastic, yet there is a hint of sarcasm in it as well. Elfman also wrote the wry and pathetic "Elsa's Song" sung by Winona Ryder at the town festival. Other songs from various sources are included, but *Frankenweenie* does not feel very musical, as in *The Nightmare before Christmas* (1993), except for the dramatic soundtrack.

Awards

Academy Award nomination: Best Animated Feature.
Golden Globe nomination: Best Animated Feature.
British Academy of Film & Television Arts (BAFTA) Award nomination: Best Animated Film.

When the movie was released in 2012, the reviews were almost unanimously complimentary. Some critics preferred the earlier twenty-nine-minute version, but most applauded the more detailed story and the excellent visuals. Both reviewers and moviegoers who were familiar with Burton's previous work cited *Frankenweenie* as one of his best, not as dark as *Corpse Bride* (2010) and funnier than *James and the Giant Peach* (1996). Audience approval allowed the film to earn over $81 million; the movie cost about $39 million. The DVD and Blu-ray editions were released in 2013.

See also *The Nightmare before Christmas*.

Did You Know . . . ?

In the pet cemetery scene, one can see a grave marked for Zero, the dog in Tim Burton's *The Nightmare before Christmas* (1993).

FRITZ THE CAT

1972
(USA: Black Ink / Fritz Productions)

Directed and written by Ralph Bakshi, based on characters created by Robert Crumb
Produced by Steve Krantz
Score by Ed Bogas and Ray Shanklin
Specs: Color and black and white; 78 minutes; traditional animation

Pushing animated films into unexplored adult territory, filmmaker Ralph Bakshi made a handful of irreverent sociopolitical movies, the best being the audacious sex and political farce Fritz the Cat.

The hip feline college student Fritz and some of his pals pick up some females in Central Park and bring them back to a friend's apartment, where they have group sex in the bathtub. Smoking grass and making a lot of noise, the party attracts the attention of some pig cops, who raid the apartment and start beating up the partygoers. Fritz grabs a gun from one of the cops and shoots the toilet, flooding the apartment and washing everyone out onto the street. Returning to his dorm, Fritz decides to give up education and sets his books on fire, causing the whole dorm to burst into flames. In a Harlem bar, Fritz meets Duke the Crow playing billiards and the two steal a car but nearly die when they drive it off a bridge. The two visit the apartment of the drug dealer Bertha and, while enjoying her drugs and her body, Fritz is inspired to start a revolution. On the street, he incites a riot in which Duke is killed. The vixen Winston Schwartz rescues Fritz and the two set

The oversexed feline Fritz (far left) has a love-'em-and-leave-'em attitude regarding the many females he encounters in this very first adult animated feature movie. *Cinemation Industries / Photofest. © Cinemation Industries*

Voice Cast

Skip Hinnant	Fritz the Cat
Judy Engles	Winston Schwartz
Rosetta LeNoire	Bertha
John McCurry	Blue and John
Ralph Bakshi	Pig Cop
Phil Sterling	Pig Cop
Charles Spidar	Duke the Crow
Mary Dean	Harriet

off on a road trip to San Francisco, but when they are conned out of their car in the desert he ditches her. Fritz then meets up with the heroin-addict rabbit biker Blue and his horse girlfriend Harriet, who bring him to the hideout of a group of revolutionaries who are planning to blow up a power station. When Harriet objects, she is gang raped by Blue and the revolutionaries. Fritz joins the anarchists and sets off the dynamite but is severely wounded. In the hospital and near death, he is nursed by Harriet and is visited by the three girls from the park. Coming back to life, Fritz has sex with the trio of females as Harriet watches.

Unconventional artist Robert Crumb introduced the character of the oversexed hipster cat Fritz in the early 1960s in a self-published comic strip produced by him and his brother Charles. By the mid-1960s Crumb and the cat were widely known within the counterculture society. Animator Ralph Bakshi, discontent with working on cartoons for Paramount, formed his own company in 1969 and approached Crumb about an animated feature centering on Fritz. Crumb was reluctant, but his wife, Dana Crumb, had power of attorney and signed with Bakshi. The screenplay, which Bakshi adapted from the Fritz the Cat comics, is true to Crumb's work visually and sociopolitically. The sex scenes are graphic, the dialogue is profane and streetwise, and the issues of race, the establishment, war, drugs, and sex are presented blatantly. The script also retains much of the crude humor of the comics. The sound in the movie is unconventional as well. The voice cast recorded their lines on the street or in other locales outside of a recording studio.

FRITZ: I know about the race problem—I've studied the race problem!

DUKE: You don't know nothing about the race problem! You've got to be a crow to know about the race problem!

The funding for *Fritz the Cat* came from various sources but did not add up to the amount an animated feature normally cost so Bakshi had to cut corners and eliminate expensive and time-consuming techniques. No preliminary pencil tests were made and the animators worked directly on cels. Photographs were combined with watercolor paintings giving the background art a semi-documentary look. The voice cast included no name stars but consisted of some very talented actors who later found fame on television, such as Skip Hinnant (Fritz) and Rosetta LeNoire (Bertha). Ed Bogas and Ray Shanklin composed the jazz-influenced soundtrack score and then published songs with low royalty costs were added. When the movie was completed and was given an X rating by the Motion Picture Association of America, Bakshi had trouble getting a distributor. When he secured the services of Cinemation, more trouble followed. Many newspapers would not print ads for *Fritz the Cat*, and some movie house chains refused to show previews for the movie. But after receiving praise at the Cannes Film Festival in 1972, the film started to get a wider release and its X rating became a selling point. Reviews in the press were mixed, but enough critics applauded the unorthodox movie that business gradually picked up. *Fritz the Cat* was made for $850,000 and earned $25 million just in the United States. To date, it is estimated that the film has made $90 million internationally. A sequel, *The Nine Lives of Fritz the Cat* (1974), retained some of the voice cast but was made without Bakshi or Crumb's participation. The exploitive movie was critically lambasted and pretty much ignored by the public. Bakshi went on to make other adult animated films, most memorably *Heavy Traffic* (1973) and *Coonskin* (1975), as well as animated fantasies, as with *Wizards* (1977) and *Lord of the Rings* (1978). But it is his first feature, *Fritz the Cat*, that enjoys a cult status and represents a bold new direction for American animation.

See also *Wizards* and *South Park: Bigger, Longer & Uncut*.

Did You Know . . . ?

Fritz the Cat was the first animated film to receive an X rating from the Motion Picture Association of America.

FROZEN

2013
(USA: Walt Disney Pictures)

Directed by Chris Buck and Jennifer Lee
Written by Jennifer Lee, based on Hans Christian Andersen's story "The Snow Queen"
Produced by John Lasseter, Peter Del Vecho, and Aimee Scribner
Score by Christophe Beck
Songs by Kristen Anderson-Lopez and Robert Lopez
Specs: Color; 102 minutes; computer animation and some traditional animation

---

A sleeper hit that surprised even the Disney studio, this animated musical fantasy, very loosely based on a Hans Christian Andersen tale, has captured the hearts of young girls who can't seem to get enough of the songs and characters.

Princess Elsa grows up in the Scandinavian kingdom of Arendelle with strange and dangerous powers, able to make things freeze by the touch of her hand. Her

Like most animated princesses, Anna has a faithful and somewhat looney sidekick, in this case the goofy snowman named Olaf. *Walt Disney Pictures / Photofest. © Walt Disney Pictures*

parents keep her powers from public knowledge and even hide her secret from her younger sister, Anna. After the King and Queen die at sea, Elsa comes of age and dignitaries from other lands arrive in Arendelle for her coronation. Anna falls in love with the visiting Prince Hans, and when she tells her sister, Elsa is furious and runs away and secludes herself in a faraway ice castle. The kingdom falls into a state of endless winter, so Anna sets out to find Elsa. On the way she is helped by the woodsman Kristoff; his faithful reindeer sidekick, Sven; and a lively snow-man named Olaf. Together they undergo harsh conditions before arriving at the ice palace. Elsa warns her sister that she is not in control of her powers, and when Anna refuses to leave, Elsa conjures up a giant snow creature to drive them away.

Voice Cast

Livvy Stubenrauch	Anna (young)
Agatha Lee Monn	Anna (teenage)
Kristen Bell	Anna (adult)
Eva Bella	Elsa (young)
Idina Menzel	Elsa (adult)
Jonathan Groff	Kristoff
Josh Gad	Olaf
Santino Fontana	Hans
Alan Tudyk	Duke
Ciarán Hinds	Pabbie
Chris Williams	Oaken
Stephen J. Anderson	Kai
Maia Wilson	Bulda
Edie McClurg	Gerda

Anna and her friends are helped by the trolls, but her hair is turning white and she is in danger of having her heart frozen by Elsa. Returning to Arendelle, Anna asks Hans to kiss her in order to break the icy spell, but he confesses he doesn't love her and only wanted her kingdom. He plans to marry Anna and then kill Elsa so he can become king, but he is stopped by Kristoff and Olaf and is sent back to his kingdom to be punished. Anna is saved from freezing to death by the strong love she has for her sister. Elsa learns how to control her powers, restores the kingdom to its natural state, and it looks like a romantic future for Anna and Kristoff.

After the success of musicalizing Hans Christian Andersen's *The Little Mermaid* (1989), it is not surprising that the Disney studio returned to the Danish author for another animated movie musical. What is surprising is that they turned to the 1845 tale of "The Snow Queen," because it is one of Andersen's longest, most complicated, and most allegorical stories. If the writers for *The Little Mermaid* had to fill out the story for the screen, the writers for *Frozen* had to carefully select which characters and episodes to use. The Andersen tale is actually seven stories that draw on native folk traditions, supernatural mythology, and Christian philosophy. The main plot centers on the youth Kai, who is entrapped by the evil Snow Queen. She has turned his heart to ice and transformed him from a fun-loving boy into a calculating man of cold reason and mathematics. His childhood playmate Gerda is determined to find Kai, travels to the Snow Queen's castle, and saves him, her tears of sympathy melting his frozen heart. This basic story is surrounded by many other characters (including animals and trolls) and episodes, the complete tale resembling a mini-epic poem. Despite its complexity, "The Snow Queen" has intrigued artists, who have used the tale to create songs, operas, ballets, orchestral suites, animated shorts and features, and even video games. It is commonly believed that C. S. Lewis was greatly inspired by the Andersen story when writing *The Lion, the Witch and the Wardrobe* (1950). The Disney studio set out to make a musical based on "The Snow Queen," but the more they worked on it, the more the story departed from Andersen's original. In fact, they dropped Andersen's title because the shooting script barely resembled his original tale. Several of Disney's top writers labored over finding a way to adapt the story, and most gave up. The songs and the added characters helped fill out this simple tale, but the plot is full of holes and unexplained complications. In fact, the more one examines the movie, the less sense it makes. Yet this didn't stop hoards of moviegoers, particularly young ones, from embracing *Frozen*.

Songs

"Let It Go"
"Love Is an Open Door"
"For the First Time in Forever"
"Do You Want to Build a Snowman?"
"Frozen Heart"
"Reindeer Are Better Than People"
"In Summer"
"Fixer Upper"

Frozen is as finely crafted as the best Disney animated musicals, particularly in its look and movement. The creation of the ice palace before our eyes is very ingenious. Ice and snow are particularly difficult to create effectively on screen yet the animators turn the problem into the movie's triumph. Elsa's frozen touch allows for some of the film's most compelling visual moments. The Nordic background art is stunning, from the cold forests to the warm interiors. The character animation is first-rate for both the humans and the trolls and even the snowman Olaf. The voice cast, mainly from Broadway, is expert in both dialogue and song. Idina Menzel shines as the moody and defiant Elsa, Kristen Bell is soft yet determined as Anna, and Jonathan Groff brings the honest but playful Kristoff to life. Josh Gad is the clownish Olaf and Santino Fontana transitions from the genial suitor Hans to the crass and heartless would-be king.

KRISTOFF: Now we just have to survive this blizzard.

ANNA: That's no blizzard. That's my sister.

The enchanting soundtrack score by Christophe Beck provides the magical atmosphere as well as the Nordic sound. The songs by Robert and Kristen Anderson-Lopez are purely in the Broadway style. The runaway hit is the catchy soaring ballad "Let It Go," which Elsa belts while building her ice castle. Also enjoyable are the comic wish song "In Summer," the childlike ditty "Do You Want to Build a Snowman?," the jaunty duet "Love Is an Open Door," and the anticipation number "For the First Time in Forever." *Frozen* may not have a classic set of songs as in the Disney movies of the distant and even recent past but the energetic pop sound was very appealing to audiences, particularly younger ones, and the score quickly became a favorite.

Frozen opened in 2013 after a lot of advance publicity and strong marketing, but even the Disney studio was surprised at how popular the movie quickly became. The $150 million project earned over $400 million just in the United States, and over $1,276 million internationally. The reasons for the film's popularity are not clear. The quality of the craftsmanship and appeal of the music are partially responsible. But a more likely explanation is less artful. Most Disney movies have a beautiful but struggling princess that little girls love to admire, imitate, and dress up like. *Frozen* has two such icons and both fascinate the young female moviegoers. The merchandizing for *Frozen* has been phenomenally successful, and the sing-along rerelease in 2014 was also very popular, as was the soundtrack recording and the 2014 DVD and Blu-ray editions. A film sequel and a Broadway version of *Frozen* are in the works.

See also *The Little Mermaid*.

Did You Know . . . ?

Jennifer Lee is the first woman to direct a Disney animated feature. She codirected *Frozen* with Chris Buck.

FUN AND FANCY FREE

1947
(USA: Walt Disney Productions)

Directed by Jack Kinney, Bill Roberts, and Hamilton Luske
Written by Homer Brightman, Tom Oreb, Harry Reeves, Ted Sears, Lance Nolley, and Eldon Dedini, based on the story "Little Bear Bongo" by Sinclair Lewis and the English fairy tale "Jack and the Beanstalk"
Produced by Walt Disney
Score by Eliot Daniel, Paul Smith, and Oliver Wallace
Songs by Ned Washington, Bobby Worth, Buddy Kaye, Eliot Daniel, Bill Walsh, Arthur Quenzer, George David Weiss, Bennie Benjamin, and Ray Noble
Specs: Color (Technicolor); 73 minutes; live action and traditional animation

Not one of the strongest Disney anthology films of the 1940s, nevertheless Fun and Fancy Free *has some first-class animation and a favorite Mickey Mouse adventure.*

Jiminy Cricket, sailing on a leaf boat and then bouncing through a private library, expresses his "no worry" philosophy in song and verse, then he introduces the story "Bongo." The popular circus bear Bongo wishes to leave the world of performing, so he escapes from the circus train and heads into the wilderness. Initially he loves the freedom of life in the woods, but soon the hardships of nature descend upon him. When he meets the female bear Lulubelle, Bongo falls in love with her but must win her from the clutches of the ferocious bear Lumpjaw before the happy ending. Jiminy then goes to a party at the home of celebrated ventriloquist Edgar Bergen, where young Disney actress Luana Patten is being entertained by the dummies Charlie McCarthy and Mortimer Snerd. Bergen then narrates the story of "Mickey and the Beanstalk," in which the land of Happy Valley is kept happy by the singing of a golden harp. When a Giant steals the harp, the land dries up and all the citizens are destitute. Among them are Mickey Mouse, Donald Duck, and Goofy, who are so hungry that Mickey decides to sell the family cow. When Mickey returns with a handful of magic beans, Donald is so furious he throws them through a hole in the floor. That night a beanstalk grows up to the Giant's castle in the sky, bringing Mickey, Donald, and Goofy with it. After a series of misadventures, the trio manage to steal the golden harp and bring life back to Happy Valley.

A feature film with Mickey Mouse as Jack in a new version of the fairy tale "Jack and the Beanstalk" had been in the planning stages since the late 1930s, and it went into production in 1941. Similarly, a feature film based on Sinclair Lewis's 1930 magazine story "Little Bear Bongo" was in preproduction by 1940 but was put on hold when the United States entered the war. Disney returned to the two projects after the war was over but felt that neither story was substantial enough

Voice Cast

Walt Disney	Mickey Mouse
James MacDonald	Mickey Mouse
Cliff Edwards	Jiminy Cricket
Clarence Nash	Donald Duck
Pinto Colvig	Goofy
Billy Gilbert	Willie the Giant
Anita Gordon	Singing Harp
Dinah Shore	Narrator ("Bongo")

Live-Action Cast

Edgar Bergen	Edgar Bergen
Edgar Bergen	Charlie McCarthy (voice)
Edgar Bergen	Mortimer Snerd (voice)
Luana Patten	Luana Patten

In the "Mickey and the Beanstalk" sequence, the famous mouse, Goofy, and Donald Duck steal the Singing Golden Harp from the Giant and use the beanstalk to escape. *RKO Radio Pictures / Photofest. © RKO Radio Pictures*

to fill out a full-length feature film. Originally the Mickey tale was to be combined with Kenneth Grahame's *The Wind in the Willows*, but the Bongo story was further along in production, so it was chosen instead. The Grahame story would show up later as part of the package feature *The Adventures of Ichabod and Mr. Toad* (1949). Because both Bongo and the beanstalk tale had originally been plotted out to be features, both had to be edited or condensed when reduced to featurettes. For example, how Mickey got the magic beans is not shown in the shortened version, just as Bongo's circus friends were eliminated for *Fun and Fancy Free*. None of the characters in the "Bongo" segment speak; instead Dinah Shore narrates with song and verse. Edgar Bergen serves as narrator of the beanstalk section, but there was plenty of dialogue for the characters as well. Just as Disney utilized live-action footage in his two Latin American anthologies—*Saludos Amigos* (1943) and *The Three Caballeros* (1945)—the scenes in *Fun and Fancy Free* with Bergen, Luana Patten, and the two dummies were not animated.

Songs

"Fun and Fancy Free" (Benjamin/Weiss)
"Fee Fi Fo Fum" (Smith/Quenzer)
"Say It with a Slap" (Kaye/Daniel)
"I'm a Happy-Go-Lucky Fellow" (Washington/Eliot)
"Too Good to Be True" (Kaye/Daniel)
"Lazy Countryside" (Worth)
"My, What a Happy Day" (Walsh/Noble)
"My Favorite Dream" (Walsh/Noble)

The "Bongo" section has such a thin story that it is difficult to imagine it was originally planned as a feature. Of course scenes and characters from the longer version were cut for *Fun and Fancy Free* so what is left is very slight indeed. Yet what is there is far from exciting. There is a cute quality to the characters, but none are very engaging and the songs seem to drag the tale out further than necessary. In truth, the "Bongo" section is far from satisfying except as a cartoon for very young children. Even the idea of bears slapping each other as a sign of affection is without wit, and for many the whole featurette is a chore to sit through. "Mickey and the Beanstalk," on the other hand, is an inspired new version of the famous fairy tale. The characters of Mickey, Donald, and Goofy are already established from their many cartoon shorts, but they also work well in the context of the story. Optimistic Mickey, complaining Donald, and clueless Goofy are ideally placed in the tale and bring humor and even some pathos to the featurette. While the animation in "Bongo" is simple and cartoonish, the artists found much more creative outlets in the beanstalk story. The most impressive section is the way the beanstalk grows overnight, taking the three heroes with it while they are sleeping. The background art in the second tale is also more masterful. The bright Happy Valley in primary colors is reduced to autumnal colors and then to no color at all as the land is changed by the loss of the magic harp. The scenes in *Fun and Fancy Free* before, between, and after the two stories are competently done but not exceptional. Movie audiences in 1947 were always pleased to see radio favorite Edgar Bergen and his dummies on screen and some of the ventriloquist's material is indeed funny, if less sarcastic than as heard on the air waves. The opening segment with Jiminy Cricket is modestly entertaining but nothing more. So why is *Fun and Fancy Free* worthy of recognition? The "Mickey and the Beanstalk" section is superlative filmmaking and a deserved classic.

MICKEY: Beans!

GOOFY: What d'you mean, "beans"?

MICKEY: Yeah, fellows. I sold the cow for some magic beans!

DONALD: Beans?

MICKEY: But Donald! These are not ordinary beans! They're magic beans! If you plant these beans in the light of a full moon, do you know what'll happen?

DONALD: Yes! We get more beans!

Unlike *Make Mine Music* (1946) and *Melody Time* (1948), music is not as integral to *Fun and Fancy Free*. In fact, most of the songs are disappointing. Jiminy's "I'm a Happy-Go-Lucky Fellow," deservedly cut from *Pinocchio* (1940), is cheerful and forgettable. So are all the numbers in "Bongo." The songs in "Mickey and the Beanstalk" are more tuneful and catchy, from the golden harp's lilting "My, What a Happy Day" to the Giant's silly "Fee Fi Fo Fum." The movie's title song, sung by a chorus during the opening credits, is a swinging song of optimism that reminds one of the kind of numbers heard in the other two package movies.

Fun and Fancy Free was well received by the press and the public, gathering plaudits for its entertainment value and earning over $2 million just in the United States. Like the other package features, the film was made on a strict budget with the idea of a guaranteed profit that could be used to get the studio through the lean 1940s. The Bongo story and the Mickey tale later appeared on Disney television shows in the 1960s, but *Fun and Fancy Free* was not rereleased in the theaters. The VHS version came out in 1982, the DVD edition in 2000, and the Blu-ray in 2014.

See also *The Adventures of Ichabod and Mr. Toad*, *Make Mine Music*, and *Melody Time*.

Did You Know . . . ?

Walt Disney voiced Mickey in the "Mickey and the Beanstalk" sequence in the early 1940s. When the piece was reworked for *Fun and Fancy Free*, actor James MacDonald was brought in to voice Mickey for the new footage. It was his first Mickey assignment. MacDonald continued to voice Mickey in various productions until he retired in 1977.

G

A GOOFY MOVIE

1995
(USA: Walt Disney Pictures)

Directed by Kevin Lima
Written by Jymn Magon, Chris Matheson, and Brian Pimental
Produced by Dan Rounds, Will Waggoner, Leslie Hough, Patrick Reagan, and Michael Serrian
Score by Carter Burwell
Songs by Tom Snow, Jack Feldman, Randy Petersen, Kevin Quinn, Patrick DeRemer, and Roy Freeland, and some song standards by various artists
Specs: Color; 78 minutes; traditional animation

After decades of bumbling his way through Disney cartoon shorts, Goofy finally was the central character in a feature film, and it allowed for a more fully developed character and a very real father-son relationship.

Single father Goofy is trying to raise his teenage son Max alone, but their relationship is an awkward one. After Max gets in trouble at school, Goofy decides a road trip with his son may help them bond. They visit an opossum-themed amusement park in which Goofy embarrasses Max and they both end up hurting each other's feelings. Camping in the woods, Goofy tries to teach Max how to fish but only succeeds in attracting Bigfoot to the campsite. Max is a big fan of the rock star Powerline, and he changes the route so that it goes to Los Angeles, where a Powerline concert is scheduled. On the way, they drive over a waterfall and the near-death experience helps the father and son reconcile their differences. At the concert, Goofy and Max end up on stage dancing to Powerline's music, which, when shown on television, impresses Max's friends, in particular Roxanne, whom he has a crush on. Back home, Max visits Roxanne and their romantic moment is ruined by Goofy's car exploding and his crashing through the roof of Roxanne's porch. Having learned to accept his father for what he is, Max introduces Goofy to Roxanne.

The 1992 television cartoon series *Goof Troop* introduced Goofy's son Max as well as other new characters. The series was so popular that a feature film starring Goofy

The troubled relationship between father and son starts to improve when Max (right) and Goofy drive off a bridge and float down the river in their car. *Buena Vista Pictures / Photofest. © Buena Vista Pictures*

and Max was planned with a script that allowed the character of Goofy to become more real while still being funny. Just as all teenagers are frequently embarrassed by their parents, Max is particularly self-conscious about his accident-prone father. Director Kevin Lima and the writers wanted to emphasize Goofy the father over Goofy the clown. He worries about his son Max and is afraid of losing his love and trust. The road trip the two embark on is filled with some farcical episodes, but it

Voice Cast

Bill Farmer	Goofy
Jason Marsden	Max (speaking)
Aaron Lohr	Max (singing)
Jim Cummings	Pete
Rob Paulsen	P. J. Pete
Kellie Martin	Roxanne
Jenna von Oy	Stacey
Wallace Shawn	Principal Mazur
Frank Welker	Bigfoot
Jo Anne Worley	Miss Maples
Kevin Lima	Lester
Pat Buttram	Possum Park Emcee
Florence Stanley	Waitress
Trevin Campbell	Powerline

is the relationship between the two that touches on reality. Several of the characters they encounter on the trip are larger than life and often very funny. The film is a comedy but one that has heart. *A Goofy Movie* is surprisingly effective as both entertainment and as a heartfelt glimpse into father-son emotions.

Songs

"On the Open Road" (Snow/Feldman)
"Stand Out" (DeRemer/Freeland)
"After Today" (Snow/Feldman)
"Lester's Possum Park" (Petersen/Quinn)
"I 2 I" (Petersen/Quinn)
"Nobody Else But You" (Snow/Feldman)

Bill Farmer had been providing the voice of Goofy since 1987, his vocals frequently heard on television series and specials, Disney shorts, and made-for-video movies. *A Goofy Movie* gave Farmer a chance to reveal the tender and vulnerable side to the character. His performance is impressive because Farmer was able to show this human side and still maintain the persona of Goofy the eternal bungler. The character of Max was in middle school in the TV series but was a teenager in *A Goofy Movie*, so a new voice actor had to be found. Sixteen-year-old Jason Marsden had been doing voice work for animation for five years when he was hired to do the vocals for Max. His performance is solid, with touches of teenage sarcasm mixed in his sincere discomfort with his dad. Some Disney voice veterans are also heard in the movie, including Pat Buttram, Jim Cummings, and Frank Welker. *A Goofy Movie* is a musical, and various songwriters contributed to the tuneful score. The catchiest number in the movie is the happy traveling song "On the Open Road," in which Goofy sings about the glories of travel while Max makes sour comments about being stuck on a road trip with a parent. Father and son are more in harmony in the duet "Nobody Else but You," which they sing while floating down a river on top of their submerged car. "After Today" is a slightly rocking number sung by Max and the high school students as they look forward to summer vacation. For the rock star Powerline are the numbers "Stand Out" and "I 2 I," and there is a silly hillbilly spoof titled "Lester's Possum Park" praising the dilapidated campsite of the title. Carter Burwell wrote the playful soundtrack score for *A Goofy Movie* and included some reflective passages without letting the music get too ponderous.

A Goofy Movie was released in 1995 and met with mixed notices. Many critics dismissed it as a TV cartoon drawn out to feature length. Others appreciated the way a classic farce character was turned into a believable father. The public reac-

---

GOOFY: This is a vacation with me and my best buddy.

MAX: Donald Duck?

GOOFY: No, silly, with you!

tion was more positive, and the film earned $35 million in its initial release. This was encouraging enough that the Disney studio made a direct-to-video sequel in 2000, *An Extremely Goofy Movie*. Most of the original cast returned for this tale about Max going to college and finding out his father has also registered for classes. The VHS edition of *A Goofy Movie* came out in 1995 and the DVD version in 2000.

Did You Know . . . ?

Although *A Goofy Movie* was completed in 1993 with plans to be released at Christmas 1994, postproduction difficulties pushed the release date to 1995. The replacement movie for Christmas 1994 was *The Lion King*.

THE GREAT MOUSE DETECTIVE

1986
(USA: Walt Disney Pictures)

Directed by Burny Mattinson, John Musker, David Michener, and Ron Clements
Written by Burny Mattinson, John Musker, David Michener, Ron Clements, Peter Young, Bruce Morris, Matthew O'Callaghan, Steve Hulett, and Mel Shaw, based on the book Basil of Baker Street by Eve Titus and Paul Galdone
Produced by Burny Mattinson
Score by Henry Mancini
Songs by Henry Mancini (music), Ellen Fitzhugh, Larry Grossman (lyrics), and Melissa Manchester
Specs: Color; 74 minutes; traditional and computer animation

This clever Disney take on the Sherlock Holmes stories is a fast-paced adventure filled with some memorable characters and scenes.

Below the 221 Baker Street residence of Sherlock Holmes in Victorian London lives the brainy mouse detective Basil. The ex-soldier mouse Dr. Dawson brings the young mouse Olivia to Basil after her father, the toy inventor Hiram Flaversham, has been kidnapped by a peg-legged bat. Basil recognizes the bat as Fidget, a henchman of the diabolical Professor Ratigan, Basil's longtime nemesis. Ratigan, a rat disguised as a mouse, has kidnapped Flaversham and forced him to create a robot-like model of the Queen of Mice, which Ratigan can use to take total control of all Mousedom. Basil and Dawson don disguises to search out Ratigan's hideout, but when they locate his lair, the twosome are captured by Ratigan and tied to a complicated contraption to kill them. Basil outwits the inventive death machine, and the two arrive in time to expose Ratigan. A frantic chase ensues, ending at the clock tower of Big Ben, where Basil engages in a life-and-death struggle with Ratigan. The rat falls to his death, Olivia is reunited with her father, and Basil and Dawson set off on other adventures.

The mouse sleuth Basil has the same ingenious detecting and forensic skills as the human Sherlock Holmes, who lives above him on Baker Street. *Walt Disney Pictures / Photofest. © Walt Disney Pictures*

Eve Titus's series of five children's books with the umbrella title *Basil of Baker Street* were published between 1958 and 1982, and the Disney studio began planning an animated feature film version in the late 1970s. The project went through many changes, as the management at the studio was in flux until 1984, when Michael Eisner was named CEO of the company. He pushed the movie forward, requesting several changes. The final screenplay was not based specifically on any one book but adapted ideas from all five. An older Olivia and her romance with

Voice Cast

Barrie Ingham	Basil of Baker Street
Val Bettin	Dr. David Q. Dawson
Vincent Price	Professor Ratigan
Susanne Pollatschek	Olivia Flaversham
Alan Young	Hiram Flaversham
Candy Candido	Fidget
Melissa Manchester	Miss Kitty Mouse
Diana Chesney	Mrs. Judson
Eve Brenner	Mouse Queen
Shani Wallis	Lady Mouse

Dr. Dawson was dropped, and the plot concentrated on Basil and his sleuthing powers. Ratigan was changed from a scrawny sewer rat to a theatrical, bigger-than-life rodent with a flashy wardrobe. Originally, the climax of the movie was to take place on the clock face of Big Ben until artist Mike Peraza suggested going inside the clockwork for the final encounter between Basil and Ratigan. The studio's new computer program was used to handle some of the action sequences as well as the climactic scene inside Big Ben. The characters were still hand drawn but the gears and cogs of the clock were computerized. This blending of the traditional and the computer animation gave *The Great Mouse Detective* a distinctive look not yet seen in the studio's work.

Songs

"The World's Greatest Criminal Mind"
"Goodbye So Soon"
"Let Me Be Good to You" (Manchester)

The re-creation of Victorian London for the movie was done with a sense of mystery with fog-filled streets and dark waterfront locales. In contrast to the London of *Peter Pan* (1953), which was set in the same time frame, the city seen in this movie was quite different even though both films shared some of the same locations. The mouse world in *The Great Mouse Detective* reflects the human one of the era. Just about all the scenes take place at night, and London is portrayed as a city of threatening shadows. The character animation in the movie is very precise yet playful. Basil can be very reserved in an English manner, then he suddenly flies off in all directions, particularly in one of his disguises. Dawson is a bouncing ball in his moves, while Fidget creeps along in a forced manner. Ratigan is the most physical character in the film, his huge body bending and stretching as he dashes through life. His thugs are a variety of creatures that seem to ricochet off of Ratigan's swift movement. A particularly unique piece of character animation in the movie is the mechanical Queen Victoria that Faversham constructs. In contrast are the fluid gyrations of the saloon singer Miss Kitty Mouse. But the animation that most impresses is more technical. The workings of the interior of Big Ben marvel with their clean lines and dazzling movements. The way the characters move in and out of this complicated clockworks remains the movie's most thrilling piece of animation.

BASIL: (examining Fidget's note) Offhand I can deduce very little, only that the words are written with a broad-tip quill pen that has spattered, twice; that the paper is of native Mongolia manufacture, no watermark; and has been gummed, if I'm very much in error . . . (smells paper) by a bat who has been drinking Rodent's Delight, a cheap brandy served only in the seediest pubs.

DR. DAWSON: Hmm. Amazing.

BASIL: Oh, not really, doctor.

British Shakespearean actor Barrie Ingram voices Basil with a blend of stuffiness and wild abandon. American actor Val Bettin is a convincing Dr. Dawson, as is Alan Young's Scottish dialect for Faversham. Scottish child performer Susanne Pollatschek is sincere and believable as Olivia. Disney veteran Candy Candido is deliciously decrepit voicing the bat Fidget. The vocal highlight of the movie is Vincent Price as Ratigan. His voice snarls, purrs, laughs, and explodes with evil. Even his singing has a touch of the macabre. Henry Mancini, one of Hollywood's most successful composers, scored his only Disney film with *The Great Mouse Detective*, and both his soundtrack score and the music for two songs are splendid. The film's main theme is urgent chase music that seems filled with glee. There are also cockeyed fanfares, honky-tonk piano music, and unsettling suspense passages. Ratigan sings the two Mancini songs, the pompous march "The World's Greatest Criminal Mind" and the mocking farewell ballad "Goodbye So Soon." Mancini also wrote an authentic music hall ditty for the saloon scene, but it was replaced by the more American and sexy "Let Me Be Good to You," written and sung by Melissa Manchester.

The Great Mouse Detective received mostly positive reviews when it was released in 1986. The reaction by the public was also favorable, helping the film to earn over $25 million on its first release. (The movie cost about $14 million to make.) When it was re-released in theaters in 1992, the film was inexplicably retitled *The Adventures of the Great Mouse Detective*. The VHS version came out that same year, the DVD edition in 2002, and the Blu-ray version in 2012.

Did You Know . . . ?

Stage and screen actor Vincent Price had wanted for many years to voice a Disney animated character. He was seventy-five years old when he got his wish and voiced Ratigan.

GULLIVER'S TRAVELS

1939
(USA: Fleischer Studios/Paramount)

Directed by Dave Fleischer
Written by Edmond Steward, Dan Gordon, Cal Howard, Tedd Pierce, and Izzy Sparber, based on the book by Jonathan Swift
Produced by Max Fleischer
Score by Victor Young
Songs by Ralph Rainger (music) and Leo Robin (lyrics)
Specs: Color (Technicolor); 76 minutes; traditional animation

---

The second animated feature made in America and the first non-Disney full-length cartoon, Gulliver's Travels *may not measure up to its only predecessor,* Snow White and the Seven Dwarfs *(1937), but it is an impressive early effort with some delightful characters and songs. Although it was popular in its day,* Gulliver's Travels *is too little known today.*

When Lemuel Gulliver is washed ashore in the land of Lilliput, the little citizens tie up the unconscious "giant" and present him to the Little King (on the balcony). *Paramount Pictures / Photofest.* © *Paramount Pictures*

The tiny Kingdom of Lilliput, ruled over by the Little King, and the Kingdom of Blefuscu, with King Bombo on the throne, have long been rivals. But when the Lilliputian Princess Glory falls in love with Prince David from Blefuscu, it looks like there will be a truce. Plans for the wedding proceed smoothly until it comes to deciding which national song will be played at the wedding: the Lilliputian anthem "Faithful" or the Blefuscu song "Forever." The dispute leads to war between the two little nations. One night the town crier Gabby discovers the giant Gulliver washed up onto the beach. The Lilliputians tie him up and transport him on a long wagon into the city. When the Blefuscians attack Lilliput, Gulliver awakes and just

Voice Cast

Sam Parker	Gulliver
Pinto Colvig	Gabby
Livonia Warren	Princess Glory (speaking)
Jessica Dragonette	Princess Glory (singing)
Cal Howard	Prince David (speaking)
Lanny Ross	Prince David (singing)
Jack Mercer	Little King
Tedd Pierce	King Bombo

his imposing size frightens the enemy away. The Lilliputians welcome Gulliver to their land and a grand celebration is held. King Bombo sends the three spies Sneak, Snoop, and Snitch to steal Gulliver's pistol in order to capture the giant. Before the plan can be accomplished, Gulliver uses his size to stop hostilities. He has Princess Glory and Prince David each sing their national songs at the same time and the two tunes blend together melodically. The wedding takes place and the Lilliputians build a boat so that Gulliver can set sail for other lands.

Gulliver's Travels was an obvious attempt to copy the success of Disney's *Snow White and the Seven Dwarfs*, yet the idea of a feature-length animated version of Jonathan's Swift's satiric novel began with producer Max Fleischer back in 1934. Swift's 1726 book consists of four adventures Lemuel Gulliver has when shipwrecked in four different lands. The episode in Lilliput is the most famous and has inspired filmmakers since 1902. Fleischer Studios was Paramount's cartoon supplier, most known for its Popeye the Sailor shorts. Because it was facing financial difficulties, Paramount vetoed Fleischer's idea of an animated feature in 1935. But once *Snow White and the Seven Dwarfs* opened and was a resounding hit, the studio contracted Fleischer to produce *Gulliver's Travels* in time for Christmas of 1939. While the Disney predecessor was in development for a year and a half and spent another eighteen months in production, *Gulliver's Travels* had to be made in half that time in order to meet the deadline. Fleischer Studios had recently moved to Miami, Florida, and was short staffed. Some eight hundred people were hired to work on *Gulliver's Travels,* and the technique of Rotoscoping was employed to save time and money. In Rotoscoping, live-action sequences with actors are filmed and the developed footage is projected onto a surface frame by frame. The artist then traces the image onto paper and then it is polished up and turned into a cel. Despite all the efforts made by the Fleischer Studio, *Gulliver's Travels* was delivered late and over budget and the studio had to pay Paramount a penalty fee of $350,000.

Songs

"Faithful"
"Forever"
"Bluebirds in the Moonlight"
"All's Well"
"I Hear a Dream (Come Home Again)"
"Faithful Forever"
"It's a Hap-Hap-Happy Day" (Timberg/Sharples/Neiburg)

Like *Snow White and the Seven Dwarfs*, *Gulliver's Travels* is a musical. Fleischer hired experienced Hollywood songwriters Ralph Rainger and Leo Robin to write the score. They had provided songs for some Shirley Temple vehicles and the *Big Broadcast* movies, one of them introducing the Oscar-winning song "Thanks for the Memory." Rainger and Robin wrote five songs for the movie, but the score's most chipper and catchy number, "It's a Hap-Hap-Happy Day" was by Al Neiburg, Sammy Timberg, and Winston Sharples. The prolific composer Victor Young was in charge of writing and conducting the soundtrack music. The studio hired notable band singers Jessica Dragonette and Lanny Ross for the singing of the prince and princess in the tale. Comic actor Pinto Colvig was cast as the excitable town crier Gabby, the movie's main comic character. Colvig was a Disney actor who had voiced Goofy and other characters. Radio announcer Sam Parker was chosen to voice Gulliver. He not only sounded right but Parker also looked the part, so he served as the human model for the live-action footage of Gulliver later used by the animators. Fleischer was able to coax some top Hollywood animators to come to Miami and work on *Gulliver's Travels,* but because the film was so rushed the animation was not as inventive and polished as the producer had hoped. *Gulliver's Travels* was completed just before it opened first in Miami, then in New York, and finally across the country right before Christmas of 1939.

> GABBY: There's a giant on the beach! There's a giant on the beach! There's a giant on the beach! There's a giant on the beach!

Among the many merits of *Gulliver's Travels* is the strong plotting. The Swift story is not very long and few characters are developed beyond types. Swift was interested in satirizing society with his depiction of Lilliput and Blefuscu and making acid comments about war by having the two nations fight over a song. There is some satire left in the screenplay, particularly in the way the Little King and King Bombo are portrayed. The three spies Sneak, Snoop, and Snitch are also caricatures, making fun of wartime espionage. The addition of Gabby (who is not in the original Swift story) and the way he is used throughout the movie helps unify the plot. Gulliver himself is not in much of the film, yet he solidifies several plot points, including the happy ending. Although all the characters in the movie are humans, Gulliver is the only one who moves in a normal manner. The lovers are rather stiff while the other characters, including Gabby and the two kings, are very agile. The background art is admirable with a storybook look that is finely detailed. Unfortunately, the actual animation movement is sometimes lacking. *Gulliver's Travels* was a rush job and nowhere is this more evident than in sections of the animation. Yet there are some striking pieces of movement, such as the rolling purple waves in the moonlight as Gulliver stares out to sea.

Awards

Academy Award nominations: Best Song ("Faithful/Forever") and Best Score.

Musically, the movie is a treat. The already-mentioned "It's a Hap-Hap-Happy Day" is a contagious celebration song that the Lilliputians sing after Gulliver scares off the Blefuscian navy. The chipper number was later recorded by name artists. So too was the double song "Faithful/Forever," which figured importantly in the plot. Each song is a flowing romantic ballad with a touch of an anthem about it. Legend has it that Rainger and Robin struggled to come up with two different ballads that could also be sung together harmoniously. They were very successful for, as pleasing as each song is, it is not until they are sung contrapuntally that the number soars. The other songs in the score are the Big Band number "Bluebirds in the Moonlight," which is used as a delicious jitterbug for the Lilliputians; the haunting "I Hear a Dream," in which voices from the sea urge Gulliver to "come home again"; and Gabby's jaunty song "All's Well," complete with sour comments on the life of a town crier.

Both critics and moviegoers could not help but compare the movie to *Snow White and the Seven Dwarfs*, the only other animated feature previously made in America. The comparisons were not altogether favorable, but *Gulliver's Travels* managed to become a major hit, earning over $3 million during its first month. The film was released internationally in 1940 but, because of the outbreak of World War II in Europe, foreign markets were limited. *Gulliver's Travels* showed up on television several times in the 1950s and 1960s then pretty much disappeared until it was put on VHS tapes and later DVDs. Today the movie has a limited but faithful following. The songs and the look of the film are a bit dated for some tastes, but there is no denying that *Gulliver's Travels* is of historical importance and still very entertaining for such an early effort in feature animation. While *Gulliver's Travels* was no threat to the Disney monopoly on highly crafted animation, the movie was impressive in its own right and did enough box office that Paramount ordered another animated feature from the Fleischer Studio for Christmas of 1941.

See also *Mr. Bug Goes to Town*.

Did You Know . . . ?

Gulliver's Travels was the first animated film to give screen credit to its voice actors. Disney and other animators never listed the vocal artists until years later.

H

HAPPY FEET

2006
(USA / Australia: Warner Brothers)

Directed by George Miller, Warren Coleman, and Judy Morris
Written by George Miller, Warren Coleman, Judy Morris, and John Collee
Produced by Dana Goldberg, Edward Jones, Bruce Berman, Graham Burke, Bill
   Miller, Doug Mitchell, and George Miller
Score by John Powell. Song "The Song of the Heart" by Prince
Specs: Color (Technicolor); 108 minutes; computer animation with some live action

Despite its cheerful sounding title, Happy Feet *is an animated film about penguins that is perhaps too intense for young children and a movie with sobering parallels to human behavior.*

The baby Mumble is born into a community of emperor penguins, where each member must find an individual "heartsong" in order to belong to the group and find a love mate. Mumble can only screech rather than sing, but he has a natural instinct for tap dancing. This makes him an outcast in the community, although the singing virtuoso Gloria secretly loves Mumble all the same. He sets off on his own and encounters a community of Adélie penguins, where he befriends the fun-loving Ramón, Nestor, Lombardo, Rinaldo, and Raul. They help Mumble woo Gloria by having the penguin lip-sync to Ramón's romantic singing, but she sees through the ruse. Mumble then teaches Gloria and the other penguins how to tap dance, but the elders of the community censure them and blame Mumble for the lack of fish in the area. Mumble has found out through the rockhopper penguin Lovelace that strange creatures are responsible for the absence of fish, and he sets off to try and reason with them to stop. He encounters a huge fishing boat taking nets full of fish out of the sea. Later, he is washed ashore near a city and taken to the local aquarium. Mumble teaches the other penguins there to tap dance, getting the humans' attention. Returned to the Antarctic with a tracking device, Mumble reaches his community and, when the human researchers arrive, leads them all in a giant tap dance routine. The film footage the humans take of the dancing penguins goes viral and soon there are debates around the world about overfishing.

131

The fact that penguins have no legs and their feet are flat and webbed does not stop them from breaking into fabulous tap dancing when they feel like it. *Warner Bros. / Photofest. © Warner Bros.*

When fishing bans in Antarctica are passed, the fish return, Mumble is the hero and wins Gloria, and all the penguins celebrate by dancing.

Early versions of the story for *Happy Feet* concentrated on aliens (humans) entering the world of the penguins in Antarctica and draining the natural resources of the land. Later versions downplayed the human aspect of the tale and centered on Mumble as an outcast in the community. As the dance aspect of the plot developed, *Happy Feet* became a musical of sorts with both singing and dancing. The songs were taken from both old standards, such as "My Way" and "Heartbreak Hotel," and more recent hits, like "Tell Me Something Good" and "Somebody to Love." When the producers tried to get permission to use Prince's song "Kiss," the artist refused. But once he saw some early footage of *Happy Feet*, Prince not only gave permission to use "Kiss" but wrote an original song, "The

Voice Cast

Elizabeth Daily	Mumble (baby)
Elijah Wood	Mumble (adult)
Alyssa Shafer	Gloria (baby)
Brittany Murphy	Gloria (adult)
Hugh Jackman	Memphis
Nicole Kidman	Norma Jean
Robin Williams	Ramón
Carlos Alazraqui	Nestor
Lombardo Boyer	Raul
Jeffrey Garcia	Rinaldo
Johnny Sanchez	Lombardo
Robin Williams	Lovelace
Anthony LaPaglia	Skua Boss
Steve Irwin	Trev
Robin Williams	Narrator

Song of the Heart," for the movie. Because tap dance became such an important element in the story, the animators were challenged to come up with both choreography and the re-creation of it on screen. It was decided to utilize the talents of Savion Glover, the preeminent tap dancer and innovator of new variations of tap set to all kinds of music. A computer program was developed that was able to film Glover in action and then translated the moves to an animated character. Because penguins have such short feet, this was all the more difficult. Yet the dancing in *Happy Feet* seems natural and, at the same time, thrilling. The computer animation throughout the film is stunning, particularly in the movement of hundreds of penguins dancing, swimming, and sliding. John Powell's soundtrack score captures the majesty of the Antarctic landscape with a rich and expansive sound that complements the visuals.

> MEMPHIS: Whatcha doin' there, boy?
>
> BABY MUMBLE: (tap dancing) I'm happy, Pa!
>
> MEMPHIS: Whatcha doin' with your feet?
>
> BABY MUMBLE: They're happy too!

Distinguishing the different characters in *Happy Feet* was a problem because within one species of penguins generally all of them look alike. It is even difficult to tell the males from the females. The animators made efforts to give certain characters identifying marks. Also, Mumble does not shed his baby feathers completely, so he is easily recognized. But it is the voice cast that not only clarifies the characters but allows them to come to life. Elijah Wood and Brittany Murphy are commendable as the grown-up Mumble and Gloria, but far more interesting are the vocals by Hugh Jackman and Nicole Kidman as Mumble's parents. Murphy, Kidman, and Jackman did their own singing, and it was in song that the characters soared. The most impressive voice in the movie is that of Robin Williams, who narrates the tale in a gruff, rustic manner, voices the demonstrative phony guru Lovelace, and does the speaking and singing vocals for the enthusiastic and out-of-control Ramón. Williams's work in *Happy Feet* compares favorably to his Genie in *Aladdin* (1992).

The look of *Happy Feet* is surprisingly realistic. The recreation of Antarctica is beautiful and accurate. The depiction of the different species of penguins, seals, and birds is equally true to life. In fact, *Happy Feet* looks like an environmental documentary film. Even the movements of the penguins are correct until they burst out tap dancing, and the incongruity of realistic birds tapping to exciting music is unforgettable. On the other hand, the harsh reality of the lives of penguins is not softened just because the movie is a musical. Frightening encounters with predators, man, and nature itself make *Happy Feet* a very intense film at times. The way the penguin community reacts to Mumble being "different" is another disturbing aspect of the movie. Sometimes the social hostilities are as dangerous as the natural ones.

Awards

Academy Award: Best Animated Feature.
Golden Globe Award: Best Song ("The Song of the Heart"); Golden Globe nomination: Best
   Animated Film.
British Academy of Film & Television Arts (BAFTA) Award: Best Feature Film; BAFTA nomina-
   tion: Best Score.

The American-Australian production cost about $100 million, but when it was
released in the United States in 2006, *Happy Feet* earned over $41 million its first
weekend. After showings in Australia and thirty-four other countries, the gross
was around $384 million. The critical reaction to the movie was mostly very ap-
preciative, the critics applauding the stunning visuals, the terrific dancing, and
the themes behind the story. The DVD and Blu-ray editions of *Happy Feet* were
released in 2007. The sequel, *Happy Feet Two*, came out in 2011 with Wood and
Williams reprising their Mumble, Lovelace, and Ramón. (It was Williams's last
animated film assignment before his death in 2014.) The sequel focuses on Erik
(voiced by Ava Acres), the son of Mumble and Gloria, who cannot dance and
experiences the same kind of estrangement that young Mumble once felt. *Happy
Feet Two* cost over $135 million, but the reviews were mixed and box office was
disappointing. It ended up earning only $15 million more than its costs.

Did You Know . . . ?

The names of Mumble's mother, Norma Jean, and father, Memphis, are tributes to Marilyn
Monroe (who was born Norma Jean) and Elvis Presley (who lived in Memphis, Tennessee).

HERCULES

1997
(USA: Walt Disney Pictures)

Directed by Ron Clements and John Musker
Written by Ron Clements, John Musker, Bob Shaw, Don McEnery, and Irene Mecchi
Produced by Ron Clements, John Musker, Alice Dewey, Noreen Tobin, and Kendra
   Haaland
Score by Alan Menken
Songs by Alan Menken (music) and David Zippel (lyrics)
Specs: Color (Technicolor); 93 minutes; traditional animation with some computer
   effects

*The Disney studio gives Greek mythology a comic and musical treatment in this adventure
favorite that satirizes everything from classical heroism to Hollywood marketing.*

A set of gospel-singing muses narrates the tale of how Hercules, the infant son of Zeus, was kidnapped by the god Hades, who orders his henchmen Pain and Panic to destroy him. But Hercules survives and is raised by the mortals Alcmene and Amphitryon. Because of his unusual strength, Hercules is a bit of an outcast from his peers, but he feels better about himself when he learns that his father is Zeus. Trained by the satyr Philoctetes, Hercules is able to do super-human stunts and soon becomes a hero in the eyes of the public. Hades sends the spy Megara to trap Hercules in situations that might destroy him, but Megara and Hercules fall in love. When Hades releases the Titans from their bondage and has them attack Mt. Olympus, Hercules saves the day and even outwits Hades by winning Megara from his clutches.

Plans to adapt various stories from Greek mythology into an animated feature began at Disney in 1992 and several treatments were written up, including versions of the Trojan War, *The Odyssey*, the labors of Hercules, and Zeus's affair with the mortal Alcmene. These were all deemed too complicated and too long for a ninety-minute feature, so codirectors Ron Clements and John Musker worked with the writers on an original tale using many elements from Greek myths. It was also decided early on that the adventure aspects of the movie would take second place to the comedy. *Hercules* ended up being a screwball farce that used the Greek stories as source material for plot, characters, and jokes. Everything in the film is anachronistic, from the gospel-singing African American Muses to the Hercules souvenirs on sale to the ancient Greek public. Even the villain Hades is a comic character with a fast-talking con-man persona. *Hercules* never takes itself seriously. The dialogue is hip, sarcastic, and very modern. The characters, be they human or gods, are funny and rarely stop to contemplate or feel anything. The directors thought of the project as a comic book, but a funny one rather than

Muscleman Hercules (right) may have exceptional strength and determination, but the god Hades has enough tricks up his sleeve to cause plenty of trouble for the mortal hero. *Walt Disney Pictures / Photofest. © Walt Disney Pictures*

Voice Cast

Josh Keaton	Hercules (young—speaking)
Roger Bart	Hercules (young— singing)
Tate Donovan	Hercules (adult)
Danny DeVito	Phil
James Woods	Hades
Susan Egan	Megara
Bobcat Goldthwait	Pain
Matt Frewer	Panic
Rip Torn	Zeus
Samantha Eggar	Hera
Hal Holbrook	Amphitryon
Barbara Barrie	Alcmene
Paul Shaffer	Hermes
Amanda Plummer	Fate
Carole Shelley	Fate
Paddi Edwards	Fate
Lillias White	Muse
Cheryl Freeman	Muse
Roz Ryan	Muse
LaChanze	Muse
Vanéese Y. Thomas	Muse

an adventure one. Although the animators visited the Greek isles and did a lot of research on the art and architecture of ancient Greece, the movie is a very cartoonish version of the past. The background art is simple and colorful, often parodying the look of ancient Greek vases. British cartoonist Gerald Scarfe was hired to make dozens of sketches for the film, and these served as the inspiration for the look of *Hercules*. The characters were animated in exaggerated and comic ways, whether humble mortals or mythical beasts. *Hercules* is never subtle, but then it is never dull either.

Songs

"One Last Hope"
"The Gospel Truth"
"Go the Distance"
"I Won't Say I'm in Love"
"Zero to Hero"
"A Star Is Born"

Although there is plenty of action in *Hercules*, the movie rests on its characters and the actors who voiced them. Hercules, played by Tate Donovan and Josh Keaton at different ages, is pretty much the straight man in the tale, although he too is funny in his naïveté. The leading lady Megara, voiced and sung with sass by Susan Egan, is no princess type. She is a sarcastic con woman and an unwilling pawn of Hades, who mocks her falling in love with Hercules. The film reaches its comic high points in the characterizations of Hades (James Woods) and Hercules's coach, Philoctetes (Danny DeVito). Both actors bring a modern slyness to the classical material. The large voice cast is filled with delicious performances that support the fast-paced comedy. The Fates (Amanda Plummer, Carole Shelley, and Paddi Edwards), the hipster Hermes (Paul Shaffer), and the henchmen Pain (Bobcat Goldthwait) and Panic (Matt Frewer) are among the standouts, but the film is often stolen by the five Muses (Lillias White, Cheryl Freeman, LaChanze, Roz Ryan, and Vanéese Y. Thomas), who sing and comment on the action with attitude.

HERCULES: You know, wh-when I was a kid, I—I would have given anything to be exactly like everybody else.

MEG: You wanted to be petty and dishonest?

HERCULES: Everybody's not like that.

MEG: Yes, they are.

HERCULES: You're not like that.

MEG: How do you know what I'm like?

The songs by Alan Menken (music) and David Zippel (lyrics) are all in the comic vein except for the stirring "Go the Distance," sung by the teenage Hercules (singing vocal by Roger Bart). The Muses let loose with the rousing "Gospel Truth," the rhythmic "Zero to Hero," and the celebratory "A Star Is Born," Megara sings the self-aware ballad "I Won't Say (I'm in Love)," and Philoctetes delivers the vaudeville ditty "One Last Hope." The way the songs are used in the movie is very clever. Rarely does the action stop for a song. Instead the musical numbers continue the story, such as "Zero to Hero" chronicling Hercules's blossoming celebrity. Menken also composed the lively soundtrack score for *Hercules*, which tosses in a few pseudo-Greek passages but mostly is modern, tuneful, and quite fun.

Awards

Academy Award nomination: Best Song ("Go the Distance").
Golden Globe nomination: Best Song ("Go the Distance").

After an extensive publicity and marketing campaign (including an electric light parade in Manhattan), *Hercules* opened in 1997 to mostly auspicious reviews. James Woods's hilarious performance received the most praise, and the other comic elements in the film were also applauded. Some critics thought the lightweight comedy too slight and inconsequential after the more deeply felt

Disney movies like *Beauty and the Beast* (1991) and *The Lion King* (1994). The Greek newspapers and commentators disdained the Disney film, calling it a sloppy and inaccurate version of their ancient culture. Moviegoers around the world thought otherwise. *Hercules* cost about $85 million but the international gross was over $250 million. The VHS version was released in 1998 and was extremely popular. The DVD edition and the Blu-ray version were available in 1999 and 2014, respectively. *Hercules* inspired a video game, a Disney on Ice show, a direct-to-video prequel *Hercules: Zero to Hero* (1998), and a television cartoon show *Hercules: The Animated Series* (1998).

See also *The Emperor's New Groove.*

Did You Know . . . ?

When *Hercules* was re-dubbed for Spanish-speaking countries, popular Latin singer Ricky Martin provided the singing for the character of Hercules.

HOME ON THE RANGE

2004
(USA: Walt Disney Pictures)

Directed and written by Will Finn and John Sanford
Produced by Alice Dewey and David J. Steinberg
Score by Alan Menken
Songs by Alan Menken (music) and Glenn Slater (lyrics)
Specs: Color; 76 minutes; traditional animation

An atypical Disney feature with the look and tone of a Warner Brothers Looney Tunes product, Home on the Range *is a merry spoof of the Old West and a film still too little known to the public.*

A region of the Old West is being terrorized by the cattle rustler Alameda Slim, who is known for stealing a whole herd of cows in a single night. The old rancher Pearl has only three cows on her farm called Patch of Heaven: the uppity and proper Mrs. Caloway, the ditzy Grace, and the wisecracking newcomer Maggie. The sheriff informs Pearl that she has to come up with the $750 that she owes the bank or her farm and all her animals will be sold at auction. When Maggie hears that the reward for capturing Alameda Slim is $750, she convinces Grace and Mrs. Caloway that their only hope in saving Patch of Heaven is to find Alameda Slim and collect the reward money. During their hunt, they encounter the bounty hunter Rico, who is working for Slim; the hyperactive horse Buck; the peg-legged rabbit Lucky Jack; and Slim's brainless stooges, the Willie Brothers. The three cows discover that Slim uses his yodeling to hypnotize the cattle and steal them and that he is also the banker who is buying up the land repossessed by the bank.

The bovines Grace, Maggie (center), and Mrs. Caloway take matters into their own hands when they band together and go in search of the cattle rustler Alameda Slim. *Buena Vista Pictures / Photofest.* © *Buena Vista Pictures*

Voice Cast

Judi Dench	Mrs. Caloway
Roseanne Barr	Maggie
Jennifer Tilly	Grace
Randy Quaid	Alameda Slim
Cuba Gooding Jr.	Buck
Charles Dennis	Rico
Carole Cook	Pearl Gesner
Sam Levine	Willie Brother
Gregory Jbara	Willie Brother
Jason Graae	Willie Brother
David Burnham	Willie Brother
Steve Buscemi	Wesley
G. W. Bailey	Rusty
Charles Haid	Lucky Jack
Richard Riehle	Sheriff Sam Brown
Charlie Dell	Ollie
Joe Flaherty	Jeb
Patrick Warburton	Patrick
Dennis Weaver	Abner

After a chase with a train filled with cattle, the three bovine heroines expose Slim, collect the reward money, and save Patch of Heaven.

Home on the Range went through more story reversals and rewrites than most animated movies. The satire of Old West clichés was originally titled *Sweating Bullets*, and the tale was about a young bull named Bullets who wishes he were a horse herding cattle. At one point it was about a Pied Piper-like character who has the power to enchant cows. Another version of the plot was about a chicken-hearted cowboy who runs up against the cattle rustler Slim, who was based on the country singer and yodeler Montana Slim. Several aspects from these versions show up in the final screenplay that emphasizes comedy over emotionally engaging characters. Even the begrudgingly reluctant friendship between Maggie and Mrs. Caloway is more sarcastic than sincere. *Home on the Range* manages to ridicule many Old West clichés and the dialogue has a modern, sitcom kind of flavor. The look of the movie is also cartoonish with exaggerated character animation and broad and artificial background art. The film is also paced like a Warner Brothers cartoon, one expecting to see Bugs Bunny or Wyle E. Coyote show up at any minute. While the characters are stereotypes, they are also very funny. The large voice cast is excellent throughout. The idea of aristocratic British actress Judi Dench and crude American comedienne Roseanne Barr in the same film is incongruously amusing. The verbal battle of wits between the two holds the silly film together. Also outstanding is Randy Quaid's farcical Alameda Slim. He speaks and sings the role with unembarrassed abandon. Similarly, Cuba Gooding Jr. gives a frantic performance voicing the high-energy horse Buck. Jennifer Tilly's low-key but hilarious Grace is also a vocal highlight in the movie. *Home on the Range* has some very celebrated actors in some very small roles. Joe Flaherty, Steve Buscemi, Pat-

---

Songs

"(You Ain't) Home on the Range"
"Little Patch of Heaven"
"Will the Sun Ever Shine Again"
"Wherever the Trail May Lead"
"Yodle-Adle-Eedle-Idle-Oo"
"Anytime You Need a Friend"

---

rick Warburton, and Dennis Weaver are heard so little one wonders how much dialogue and how many scenes were left on the cutting room floor.

Working with up-and-coming lyricist Glenn Slater, composer Alan Menken wrote a delectable set of songs as well as the lively soundtrack score. The music sometimes mocks familiar songs of the West as well as famous western movie themes. The tender ballad "Will the Sun Ever Shine Again," sung by Bonnie Rait on the soundtrack, is the score's only quiet moment, and it is so heartbreaking that one wonders if it belongs in this movie. (Menken and Slater wrote the number soon after the tragic events of 9/11.) The opening "(You Ain't) Home on the Range" is a vigorous cowboy ballad with a prankish lyric, while "Wherever the Road May Lead" and "Little Patch of Heaven" are both pleasing country numbers. The most raucous song in the film is the buffoonish "Yodle-Adle-Eedle-Idle-Oo" sung by Slim as he rounds up cattle and yodels familiar passages by Tchaikovsky, Wagner, and others. All in all, the music in *Home on the Range* is a wonderful fusion of the western and Broadway sounds.

MAGGIE: I got it! Why don't we go nab that Alameda Slim and use the reward money to save the farm?

MRS. CALOWAY: Oh, that *is* a sensible idea.

MAGGIE: I knew you'd love it!

MRS. CALOWAY: Don't they have sarcasm where you come from?

Because there were so many script problems, *Home on the Range* ended up costing $110 million. The film made just shy of $104 million and was considered a financial flop. The reviews were decidedly mixed. Some critics appreciated the breezy, unpretentious nature of the movie, while others thought it soulless and empty. Audiences responded with lukewarm box office numbers. *Home on the Range* was the last Disney film offered on VHS; DVD sales were promising but ultimately disappointing. The Blu-ray edition came out in 2012. The movie's failure to catch on has been attributed to its lack of warm and engaging characters, its PG rating, and the public's disinterest in or ignorance of the Hollywood westerns that are being spoofed. But for moviegoers wanting a daffy alternative to the typical Disney product, *Home on the Range* is a joyous romp.

See also *Rango*.

Did You Know . . . ?

Because of a joke about the cow Maggie's udders, the movie received a PG rating.

HOW TO TRAIN YOUR DRAGON

2010
(USA: DreamWorks Animation)

Directed by Dean DeBois and Chris Sanders
Written by William Davies, Dean DeBois, and Chris Sanders, based on the book by
   Cressida Cowell
Produced by Kristine Belson, Tim Johnson, Bonnie Arnold, Michael A. Connolly, Roy
   Lee, Bruce Seifert, Karen Foster, Suzanne Buirgy, and Doug Davison
Score by John Powell
Songs "Sticks and Stones" by Jon Thor Birgisson and "A Beautiful Lie" by Jared Leto
Specs: Color; 98 minutes; computer animation

Part adventure film, part coming of age movie, How to Train Your Dragon *succeeds on both levels, helped by imaginative animation, evocative background art, and a solid voice cast.*

In the Viking village of Berk, the teenage Hiccup does not have the brawn or the killing instinct that is expected of a Viking, especially the son of the chieftain Stoick. But Hiccup has plenty of brains and designs a flying contraption that manages to catch an elusive Night Fury dragon in a net and bring him down in a nearby forest. When Hiccup discovers the trapped creature, he doesn't have the heart to kill it but frees the dragon from the net and befriends it, naming it Toothless because it can retract all its teeth. Toothless has lost a fin and cannot fly, so Hiccup makes an artificial fin and the two ride through the skies together. In doing so, Hiccup discovers that all the dragons that attack the village are looking for sheep and other food to feed to the gigantic dragon Red Death. Stoick finds out about the mountain in which the dragons nest and all the Vikings set sail to destroy Red Death. But Hiccup has learned how to befriend the other dragons and, with his teen crush Astrid and his fellow teenagers, they fly to the mountain where Hiccup and Toothless cleverly destroy Red Death. Hiccup loses part of his leg in the battle but survives to see the Vikings and the dragons living together in harmony.

   British author Cressida Cowell's *How to Train Your Dragon* was published in 2003 and has been followed by fifteen sequels. DreamWorks was immediately interested, but development of a film version was slow because of script problems. The original book was considered too sentimental and soft by studio executives, so changes were made to the story, the most important being the dragon Toothless. A small and ordinary dragon in the book, Toothless was turned into an elu-

The young Viking named Hiccup befriends and trains the dragon Night Fury, then they set off to save the village of Berk from the fierce dragon Red Death. *Paramount Pictures / Photofest.* © *Paramount Pictures*

sive Night Fury that was large enough that Hiccup could ride on its back. A love interest was created with the female Viking Astrid, and Hiccup's losing part of his leg was added to bring a dose of reality to the movie. A good portion of the film involves Toothless and Hiccup flying, and they are among the most beautiful and exciting sequences in *How to Train Your Dragon*. The script has several characters, but it is the unspoken bond between Hiccup and Toothless that is most rewarding. Voiced by Canadian actor Jay Baruchel, Hiccup is an engaging, funny, and sympathetic character who holds the film together. The animators managed to convey Toothless's many moods with only minimal sounds but wonderful facial expressions. Much of the dialogue in the movie is anachronistic with very modern jokes and comments, but there is still plenty of heart in some conversations, particularly between Hiccup and his father, Stoick. The coming-of-age plot may be familiar, but there is much originality in the telling of it.

Voice Cast

Jay Baruchel	Hiccup
America Ferrera	Astrid
Gerard Butler	Stoick
Craig Ferguson	Gobber
Jonah Hill	Snotlout
Christopher Mintz-Plasse	Fishlegs
T. J. Miller	Tuffnut
Kristen Wiig	Ruffnut
Robin Atkin Downes	Ack
Philip McGrade	Starkard
David Tennant	Spitelout
Kieron Elliott	Hoak the Haggard
Ashley Jensen	Phlegma the Fierce

> HICCUP: Three hundred years, and I'm the first Viking who wouldn't kill a dragon!
>
> ASTRID: First to ride one, though. So . . . ?
>
> HICCUP: I wouldn't kill him, because he looked as frightened as I was. I looked at him . . . and I saw myself.

How to Train Your Dragon is an adventure film with plenty of action that, as originally seen in 3-D, resembled a theme park ride at times. There is so much movement that it is sometimes difficult to appreciate the fine computer animation. The Vikings are mostly oversized hulks with wild hair and beards and with vibrant facial expression. The variety of dragons portrayed is impressive, but they are so active that one rarely gets to enjoy the intricate details in their look. Also sometimes lost in all the flying and fighting is the expert decor and background art. The village of Berk is both crude and poetic as it perches high in the Nordic landscape. The interiors are often oversized, like a vast, empty cathedral. The re-creation of the sea and the rocky shores is majestic and mythic, as in a Scandinavian epic picture book. Also majestic is John Powell's stirring soundtrack score, which utilizes Irish and Scottish folk instruments such as the bagpipe, harp, fiddle, and penny whistle to capture a rustic and primitive sound at times. Other times, a full orchestra soars with enthralling bombast, as in some of the flying sequences. *How to Train Your Dragon* looks and sounds like a colorful legend come to life.

Awards

Academy Award nominations: Best Animated Feature and Best Score.
Golden Globe nominations: Best Animated Feature.
British Academy of Film & Television Arts (BAFTA) Award nominations: Best Animated Film and Best Score.

The first release of *How to Train Your Dragon* in 2010 was offered in 3-D but there was a scarcity of theaters equipped with 3-D screens because *Clash of the Titans* and *Alice in Wonderland*, also 3-D films, opened around the same time. Once widely released in conventional theaters, the movie managed to find an audience and ended up earning over $200 million in domestic sales, eventually close to $500 million internationally. The movie was greeted with mostly favorable reviews and several award nominations. The DVD version, released in late 2010, was also very popular, as was the 2014 Blu-ray release. *How to Train Your Dragon* inspired four short films, a television series titled *DreamWorks Dragons*, video games, and even a live-action arena show in Australia in 2012 with acrobats, projections, and animatronic dragons. The sequel *How to Train Your Dragon 2* was released in theaters in 2014 and was also very popular. Many of the same voice actors returned for this tale, which takes place five years later. Hiccup, now twenty years old, discovers that his long lost mother is alive and is the dragon rider Valka (voiced by Cate Blanchett). Hiccup and his friends also have to battle the power-hungry warlord Drago Bludvist (voiced by Djimon Hounsou), who tries to take over the world with his army of ruthless dragons. Some critics thought the sequel as satisfying as the original, and audiences must have agreed; the movie earned over $100 million more than *How to Train Your Dragon*. Another sequel, *How to Train Your Dragon 3*, is set to be released in 2019.

Did You Know . . . ?

In creating the look for the dragon Toothless, the animators combined characteristics of a dog, a cat, a horse, and a salamander.

THE HUNCHBACK OF NOTRE DAME

1996
(USA: Walt Disney Pictures)

Directed by Gary Trousdale and Kirk Wise
Written by Tab Murphy, Irene Mecchi, Noni White, Jonathan Roberts, and Bob Tzu-diker, based on the novel by Victor Hugo
Produced by Don Hahn, Roy Conli, and Philip Lofaro
Score by Alan Menken
Songs by Alan Menken (music) and Stephen Schwartz (lyrics)
Specs: Color; 91 minutes; traditional and computer animation

Much darker and more sensual than perhaps any other Disney movie, this version of the French literary classic is not always faithful to its source but is never less than riveting.

Quasimodo is a deformed orphan who rings the bells of Notre Dame Cathedral in sixteenth-century Paris. His guardian is Judge Frollo, the evil Minister of Justice, who is intent on driving out all the gypsies in Paris. Quasimodo's only friends are the three talking Gargoyles—Victor, Hugo, and Laverne—who urge him to leave the cathedral to celebrate the annual Festival of Fools taking place in the plaza below. Quasimodo's grotesque appearance is mistaken as a costume and he is crowned King of Fools. But when it is revealed that his face is no mask, the crowd turns on Quasimodo and only the gypsy girl Esmeralda takes pity on him. Frollo orders the guards to arrest Esmeralda, but Quasimodo helps her escape into the cathedral where she is safe under the law of sanctuary. The two become friends, but Esmeralda falls in love with Phoebus, the kind-hearted Captain of the Guard, who allows her to return to the gypsy hideout. While Quasimodo glows in Esmeralda's friendship, Frollo lusts after her and, because he cannot have her, vows to destroy the gypsy girl. The gypsies and the citizens rise up against Frollo, who is killed when Quasimodo and the three gargoyles pour molten lead down on the soldiers trying to storm the cathedral. Esmeralda and Phoebus are united, and Quasimodo is declared a hero by the people of Paris.

The three comic gargoyles Victor, Hugo, and Laverne encourage the deformed Quasimodo to woo the fiery gypsy girl Esmeralda, with whom he is smitten. *Walt Disney Pictures / Photofest. © Walt Disney Pictures*

Director-animators Gary Trousdale and Kirk Wise were in the early development stage for a film about a humpback whale when Disney producer Jeffrey Katzenberg assigned them to a different film about a humpback hero, *The Hunchback of Notre Dame*. Production began in 1993 when the staff visited Paris and made hundreds of sketches of the cathedral of Notre Dame and other medieval buildings. Meanwhile the writers struggled with ways to make a family-friendly film of Victor Hugo's 1831 classic novel without omitting the dark themes in the story. The archdeacon Frollo was turned into a judge, the soldier Phoebus became Esmeralda's love interest, and a romantic triangle was fashioned for Quasimodo, Phoebus, and Esmeralda. The biggest departure in the script was the creation of the three gargoyles, who speak to Quasimodo and give the disfigured hero someone to confide in. Among the difficult elements in the novel that were retained

Voice Cast

Tom Hulce	Quasimodo
Tony Jay	Frollo
Demi Moore	Esmeralda (speaking)
Heidi Mollenhauer	Esmeralda (singing)
Kevin Kline	Phoebus
Paul Kandel	Clopin
Jason Alexander	Hugo
Charles Kimbrough	Victor
Mary Wickes	Laverne
David Ogden Stiers	Archdeacon

Songs

"The Bells of Notre Dame"
"Topsy Turvy"
"Out There"
"God Help the Outcasts"
"A Guy Like You"
"Heaven's Light/Hellfire"
"The Court of Miracles"
"Someday"

in the screenplay were the persecution of the gypsies and Frollo's lust for Esmeralda. While the gargoyles provide some comic relief, *The Hunchback of Notre Dame* turned out to be one of the most serious and disturbing Disney productions.

The animation and background art in the movie are both extraordinary. The Paris of the 1500s is depicted with realistic details yet there is a romanticized flavor to it as well. The scenes in various locales inside the cathedral are atmospheric and accurate. Some computer animation was used for these sections, particularly in scenes utilizing the famous bells of Notre Dame. Character animation is ingenious throughout. Quasimodo was the most challenging character to portray, but the artists came up with a grotesque look that still allowed his eyes and smile to indicate the person under the hideous exterior. Quasimodo has almost a weightlessness as he climbs and swings through the Medieval church, looking as if one of the gargoyles has broken loose and come to life. Frollo is one of Disney's most malevolent villains, without a trace of humor or compassion. The artists portray him with severe lines and dark colors. In a way, Frollo also is like one of the cathedral's gargoyles, but not an exuberant and very physical one like Quasimodo. Phoebus and Esmeralda are drawn as conventional lovers, although he is funnier than most and she is more sensual than any of her predecessors. The depiction of the gargoyles Victor, Hugo, and Laverne is not at all like solid stone. The trio bend, jump, and twist themselves as if they were human children. The three statues only move and talk when they are alone with Quasimodo, so one can assume that they come alive only in his imagination. It makes sense that his inanimate friends would have such sportive behavior.

The voice work in *The Hunchback of Notre Dame* is uneven. Film and television veterans Jason Alexander, Charles Kimbrough, and Mary Wickes are perhaps too vaudevillian as the gargoyles, Demi Moore is an unimaginative Esmeralda, and Kevin Kline a bit too modern sounding for Phoebus. But Tom Hulce's Quasimodo is touching, Tony Jay's interpretation of Frollo is chilling, and there is a lively voice performance by Paul Kandel as the narrator-puppeteer-ringleader Clopin. All the principals did their own singing except for Moore, whose Esmeralda was sung by Heidi Mollenhauer. Hulce surprises with his strong singing for Quasimodo, Jay manages to be even more sinister when he sings, and Kandel handles his songs splendidly.

Alan Menken (music) and Stephen Schwartz (lyrics) wrote the songs for the film, some of which, such as the opening "The Bells of Notre Dame," combined narrative and character effectively. Quasimodo yearns for life in the soaring ballad "Out There," Esmeralda prays with fervor in "God Help the Outcasts," the three gargoyles ham it up with the anachronistic "A Guy Like You," and the crowd cel-

FROLLO: I should have known you'd risk your life to save that Gypsy witch! Just as your own mother died trying to save you.

QUASIMODO: (shocked) What?

FROLLO: Now, I'm going to do what I should have done . . . twenty years ago!

ebrates a festival where everything turns dangerously "Topsy Turvy." The most potent number in the movie is the contrasting songs "Heaven's Light," sung by Quasimodo as he basks in the warmth of Esmeralda's smile, and "Hellfire," in which the villainous Frollo sings about both his hatred and lust for the gypsy girl as the flames in his fireplace conjure up erotic images of passion and punishment. The songwriters also wrote the hymn-like "Someday," a plea for acceptance, to be sung in the cathedral. The song was cut from the story but was sung by the rhythm and blues group All-4-One over the final credits. The superb soundtrack score by Menken includes some Gregorian chant, passages from Mozart's Requiem, period festival music, and deep foreboding themes for the film's darkest scenes.

Awards

Academy Award nomination: Best Score.
Golden Globe nomination: Best Score.

An animated movie dealing with prejudice, infanticide, sexual obsession, religious persecution, and other issues was a tricky proposition, and one has to salute the Disney studio for making such a film, especially at a price tag of $100 million. But *The Hunchback of Notre Dame* received mostly approving reviews, and the public turned the film into a considerable hit. While some critics scolded the filmmakers for the changes they made to Hugo's original, in particular the talking gargoyles, nearly all the notices complimented the artistic look of the movie and the portrayal of Quasimodo. There was also applause for the score and the voice cast. Even in France, the press generally approved of the movie. Some church groups in the United States and Great Britain thought the sensuality in *The Hunchback of Notre Dame* was scandalous and boycotted the film. But most of the public embraced the film and it ended up earning $325 million internationally. A stage musical version of the movie was a success in Germany in 1999 and finally opened regionally in the United States in 2014. There was a direct-to-video sequel titled *The Hunchback of Notre Dame II* in 2002 as well as a video game. The VHS edition of the original move came out in 1997, the DVD in 2000, and the Blu-ray in 2013.

Did You Know . . . ?

The film originally opened with scenes of dialogue and unsung exposition. The result was not very interesting, so Alan Menken and Stephen Schwartz wrote the opening number, "The Bells of Notre Dame," which incorporated all the necessary exposition in song. It is considered one of the most complex yet finest opening numbers in any Disney film.

I

ICE AGE

2002
(USA: Blue Sky Studios/20th Century Fox)

Directed by Chris Wedge and Carlos Saldanha
Written by Michael Berg, Michael J. Wilson, and Peter Ackerman
Produced by Christopher Meledandri, Lori Forte, and John C. Donkin
Score by David Newman
Specs: Color; 81 minutes; computer animation

A prehistoric adventure film with more than its fair share of comedy, Ice Age *was a surprise hit and launched one of the biggest movie franchises of the new century.*

As the Ice Age begins on planet Earth, all the prehistoric animals are migrating south to survive. Among them are the scatterbrained sloth Sid and the woolly mammoth Manfred, who always quarrel with each other but join forces when they rescue a human infant from the Smilodon Soto and his henchman Diego. Sid and Manfred bring the baby to the human settlement, but the village has been abandoned so Diego offers to track the humans. What he really plans is to lead them into a trap. As they travel on, Sid and Manfred discover a cave in which humans have painted scenes on the walls that depict the slaughter of Manfred's wife and child. The group then encounters a lava stream in which Diego is nearly killed but is rescued by Manfred. With a change of heart, Diego warns the others about the trap that is set for them. Soto and his herd attack, Diego is wounded, and Manfred pushes Soto to his death. When the herd finally arrives at the human settlement to return the baby to the tribe, a recovered Diego is there to meet them. Together they all continue south in search of a warmer climate.

Early drafts for an animated movie set during the prehistoric age were very serious in tone and sought to be anthropologically accurate. Veteran animator-director Don Bluth was heading the project until 20th Century Fox insisted that the film be computer generated. Bluth, who despised CGI movies, quit the production and it was turned over to Chris Wedge, who codirected *Ice Age* with Carlos Saldanha. The script went through several changes during production in efforts to make the film primarily a comedy. The villain-turned-hero Diego died

With their homeland frozen by the approaching Ice Age, the saber-toothed tiger Diego, the sloth Sid, and the woolly mammoth Manfred head south searching for a warmer climate. *20th Century Fox Film Corporation / Photofest. © 20th Century Fox Film Corporation*

in the final screenplay but children's reactions at the test screenings made it clear they liked the Smilodon, so the ending was redone. The character of the sloth Sid was originally a slick con man and a bit of a womanizer. He was softened into a bumbling smart aleck. A very minor character in the plot, a half-squirrel, half-rat critter called Scrat, was introduced late in the film. This nonspeaking creature with a penchant for failure in getting acorns, quickly caught on with the artists, and his role was increased until he became a silent narrator of sorts. The unlucky Scrat eventually became the unofficial symbol of the whole *Ice Age* franchise. All of the animal characters were rendered as realistically as possible. Creatures not existing during the first Ice Age, such as dinosaurs, were not included in the film.

Voice Cast

Ray Romano	Manfred
John Leguizamo	Sid
Denis Leary	Diego
Goran Visnjic	Soto
Jack Black	Zeke
Cedric the Entertainer	Carl
Stephen Root	Frank
Lorri Bagley	Jennifer
Jane Krakowski	Rachel
Diedrich Baer	Saber-Toothed Tiger
Alan Tudyk	Lenny
Chris Wedge	Dodo
P. J. Benjamin	Dodo
Josh Hamilton	Dodo
Peter Ackerman	Dodo

The animals animated in *Ice Age* moved in the way archeologists believe they moved. The human characters in the story are nameless and speechless, only the infant making human baby noises. The artists' depiction of the landscape during the coming of the Ice Age is also as accurate as possible.

SID: You know? This whole Ice Age thing is getting old. You know what I could go for? A global warming.

DIEGO: Keep dreaming.

SID: No really . . .

Ice Age may look more like a nature documentary than a comedy but the vibrant voice cast changes everything. The animal characters speak in very modern terms, the dialogue filled with sarcasm and hip humor. Comic actors with a gift for ad-libbing were hired and encouraged to turn the written lines into stand-up comedy. The edgy Hispanic comic John Leguizamo, who is a master in creating different voices in different dialects, experimented with various sounds in voicing Sid and, learning that sloths spent most of their lives eating something very slowly, he did his lines as if his mouth were filled with food. Television favorite Ray Romano voices Manfred with a deep, lazy sound that allows his wry comments to land softly but effectively. Other memorable performances are given by Denis Leary, who gives Diego a rural, raspy kind of voice, and Cedric the Entertainer and Stephen Root as the pseudo-sophisticated rhinos Carl and Frank.

Award

Academy Award nomination: Best Animated Feature.

Made for $59 million, *Ice Age* surprised everyone and grossed over $383 million internationally. The reviews were positive if not outstanding, but the unpretentious comedy had wide audience appeal. Moviegoers and critics were particularly taken with Scrat, who was later featured in a series of animated shorts and made appearances in the four sequels. *Ice Age: The Meltdown* (2006), *Ice Age: Dawn of the Dinosaurs* (2009), *Ice Age: Continental Drift* (2012), and *Ice Age: Collision Course* (2016) reunited several of the characters and voices from the original, and each movie was a major box office hit. It is estimated that the five *Ice Age* films have earned over $3 billion internationally. Add to that the DVD and Blu-ray versions, video games, television specials, and animated shorts and the *Ice Age* franchise is one of the most lucrative in modern Hollywood history.

See also *Dinosaur*.

Did You Know . . . ?

A variety of prehistoric animals were developed and designed for the movie but were cut from the final print. These animals later appeared in the film's many sequels.

THE INCREDIBLES

2004
(USA: Pixar Animation Studios/Disney)

Directed and written by Brad Bird
Produced by John Lasseter, John Walker, Katherine Sarafian, Kori Rae
Score by Michael Giacchino
Specs: Color; 115 minutes; computer animation

A clever and entertaining movie on several levels, The Incredibles *offers a superhero adventure with a fresh point of view.*

Because some bad publicity has turned public opinion against them, various superheroes have retired from saving mankind and now live incognito among ordinary people. Mr. Incredible and his wife, Elastigirl, take on the identity of Bob and Helen Parr, with their three children Dash, Violet, and Jack-Jack. When the elusive and alluring woman Mirage urges Bob to use his superpowers to destroy the spider-like robot Omnidroid, Mr. Incredible is happy to return to his former life. But Mirage is working for the master criminal Syndrome, a former superhero fan who has developed sinister weapons of destruction. With new superhero costumes designed by the fashion icon Edna, the entire Incredible family gets involved in the hunt for Syndrome, each one using his or her specific superpower to eventually kill him and become popular heroes again.

Animator-director Brad Bird brought his idea of a movie about retired superheroes to producer John Lasseter at Pixar in 2000 and both the concept and Bird were taken on and development started. In an unusual move for animation, Lasseter named Bird sole writer and director of *The Incredibles*. Also unusual for Pixar, there are no animal characters in the film. Bird created original superheroes for the story but acknowledged that his inspiration came from 1960s comic

The Parr family members (left to right) Dash, Violet, Bob, and Helen come out of retirement to become superheroes once again and destroy the villain Syndrome. *Pixar Animation Studios/Walt Disney Pictures / Photofest. © Pixar Animation Studios/Walt Disney Pictures*

Voice Cast

Craig T. Nelson	Bob Parr/Mr. Incredible
Holly Hunter	Helen Parr/Elastigirl
Jason Lee	Buddy Pine/Syndrome
Samuel L. Jackson	Lucius Best/Frozone
Dominique Louis	Bomb Voyage
Brad Bird	Edna E. Mode
Wallace Shawn	Gilbert Huph
Sarah Vowell	Violet Parr
Spencer Fox	Dashiell Parr
Lou Romano	Bernie Kropp
Jean Sincere	Mrs. Hogenson
Elizabeth Peña	Mirage
Wayne Canney	Principal
Bud Luckey	Rick Dicker
Michael Bird	Tony Rydinger
Eli Fucile	Jack-Jack Parr
Maeve Andrews	Jack-Jack Parr
Teddy Newton	Newsreel Narrator

books. Although he had directed the animated movie *The Iron Giant* (1999), Bird had not worked in computer animation before and had to learn how to translate his visual ideas to the new medium. Production was very slow due to this and because of the unique demands in the look of the film. Although the animators wanted the color and design of a 1960s comic book, the texture of the visuals was much different from hand-drawn animation. The superheroes' suits, for example, required an elastic, other-worldly appearance that did not resemble everyday cloth. Animating each hero's power was also a challenge, particularly Elastigirl's expanding appendages. Because of its many locations and special effects, *The Incredibles* turned into Pixar's most complex and labor-intensive project yet, eventually costing over $92 million.

EDNA: This is a horrible suit, darling. You can't be seen in this. I won't allow it. Fifteen years ago, maybe, but now? Feh!

BOB: Wait, what do you mean? You designed it.

EDNA: I never look back, darling! It distracts from the now.

While *The Incredibles* is set in a comic-book world, the characters are very human and much more complicated than one usually finds in the action comics genre. The Parr family is trying to live like ordinary people, ignoring their super powers as much as they can. Bob Parr, who has a dreary job with an insurance company, is particularly unhappy, his muscular body turned fat and wasted. His decision to return to his superhero persona is not made easily, because he has his family to consider. Yet each of the Parrs is undergoing some kind of discontent, and their return to fighting super villains helps them bond as a family. The movie's villain, Syndrome, is a classic evildoer yet is driven by very human emotion: revenge for being overlooked in his youth by the reigning superheroes. The Parrs are surrounded by a variety of interesting characters, but the most original and hilarious is the fashion designer Edna Mode, who is concerned with style as well as practicality in her superhero suits. A spoof of the celebrated Hollywood designer Edith Head, Edna offers a whole new viewpoint to the world of superheroes. Director Bird voices Edna himself, and in some ways, this supporting character represents the oddball silliness of *The Incredibles*. Craig T. Nelson voices Bob Parr with a dashing hero voice undercut by frustration. Holly Hunter is vivacious yet very human as Helen Parr, and Spencer Fox and Sarah Vowell have a sitcom-like attitude in playing the offspring Dash and Violet. Among the splendid supporting cast, Samuel L. Jackson stands out voicing the reluctant Lucius Best, who leaves his nagging wife and returns to his Frozone persona. Many of the characters in *The Incredibles* sound like the people in 1960s TV action cartoons. Composer Michael Giacchino captures that sound in his vibrant soundtrack score. Blues and jazz are used throughout, often in a propulsive manner that recalls the James Bond scores of the era and TV themes like that for *Mission: Impossible*. There is also humor in the music, subliminally reminding the moviegoer that this is all a comic-book spoof.

Awards

Academy Awards: Best Animated Film and Best Sound Editing. Oscar nominations: Best Screenplay and Sound Mixing.
Golden Globe nomination: Best Feature Film.
British Academy of Film & Television Arts (BAFTA) Award: Best Feature Film.

Critical reaction to *The Incredibles* when it was released in 2004 was overwhelmingly laudatory, the press approving of the film as a summer action movie and a clever commentary on the comic-book genre. The public was equally impressed and the film paid back most of its cost in the first weekend. Internationally *The Incredibles* grossed over $633 million. The 2005 VHS and DVD releases and the Blu-ray edition in 2011 were also very successful, as was a video game. A sequel, a long time in the works, is expected in 2018.

See also *Big Hero 6* and *The Lego Movie*.

Did You Know . . . ?

Actress-comedienne Lily Tomlin was approached to voice Edna, the fashion expert, but when director-writer Brad Bird demonstrated for her what Edna should sound like, Tomlin said he had the perfect character voice for Edna and suggested he do the vocals himself. So he did.

INSIDE OUT

2015
(USA: Pixar Animation Studios/Disney)

Directed by Pete Docter and Ronnie Del Carmen
Written by Pete Docter, Meg LeFauve, and Josh Cooley
Produced by John Lasseter, Andrew Stanton, Jonas Rivera, and Mark Nielsen
Score by Michael Giacchino
Specs: Color; 95 minutes; computer animation

An often somber Pixar film about the heartaches of growing up, Inside Out *is one of the most abstract of animated movies, focusing on the psyche rather than the exterior life of an adolescent.*

Eleven-year-old Riley Anderson moves with her parents from Minnesota, where they all enjoy winter sports, to San Francisco, where the father is starting a new business. The transition is difficult for Riley, especially when her new unfurnished home is depressing, her first days of school are unsuccessful, and she fails to make the girls' hockey team. Missing her old home, Riley steals her mother's credit card and buys a bus ticket to Minnesota. But at the last minute she returns home, expresses her sadness with the situation, and the family starts to bond again. This story is all told from the point of view of Riley's brain, which is controlled by five emotions: the ever-cheerful Joy, the depressed Sadness, the neurotic Fear, the short-tempered Anger, and the sarcastic Disgust. With Riley's emotional crises,

The personified emotions (left to right) Fear, Joy, and Disgust, who work inside the brain center of the preteen Riley, rarely agree on which psychological direction to take next. *Walt Disney Pictures / Photofest.* © *Walt Disney Pictures*

Voice Cast

Kaitlyn Dias	Riley
Amy Poehler	Joy
Phyllis Smith	Sadness
Bill Hader	Fear
Lewis Black	Anger
Mindy Kaling	Disgust
Richard Kind	Bing Bong
Diane Lane	Mom
Kyle MacLachlan	Dad

the controls in her brain misfire and Joy and Sadness are thrust deep into Riley's memory storage. There they meet her old imaginary companion, Bing Bong, who helps the two emotions return to the headquarters in Riley's brain. Realizing that Riley cannot continue to hide her emotions, Joy lets Sadness take over, allowing Riley to weep and tell her parents how she feels.

The idea for *Inside Out* came from two life experiences of director-animator Pete Docter: his feeling of loneliness when his family moved to a new city and, years later, the emotional roller coaster his daughter experienced when she approached puberty. Noted psychologists were consulted in the process of turning Docter's life experiences into a movie, but the script went through many variations until a workable screenplay was developed. Because most of the film takes place in the world of Riley's brain, *Inside Out* also called for an imaginative approach to personifying the key emotions and creating a landscape that included islands of past experiences and a warehouse for various memories. The concept of memories being stored in shiny balls of color set the look for the movie, the warehouse of memories resembling thousands of color gum balls in plastic storage units. Other locations included the creepy land containing Riley's subconscious, a literal Train of Thought, a Land of Imagination from young childhood, and a Memory Dump where some recollections are lost forever. While some emotions, such as Joy, Sadness, and Disgust were very human in their appearance, Anger and Fear were more abstract. The commendable voice cast was responsible for keeping the many characters distinct, often taking their characterization from a single emotion. Yet as the story progresses, Joy actually breaks down and cries and Anger finds a soft spot in its heart. *Inside Out* was filled with risks for all concerned, and the Pixar staff were quite unsure about how marketable such an unusual film would be.

JOY: Hey, look! The Golden Gate Bridge! Isn't that great? It's not made out of solid gold like we thought, which is kind of a disappointment, but still!

FEAR: I sure am glad you told me earthquakes are a myth, Joy, otherwise I'd be terrified right now.

JOY: Uh . . . yeah . . .

The animation for the movie called for a great deal of original images, both for the characters and the landscape of a girl's brain. Rather than go completely abstract, the animators chose to take images from the real world and extrapolate them into a surreal world. The islands of past experiences resemble mini theme parks, the memory storage bins remind one of candy containers, the headquarters recalls the command tower at an airport, and the memory pit has the desolated feel of a burned-out garbage dump. Everything in *Inside Out* looks familiar yet defies logic and, sometimes, physics. The real-life story of Riley and her parents is presented mostly with poetic realism. Happy scenes in Minnesota are contrasted with a very grim and sobering San Francisco. There is a glow to the pleasant scenes (similar to the glow that always surrounds Joy), but a coldness to the city that is the Andersons' new home. Similarly, Michael Giacchino's soundtrack score is filled with contrasts. The music often echoes the emotion that is dominant at that point, quickly changing and going in a new direction as the story is tossed on a sea of emotions.

Awards

Academy Award: Best Animated Feature. Oscar nomination: Best Screenplay.
Golden Globe Award: Best Motion Picture—Animated.
British Academy of Film & Television Arts (BAFTA) Award: Best Animated Film and BAFTA nomination for Best Screenplay.

Inside Out was a pleasant surprise for Pixar and Disney when it was released in 2015. They knew the movie would not appeal to very young children but hoped audiences who were Riley's age and higher would identify with the themes in the story. The audience response was immediately enthusiastic, the box office bringing in over $90 million the first weekend. The complicated movie cost $175 million to make, but within a year it grossed over $850 million worldwide. Critics were as happy with *Inside Out* as audiences were. It received almost unanimous raves from the press and won many awards. The release of the DVD and Blu-ray editions late in 2015 added to the movie's popularity and financial success. The film has quickly become a kind of classic in the genre.

Did You Know . . . ?

Because all of the conflicts in the movie are inside Riley's head, *Inside Out* is the only Pixar film with no overt villain.

J

JAMES AND THE GIANT PEACH

1996

(UK / USA: Skellington Productions / Disney)

Directed by Henry Selick
Written by Karey Kirkpatrick, Steve Bloom, and Jonathan Roberts, based on the book
  by Roald Dahl
Produced by Jake Eberts, Tim Burton, Denise Di Novi, John Engel, Brian Rosen, and
  Henry Selick
Score and songs by Randy Newman
Specs: Color (Technicolor); 79 minutes; stop-motion animation and live action

Roald Dahl's whimsical children's books are ideal sources for animated features and this delightful fantasy, with an offbeat tone, successfully combines live action and animation.

The orphaned boy James, who has always dreamed of visiting New York City, lives with his nasty aunts Spiker and Sponge by the sea in England. One day a mysterious man gives him a bag of "crocodile tongues" to keep safe. James accidentally drops the bag and the tongues creep into the ground, growing into a giant peach on a stem. The peach becomes a tourist attraction bringing in money for the greedy aunts until James burrows into the giant fruit and it breaks from the stem and rolls into the sea. Inside the peach are Miss Spider, Mr. Grasshopper, Mr. Centipede, Glowworm, Earthworm, and Ladybug, who befriend James and decide to join him on a journey to New York City. Miss Spider spins silk strings that are attached to seagulls that carry the peach over the Atlantic Ocean. But the peach gets off course and they find themselves in the Arctic. Grasshopper says they need a compass, so Centipede dives into the ocean to find one in a sunken pirate ship. The pirate skeletons capture Centipede, but he is rescued by James and Miss Spider. As the peach approaches New York, a storm rises and lifts the peach up high so that it lands on the top of the Empire State Building. James becomes a celebrity and his two aunts arrive and try to cash in on the glory. Miss Spider ties Spiker and Sponge into a silk web, and James offers the peach to the children to eat. The remaining peach pit is turned into a home for James and his insect friends.

The boy James (center) flies away from home on a magical giant peach with an oddball group of friends, including Grasshopper (left) and Centipede. *Walt Disney Pictures / Photofest.* © *Walt Disney Pictures*

Popular British author Roald Dahl did not think his 1961 book *James and the Giant Peach* would make an effective movie and refused all offers from different studios to film it. After Dahl died in 1990, his widow, Felicity "Liccy" Dahl, sold the rights to Disney in 1992 with the idea of making a live-action movie. Henry Selick, who had directed *The Nightmare before Christmas* (1993), thought the whole idea of a giant peach could be handled best with animation. *James and the Giant Peach* ended up being both live action and animated. The first twenty minutes of the film are done

Voice Cast

Paul Terry	James
Simon Callow	Grasshopper
Richard Dreyfuss	Centipede
Jane Leeves	Ladybug
Susan Sarandon	Spider
David Thewlis	Earthworm
Miriam Margolyes	Glowworm

Live-Action Cast

Paul Terry	James
Joanna Lumley	Aunt Spiker
Miriam Margolyes	Aunt Sponge
Pete Postlethwaite	Old Man

with live actors and real (though hardly realistic) sets and costumes. Once James and the peach escape from his aunts and the animal characters are introduced, the film becomes stop-motion. The transition is effective without being too jarring. The "real" world in England has surreal houses, impressionistic trees, and grotesque people. The animated world on the giant peach has insects that are surprisingly realistic even if the Centipede smokes a cigar and the Grasshopper sports a morning coat. While crossing the Atlantic, James and the insects encounter a shark, which is rendered as a mechanical creature, far from zoologically accurate. The animated version of James does not exactly resemble the live-action actor, Paul Terry. His head is disproportionately large, and his facial expressions are stylized. Putting a live-action James in the stop-motion world of the movie might have worked, as it did in *Song of the South* (1946), but the animated James makes the film unique. For the most part, the screen version of *James and the Giant Peach* follows the book closely. The biggest change was not having the two aunts killed by the rolling peach, as in the book.

Songs

"Family"
"My Name Is James"
"That's the Life"
"Good News"
"Eating the Peach" (lyric by Roald Dahl)

The voice cast for *James and the Giant Peach* is diverse, with accents from all over the map. Paul Terry's James has a very proper British dialect in contrast to the crass and low-class language of his obnoxious aunts (Joanna Lumley and Miriam Margolyes). The Grasshopper (Simon Callow) has an Oxbridge dialect while the Centipede (Richard Dreyfuss) is very New Yorkese in speech. Susan Sarandon gives the Spider an exotic, thick but indistinguishable foreign accent, David Thewlis gives the Earthworm a working-class British voice, and Jane Leeves voices the Ladybug with a prim and proper demeanor. In the live-action section, Pete Postlethwaite is mesmerizing as the strange Old Man who gives James the bag of crocodile tongues that later produce the giant peach. All in all, it is a splendid voice cast, each one doing his or her own singing as well.

CENTIPEDE: I've sailed all the five seas. From the land of Bora Bora to the icy shores of Tripoli. Commodore Centipede, they used to call me.

GRASSHOPPER: Seven.

CENTIPEDE: Huh?

GRASSHOPPER: There are seven seas, and Tripoli is in the Sub-Tropics, Commodore!

CENTIPEDE: Trim the sails!

LADYBUG: There are no sails.

CENTIPEDE: Start the engines!

EARTHWORM: There are no engines.

CENTIPEDE: I can't work with this miserable crew!

Randy Newman wrote the masterful soundtrack score and five songs for the film. With a lyric by Dahl, "Eating the Peach" is a fun music-hall number in the British manner with James and the insects listing their favorite foods. The plaintive ballad "My Name Is James" is sung by the friendless James near the beginning of the film. This is later contrasted by "Family," a breezy number sung by the violin-playing Grasshopper, the insects, and James about their mutual admiration for each other. Newman sings the catchy song "Good News" over a montage of newspaper headlines about the giant peach, and James and his friends sing "That's the Life" anticipating their arrival in New York City. The soundtrack score is even more impressive. The main theme is a simple string duet that aches with loneliness. Some sections of the score have a magical and dreamy quality, but for the action scenes there is restless and furtive music that overflows with adventure.

Award

Academy Award nomination: Best Score.

The reviews for *James and the Giant Peach* when it opened in 1996 were almost all favorable. Critics enjoyed the technical aspects of the movie, such as the stop-motion animation, but also thought the story had heart and wide appeal. Oddly, the film did only modest box office. The elaborate movie cost around $38 million but earned just under $30 million in the United States. With foreign box office and the VHS, DVD, and Blu-ray sales, the film eventually made a profit, but it did not join the ranks of Disney successes of the 1990s. Yet *James and the Giant Peach* now has a strong following, which will grow as each new generation discovers it.

See also *Fantastic Mr. Fox*.

Did You Know . . . ?

The head of Jack Skellington from *The Nightmare before Christmas* (1993) shows up in the underwater pirate ship in this film.

THE JUNGLE BOOK

1967
(USA: Walt Disney Productions)

Directed by Wolfgang Reitherman
Written by Larry Clemmons, Vance Gerry, Ken Anderson, and Ralph Wright, based
   on the book of stories by Rudyard Kipling
Produced by Walt Disney
Score by George Bruns
Songs by Richard M. and Robert B. Sherman, and Terry Gilkyson
Specs: Color (Technicolor); 78 minutes; traditional animation

Music and character take precedence over plot in this spirited Disney version of the famous tales set in the wilds of India. More Disney than Kipling, The Jungle Book *is one of the studio's most slaphappy and freewheeling movies.*

The orphaned baby Mowgli is rescued in the Indian jungle by the panther Bagheera and turned over to a family of wolves to raise him. As a young boy, he is very happy in the wolfpack, but when the man-eating tiger Shere-Khan returns to the area, Bagheera realizes that it is not safe for the boy and makes plans to bring him to the Man-Village, where he can be with his own kind. Mowgli wishes to remain in the jungle, but after a near-death encounter with the snake Kaa and a merry frolic with a herd of elephants, Bagheera is more convinced than ever that the boy must join the humans. When Mowgli meets the fun-loving bear Baloo, the two become fast friends and plan to remain together in the wild. But an episode with the orangutan King Louie turns dangerous, and Baloo admits that Mowgli belongs in the Man-Village. Furious with Baloo, Mowgli runs away, only to face Shere Khan. With the help of Baloo and four vultures, Mowgli attaches a burning twig to Shere Khan's tail and he runs off in a panic. Baloo is wounded in the struggle but survives to bring the boy to the village. At the edge of the Man-Village, Mowgli is smitten with a young girl who gathers water from the river. He willingly follows her back to the village, and Baloo and Bagheera are content to know Mowgli is finally safe.

Rudyard Kipling's *The Jungle Book*, first published in Britain in 1894, had long been a favorite in the United States and there was a popular live-action movie version made in 1942. Studio writer Bill Peet suggested an animated version of the stories to Walt Disney, who was excited about the idea until he saw Peet's storyboards, which were dark and mysterious as in the book. Peet abandoned the project (and the studio) and Disney supervised a more comic and playful approach to the tales. The writers struggled in trying to turn several individual stories into a unified screenplay. The result was a plot that was motivated by the panther Bagheera's efforts to deliver the "man cub" Mowgli to the Indian village before the tiger Shere Khan can get to him. Mowgli is opposed to the idea, especially when he becomes

Voice Cast

Bruce Reitherman	Mowgli
Phil Harris	Baloo
Sebastian Cabot	Bagheera
George Sanders	Shere Khan
Sterling Holloway	Kaa
J. Pat O'Malley	Colonel Hathi
Louis Prima	King Louis
Clint Howard	Elephant Junior
Chad Stuart	Vulture
Lord Tim Hudson	Vulture
Digby Wolfe	Vulture
Leo DeLyon	Vulture

The orphan boy Mowgli has been told by the other animals in the jungle that he must go and live in the Man-Village, but he is having too much fun with the bear Baloo to leave. *Walt Disney Pictures / Photofest. © Walt Disney Pictures*

pals with the bear Baloo, so a conclusion with Mowgli attracted by a young Indian girl was devised. Many changes were made to Kipling's book, such as turning Kaa the snake from a friend to an enemy of Mowgli's and the invention of the orangutan King Louis. *The Jungle Book* has less plot than any other Disney feature, but it is filled with unforgettable characters. In fact, the simple narrative is interrupted several times for scenes in which these characters get to shine, often with song and dance.

Songs

"I Wanna Be Like You"
"Trust in Me"
"That's What Friends Are For (The Vulture Song)"
"My Own Home"
"Colonel Hathi's March"
"The Bare Necessities" (Gilkyson)

The background art in *The Jungle Book* is lush and painterly with wonderful uses of light and dark locations. The rich verdant forest moves from a happy place to a sinister one with a change of light. The character animation set against these backgrounds is endlessly creative and boasts some of the best animal movement in the Disney canon. Baloo and King Louie are perhaps the most physical, and Mowgli manages to keep up with them both. The animation for Kaa is smooth and intricate, whereas Shere Khan's animation is formal and statuesque. There is a particular kind of silliness in the movement of the elephants, a satire on military maneuvers. Finally, Bagheera's moves are lyrical and flowing. All of the animals have distinctive facial animation, filled with broad humor and some subtle nuances. The animators sometimes drew their inspiration from the voice actors, particularly in the case of George Sanders as Shere Khan, Phil Harris as Baloo, and Louis Prima as King Louie. *The Jungle Book* has a superior cast. Director Wolfgang Reitherman's son Bruce gives a bright and lively performance as Mowgli. Harris's raspy voice is ideal for Baloo, Sanders's voice drips with sneers as Shere Khan, Sterling Holloway lisps through his performance as Kaa, J. Pat O'Malley blusters gruffly as Colonel Hathi, and Sebastian Cabot as Bagheera narrates the tale with solid vocals that suggest authority. An amusing touch is having the four vultures sport Liverpool accents. With such vocal talents and with such fine animation, the characters make *The Jungle Book* soar without a gripping plot.

MOWGLI: Run? Why should I run?

SHERE KAHN: Why should you run? Is it possible that you don't know who I am?

MOWGLI: I know you alright. You're Shere Khan.

SHERE KAHN: Precisely. And you should know that everyone runs from Shere Khan.

MOWGLI: You don't scare me. I won't run from anyone.

SHERE KAHN: Ah, you have spirit for one so small. And such spirit is deserving of a sporting chance. Now, I'm going to close my eyes and count to ten. It makes the chase more interesting . . . for me. One . . .

Perhaps no other Disney animated film of the period placed as much emphasis on the songs as in this movie. Terry Gilkyson wrote several songs for *The Jungle Book* but Disney thought most of them too heavy and ponderous. Only "The Bare Necessities" was retained, and it turned out to be the musical highlight of the film. The jazzy number is far from appropriate for a tale set in the forests of India, but as a vaudevillian turn it is priceless. Disney brought in studio songwriters Richard M. and Robert B. Sherman to write the rest of the songs, and they are similarly non-Asian as well. Kaa's seductive "Trust in Me" has a touch of the exotic, but the rousing "I Wanna Be Like You" is Dixieland jazz at its best. Also enjoyable are the barbershop quartet "That's What Friends Are For" for the vultures and the brusque "Colonel Hathi's March" for the elephants. Only the haunting "My Own Home," sung by the Indian girl, has the flavor of the Indian locale. George Bruns used it effectively throughout his soundtrack score. In fact, any sense of the exotic jungle setting is heard more in Bruns's splendid music than in the songs.

Award

Academy Award nomination: Best Song ("The Bare Necessities").

Walt Disney died of lung cancer while *The Jungle Book* was nearing completion, so it is the last animated feature to have his mark on it. The studio was thrown into such uncertainty at the death of its founder and leader that there was talk of discontinuing the animation division and concentrating on the theme parks and live-action movies. Luckily, when *The Jungle Book* opened in 1967 it was very well received by the press and the public. Some critics carped over the film's many departures from the Kipling stories, but generally the reaction was enthusiastic. The studio spent $4 million on the movie, but it ended up earning four times that on its first release. Had *The Jungle Book* failed at the box office, the history of the studio might have been much different. The movie was rereleased in 1978, 1984, and 1990 before coming out on VHS in 1991. The DVD edition was released in 1999 and the Blu-ray in 2014.

Did You Know . . . ?

The four vultures were designed with the hope that the four Beatles would do the voices. The deal fell through, but the characters still sport Beatles haircuts and Liverpool accents.

K

KUBO AND THE TWO STRINGS

2016
(USA: Laika Entertainment)

Directed by Travis Knight
Written by Marc Haimes and Chris Butler
Produced by Arianne Sutner, Travis Knight, and Jocelyn Pascall
Score by Dario Marianelli
Specs: Color; 101 minutes; stop-motion animation

There are dozens of animated features about Japanese samurai and magical deeds, but Kubo and the Two Strings *is unique in that it is an American production with an original story. The subject may recall Asian anime cinema, but the film is clearly a Hollywood product.*

The Japanese village boy Kubo has magical powers and is able to create origami images when he plays his stringed shamisen. But he has only one eye because when he was a baby his evil grandfather, the Moon King, and his sinister aunts stole the other. Kubo's sickly mother, Sariatu, tells him stories of his warrior father, Honzo,

The Japanese youth Kubo sets out to find his late father's sword and armor in order to slay the evil Moon King, so the wooden Monkey comes to life and aids him in his quest. *Focus Features / Photofest. © Focus Features*

Voice Cast

Art Parkinson	Kubo
Charlize Theron	Sariatu/Monkey
Matthew McConaughey	Beetle/Hanzo
Ralph Fiennes	Moon King
Rooney Mara	The Sisters
Brenda Vaccaro	Kameyo
Cary-Hiroyuki Tagawa	Hashi
Meyrick Murphy	Mari
George Takei	Hosato

who was defeated by her sisters and the grandfather. When the sisters attack and kill Sariatu, Kubo saves a strand of her hair and sets out to find his father's sword, armor, and helmet in order to slay the Moon King. He is helped by the wooden Monkey that has come to life and by Beetle, a samurai who cannot remember his own past. The threesome encounter the Skeleton Demon, the sisters, and the Moon King himself. It is revealed that Monkey is the spirit of Kubo's mother and that Beetle is Honzo, although he did not know it. Kubo defeats the Moon King not through battle but by adding a strand of Honzo's hair to his shamisen and playing music that turns the Moon King into a mortal who cannot recall any of his evil past deeds.

Animator Shannon Tindle came up with the original story for *Kubo and the Two Strings*, written in the style of an ancient Japanese legend but not based on known mythology. Marc Haimes and Chris Butler wrote the screenplay based on the story, and Travis Knight made his directorial debut with the stop-motion movie. Because of the trick photography and many visual effects in the film, *Kubo and the Two Strings* does not always look like stop-motion, especially when characters like the Moon King and his mortal self have a hologram appearance. The way the sea and the sky are portrayed is also mindful of computer animation. Yet most of the characters are indeed 3-D figures and full of expression, in particular Kubo and Monkey. Despite some joking by Beetle and the sarcasm of Monkey, much of the film is very serious, solemn even. Yet the action scenes are thrilling and the two sisters are visually and vocally compelling and among the most sinister of villains to be seen in an animated feature.

BEETLE: Stealth is my middle name.

MONKEY: You don't even have a first name.

While the plotting of *Kubo and the Two Strings* is a bit confusing and the philosophy behind all the magic a bit convoluted, the movie is a visual feast of images. The origami creatures have a life to them that is dazzling and the human characters are rendered with energy and emotion. The decor is also superior, including the detailed Japanese village, the stark mountain home of Sariatu, the ship made out of leaves, and the gruesome caves and lairs of the demons. There are also scenes that seem to defy stop-motion animation and take on a life of their own, such as the dozens of floating lanterns to commemorate the dead. While the facial portrayal of Beetle and his smart-aleck vocals by Matthew McConaughey are disappointing, there is fine work by Charlize Theron doing the vocals for the dying Sariatu and the lively Monkey. Art Parkinson as the boy Kubo is feisty and confident. Ralph Fiennes does well with the snarling Moon King and with his gentle grandfather side, and Brenda Vaccaro turns the village widow Kameyo into a charming pixie of a character.

Awards

Academy Award nominations: Best Animated Feature and Best Visual Effects.
Golden Globe nomination: Best Picture—Animated.
British Academy of Film & Television Arts (BAFTA) Award: Best Animated Feature.

Dario Marianelli's soundtrack score is a lovely mixture of Asian sounds and Hollywood bombast. The mystical passages in the score are perhaps the most captivating, as when the ship of leaves is created and the lanterns are lit. Yet there is a particular quality to Kubo's string playing and the way it brings the origami creatures to life. George Harrison's song standard "While My Guitar Gently Weeps" is sung eerily during the end credits by Regina Spektor and it concludes the film with its own bittersweet note.

Critics and moviegoers familiar with such original Laika Entertainment works as *Coraline* (2009) and *The Boxtrolls* (2014) were surprised and mostly delighted with the new direction the animators took with *Kubo and the Two Strings* when it opened in 2016. Those movies were small, intimate, and quirky in different ways; the new film was on a grand scale, with an expansive spirit and a mythic flavor. The reviews were mostly raves and *Kubo and the Two Strings* did well domestically and internationally. The film cost $60 million, but within a year it had grossed over $73 million before the DVD and Blu-ray editions were released.

See also *Kung Fu Panda*.

Did You Know . . . ?

The Skeleton Demon model was sixteen-feet tall, the largest puppet yet created for a stop-motion film.

KUNG FU PANDA

2008
(USA: DreamWorks Animation)

Directed by Mark Osborne and John Stevenson
Written by Jonathan Aibel and Glenn Berger
Produced by Bill Damaschke, Melissa Cobb, Kristina Reed, Glenn Berger, and Jonathan Aibel
Score by John Powell and Hans Zimmer
Specs: Color; 92 minutes; computer and traditional animation

The clumsy panda Po is not ideal hero material, but, under the kung fu training of the red panda Master Shifu (left), Po is able to battle the evil snow leopard Tai Lung. *DreamWorks / Photofest.* © *DreamWorks*

A slick action comedy set in ancient China, the martial arts movie goes beyond a fast-paced adventure and has some engaging characters and stunning visuals.

In a Chinese valley populated by various animal citizens, the red panda Master Shifu trains the kung fu warriors Tigress, Crane, Mantis, Monkey, and Viper with the hope that one will become the Dragon Warrior who will protect the village from the demon snow leopard Tai Lung. The aged Grand Master, the tortoise Oogway, has a vision that Tai Lung will escape from prison and return to destroy the valley. Instead of making one of Shifu's five students the Dragon Warrior, Oogway selects the overweight panda Po when he accidentally crashes before the Jade Temple on the seat of some fireworks. Po idolizes the five pupils of Shifu, who look upon the panda with disdain. Shifu eventually believes Po can become a great kung fu warrior because Oogway believes it. When Oogway dies, Shifu trains Po into a unique kind of warrior with unconventional methods of fighting. As foretold, Tai Lung escapes from prison and returns to the valley to get revenge for being denied the title of Dragon Warrior. The five kung fu students try but fail to stop Tai Lung, but Po, using his weight and ingenuity, manages to conquer the demon and bring peace to the community.

Voice Cast

Jack Black	Po
Dustin Hoffman	Master Shifu
Lucy Liu	Viper
Jackie Chan	Monkey
Angelina Jolie	Tigress
Seth Rogen	Mantis
David Cross	Crane
Ian McShane	Tai Lung
Randall Duk Kim	Oogway
Dan Fogler	Zeng
James Hong	Mr. Ping
Michael Clarke Duncan	Commander Vachir

Kung Fu Panda started out as a spoof of martial arts movies, with different animals playing the Chinese characters. Yet as the project developed, it moved closer to an actual kung fu film with a modern sense of humor. The script retained the mystical aspect of the ancient Chinese art of fighting and even embraced some of the philosophy of that culture. Just as the look of the landscape was accurate to Chinese painting, the actual martial arts moves were authentic. Each of Shifu's five pupils represents a specific type of kung fu movement, while Po's actions are an oddball mixture of several forms. Characterization also went through changes, such as Po moving from a goofball jerk to a youth who dreams of becoming a kung fu warrior even though he is just a fat panda working in his father's noodle restaurant. Also firmly developed is the character of Master Shifu, who reveals different aspects of his personality as the story progresses. As in real martial arts films, there is plenty of action in *Kung Fu Panda* but there are also plenty of quiet and reflective moments as well. What started as a one-joke movie turned into a very intricate and engrossing adventure saga.

> PO: Maybe I should just quit and go back to making noodles.
>
> OOGWAY: Quit, don't quit. . . . Noodles, don't noodles. . . . You are too concerned about what was and what will be. There is a saying: yesterday is history, tomorrow is a mystery, but today is a gift. That is why it is called the present.

In many ways, *Kung Fu Panda* was the most complex and difficult animated movie yet attempted by DreamWorks. The film opens with traditional animation as Po dreams of being a famous warrior, the images mostly using the art of Chinese puppetry. The computer animation for the rest of the film requires intricate character movement as the various forms of martial arts are illustrated. As with live-action kung fu films, the action often shifts into slow motion for a few seconds to emphasize the poetic moves of the characters. The five kung fu pupils are particularly impressive, as the human martial arts moves are adapted to the different animal shapes. The facial animation throughout the movie is also impressive, as with the wizened tortoise Oogway and the fiery demon Tai Lung. Po himself is masterfully animated, his round face and body full of expression as it rolls and twists about. The special effects and tricky action scenes in *Kung Fu Panda* are often compelling. The scene in which the five warriors battle Tai Lung on a long rope bridge is as poetic as it is exciting. Similarly, the sequence inside the prison in which Tai Lung is kept is gripping filmmaking, with an almost surreal flavor. The background art in the movie is stylized, with beautiful vistas as seen in Asian watercolors and prints. The architectural details also invoke the fanciful Chinese look, particularly inside the Jade Temple. It seems like the artists created a serene and mystical world rather than the backdrop to an action movie. Just as *Kung Fu Panda* looks like a Chinese epic, it also sounds like one. The soundtrack score by Michael Powell and Hans Zimmer is a successful blend of Asian and Western sounds. Some Chinese instruments are used, but mostly it is the chords and repetition of Asian music that gives the movie such a glorious sound. Some action sequences are scored with traditional Hollywood action music, but much of the soundtrack has the temperament of the East, an homage to the Asian sound without trivializing it.

Awards

Academy Award nomination: Best Animated Feature.
Golden Globe nomination: Best Animated Film.

Comic actor Jack Black was cast as Po early in the development of *Kung Fu Panda* and his vocals shaped much of the movie. Po is sometimes anachronistic and full of jokes, yet there is a lot of heart in the character and Black is responsible for much of it. Dustin Hoffman gives a splendid performance as Shifu, his vocals ranging from frustrated sarcasm to sincere and deeply moving readings. Among the Asian actors who contributed effectively to the film are Randall Duk Kim as the wise old Oogway, Jackie Chan as the Monkey warrior, Lucy Liu as the viper, and James Hong as Po's simple but dedicated father, Mr. Ping. Ian McShane makes a rousingly evil Tai Lung, and Angelina Jolie purrs and sneers admirably as the Tigress warrior.

Kung Fu Panda previewed at the Cannes Film Festival in 2008 and later that year was given a wide release in the United States and in Great Britain. Most of the reviews were highly favorable, the critics taken by surprise when the title suggested a silly spoof. The movie was an immediate hit at the box office. Although it cost a hefty $130 million to make, it brought in more than half that during the opening weekend. When released in China, *Kung Fu Panda* broke the record as the most profitable animated film to come from Hollywood. International sales eventually topped $600 million. Within a year, the movie was available on DVD and Blu-ray. In 2011 DreamWorks released *Kung Fu Panda 2*, in which Po battled a new villain, a diabolical peacock named Lord Shen. Most of the characters and voice cast from the original were in the sequel. They also returned for *Kung Fu Panda 3* in 2016. In this installment, Po has to organize an army of pandas to defeat the spirit warrior Kai. Both sequels were given approving notices by the critics and were as financially successful as the original, making the Kung Fu franchise (including a video game and a television series) one of the most profitable in the new century.

See also *Kubo and the Two Strings*.

Did You Know . . . ?

To get the martial arts moves of the characters correct, the animators of the film took kung fu lessons.

L

LADY AND THE TRAMP

1955
(USA: Walt Disney Productions)

Directed by Clyde Geronimi, Wilfred Jackson, and Hamilton Luske
Written by Erdman Penner, Joe Rinaldi, Ralph Wright, and Don DaGradi, loosely
    based on the story "Happy Dan, the Whistling Dog" by Ward Greene
Produced by Walt Disney and Erdman Penner
Score by Oliver Wallace
Songs by Sonny Burke and Peggy Lee
Specs: Color (Technicolor); 76 minutes; traditional animation

Small-town America at the turn of the twentieth century is viewed from a canine point of view in this Disney favorite that was nostalgic in 1955 and is even more so today.

For Christmas of 1909, Jim Dear gives his wife, Darling, a cocker spaniel puppy that they name Lady. When she is full grown, the pampered but affectionate Lady feels on the outs when a new human baby in the household usurps her position as the family's only pet. When Jim and Darling go out of town, Aunt Sarah takes over the house and her two spoiled Siamese cats wreak havoc and make it look like Lady is the culprit. Sarah puts a muzzle on Lady, who escapes but soon finds the outside world is even less accepting. Only the wily street mutt Tramp helps her, getting rid of the muzzle and bringing her to dine in the alley behind Tony's restaurant. On the way home, Lady is picked up by the dog catcher and spends the night in the pound before being claimed by Sarah. Chained in her backyard, Lady sees a rat climb up the side of the house and into the baby's bedroom. Tramp comes on the scene, kills the rat, but then is taken away by the dogcatcher. Lady shows the returning Jim and Darling the dead rat and all go to rescue Tramp. By the next Christmas, Tramp and Lady have three puppies, two girls who look like Lady and a male who looks like Tramp.

Lady and the Tramp is unique in the Disney catalog in that it was not based on an existing book but was the creation of various Disney artists. Story director Joe Grant found that his canine pet Lady was quite put out when a baby was added to the household and he developed a storyboard about a cocker spaniel who feels she has

172

The street-smart mutt Tramp (left) and the domesticated cocker spaniel Lady partake of the most famous spaghetti dinner in the history of the movies. *Buena Vista Pictures / Photofest. © Buena Vista Pictures*

been cast aside for the new arrival. Walt Disney liked the idea, but after many plot ideas he realized that there was not enough of a story for a feature film. The project was put aside and, years later after Grant had left the studio, Disney read a short story in *Cosmopolitan* magazine titled "Happy Dan, the Whistling Dog." The hero was a cynical and street-smart dog who lived by his wits and Disney thought he would be a perfect foil for the pampered Lady. Various writers then contributed to what became *Lady and the Tramp*. (Ward Greene, the author of the magazine story,

Voice Cast

Barbara Luddy	Lady
Larry Roberts	Tramp
Bill Baucom	Trusty
Bill Thompson	Jock
Dal McKennon	Toughy
Peggy Lee	Peg
George Givot	Tony
Lee Millar	Jim dear
Peggy Lee	Darling
Verna Felton	Aunt Sarah
Peggy Lee	Si and Am
Stan Freberg	Beaver

Songs

"He's a Tramp"
"What Is a Baby?"
"La La Lu"
"Bella Notte (This Is the Night)"
"The Siamese Cat Song"
"Peace on Earth"

wrote a novelization of the film's plot and titled it *Lady and the Tramp.* It was published before the movie was released, but it was not the source for the film.)

The Disney artists decided to set the tale in a small American city soon after the turn of the twentieth century, which echoed Disney's hometown of Marceline, Missouri. The animators studied all kinds of dogs for their research, wanting to get their movements as natural as possible. The humans are seen only as the dogs see them, often limited to feet and tall figures. The sharp, truthful characterizations of the canine characters and the very human feelings of rejection and love that they possess keep the movie potent and enjoyable for each new generation that experiences it. The supporting characters are a colorful crew: the aging bloodhound Trusty, the wiry Scottish terrier Jock, the sassy, sexy canine Peg, and two stuck-up Siamese cats. The plotting in the film is solid, mixing humor and pathos. There are also some very disturbing scenes, such as the rat in the nursery and the image of a dog at the pound being led to be euthanized. *Lady and the Tramp* is also a very romantic movie, with one of the most memorable love scenes in all cinema: the spaghetti dinner outside Tony's Restaurant. Disney thought the idea of two canines devouring pasta was far from romantic, but animator Frank Thomas turned it into a funny and touching love scene. The background artists captured the late-Victorian houses and other buildings in the town, giving the movie a very nostalgic feeling for a time long gone. Halfway through production, the studio decided to release the film in the standard format as well as in the new wide-screen cinemascope process. This meant that the artists had to add more width to all the already completed background art.

The voice cast for *Lady and the Tramp* included some Disney regulars, but the new voice that was so impressive was that of popular singer Peggy Lee. She played the human Darling as well as the Siamese felines Si and Am and the saucy canine Peg.

LADY: What's a . . . baby?

JOCK: Well, they . . . they resemble humans.

TRUSTY: But I'd say a mite smaller.

JOCK: Aye, and they walk on all fours.

TRUSTY: And if I remember correctly . . . they beller a lot.

JOCK: Aye, and they're very expensive. You'll no be permitted to play wi' it.

TRUSTY: But they're mighty sweet.

JOCK: And very very soft.

TRAMP: Just a cute little bundle . . . of trouble!

Barbara Luddy's vocals for Lady are very soft and engaging, while Larry Roberts's Tramp is cocky and sarcastic. The other dogs are voiced with glee by expert character actors who used a variety of dialects as suggested by the nationality of the canines' names. Oliver Wallace wrote the evocative soundtrack score that often felt old-fashioned and quaint but was very dramatic for some of the action scenes. The songs by Lee and Sonny Burke are mostly true to the period. The lullaby "La La Lu," the inquisitive lament "What Is a Baby?," and the hymn-like "Peace on Earth" set the time frame. The Italianate ballad "Bella Notte" is the film's most famous song, a flowing number that oozes with romance. There is even a quasi-Oriental song for the Siamese cats, "The Siamese Cat Song," which is also accurate to the kind of exotic Asian songs popular in America early in the century.

Award

British Academy of Film & Television Arts (BAFTA) Award nomination: Best Animated Film.

When *Lady and the Tramp* was released in 1955, the critical reaction was supportive but not all reviews were enamored of the canine love story. The public, on the other hand, embraced the movie without hesitation, making it the most successful Disney feature since *Snow White and the Seven Dwarfs* (1937). Production costs were about $4 million, but on its first release *Lady and the Tramp* earned over $7 million just in the United States. The studio rereleased the film in 1962, 1972, 1980, and 1986. The next year the VHS version was on sale, followed by the DVD in 2006 and Blu-ray in 2012. A sequel, titled *Lady and the Tramp II: Scamp's Adventure*, was a made-for-video feature by the Disney studio.

See also *101 Dalmatians*.

Did You Know . . . ?

In the original version of the film, the old hound Trusty was killed when he was hit by the wagon. Walt Disney and others thought it too traumatic and had the animators add a bandaged Trusty to the final scene on Christmas morning.

THE LAND BEFORE TIME

1988
(USA/Ireland: Sullivan Bluth Studios/Universal)

Directed by Don Bluth
Written by Stu Krieger
Produced by Steven Spielberg, George Lucas, Kathleen Kennedy, Frank Marshall, Don Bluth, John Pomeroy, Gary Goldman, and Deborah Jelin Newmyer
Score by James Horner
Song "If We Hold on Together" by James Horner and Will Jennings
Specs: Color (Technicolor); 69 minutes; traditional animation

During their long journey to the Great Valley, the young dinosaur Little Foot (left) and his friend Cera run up against a myriad of obstacles from nature and other dinosaurs. *Lucasfilm Ltd/Universal Pictures / Photofest.* © *Lucas Film Ltd/Universal Pictures*

A simple but effective children's tale about young dinosaurs, The Land before Time *spawned a long series of popular made-for-video sequels.*

A drought has forced the dinosaurs to seek a place known as the Great Valley, where there is water and vegetation. A "Longneck" mother explains to her son, called Little Foot, that they must migrate with the others, but before they can start a "Sharptooth" attacks Little Foot and his female friend Cera, and the mother dies when she saves them. An earthquake creates a wide chasm that divides Little Foot and some other young dinosaurs from the adults, leaving the children to search

VOICE CAST

Gabriel Damon	Littlefoot
Judith Barsi	Ducky
Candy Hutson	Cera
Frank Welker	Spike
Will Ryan	Petrie
Bill Erwin	Grandfather
Helen Shaver	Littlefoot's Mother
Pat Hingle	Narrator

out the Great Valley on their own. Little Foot and Cera are joined by the swimming dinosaur Ducky and the flying dinosaur Petrie as they are guided by the voice of Little Foot's mother to find the Great Valley. Along the way they befriend the "Spiketail" Spike, escape from a tar pit, outwit a predatory Sharptooth, run from a couple of "Boneheads," and eventually reach the Great Valley, where they are reunited with surviving relatives.

Producers Steven Spielberg and George Lucas, who teamed up for the animated feature *An American Tail* (1986), wanted to make a dinosaur film without dialogue, letting the actions of the creatures tell the story. Afraid that such a movie would not appeal to children, they accepted the idea of talking dinosaurs who were also children so that the young audience could empathize with them. They hired Don Bluth, who had made *An American Tail*, to direct and recruited a team of animators who researched the many kinds of dinosaurs from which to create characters. All of the scientific names for the dinosaurs were replaced by kid-friendly, self-explanatory titles: long necks, sharptooths, boneheads, spike tails, and so on. The plot takes the form of a journey and allows for the young characters to overcome various obstacles along the way. Also, the child dinosaurs sound like human kids and quarrel and joke as kids do. It is far from an engrossing tale for adults, but as a children's story it works. The same could be said for the animation and the background art. Both are simple and uncomplicated. The drought-ridden land, the dark swamps, and the fertile Great Valley are all portrayed in primary colors and uncomplicated images. The most interesting piece of art is the way clouds suggest the form of dinosaurs when Little Foot remembers his mother. The movement of the young dinosaurs is often rambunctious and playful, while the adults are stately and slow. The vicious predators in the story are exaggerated and fierce, yet there is little bloodshed or graphic violence. In fact, the final print was severely edited when it was thought some scenes were too disturbing for children. *The Land before Time* aims directly at its young audience and often there is little to keep adult viewers interested. Yet children immediately connect to the film and it still entertains young audiences on home video.

LITTLEFOOT: Have you ever seen the Great Valley?

LITTLEFOOT'S MOTHER: No.

LITTLEFOOT: Well, how do you know it's really there?

LITTLEFOOT'S MOTHER Some things you see with your eyes, others you see with your heart.

LITTLEFOOT: I don't understand, Mother.

LITTLEFOOT'S MOTHER: You will, my son. You will.

The voice actors for *The Land before Time* included some screen veterans, such as Pat Hingle (Narrator and Rooter), Helen Shaver (Mother), and Bill Erwin (Grandfather), but most of the dialogue in the movie was handled by unknown child actors, who are expressive, lively, and far from subtle. The music soundtrack by James Horner is rich and stirring, especially when Britain's King's College Choir sings with the London Symphony Orchestra. One might argue that the score is too sophisticated and "adult sounding" for a children's movie, but it is glorious music and something most enjoyed by older audiences. Horner collaborated with Will Jennings on the ballad "If We Hold on Together," and it was sung by Diana Ross on the soundtrack; the recording was later a chart hit.

When the film was released in 1988, the critics treated it as a children's movie and most thought it was above average fare. The press thought it still lagged behind the Disney products (*Oliver & Company* was released on the same day) but the public was not so critical, and *The Land before Time* was a huge hit. Made for around $12 million, the movie ended up grossing over $84 million. Even more lucrative, the film inspired a 2007 television series and thirteen direct-to-video sequels and spinoffs between 1988 and 2016. Many of these movies were musicals with songs that appeared in a series of sing-along albums. With the video games and VHSs, DVDs, and Blu-ray editions, *The Land before Time* is one of Hollywood's most successful franchises.

See also *Dinosaur*.

Did You Know . . . ?

Over two dozen different kinds of dinosaurs are seen in the film. At least five of them were extinct before the time period of the movie.

THE LAST UNICORN

1982
(USA/UK/Japan/West Germany/France: Rankin/Bass Productions)

Directed by Jules Bass and Arthur Rankin Jr.
Written by Peter S. Beagle, based on his novel. Score and songs by Jimmy Webb
Produced by Martin Stager, Michael Chase Walker, Jules Bass, and Arthur Rankin Jr.
Specs: Color; 92 minutes; traditional animation

The clever and successful team of Rankin and Bass, who had made many animated television specials, turned to the big screen for this fanciful fable that blended magic, adventure, and song into a pleasing feature film.

A unicorn living in an enchanted region where it is always spring learns from a butterfly that she is the last surviving unicorn in the world because a Red Bull has chased all the others into the kingdom of King Haggard. The unicorn sets out to find the Red Bull and any surviving fellow unicorns. She is captured by the sorceress Mommy Fortuna and put in her Midnight Carnival filled with mythical beasts. With the help of the bumbling wizard Schmendrick she escapes, and he accompanies the unicorn on her quest. Also joining them is the cook Molly Grue, who is impressed with Schmendrick's magical powers. When the threesome arrive at the

Told that she is the last unicorn left, the heroine cannot believe it, so she travels to the Kingdom of King Haggard to find the other unicorns captured by the Red Bull. *Incorporated Television Company (ITC) / Photofest. © Incorporated Television Company (ITC)*

kingdom of Haggard, the Red Bull appears and tries to capture the unicorn, but Schmendrick turns her into a human and the bull runs away. Schmendrick gets a job as Haggard's magician and jester, and the unicorn, now a beautiful young woman named Amalthea, falls in love with the king's son, Prince Lir. She learns from Haggard that all the unicorns the Red Bull has collected are now creatures of the sea, and, guessing her true identity, he threatens to imprison her as well. Molly finds the location of the Red Bull, and Amalthea, Prince Lir, and Schmendrick join Molly and face the creature. The wizard changes Amalthea back into a unicorn, and the Red Bull tries to drive her into the sea. Prince Lir battles the bull but is killed, and it is the unicorn that drives the Red Bull into the sea and frees all the other unicorns. Using her magical unicorn powers, she restores Prince Lir to life and then joins the other unicorns in their journey back to the enchanted forest.

Voice Cast

Mia Farrow	Unicorn/Amalthea
Alan Arkin	Schmendrick
Tammy Grimes	Molly Grue
Jeff Bridges	Prince Lir
Christopher Lee	King Haggard
Robert Klein	Butterfly
Angela Lansbury	Mommy Fortuna
Keenan Wynn	Captain Cully/Harpy
Paul Frees	Mabruk
René Auberjonois	Skull

Peter S. Beagle's 1968 fantasy novel *The Last Unicorn* had interested several movie studios, so it was surprising when the television producers Jules Bass and Arthur Rankin Jr. gained the rights to turn the tale into an animated film. Beagle wrote the screenplay, so the movie is very faithful to the book, much of the dialogue coming from the printed page. Rankin and Bass hired the Japanese studio Topcraft to do the animation, so the film often resembles an anime product. But the cast of American voice actors gives *The Last Unicorn* a very Western sound and an American sense of humor. The background art is exceptional, full of color, twinkling accents, and stylized nature. No attempt at reality was made, and often the settings resemble a colorful Asian print. The character animation is uneven. The movement of the animals and nonhuman creatures is very accomplished, but the animation of the humans is simple to the point of being primitive. Body movements are impressive but facial animation is often crude. American songwriter Jimmy Webb wrote the score and the songs heard on the soundtrack. The soundtrack is filled with diverse musical passages, but the songs tend to be in the urban folk mode, most of them sung on the soundtrack by the group America. The soundtrack for *The Last Unicorn* was later quite popular in Great Britain and Germany.

Songs

"The Last Unicorn"
"Man's Road"
"Now That I Am a Woman"
"That's All I've Got to Say"
"In the Sea"

The star-studded voice cast for the movie contributed greatly to the success of *The Last Unicorn*. Mia Farrow's unicorn is vocally naive and sincere, while there is a sly sense of satire in Alan Arkin's Schmendrick. Christopher Lee brings a weighty villainy to the voice of King Haggard, but his son, Prince Lir, is played with casual charm by Jeff Bridges. Tammy Grimes provides vocal energy as the cook Molly, her distinctive voice working well with the comedy and the pathos. First-rate actors were hired for even the secondary characters and all gave splendid performances, including Angela Lansbury's cackling Mommy Fortuna, Robert Klein's daffy Butterfly, René Auberjonois's jocular Skull, and Paul Frees as the loony magician Mabruk. Farrow and Bridges did their own singing in the film and are far from polished but still effective.

The Last Unicorn was given a limited released in 1982 and managed to earn over $2.5 million in its first weekend. Helped by approving reviews, the movie

SCHMENDRICK: The magic chose the shape, not I. I am a bearer, I am a dwelling, I am a messenger . . .

MOLLY: You are an idiot!

eventually grossed over $6 million. The VHS edition was released in 1983 and sold well, but the 2004 DVD edition was made from an inferior print and did not do the film justice. It was restored and reissued on DVD in 2007, followed by the Blu-ray edition in 2011.

See also *Wizards*.

Did You Know . . . ?

Actor Christopher Lee loved the original novel so much that he brought a copy to his recording sessions and insisted that certain lines of King Haggard be included in the film.

THE LEGO MOVIE

2014
(Australia/USA/Denmark: Warner Brothers)

Directed and written by Phil Lord and Christopher Miller
Produced by Kathleen Fleming, Allison Abbate, Benjamin Melniker, etc.
Score by Mark Mothersbaugh
Song "Everything Is Awesome" by Shawn Patterson and song standards by various artists
Specs: Color (ACES); 100 minutes; computer and stop-motion animation with some live-action sequences

---

A frenetic, action-packed feature, The Lego Movie *is unique in that its visuals are limited to images than can be created using the internationally popular toys known as Legos.*

A world of Lego figures is ruled by Lord Business, who has a secret weapon: the Kragle, which is actually Krazy Glue that can "freeze" people into one position forever. An underground movement led by the wizard Vitrivius knows there exists a Piece of Resistance that can stop the Kragle and Lord Business. The Piece is found by the ordinary construction worker Emmet Brickowski, who is told he is "special" and can bring about the downfall of Lord Business. With the help of Vitruvius, the pretty rebel Wyldestyle, and the pirate Metal Beard, Emmit goes through a series of dangerous confrontations with Lord Business and his henchman Bad Cop/Good Cop. It turns out that this Lego world is the work of the human Man Upstairs and the undoing of Lord Business is encouraged by the Man's son Finn as they play with the Legos in their basement.

Making an adventure film using Lego bricks for characters, settings, and even special effects was costly (around $100 million) and required financing from Warner Brothers, Australia (where production took place), and Denmark (where the corporate offices for Legos are located). The decision to not use actual Legos in a stop-motion film but to computer animate the movie so that it looked like

In a world in which everything is made of Lego pieces, the construction worker Emmet Brickowski (center) finds himself in the middle of revolution and danger. *Warner Bros. / Photofest.* © *Warner Bros.*

stop-motion was intriguing but problematic. The animators even went so far as to create cracks, chips, and fingerprints on the computerized Legos. When special effects were called for, such as smoke, waves, lasers, and explosions, they were rendered with pieces of Legos giving the movie a very distinctive look. The script followed the pattern of many sci-fi adventures, but the dialogue is more sarcastic and there are in-jokes about the plastic world of Legos. Also, characters from comic books, *Star Wars*, and *The Lord of the Rings* films made appearances in *The*

Voice Cast

Chris Pratt	Emmet Brickowski
Will Ferrell	Lord Business
Elizabeth Banks	Wyldstyle
Liam Neeson	Bad Cop/Good Cop
Morgan Freeman	Vitruvius
Will Arnett	Batman
Alison Brie	Unikitty
Graham Miller	Duplo
Nick Offerman	Metal Beard

Live-Action Cast

Will Ferrell	The Man Upstairs
Jadon Sand	Finn

Lego Movie, always in a satirical mode. The live-action sequence at the end of the film reduced all the Legos to toys once again, and the soppy message of universal brotherhood was laid on very thick. But much of *The Lego Movie* moves along at such a frantic pace and the effects and words come so fast that there is barely time to enjoy all the dazzling visuals the film offers.

> EMMET: Uh, guys? We're about to crash into the sun.
>
> BATMAN: Yeah, but it's gonna look really cool.

The American and British voice cast for *The Lego Movie* came from a wide variety of media. Film actor Chris Pratt plays the everyman Emmet in a silly optimistic manner in which he accepts the Lego world without question until he is convinced he is someone special. Morgan Freeman brings a playful solemnity to the mystic Vitruvius, Liam Neeson is very funny as the bipolar Bad Cop/Good Cop, and Will Ferrell is gleefully evil as Lord Business. Canadian comic Will Arnett voices the pompous Batman and TV favorite Nick Offerman is blustering as the kookie pirate Metal Beard. Composer Mark Mothersbaugh came up with a high-speed score that added to the film's fast-paced tempo. Even the movie's one song, the catchy and satiric "Everything Is Awesome" by Shawn Patterson, moves as quickly along as the Lego characters and machines. While *The Lego Movie* strikes some as a blast of animation energy, others might find it rather exhausting.

Awards

Academy Award nomination: Best Song ("Everything Is Awesome").
Golden Globe nomination: Best Animated Feature.
British Academy of Film & Television Arts (BAFTA) awards: Best Animated Feature and Children's Award: Best Feature Film.

The Lego Movie received mostly rave notices from the critics and big box office from the public. The film earned over $250 million in North America and another $200 million overseas. The merchandizing connected to the movie was also considerable: action figures, Lego kits recreating scenes from the film, and video games were all very successful. *The Lego Movie* was on sale on DVD and Blu-ray three months after its initial release and sold very well. The spin-off film *The Lego Batman Movie* was released in 2017 and sequels to *The Lego Movie* are planned for 2018 and 2019.

See also *The Incredibles*.

Did You Know . . . ?

Except for a handful of specially designed hair and helmet pieces for some characters, all of the Lego pieces seen in the movie actually exist and can be purchased in Lego kits.

LILO & STITCH

2002
(USA: Walt Disney Pictures)

Directed and written by Dean DeBlois and Chris Sanders
Produced by Lisa M. Poole and Clark Spencer
Score by Alan Silvestri
Song "He Mele No Lilo" by Alan Silvestri and Mark Keali'i Ho'omalu
Specs: Color (Technicolor); 85 minutes; traditional animation

A mix of science fiction fantasy and very real domestic life, Lilo & Stitch *is unusual for its setting, the bond between two sisters, and a very odd little creature from out of this world.*

In outer space, the scientist Dr. Jumba Jookba has accidentally created an uncontrollable creature known as Experiment 626. The Galactic Federation orders the chaotic critter exiled to a distant asteroid, but 626 manages to take over the spaceship and heads to Earth, where he crashes on the Hawaiian island of Kaua'i. Injured by a passing truck, 626 is brought to an animal shelter where he passes himself off as a dog and is adopted by the little orphan girl Lilo. She names him Stitch and tries to train him like a dog, but 626 is too crazy and destructive to be domesticated. Jumba and the agent Pleakley arrive in Hawaii and try to capture Stitch and take him away from Earth, but the critter is too smart for them. He also causes so much mischief on the beach that Lilo is taken from the custody of her older sister Nani and scheduled to be put in a foster home. Captain Gantu from the Federation arrives on Earth to capture Stitch, but before the spaceship can take off Stitch explains that he has found a family with Lilo and Nani and has become civilized. Gantu allows Stitch to remain on Earth, Lilo is allowed to stay with Nani, and they all become a family.

The frenetic space alien creature Stitch (left) learns from the Hawaiian girl Lilo all about the planet Earth, including the music of Elvis Presley. *Walt Disney Pictures / Photofest.* © *Walt Disney Pictures*

Voice Cast

Daveigh Chase	Lilo
Chris Sanders	Stitch
Tia Carrere	Nani
David Ogden Stiers	Jumba
Kevin McDonald	Pleakley
Ving Rhames	Cobra Bubbles
Zoe Caldwell	Grand Councilwoman
Jason Scott Lee	David Kawena
Kevin Michael Richardson	Captain Gantu
Amy Hill	Mrs. Hasagawa

Artist Chris Sanders created the critter Stitch in 1985 as the central character in a children's book. No publisher was interested in the creature or the book. Fifteen years later, Sanders was working for Disney and proposed an animated film based on his idea of the mischievous intergalactic Stitch. Working with Dean DeBlois, Sanders went through many possible scenarios. At one point Stitch was a gangster who gets left on Earth after a heist. Eventually the character of Stitch was made more troublesome than dangerous and the action was set in present-day Hawaii. The plot was unique in that there is no central love story. Instead, the strong relationship between the little girl Lilo and her older sister Nani was emphasized. The studio decided that *Lilo & Stitch* would be a small, low-budget film like *Dumbo* (1941), which was made inexpensively during hard times and ended up earning a lot of money for the studio. Sanders and DeBlois liked the simple and colorful look of *Dumbo* and made efforts to reproduce the same quality as that earlier classic. The background art, for example, was done with watercolor sketches rather than detailed computerized or hand-painted renderings. The characters, both human and alien, were designed by Sanders to be two-dimensional cartoon images with uncomplicated facial movements. Stitch was particularly unusual because, in an effort to make him unlike an animal, he has no pupils in his eyes. The animators compensated by making Stitch very physical and expressive in other ways. The spaceships in the movie are playfully fantastical, resembling marine creatures rather than mechanical vehicles. Yet as fantastical as *Lilo & Stitch* is, the artists were very diligent in rendering the island of Kaua'i accurately. Even the hula dancing in the movie is authentic.

LILO: David! I got a new dog!

DAVID: Auwe . . . You sure it's a dog?

LILO: Uh huh . . . He used to be a collie before he got ran over.

Casting *Lilo & Stitch* centered on finding authentic Hawaiian voices for the humans and bizarre and unworldly vocals for the intergalactic characters. Tia Carrere, who voiced Nani, and Jason Scott Lee, who did the vocals for her boyfriend David Kawena, were natives of Hawaii and not only gave authentic readings but contributed changes in the dialogue to make it more accurate. The eleven-year-old actress Daveigh Chase gives a funny and sincere performance as Lilo, while character actors David Ogden Stiers, Ving Rhames, and Kevin Michael Richardson let loose with jocular interpretations for the aliens. Renowned stage actress Zoe Caldwell is particularly effective as the Grand Councilwoman. The most difficult voice task was Stitch but Sanders had been working on the character for years and came up with a sparkling vocal that merged animal and alien sounds. Alan Silvestri's soundtrack score for *Lilo & Stitch* is not particularly Hawaiian, as it transitions from lyrical passages to action music with plenty of percussion.

The authentic sound of the Hawaiian Islands is captured in the song "He Mele No Lilo" (lyric by Mark Keali'i Ho'omalu), a rousing rhythmic chant sung on the soundtrack by Ho'omalu and the Kamehameha Schools Children's Chorus. Silvestri and Ho'omalu also wrote the song "Hawaiian Roller Coaster Ride," a vigorous piece that sweeps along in a carefree and joyous manner.

Award

Academy Award nomination: Best Animated Feature.

The costs for *Lilo & Stitch* were not as low as the studio had hoped. The final price tag for the film was $80 million, but it made more than half of that during the first weekend of its release. The international income for the movie was over $273 million. The reviews were mostly positive, though some critics found the character of Stitch less than endearing. The public disagreed and the intergalactic little fellow soon became a kids' favorite. The franchise built around *Lilo & Stitch* was very successful, including toys and stuffed animals, several video games, and three television cartoon series: *Lilo & Stitch: The Series* (2003), *Stitch!* (2008), and *Stitch and Ai* (2017). There have also been two direct-to-video movie sequels, *Stitch! The Movie* (2003) and *Lilo & Stitch 2: Stitch Has a Glitch* (2005).

Did You Know . . . ?

In early drafts of the story, the alien Stitch landed in Kansas. It was in later versions that the setting was changed to Hawaii.

THE LION KING

1994
(USA: Walt Disney Pictures)

Directed by Roger Allers and Rob Minkoff
Written by Irene Mecchi, Jonathan Roberts, and Linda Woolverton
Produced by Thomas Shumacher, Sarah McArthur, Don Hahn, and Alice Dewey
Score by Hans Zimmer
Songs by Elton John (music) and Tim Rice (lyrics)
Specs: Color (Technicolor); 89 minutes; traditional and computer animation

The young lion cub Simba (right) is in line to be the next Lion King but his uncle, the conniving Scar (left), has regal ambitions of his own. *Walt Disney Pictures / Photofest.* © *Walt Disney Pictures*

One of the biggest "sleepers" in the history of Disney animation, The Lion King *was a surprise hit that broke box office records and illustrated the creative power of the studio during the Disney renaissance.*

The lion patriarch King Mufasa rules from Pride Rock over all the animals on the African savanna, and the birth of his son Simba is celebrated by all the creatures. Young Simba grows to be a playful but impatient cub who eagerly looks forward to being the lion king someday. During a stampede of wildebeests, Mufasa is pushed into the path of the herd and is trampled to death. Simba is convinced

Voice Cast

James Earl Jones	Mufasa
Jonathan Taylor Thomas	Simba (young—speaking)
Jason Weaver	Simba (young—singing)
Matthew Broderick	Simba (adult)
Robert Guillaume	Rafiki
Jeremy Irons	Scar (speaking)
Jim Cummings	Scar (singing)
Nathan Lane	Timon
Ernie Sabella	Pumbaa
Niketa Calame	Nala (young)
Moira Kelly	Nala (adult)
Rowan Atkinson	Zazu
Whoopi Goldberg	Shenzi
Cheech Marin	Banzai
Jim Cummings	Ed
Madge Sinclair	Sarabi

by his evil uncle Scar that the cub was responsible for the death of his father, when it was Scar himself who murdered his brother in order to take over the pride. Simba runs away and grows up under the "no worries" philosophy of the meerkat Timon and the warthog Pumbaa. Scar proves to be a neurotic, ineffective king, and his allies the hyenas are starting to turn against him. Simba is encouraged by the wise old baboon Rafiki to return home and avenge his father's death, and in the battle that follows, the truth of who really murdered Mufasa is revealed. Scar is destroyed, Simba mates with his childhood sweetheart, and the animals once again come to pay homage when the couple presents their newborn cub to the pride.

Most Disney animated films are based on a preexisting book or fairy tale so it is surprising that one of the studio's most successful animated features had an original story. The screenplay by Irene Mecchi, Jonathan Reynolds, and Linda Woolverton may have borrowed generously from *Hamlet* and the studio's own *Bambi* (1942) but the story and characters were solid and engaging and lent themselves to an often serious musical film. No animated film had taken on so many heavy issues, met them head on, and succeeded like *The Lion King*. The stampede in which Mufasa died was as powerful as any live-action adventure, yet the comedy of Timon and Pumbaa had the heart and soul of vaudeville. Directors Roger Allers and Rob Minkoff captured not only the look and feel of the African savanna but also the kinship of community that drives the plot. The depiction of the many different kinds of animals that are connected to the pride is both lyrical and stunning, like a ballet of nature enfolding before our eyes. The background art and animation are equally as evocative. The animals are not given human clothes and postures but they are indeed human when it comes to the empathy the audience has for them. Each major character has a distinctive look and sound and several of the animals have joined the ranks of the most memorable Disney characters: the regal and dignified King Mufasa, the conniving Scar, the wise but silly mandrill Rafiki, the wisecracking Timon, the dense Pumbaa, and the harried hornbill Zazu. Simba, the central character, grows from an anxious child to a responsible adult right before our eyes. *The Lion King*'s portrayal of an animal culture viewed through human sympathies is what makes the film so compelling.

Ironically, the Disney studio at the time put most of its resources and top animators on *Pocahontas* (1995) and considered *The Lion King* of secondary importance. So it is somewhat surprising that *The Lion King* is so outstanding in its artistry. The African savanna is depicted as a warm nurturing place, a lyrical land, and

Songs

"Circle of Life"
"Be Prepared"
"I Just Can't Wait to Be King"
"Can You Feel the Love Tonight"
"Hakuna Matata"

sometimes a cruel place of survival. These many moods are rendered beautifully on screen. The background artists and animators traveled to Kenya for research, observing the land and the animals so that the movie was accurate. Then they brought both scenery and animals to life using the magic of animation. Of the many notable scenes in *The Lion King*, two sequences stand out regarding the blend of art and movement: the stunning opening scene, in which the animals on the savanna gather to pay homage to the baby Simba, and the stampede by the wildebeests. The later sequence used the computer to duplicate the hundreds of stampeding animals yet it looks hand-drawn and far from mechanical. When the story moves into the jungle, where Simba meets Timon and Pumbaa, a very different world is presented. Lush and green with colorful flora, this background is the setting for the movie's comic turns as well as the romantic scenes. Another vivid setting is the elephant graveyard, which is creepy yet fascinating. One can understand why the young Simba is so drawn to it. Not since *Bambi* had the studio made an animated film in which there was so much focus on nature.

YOUNG SIMBA: Hey, Uncle Scar, guess what?

SCAR: I despise guessing games.

YOUNG SIMBA: I'm gonna be King of Pride Rock.

SCAR: Oh, goody.

YOUNG SIMBA: My dad just showed me the whole kingdom. And I'm gonna rule it all. He-heh.

SCAR: Yes. Well, forgive me for not leaping for joy. Bad back, you know.

YOUNG SIMBA: Hey Uncle Scar, when I'm King, what'll that make you?

SCAR: A monkey's uncle.

YOUNG SIMBA: (laughs) You're so weird.

SCAR: You have no idea.

The voice talents recruited for the movie came from the theater, television, and live-action films. The renowned, deep-voiced actor James Earl Jones was the studio's choice for Mufasa from the beginning, and his sense of dignity in his performance solidified the majesty of the role. British actor Jeremy Irons's sly Scar is very funny yet never loses its deadly sting. Robert Guillaume is quixotic as Rafiki, alternately playing both the fool and the wise man. Nathan Lane and Ernie Sabella, who had performed on Broadway together, brought their precise comic timing to the roles of Timon and Pumbaa. Oddball British comic Rowan Atkinson is ideal as the frustrated Zazu, and the three principal hyenas were voiced with panache by Jim Cummings, Cheech Marin, and Whoopie Goldberg. The hero Simba was portrayed by TV child actor Jonathan Taylor Thomas as a youth and stage-screen star Matthew Broderick as an adult, both turning in proficient performances.

Elton John (music) and Tim Rice (lyrics) wrote a pop score that sometimes bordered on the fervent, especially in the opening number "The Circle of Life," which combined music, animation, and ritual in a way rarely seen on the screen before. The other songs are Timon and Pumbaa's freewheeling "Hakuna Matata," Scar's Fascist creed "Be Prepared," young Simba's ambitious "I Just Can't Wait to Be King," and the Oscar-winning ballad "Can You Feel the Love Tonight" used behind the romantic scenes between adult Simba and Nala. The superb musical background score by Hans Zimmer gave the movie an authentic-sounding African rhythm not found in the songs, particularly the choral sections arranged and conducted by African maestro Lebo M. Since most of the singers were Broadway veterans, there was a polished showbiz quality to the singing. This was in contrast to the tribal chanting on the soundtrack. Never before had moviegoers been so enthralled by the musical sounds of Africa. The soundtrack recording was very popular and some of the songs quickly entered the league of Disney's most recognized tunes.

Awards

Academy Awards: Best Song ("Can You Feel the Love Tonight") and Best Score. Oscar nominations: Best Song ("Hakuna Matata" and "Circle of Life").
Golden Globe Awards: Best Picture—Comedy or Musical, Best Score, and Best Song ("Can You Feel the Love Tonight").
British Academy of Film & Television Arts (BAFTA) Interactive Award. BAFTA nominations: Best Score and Best Sound.

The Lion King was released in 1994 and eventually broke all box office records, grossing over $960 million internationally. The VHS version released in 1995 and the DVD in 2003 went on to become the biggest-selling home videos of all time. Equally impressive was the round of laudatory reviews that the movie received from the press. *The Lion King* was instantly recognized as a classic and remains among the artistic high points in the Disney canon. The direct-to-video sequels *The Lion King II: Simba's Pride* (1998) and *The Lion King 1 1/2* (2004) were very popular, and the 1997 Broadway version has become one of the longest-running and most successful musicals in New York, London, and on tour.

See also *Bambi*.

Did You Know . . . ?

The love scene in which "Can You Feel the Love Tonight" is sung was cut from the film just before it was released. Composer Elton John convinced the studio to reinstate it. The song went on to win the Oscar.

> # THE LITTLE MERMAID
>
> 1989
> (USA: Walt Disney Pictures)
>
> Produced by Howard Ashman, Maureen Donley, and John Musker
> Directed and written by Ron Clements and John Musker, based on the story by Hans Christian Andersen
> Score by Alan Menken
> Songs by Alan Menken (music) and Howard Ashman (lyrics)
> Specs: Color (Technicolor); 83 minutes; traditional animation

The movie that began the Disney renaissance in animated musicals in the 1990s, The Little Mermaid *offers a classic story, superb animation, vibrant characters, and a Broadway-like score full of memorable songs.*

The mermaid Ariel is not happy in her underwater world, even though she is the daughter of King Triton. She has often swum to the surface and observed humans, even collecting the objects from their world that have sunk into the sea. Despite the arguments of the crab Sebastian that life under the sea is the best of all exis-

The evil sea witch Ursula (right) promises the mermaid princess Ariel to turn her into a human, but there is an awful price to be paid. *Buena Vista Pictures / Photofest.* © *Buena Vista Pictures*

Voice Cast

Jodi Benson	Ariel
Pat Carroll	Ursula
Samuel E. Wright	Sebastian
Christopher Daniel Barnes	Eric
Buddy Hackett	Scuttle
Jason Marin	Flounder
Kenneth Mars	King Triton
René Auberjonois	Louis
Paddi Edwards	Flotsam and Jetsam
Ben Wright	Grimsby

tences, Ariel yearns to be human, especially when she sees and falls in love with Prince Eric. After a fight with her father, Ariel makes a pact with the sea witch Ursula to exchange her beautiful voice for human legs. The deal involves Ariel getting Eric to kiss her or else she becomes the slave of the witch. Ursula tricks Ariel by appearing as a beautiful woman with Ariel's voice, but the plot is uncovered just in time. Eric slays the sea witch, and Ariel becomes a mermaid again. Triton, seeing how much Ariel loves Eric, uses his powers to make her human once again, and she is reunited with Eric.

The idea of turning Hans Christian Andersen's story into an animated feature goes back to the late 1930s when Walt Disney was considering projects to follow *Snow White and the Seven Dwarfs* (1937). The dark tale was considered and then shelved many times until 1985 when directors Ron Clements and John Musker resuscitated the project and studied some of the studio's earlier drafts of the story. Writer-lyricist Howard Ashman joined the team and was responsible for several changes, such as turning the very-British crab Clarence into the Jamaican singer Sebastian. Ashman brought his theater collaborator, composer Alan Menken, into the project and the songs the two men wrote also changed the tone of the movie. The final script stays close to Andersen's 1837 fairy tale until the ending. In the original story, the prince is forced to marry another princess and Ariel can only save herself by killing the prince and letting his blood drip onto her feet. But Ariel still loves the prince so she returns to the sea, where she is turned into foam and vanishes. In Andersen's version, Ariel's confidant is her grandmother, who counsels her and warns her about the sea witch. As the Disney studio had done so well in the past, the writers created an array of colorful new characters, such as Ariel's fearful pal Flounder, the cockeyed seagull Scuttle, and the disapproving music-master crab Sebastian. Also a tradition, the villainess had her henchmen, two slithering, demonic eels named Flotsam and Jetsam. *The Little Mermaid* may have been a Disney-fied version of the Danish original, but it was superior filmmaking in all aspects.

Songwriters Menken and Ashman had found some success in the theater, mostly with *Little Shop of Horrors* (1982), and were invited to the Disney studio when Walt's nephew Roy Disney wanted to build up the animation department. The splendid score Menken and Ashman wrote for *The Little Mermaid* reminded

Songs

"Part of Your World"
"Under the Sea"
"Poor Unfortunate Souls"
"Kiss the Girl"
"Les Poissons"
"Fathoms Below"
"The Daughters of Triton"
"Vanessa's Song"

audiences of what a top-notch Broadway score used to sound like. Not only were the musical numbers tuneful and imaginative, they were also marvelous character pieces that moved the story along effectively. Ariel's wistful "Part of Your World," the Oscar-winning calypso number "Under the Sea," the bombastic aria "Poor Unfortunate Souls," and the romantic Caribbean-flavored "Kiss the Girl" were more than musical diversions; they were the heart of the movie. Menken's soundtrack score was equally enthralling, with sea chanty tunes, Caribbean calypso music, and an eerie suspense theme for the sea-witch Ursula. *The Little Mermaid* launched the incredibly successful collaboration of Menken and Disney.

> URSULA: Well, angelfish, the solution to your problem is simple. The only way to get what you want is to become a human yourself.
>
> ARIEL: Can you do that?
>
> URSULA: My dear, sweet child. That's what I do. It's what I live for, to help unfortunate merfolk, like yourself, poor souls with no one else to turn to.

The studio spent more money on the film than they had on any other since the 1960s. The animation was so complex that the work was farmed out to studios in Glendale, California, and Orlando, Florida. Because it was the last animated movie to use hand-painted cels and the story required over a million cels, work was also sent to a studio in Bejing, China. In fact, when the Tiananmen Square protests broke out in China, thousands of completed cells were trapped in a vault before peace was restored and the cels could be shipped to the United States. The resulting animation makes *The Little Mermaid* one of the most visually dazzling of all Disney films. The background art is colorful and fairy tale–like and the animation is buoyant and playful. Since much of the story takes place underwater, the artists strove to create bubbles, light seen through water, and other underwater effects with meticulous detail. The character animation is equally impressive. The way Ariel moves through the water is as poetic as it is fascinating. The movement of Ursula is just as compelling, though in a slick and uncomfortable way. Her two eel-henchmen are masterfully animated as well, sliding through the water and around objects and other characters in a menacing way. Sebastian is not limited in his movements because he is a crab; instead, he is very physical and versatile.

The vocals by Samuel E. Wright are superb, turning the frustrated little crab into a favorite Disney character. Theater singer Jodi Benson does the speaking and singing voice of Ariel and brings a new level of empathy to a Disney princess. Prince Eric, voiced by Christopher Daniel Barnes, is perhaps the first Disney prince with an engaging character and not merely a romantic figure. Pat Carroll, a theater veteran, created a delightful villainess in Ursula, alternating between a purring seductress and a violent thunderbolt. Carroll's rendition of "Poor Unfortunate Souls" is arguably the best musicalization of a Disney villain.

Awards

Academy Awards: Best Song ("Under the Sea") and Best Score. Oscar nominations: Best Song ("Kiss the Girl").

Golden Globe Awards: Best Song ("Under the Sea") and Best Score. Golden Globe nominations: Best Motion Picture—Comedy or Musical and Best Song ("Kiss the Girl").

The Little Mermaid opened in 1989 to the best reviews that the studio had received in years. Praise for the storytelling, the animation, and the songs was nearly unanimous and the movie was a box office hit from the start. The expensive film, costing around $40 million, was the first animated movie to earn over $100 million. The VHS version in 1990 and the 1997 rerelease in theaters helped *The Little Mermaid* double that amount. It was by far the most successful animated movie yet made. The DVD version in 1999 and the Blu-ray edition in 2013 continued the film's success story. *The Little Mermaid* opened the door for an exciting decade of musical animation from the Disney studio. The movie was popular enough to inspire a cartoon series on television, some made-for-video sequels, and a Broadway show in 2007. Yet the original is now considered a Disney classic and joins the ranks of the most beloved products to ever come out of the studio.

See also *Moana*.

Did You Know . . . ?

The animators gave Ariel red hair because they did not want there to be comparisons made with the mermaid that blonde Daryl Hannah played in the popular live-action comedy *Splash* (1984).

M

MADAGASCAR

2005
(USA: DreamWorks Animation)

Directed by Eric Darnell and Tom McGrath
Written by Mark Burton, Billy Frolick, Eric Darnell, and Tom McGrath
Produced by Teresa Cheng and Mireille Soria
Score by Hans Zimmer
Song standards by various artists
Specs: Color; 86 minutes; computer animation

A slaphappy animated adventure with some enjoyable vocals, Madagascar *was a surprise hit that spawned a series of successful sequels.*

The zebra Marty lives at Manhattan's Central Park Zoo with his friends the boastful lion Alex, the no-nonsense hippo Gloria, and the neurotic giraffe Melman. While each is considered a celebrity and is pampered by the zoo's staff, Marty yearns to live in the wild. When he escapes from the zoo to pursue his dream, his three friends follow, but all four animals are captured in Grand Central Station and put in crates, which are shipped to a wildlife preserve in Kenya. Also escaping are four clever penguins—Skipper, Private, Kowalski, and Rico—who stow away on the same ship. The penguins hijack the freighter and head toward Antarctica but in a storm the crates containing Marty, Alex, Gloria, and Melman are washed overboard and end up on the shores of Madagascar, which they think is the San Diego Zoo. King Julien XIII, leader of the pack of lemurs on the island, plans to use Alex to scare off the predatory fossa. But Alex, having gone days without eating meat, starts to turn primitive and finds himself craving Marty as a meal. The penguins, finding Antarctica too cold and bleak, arrive by ship at Madagascar, which is more to their liking. When the fossa try to kill Marty, Gloria, and Melman, Alex rescues them, frightens the fossa out of the lemurs' territory, and the four mammals board the ship to return to New York City.

The script for *Madagascar* went through many changes during development. Originally an animal rights group freed the four mammals from the zoo, setting off the adventure. In one treatment Melman was an okapi and in another Gloria

The zebra Marty, the lion Alex, the hippo Gloria, and the giraffe Melman are residents of the Central Park Zoo, but a series of mishaps lands them on the shores of Madagascar. *DreamWorks / Photofest.* © *DreamWorks*

was pregnant and gave birth to a baby hippo on the island. The final screenplay is a fairly simple and straightforward journey of four friends, improbable as the details were. The script is filled with jokes and references to human society, yet many of the characters are well enough developed that they are individual and even engaging. This was helped by some superior voicing, in particular Chris Rock's hip Marty, Sacha Baron Cohen's Indian-accented Julien, Tom McGrath's gruff Skipper, and David Schwimmer's neurotic Melman. The story for *Madagascar* does not aim very high, content to be a fast-paced comedy, and on that level it succeeds.

Voice Cast

Ben Stiller	Alex
Chris Rock	Marty
David Schwimmer	Melman
Jada Pinkett Smith	Gloria
Sacha Baron Cohen	Julien
Cedric the Entertainer	Maurice
Andy Richter	Mort
Conrad Vernon	Mason
Tom McGrath	Skipper
Christopher Knights	Private
Chris Miller	Kowalski

ALEX: The wild? Are you nuts? That is the worst idea I have ever heard!

MELMAN: It's unsanitary!

MARTY: The penguins are going, so why can't I?

ALEX: The penguins are psychotic!

The computer animation, on the other hand, is very accomplished as is the background art. The characters do not walk or move like animals (only Gloria walks on all four legs) but rather like high-strung humans. The body movements are broad and funny, particularly in the case of the gangly giraffe Melman. Facial expressions and animation details are also first-rate, such as the behavior of Alex's spiky mane and Julien's wide-eyed hysterics. The rendering of both contemporary New York City and the wilderness on Madagascar is expertly done, filled with detail and color. Both city and nature are romanticized and suggest a high-quality illustrated children's book. The clean angles of the zoo buildings and Grand Central contrast with the free-flowing depiction of the Madagascar beaches and jungle. Because of the frenetic action, only occasionally are these beautiful backgrounds given primary focus. Hans Zimmer's vigorous score is interrupted by well-known songs or movie themes, adding to the jokey nature of the movie. The most effective use of music standards is Louis Armstrong's recording of "What a Wonderful World" during a montage of frolicking in the jungle.

Madagascar was given a wide release in 2005 and met with very mixed reviews, many critics placing it in the second ranks of recent animated movies. Yet box office was strong from the start, and the $75 million film ended up grossing over $500 million worldwide. Its popularity encouraged DreamWorks to produce three sequels. *Madagascar: Escape 2 Africa* (2008) began where the original film ended and followed the same characters (voiced by the same cast) as they try to return to New York but end up in Africa. *Madagascar 3: Europe's Most Wanted* (2012) also featured the same major characters but introduced many new animals when the foursome joins a European circus. More a spin-off than a sequel, *The Penguins of Madagascar* (2014) concentrated on the four penguins from the original movie. There have also been three animated shorts—*The Madagascar Penguins in a Christmas Caper* (2005), *Merry Madagascar* (2009), and *Madly Madagascar* (2013)—and a television cartoon series *The Madagascar Penguins* (2008–2015).

See also *Rio*.

Did You Know . . . ?

Julien, the King of the Lemurs, was a very minor role in the original script, but when Sacha Baron Cohen was in the recording studio he improvised eight minutes of material using an Indian accent. The animators built up the role so they could use more of Cohen's voice work.

MAKE MINE MUSIC

1946
(USA: Walt Disney Productions)

Directed by Joshua Meader, Hamilton Luske, Robert Cormack, Jack Kinney, and Clyde Geronimi
Written by Erdman Penner, Homer Brightman, Tom Oreb, Dick Kinney, Dick Kelsey, Cap Palmer, James Bodrero, Dick Shaw, John Walbridge, Eric Gurney, Dick Huemer, Jesse March, Erwin Graham, Roy Williams, Sylvia Moberly-Holland, and T. Hee
Produced by Walt Disney
Score by Eliot Daniel, Oliver Wallace, and Charles Wolcott
Songs by Ken Darby, Eliot Daniel, Al Cameron, Ted Weems, Osvaldo Farrés, Bobby Worth, Ray Gilbert, Charles Wolcott, Eddie Sauter, Alec Wilder, Allie Wrubel, Turner Leighton, and Henry Creamer
Specs: Color (Technicolor); 75 minutes; traditional animation

---

Top-flight music performances and music ranging from classical to bebop were matched by superb animation in this anthology feature, which is still highly entertaining after seventy years.

The tale of the legendary Hatfield and McCoy feud is given a farcical treatment in the musical number "The Martins and the Coys," sung by the vocal group the King's Men. "Blue Bayou" is a dreamy lullaby performed by the Ken Darby Singers as two egrets wade in the water and float through the air in a romantic setting in the Everglades. Swing music comes to life while the Benny Goodman Orchestra plays, "All the Cats Join In" and hip teenagers gather at the local malt shop and dance to the jukebox. The teary torch song "Without You" is crooned by tenor Andy Russell as the rain pours down and turns images in the park into an impressionist painting. The famous poem "Casey at the Bat" is given a silly rendering in song, narration, and farcical animation. Two ballet dancers perform the heartthrob ballad "Two Silhouettes" in a fanciful setting while Dinah Shore sings on the soundtrack. Sergei Prokofiev's classic *Peter and the Wolf* is performed,

Voice Cast

Nelson Eddy	Willie the Whale
Sterling Holloway	Narrator (*Peter and the Wolf*)
Jerry Colonna	Narrator (*Casey at the Bat*)
Dinah Shore	Soundtrack singers
Andy Russell	Soundtrack singers
The Andrews Sisters	Soundtrack singers
The Pied Pipers	Soundtrack singers
The King's Men	Soundtrack singers
Ken Darby Chorus	Soundtrack singers

In the memorable *Peter and the Wolf* section, the young Russian boy Peter sets off with his toy gun to find and slay the wolf that has been sighted in the forest. *RKO Radio Pictures / Photofest.* © *RKO Radio Pictures*

narrated by Sterling Holloway. The song standard "After You've Gone" is given a jazz treatment by the Benny Goodman Quartet as various musical instruments come alive as characters in an abstract setting. The Andrews Sisters sing the story of "Johnny Fedora and Alice Bluebonnet," the bittersweet tale of two hats who fall in love but are separated until the end of the song. The anthology film ends with the opera spoof "The Whale Who Wanted to Sing at the Met," in which Nelson Eddy sings all the roles in the story of an opera-loving whale.

Sometimes called a package movie, *Make Mine Music* was one of eight anthology films made by Disney in the 1940s when the studio was understaffed and financially strapped, particularly during World War II. This feature included ten

Songs

"Make Mine Music" (Darby/Eliot)
"The Martins and the Coys" (Cameron/Weems)
"All the Cats Join In" (Sauter/Wilder/Gilbert)
"Without You" (Farrés/Gilbert)
"Blue Bayou" (Worth/Gilbert)
"Two Silhouettes" (Wolcott/Gilbert)
"After You've Gone" (Leighton/Creamer)
"Johnny Fedora and Alice Bluebonnet" (Wrubel/Gilbert)
"The Whale Who Wanted to Sing at the Met" (various opera composers)

very diverse sequences built around music. Unlike *Fantasia*, the feature included recent hit songs, original numbers, and top recording stars as well as some classical music. Benny Goodman, the Andrews Sisters, Dinah Shore, Andy Russell, and other current stars of the pop musical scene were recruited to provide the vocals and instrumentals and *Make Mine Music* boasts a superior soundtrack. But equally impressive is the animation and art work throughout. The style, temperament, tone, and look of each segment is individual, each inspired by the music at hand. One might describe the film as a "pop *Fantasia*."

The most famous sequence in *Make Mine Music* is the "Peter and the Wolf" story because of the renowned Prokofiev music but also because the segment was shown many times years later on Disney television. The animation is playful rather than poetic, and the background art is simple even as it is atmospheric, particularly in conveying a frightening Russian forest. Also cartoonish is the "Casey at the Bat" segment, which starts out with some Currier and Ives–like lithographs then turns to farce for the robust and exaggerated characters. The two Benny Goodman selections have the most original animation. The artist's paintbrush creates the characters and setting for "All the Cats Join In" as quickly and rhythmically as Goodman's swing music. "After You're Gone" is even more creative, moving into abstract art as the musical instruments take their cue from the jazz music and cut loose in delightful ways. The musical satire "The Whale Who Wanted to Sing at the Met" is traditionally illustrated and the focus is on the various opera passages that Nelson Eddy performs with a less-than-serious tone. Also very traditional looking is "Johnny Fedora and Alice Bluebonnet," complete with a sense of nostalgia for the past time. "The Martins and the Coys" section has dated poorly. The gunplay is supposed to be good hillbilly humor, but modern audiences are not amused; the sequence is edited out of most DVD editions of *Make Mine Music*. "Two Silhouettes," "Without You," and "Blue Bayou" are perhaps the least impressive sequences. The songs are pleasing without being memorable but the animation is very sophisticated if a bit dull. The rotoscoping of two actual ballet stars in "Two Silhouettes" is engaging at first but soon gets repetitive. The poetic recreation of the Florida bayou in "Blue Bayou" is quite accomplished but less than exciting, just as the rain-drenched images in "Without You" are expert without being compelling. Yet there are so many wonderful things in *Make Mine Music* that the overall experience is still a resplendent one.

NARRATOR: Now Willie will never sing at the Met. But don't be too harsh on Tetti-Tatti; he just didn't understand. You see, Willie's singing was a miracle, and people aren't used to miracles.

When the film was released in 1946, critical reaction was mostly appreciative if not enthusiastic. Audience reaction was also mixed and the movie was a modest box office success. It took a while for the $1.35 million film to pay for itself but eventually it earned over $2 million. Unlike the Disney features with a plot, *Make Mine Music* was never rereleased in theaters. Instead the different sequences were shown separately on Disney's television shows in the 1950s and 1960s. Years later, the entire movie (minus "The Martins and the Coys") was released on VHS and DVD in the States; it is still difficult to find overseas.

See also *Melody Time* and *Fun with Music*.

Did You Know . . . ?

The animation for the poetic "Blue Bayou" sequence was completed for *Fantasia* (1940), where it was matched with Claude Debussy's "Clair de Lune." The section was cut from *Fantasia* and reused in this film with an original song, "Blue Bayou."

THE MANY ADVENTURES OF WINNIE THE POOH

1977
(USA: Walt Disney Productions)

Directed by John Lounsbery and Wolfgang Reitherman, based on the stories by A. A. Milne
Written by Ken Anderson, Larry Clemmons, Xavier Atencio, Julius Svendsen, Vance Gerry, Ralph Wright, Eric Cleworth, Ted Berman, and Winston Hibbler
Produced by Wolfgang Reitherman
Score by Buddy Baker
Songs by Richard M. and Robert B. Sherman
Specs: Color (Technicolor); 74 minutes; traditional animation

---

The first appearance of the famous A. A. Milne characters in a feature film, The Many Adventures of Winnie the Pooh *is generally considered the most satisfying Winnie the Pooh movie and the one that remains closest to the original stories.*

The stuffed bear Winnie the Pooh and his friends in the Hundred Acre Woods are all toys belonging to the British youth Christopher Robin, who imagines them coming alive and sharing adventures with him. The episodic plot includes Pooh's attempt to get honey from a bees' nest by using a helium balloon and disguising

Voice Cast

Sterling Holloway	Winnie the Pooh
Junius Matthews	Rabbit
Paul Winchell	Tigger
Ralph Wright	Eeyore
John Fielder	Piglet
Hal Smith	Owl
Barbara Luddy	Kanga
Dori Whitaker	Roo
Clint Howard	Roo
Howard Morris	Gopher
Bruce Reitherman	Christopher Robin
Jon Walmsley	Christopher Robin
Timothy Turner	Christopher Robin
Sebastian Cabot	Narrator

The Pooh bear Winnie has eaten so much honey at Rabbit's house that he gets stuck in the doorway and needs help from (left to right) Christopher Robin, Kanga, and Eeyore. *Buena Vista Pictures / Photofest. © Buena Vista Pictures*

himself as a "little black rain cloud"; a flood in the Hundred Acre Woods that leaves Piglet homeless; a wind storm that blows over the tree where Owl lives; an attempt by Rabbit to lose Tigger in the forest but Rabbit ends up getting lost himself; and Pooh's getting stuck in the entrance to Rabbit's burrow because he ate too much honey. By the end of the movie, Christopher has to go away to school, but he promises to return to the Hundred Acre Wood and his stuffed toys.

Walt Disney had success in turning the Milne stories into three featurettes: *Winnie the Pooh and the Honey Tree* (1966), *Winnie the Pooh and the Blustery Day* (1968), and *Winnie the Pooh and Tigger Too* (1974). He had always intended to make a feature film with the Pooh characters, but it didn't happen until a decade after he died. *The Many Adventures of Winnie the Pooh* incorporates footage from those three shorts tied together with scenes with Christopher Robin and adding a new ending to the episodic plot. Also uniting the movie are sections showing the original Milne illustrated books and having fun with the pages, such as having characters jump from page to page and letting the wind and the water blow and wash away words from the text. The result is a delightful children's movie that feels like an animated feature rather than a series of cartoons.

The original A. A. Milne books were illustrated by Ernest Shepard in a colorful sketch-like style that is whimsical rather than realistic. The Disney animators and the background artists did not copy Shepard's work closely but suggested it in the movie version. The bucolic English countryside is rendered with watercolors and

Songs

"Winnie the Pooh"
"Like a Rather Blustery Day"
"Rumbly in My Tumbly"
"Mind over Matter"
"(I'm Just a) Little Black Raincloud"
"The Wonderful Thing about Tiggers"
"Heffalumps and Woozles"
"The Rain, Rain, Rain Came Down, Down, Down"
"Up, Down, Touch the Ground"
"Hip-Hip Pooh-ray!"

a lot of pen lines that give the locations plenty of details without being realistic. In particular, the interiors of the various characters' homes are filled with vigorous lines and rustic touches. Pooh, Eyeore, Tigger, and others are animated not as animals but as toys, their movement playfully suggesting stuffed creatures who defy the rules of physics. Falling from trees or floating in raging rivers, these characters' adventures never alarm the viewer because they seem destined to survive in a way humans or animals cannot. While many cartoons include violence and disaster in which the characters illogically spring back to life, the action scenes in *The Many Adventures of Winnie the Pooh* are more gentle and consequently far from frightening.

The voice cast for the film is exceptional, filled with many Disney regulars. Sterling Holloway's Pooh is so distinctive and cherished that moviegoers cannot imagine the bear sounding like anyone else. This film was Holloway's last project before retirement, and subsequent actors voicing Pooh wisely imitated him. Paul Winchell's Tigger is a spontaneous delight. He ad-libbed two of the character's most famous sounds: the giggle and the exit line "TTFN—Ta Ta for Now. " John Fiedler's nervous Piglet and Ralph Wright's fatalistic Eyeore are also standouts in the vocals. Setting the right tone throughout is Sebastian Cabot in his last movie performance as the wry Narrator.

TIGGER: (sitting on Pooh's stomach) And who are you?

WINNIE: I'm Pooh.

TIGGER: Oh, Pooh. (giggles) Sure! Uh—what's a pooh?

WINNIE: You're sitting on one.

Just as the Pooh books are aimed at young children and can be enjoyed by having the tales read to them, the movie also focuses on its youthful audience. If adults enjoy the books and the film versions, it is because there is nostalgia for a time when one was young and was first enamored with Milne's characters. Things are kept simple in the movie. Each storyline is straightforward and not complicated by a subplot or any tangent that takes away from the thrust of the action. The handful of songs written by Richard M. and Robert B. Sherman are also simple, with cute but playful lyrics and catchy music. Each musical number is short yet is so tuneful that most moviegoers (in particular, children) can easily recall and hum each ditty. "Winnie the Pooh" is instantly likable and has served as the theme song for all the many Pooh shorts and features. The silly "Rumbly in My Tumbly" and the plaintive "(I'm Just a) Little Black Raincloud" are also easily remembered, and the rhythmic "The Rain, Rain, Rain Came Down, Down, Down" has the quality of a sing-along number and seems to bounce along as gleefully as the character does. "Heffalumps and Woozles," heard during a dream sequence when Pooh imagines various hybrid animals, is a cockeyed march, as is the finale number, "Hip-Hip Pooh-ray!" The Sherman Brothers wrote many noteworthy scores for Disney, but the songs from the Pooh stories are perhaps the simplest and most accessible.

The Many Adventures of Winnie the Pooh received favorable if not rave reviews and did modest box office when released in 1977. The movie was even more popular on VHS in 1982 and on DVD in 2002. Disney returned to the Pooh characters several times over the years, including such feature films as *Pooh's Grand Adventure: The Search for Christopher Robin* (1997), *The Tigger Movie* (2000), *A Very Merry Pooh Year* (2002), *Piglet's Big Movie* (2003), *Springtime with Roo* (2004), *Pooh's Heffalump Movie* (2005), and *Tigger & Pooh and a Musical Too* (2009). Many of these had original plots that strayed far from the original books. For most, *The Many Adventures of Winnie the Pooh* remains the best animated version of the beloved stories.

Did You Know . . . ?

Gopher is the only character in the film who is not in Milne's stories. He is a creation of the Disney artists and was introduced in *Winnie the Pooh and the Honey Tree* (1966).

MEET THE ROBINSONS

2007
(USA: Walt Disney Animation Studios)

Directed by Stephen Anderson
Written by Stephen Anderson, Don Hall, Joseph Mateo, Jon Bernstein, Michelle Bochner Spitz, and Aurian Redson, based on the book *A Day with Wilbur Robinson* by William Joyce
Produced by John Lasseter, Clark Spencer, William Joyce, Dorothy McKim, Bill Borden, Makul Wigert, and Monica Lago-Kaytis
Score by Danny Elfman
Songs by Danny Elfman, Rufus Wainwright, Rob Thomas, and Marius De Vries
Specs: Color; 95 minutes; computer animation

A time-traveling animated fantasy that is frequently frenetic, Meet the Robinsons *also has plenty of heart. It is one of the most complicated movies, plot-wise, but is filled with amusing characters.*

The twelve-year-old orphan Lewis and his nerdy roommate Michael "Goob" Yagoobian have been at the orphanage for years because they are both too weird to get adopted. Lewis is a whiz at inventing things, though rarely do they work. To help him picture his mother, who abandoned him as an infant, Lewis creates a "memory scanner" and brings it to the school's science fair. There he meets thirteen-year-old Wilbur Robinson, who has come from the future to keep Lewis's invention from falling into the hands of the devious Bowler Hat Guy. To convince Lewis that he is from the future, Wilbur takes Lewis to the year 2037 in his father's time machine. The machine crashes and Lewis agrees to fix it if Wilbur will take him back in time so he can see his mother. Before Lewis can repair the machine, he is welcomed into Wilbur's screwball family and bonds with them. Bowler Hat Guy, who is dictated to by a computerized bowler hat named Doris, tries to steal the time machine. It turns out that Wilbur's father, Cornelius Robinson, is not only a genius inventor but is also Lewis in the future, making Wilbur his son. Lewis also learns that Bowler Hat Guy is the frustrated adult that Goob became in the future. Lewis fixes the time machine and returns to the science fair, where he is discovered by a scientist couple who adopt him and set him on his way to becoming a renowned scientist.

The original screenplay for *Meet the Robinsons* followed William Joyce's book closely and production was over half completed when there was a shake-up at the Disney studio. John Lasseter, the founder of Pixar, was put in charge of all Disney animation. Lasseter was not pleased with the completed footage of the movie and made several demands of director Stephen J. Anderson, including the rethinking

Lewis is a science whiz who has invented a "memory scanner" which he hopes to use to go back in time and see his mother who left him as a baby at the orphanage. *Buena Vista Pictures / Photofest.* © *Buena Vista Pictures*

Voice Cast

Daniel Hansen	Lewis
Jordan Fry	Lewis
Wesley Singerman	Wilbur
Matthew Josten	Michael "Goob" Yagoobian
Angela Bassett	Mildred
Stephen Anderson	Bowler Hat Guy
Dara McGarry	Mrs. Harrington
John H. H. Ford	Mr. Harrington
Laurie Metcalf	Lucille Krunklehorn
Paul Butcher	Stanley
Tracey Miller-Zarneke	Lizzy
Tom Kenny	Mr. Willerstein
Jessie Flower	Franny (young)
Nicole Sullivan	Franny (adult)
Don Hall	Coach
Adam West	Uncle Art
Tom Selleck	Cornelius

of Bowler Hat Guy and adding Doris and a chase sequence with a dinosaur. Most of the finished scenes were scrapped, then production resumed as costs escalated, with the final budget estimated at $150 million. Production continued so long that boy actor Daniel Hansen's voice broke and the vocals for Lewis were completed by Jordan Fry. Because of other production delays, the release date for *Meet the Robinsons* was moved from 2006 to 2007.

Songs

"The Motion Waltz" (Wainwright)
"Where Is Your Heart At?" (Wainwright)
"The Future Has Arrived" (Elfman)
"Little Wonders" (Thomas)
"Another Believer" (Wainwright/De Vries)

Meet the Robinsons has one of the most confusing plots of any Disney movie, and the audience is kept in the dark for much of the film as to who certain characters are and what forces are at work on those characters. Yet by the end of the movie, the pieces of the plot come together and everything is explained. Some find this kind of storytelling intriguing, others think it irritating. In either case, there is so much action in the film that one is not given much time to ponder what is happening. Similarly, some characters are introduced so quickly that the viewer may have trouble keeping track of who is who, even though many of the characters (especially the Robinsons) are silly and engaging. For all the time traveling and chases in the movie, *Meet the Robinsons* has some touching character scenes involving

Lewis and Goob. The unwanted Lewis is not pathetic but spunky and determined. The sleep-deprived Goob is funny even in his failures. The high-energy Wilbur is not as endearing as the story expects him to be, particularly since one is never sure of his mission until late in the film. A nice touch of real warmth is provided by the orphanage worker Mildred, voiced with affection by Angela Bassett. Perhaps the liveliest voice performance is given by director Anderson as Bowler Hat Guy, a comic villain who is more foolish than threatening.

> WILBUR: Five years ago, Dad wakes up in the middle of the night in a cold sweat. Wants to build a time machine. So he starts working! We're talking plans, we're talking scale models, we're talking prototypes! (shows Lewis a small scrap of metal)
>
> LEWIS: That's a prototype?
>
> WILBUR: The very first! . . . Or, what's left of it.
>
> LEWIS: Yikes.
>
> WILBUR: Yeah. Dark day at the Robinson household.

The computer animation in *Meet the Robinsons* is as swift and frantic as the story-telling. Facial movements and character animation are broad and very cartoon-like with little effort to convey realism. The background art is bright and colorful as in a cartoon as well. The settings in the present are detailed and real enough, while the locations in 2037 are purposely artificial looking, with structures that resemble a theme park. The topiary gardens in the future are playful, but the interiors of the Robinsons' house and lab are streamlined to the point of sterility. The contrast between the present and the future is very clear if not overstated. Ironically, one longs to return to the city of 2007 because it seems more grounded and tangible than a future filled with Cornelius Robinson's inventions. The soundtrack score by Danny Elfman does not distinguish much between the two worlds, since much of the music is in keeping with the brisk pace of the movie. It is a breathless score that only quiets down for a few scenes. There are also some pop songs by Elfman and others that provide some color during a montage or over the final credits.

Meet the Robinsons opened in 2007 to mixed reviews. Some critics applauded the movie's energy and visual presentation. Others thought the film rushed and empty. Audiences were not so divided. The fantasy started strong and did good box office (particularly at 3-D showings), eventually earning nearly $170 million internationally. This would be an impressive number if the movie had not cost so much to make. The number of DVDs and Blu-ray copies sold was significant when released late in 2007 but they were not best sellers. Also modestly popular was a video game based on *Meet the Robinsons*. Plans for a sequel to the film were scrapped in 2008 by Lasseter. While *Meet the Robinsons* does not compare favorably with some of the other animated features released early in the new century, the movie is still a significant contribution to the art form. The expected Disney polish is there, as is the high craftsmanship in computer techniques. The studio would take a few years before its computer animated films reached the level that Pixar had offered since the late 1990s.

Did You Know . . . ?

When Wilbur travels to the year 2037, one can see Space Mountain and the Rocket Jets from the Walt Disney World's Magic Kingdom theme park.

MELODY TIME

1948
(USA: Walt Disney Productions)

Directed by Jack Kinney, Wilfred Jackson, Clyde Geronimi, and Hamilton Luske
Written by Erdman Penner, Winston Hibbler, Joe Rinaldi, Ted Sears, Art Scott, John Walbridge, Ken Anderson, Jesse Marsh, Harry Reeves, Homer Brightman, William Cottrell, and Bob Moore
Produced by Walt Disney
Score by Eliot Daniel and Paul J. Smith
Songs by Eliot Daniel, Johnny Lange, Ernesto Nazareth, Kim Gannon, Ray Gilbert, Joyce Kilmer, Oscar Rasbach, Walter Kent, Bobby Worth, George David Weiss, Allie Wrubel, and Bennie Benjamin
Specs: Color (Technicolor); 75 minutes; live action and traditional animation

---

Disney's final musical anthology movie of the 1940s, Melody Time *is arguably the best in the series with memorable music and glittering animation.*

In the nostalgic "Once Upon a Wintertime," a young courting couple takes a sleigh ride and goes ice skating. The memorable day is remembered years later by the married couple. Bandleader Freddie Martin gives the Russian classic "Flight of the Bumble Bee" by Rimsky-Korsakov a jazz interpretation as a beleaguered bee is caught in a world of animated musical instruments. "The Legend of Johnny Appleseed" is told in song and spoken narration, from his calling as a young man to plant apple trees throughout Ohio and Indiana until his death as a satisfied old man. The harmonizing trio the Andrews Sisters sings the tale of "Little Toot," the son of a mighty tugboat in the New York City harbor, who gets into mischief until he clears his name by saving a ship at sea. Joyce Kilmer's beloved poem "Trees" is sung in a hymn-like arrangement by Fred Waring's chorale, the Pennsylvanians. Donald Duck, Joe Carioca, and the Aracuan Bird from *The Three Caballeros* (1944) frolic while organist Ethel Smith (in live action) plays the Latin American song "Blame It on the Samba." The film ends with Roy Rogers and the singing Sons of the Pioneers, sitting around the campfire with Disney child stars Luana Patten and Bobby Driscoll in live-action footage, performing the cowboy ballad "Blue Shadows on the Trail." Then Rogers narrates the legend of "Pecos Bill," a wild frontiersman who is finally tamed when he falls in love with the pretty Slue Foot Sue. When Bill loses Sue, he howls at the moon and all the coyotes copy him to this day.

Among the tales of Americana told in this anthology film is that of the factual Johnny Appleseed, who planted thousands of apple trees in Ohio and Indiana in the nineteenth century. *RKO Radio Pictures / Photofest.* © *RKO Radio Pictures*

Voice Cast

Dennis Day	Johnny Appleseed
Buddy Clark	Master of Ceremonies
Roy Rogers	Soundtrack singer
Bob Nolan	Soundtrack singer
The Andrews Sisters	Soundtrack singers
Sons of the Pioneers	Soundtrack singers
Dinning Sisters	Soundtrack singers
Fred Waring's Pennsylvanians	Soundtrack singers

Live-Action Cast

Roy Rogers	Roy Rogers
Bobby Driscoll	Bobby Driscoll
Luana Patten	Luana Patten

More so than any of the other Disney package films, *Melody Time* concentrates on American stories and American music. Even the Russian "Flight of the Bumble Bee" comes out sounding very American when turned into a jazz number. The animation in this segment is the most imaginative in the film. The musical instruments and, in particular, the piano keys explode with life in time to the rapid music. The art work in "Once Upon a Wintertime" is nostalgic with a Christmas-card look, while "The Legend of Johnny Appleseed" utilizes an American Primitive design with simple shapes and bright colors. The animation for "Blame It on the Samba" recalls the lively numbers from Disney's two Latin American movies, *Saludos Amigos* and *The Three Caballeros*, including the clever mixing of live-action and animated characters. The images of trees in the "Trees" segment are very stylized, the trunks and branches resembling modern sculpture. "Little Toot" and "Pecos Bill" are the most cartoon-like in design and movement, both sections having plenty of action. Because all the movie's sequences are very much exercises in Americana, *Melody Time* doesn't have the visual variety of some of the other anthology films.

Songs

"Melody Time" (Weiss/Benjamin)
"Once Upon a Wintertime" (Worth/Gilbert)
"Johnny Appleseed" (Gannon/Kent)
"Trees" (Kilmer/Rasbach)
"Little Toot" (Wrubel)
"Pecos Bill" (Daniel/Lange)
"Blame It on the Samba" (Nazareth/Gilbert)
"Blue Shadows on the Trail" (Daniel/Lange)

The music, on the other hand, is very diverse, even keeping within American musical forms. The title number is a slightly swinging number sung by a chorus over the opening credits and it is pure 1940s in temperament. There is also a Big Band sound to the musical narration for "Little Toot," especially when sung by the rhythmic Andrews Sisters. The Johnny Appleseed music is filled with variety, including a fervent hymn and a hoe-down number. The smooth ballad heard in "Once Upon a Wintertime" is decidedly old-fashioned, as befits the period illustrated. Similarly, "Pecos Bill" includes gentle cowboy songs, a robust yodeling number, and a lullaby-like love song. The most memorable song in the movie is the intoxicating Latin number "Blame It on the Samba," which moves along in a rhythmic manner that is both festive and sexy.

MASTER OF CEREMONIES: Here's a tall tale straight from the chuck wagon, just the way the old-timers used to tell it. According to them, Pecos Bill was the roughest, toughest, rootin'est, tootin'est, shootin'est cowpoke that ever lived. Well, any story about old Pecos is bound to be right strong medicine, so maybe it's best to sashay into it kinda gentle-like.

Melody Time was released in the States, Brazil, and Argentina in 1948, with openings around the world within the next two years. The reviews were mixed, the movie getting more praise for the songs and singers than the film itself. Costing about $1.5 million, the film paid back its investment and then some. The studio did not rerelease *Melody Time* in theaters but the movie's segments were turned into shorts to be shown on television and later in video collections. Because Pecos Bill is constantly smoking in his story, that segment was edited to remove some of the cigarette images when *Melody Time* was released on video in 1998. The DVD edition came out two years later.

See also *Make Mine Music* and *Fun with Music*.

Did You Know . . . ?

The song "Blame It on the Samba" was a popular Latin number titled "Apanhei-te, Cavaquinho" by composer Ernesto Nazareth. Ray Gilbert wrote an English lyric for this movie and the song became a big hit in the States.

MOANA

2016
(USA: Walt Disney Animation Studios)

Directed by Ron Clements, John Musker, Chris Williams, and Don Hall
Written by Jared Bush
Produced by John Lasseter and Osnat Shurer
Score by Mark Mancina
Songs by Opetaia Foa'i, Lin-Manuel Miranda, and Mark Mancina
Specs: Color; 103 minutes; computer and traditional animation

---

Disney's animation department, under Pixar's John Lasseter, moved more and more into computerized animation in the new century and reached a technological high point with Moana, *a film that rivals Pixar's finest works even as it retains a very Disney tone.*

On the ancient Polynesian island of Motunui, the natives remain inside the reef and live happily off the plants and fish that surround them. But in the past, the people were sea voyagers and Gramma Tala tells the children tales from those days of navigation. The Chieftain Tui's only offspring, the eager teenager Moana, yearns to travel outside the reef but is discouraged by her parents and encouraged by her Gramma. When the crops fail and the fish disappear, Moana knows it is because years ago the demigod Maui stole the heart of the goddess Te Fiti and gave it to the lava monster Te Ka. Moana sets off alone on a canoe with the silly chicken Heihei to find Maui and force him to return the heart to Te Fiti. She finds Maui, but he is a self-absorbed, sarcastic egomaniac who refuses to cooperate. The seas give Moana enough power to convince Maui to

Maui is a self-centered former demigod who meets his match in the young Polynesian girl Moana, who insists that he help her find and return the heart of the goddess Te Fiti. *Walt Disney Pictures / Photofest.* © *Walt Disney Pictures*

help her, however, and thereby reclaim his lost powers. They outwit the vicious Kakamora creatures, outmaneuver the crab monster Tamatoa, get the heart from fiery Te Ka, and return it to Te Fiti, who is very grateful. Maui is once again a powerful demigod and Moana is a hero when she returns to Motunui, where everything is blossoming and the fish are plentiful.

John Musker and Ron Clements, who had directed such traditionally animated Disney films as *The Little Mermaid* (1989) and *Hercules* (1997), moved into computerized animation with *Moana* and, with codirectors Chris Williams and Ron Hall, captured much of the magic of those past works in the computerized *Moana*. The script, based on Polynesian mythology, follows the useful premise of a journey in which an unlikely heroine faces incredible odds to save her community. What is unusual in *Moana* is that there is no romantic relationship in the tale. Moana loves her Gramma, her parents, her people, and even the cockeyed chicken Heihei, but there is only the hint of friendship with the demigod Maui. He is far from the leading man type. In most Disney films, Maui would be the secondary character used for comic relief. As voiced by the wrestler-actor Dwayne Johnson, Maui is indeed funny and provides a sassy modern attitude that contrasts with the reverent tone of the natives of Motunui. Moana is a smart and passionate sixteen-year-old and a bridge between the solemn folklore and Maui's hip approach to life. The villains,

Voice Cast

Louise Bush	Moana (toddler)
Auli'i Cravalho	Moana (teenager)
Dwayne Johnson	Maui
Rachel House	Gramma Tala
Temuera Morrison	Chief Tui
Nicole Scherzinger	Sina
Jemaine Clement	Tamatoa
Alan Tudyk	Heihei

such as the lava-spewing Te Ka and the dart-throwing Kakamoras, as well as the divine force Te Fiti, do not speak and are visual creations. Only the crab monster Tamatoa is heard in a calypso number. Also, the chicken Heihei, the pig Pua, and the other animals in the film do not talk. *Moana* has fewer speaking roles than just about any Disney animated movie. This is a story that is seen more than heard.

Songs

"We Know the Way"
"How Far I'll Go"
"You're Welcome"
"Shiny"
"Tulou Tagaloa"
"An Innocent Warrior"
"Where You Are"
"Logo Te Pate"
"I Am Moana (Song of the Ancestors)"
"Know Who You Are"

The creative team visited some Polynesian islands in preparation for the film and the results on the screen are exceptional. Unlike the fantasy "under the sea" world of *The Little Mermaid*, the ocean in *Moana* is both frightening and seductive. Much of the film takes place on the canoe at sea but the background artists and animators find a variety of looks, moods, and movement. The movie pretty much consists of only two characters, Moana and Maui. The visualization of each is quite different. Moana is one of the most realistic of all Disney heroines. She has no exaggerated features and her beauty is simple and accessible. Maui, on the other hand, is a giant-sized athletic type whose broad torso and arms are large enough to sport many tattoos, some telling stories as in an ancient wall painting. While all of his movements are computer generated, the tattoos that move are done with traditional animation, turning Maui's body into a kind of movie screen. While Maui's periodic transformation into a hawk is impressive, it is his human form and the way he moves that are most interesting.

MOANA: I am not a princess.

MAUI: If you wear a dress and have an animal sidekick, you're a princess.

The voice work in Moana is top-notch, although it really comes down to two performers. Hundreds of teenagers were auditioned before the fourteen-year-old Hawaiian Auli'i Cravalho was cast, even though she had no professional acting or singing experience. Moana is a spunky heroine but Cravalho's performance goes beyond the usual liberated female. She has her doubts and fears yet draws her courage from within herself. The hipster Maui calls for the quick delivery of a stand-up comic and Johnson does not disappoint. Like Cravalho, he does his own

Awards

Academy Award nominations: Best Animated Feature and Best Song ("How Far I'll Go").
Golden Globe nominations: Best Picture—Animated Film, and Best Song ("How Far I'll Go").
British Academy of Film & Television Arts (BAFTA) nomination: Best Animated Feature.

singing and manages to spit his wordy lyrics out with panache. The only other developed character in the movie is Gramma Tala. Rachel House voices her with a wistful yet quixotic playfulness that makes all of her scenes glow with warmth.

The one disappointing aspect of *Moana* is the songs. While Mark Mancina's soundtrack score is rich with tribal sounds and a sense of mystery and majesty, the songs are lackluster, especially considering the musical possibilities the story offers. The heroine's "I Am Moana" is a cliché-ridden anthem given some power by the tribal chanting behind it. Maui's pop number "You're Welcome" is cute but goes nowhere. "We Know the Way" is a routine call-and-response number for the tribal voyagers of the past, while "Shiny" is a pseudo-calypso number with a rap lyric that is neither funny nor interesting. More appealing are Moana's driven ballad "How Far I'll Go" and the rhythmic "Logo Te Pate," which captures the spirit of Polynesia even as it is very accessible and engaging.

Perhaps it is too soon to determine if *Moana* will have the long-lasting appeal of some of the Disney classics but it has been extremely successful domestically and internationally. Its folk-tale story has a wide appeal and the exotic charm of the Polynesian setting is timeless.

See also *The Little Mermaid*.

Did You Know . . . ?

The title of the film and the heroine's name had to be changed when *Moana* was released in some foreign countries. Although *moana* means "blue" in Polynesian, in Italy and France the name is most associated with the infamous porno star Moana Pozzi. The heroine is called Vaiana in the European version and the film is often titled *Oceania*.

MONSTERS, INC.

2001
(USA: Pixar Animation Studios/Disney)

Directed by Pete Docter, David Silverman, and Lee Unkrich
Written by Andrew Stanton and Daniel Gerson
Produced by John Lasseter, Andrew Stanton, Darla K. Anderson, Kori Rae, and
   Karen Dufilho-Rosen
Score by Randy Newman
Song "If I Didn't Have You" by Randy Newman
Specs: Color; 92 minutes; computer animation

One of the comic ironies in the story is that the monsters, such as Mike Wazowski (left) and James P. "Sulley" Sullivan, are actually afraid of humans, even young children. *Pixar Animation Studios/ Walt Disney Pictures / Photofest. © Pixar Animation Studios/Walt Disney Pictures*

With its unusual premise and delightful characters, this Pixar entry is surprisingly engaging, one of the best computerized features of the new century.

The screams of human children are needed to power the city of Monstropolis, so the factory Monsters, Inc. employs various monsters to enter the human world through special doors and scare children to get the needed screams. The top "scarer" at the factory is the large furry blue monster James P. Sullivan, known as Sulley to his friends, including his pal Mike Wazowski, a short, green monster with only one eye. The lizard monster Randall Boggs is Sulley's rival and plots

Voice Cast

Billy Crystal	Mike Wazowski
John Goodman	James P. "Sulley" Sullivan
Steve Buscemi	Randall Boggs
Mary Gibbs	Boo
Jennifer Tilly	Celia
Bob Peterson	Roz
James Coburn	Henry J. Waternoose
Frank Oz	Fungus
Daniel Gerson	Needleman
Bonnie Hunt	Flint
Jeff Pidgeon	Bile
Samuel Lord Black	George Sanderson
John Ratzenberger	Abominable Snowman
Steve Susskind	Floor Manager

with the company CEO, Waternoose, to depose Sulley and harness screams by kidnapping children. When one of the door portals to the human world is accidentally left open, the little girl Boo enters the factory. She is discovered by Sulley and Mike, who hide her from the monster community. Randall finds out about Boo and kidnaps her, then sends Mike and Sulley to the Himalayas. The Abominable Snowman helps the two monsters return to the factory where they rescue Boo. The two monsters then destroy Randall by sending him to the Everglades, where he is mistaken for an alligator and killed. The monster duo also reveal Waternoose's kidnapping plot. Sulley is made CEO of Monsters, Inc. and changes the process to collecting children's laughter to power the city.

The fear that there is a monster in your closet is an idea that just about every child experiences. Director-animator Pete Docter first proposed a film about such a phobia to the Pixar staff in 1996. During the next six years the premise went through many versions and characters until the final screenplay was solidified. The idea of a young child making friends with one of the closet monsters is at the heart of the story, but the friendship between Sulley and Mike gives the tale its structure. The writers and designers were faced with some very particular challenges in creating *Monsters, Inc.* It was decided early on that none of the many monster characters in the movie would look alike, so dozens of different kinds of creatures had to be designed. Both Sulley and Mike went through many different designs before the blue-furred Sulley and the one-eyed Mike were finalized. Also, giving the fur on the many different monsters the look and texture of real fur required a new and unique program on the computer. The artists had to create the whole new world of Monstropolis, a city that resembled a human environment yet had its own cockeyed look. Similarly, the monster characters had to have enough human qualities so that the audience would accept them as more than oddball creatures. Because of the number of characters, the many locations, and the special effects needed, *Monsters, Inc.* became the most complex movie yet attempted by Pixar. It is also the first Pixar film not directed by John Lasseter. Docter codirected it with Lee Unkrich and David Silverman.

> MIKE: Can I borrow your odorant?
>
> SULLEY: Yeah, I got, uh, Smelly Garbage or Old Dumpster.
>
> MIKE: You got, uh, Low Tide?
>
> SULLEY: No.
>
> MIKE: How about Wet Dog?
>
> SULLEY: Yep. Stink it up.

Just as the major monster characters went through many changes during development and production, many actors were considered to voice them. Bill Murray was approached to voice Mike but miscommunication ruined the deal. Billy Crystal, who, to his everlasting regret, had turned down the role of Buzz Lightyear in *Toy Story* (1995), eagerly accepted when offered to voice Mike. Crystal's experience as a stand-up comic added to the character, allowing Mike to joke and kid the other characters in an endearing way. Character actor John Goodman's full, deep voice was ideal for Sulley, providing a contrast to Mike's high-pitched wise-cracking. Goodman had acted with Steve Buscemi before and recommended him for the role of the snide monster Randall. The producers found Buscemi's creepy vocal quality perfect for Randall. The many supporting characters in *Monsters, Inc.* are well voiced, but the standout is Bob Peterson's Roz, a small but memorable role of the disapproving secretary at the factory. Pixar animator and writer Peterson provided the temporary voice for Roz until an actor was assigned. The producers thought his raspy vocals could not be bettered and used his recording. Randy Newman, who had scored all the previous Pixar films, composed the soundtrack score for *Monsters, Inc.* It is a very playful mix of jazz, blues, eerie atmosphere music, light-hearted child-like passages, and vigorous action scoring. At one point, there is a stirring anthem in which the monsters are presented as noble heroes. The film is not a musical, but Newman wrote a catchy song for Crystal and Goodman to sing over the closing credits. "If I Didn't Have You" is a breezy buddy ditty that gave the two actors a chance to ad-lib and improvise. The song was Newman's sixteenth Oscar nomination and his first win.

Awards

Academy Award: Best Song ("If I Didn't Have You"). Oscar nominations: Best Animated Feature and Best Sound Editing.
British Academy of Film & Television Arts (BAFTA) Children's Award: Best Feature Film.

On its release in 2002, *Monsters, Inc.* received a round of rave reviews for its clever premise, sprightly characters, and sportive voice performances. The expensive movie, which cost around $115 million, had been widely promoted by the studio, helping it earn $62 million during its first weekend. Domestic and international earnings were over $577 million. The 2002 VHS and DVD sales were also big sellers, as were the earnings of the 2012 rerelease in 3-D and the Blu-ray edition in 2013. Video games, comic books, and an animated short, *Mike's New Car* (2002), followed. A much anticipated prequel, *Monsters University*, was released in theaters in 2013 and was even more successful than the original. Because the story was set back in time when Mike and Sulley were both college students, only a few characters from the original movie returned. But dozens of new monsters were introduced, most memorably the hard-nosed Dean Hardscrabble (voiced by Helen Mirren). Mike and Sulley were such close friends in *Monsters, Inc.* that it was surprising to find out that they were enemies back in college. But they eventually have to join forces to become Scarers and, consequently, friends. Rather than a retread of the premise of the first movie, *Monsters University* was clever and original in its own way. Crystal, Goodman, Buscemi, and Peterson reprised their Mike, Sulley, Randall, and Roz, and the Dan Scanlon–directed film was received as enthusiastically as the original. *Monsters University* cost $200 million but ended up earning over $744 million.

MR. BUG GOES TO TOWN

1941
(USA: Fleischer Studios/Paramount)

Directed by Dave Fleischer and Shamus Culhane
Written by Cal Howard, Tedd Pierce, Graham Place, Dan Gordon, Carl Meyer, Izzy Sparber, Bob Wickersham, and Bill Turner
Produced by Max Fleischer
Score by Leigh Harline
Songs by Hoagy Carmichael, Frank Loesser, and Sammy Timberg
Specs: Color (Technicolor); 78 minutes; traditional animation

Too little known today, this early animated feature is a pleasant surprise and very revealing of what another studio was capable of doing even as Disney dominated the field. Mr. Bug Goes to Town *is original, tuneful, and still entertaining.*

In a vacant lot in the middle of a large city, an insect community called Buggsville is suffering from humans who trespass through a broken fence and smash their houses with their feet. The popular grasshopper Hoppity returns to Buggsville to seek out his sweetheart, the bee Honey, only to find her family's Honey House threatened by a tossed away cigar butt. Also hoping to wed Honey is the greedy beetle entrepreneur C. Bagley Beetle, who uses his henchmen Swat the Fly and Smack the Mosquito to get rid of Hoppity but the two incompetent stooges fail. Next to the lot is a house where the human songwriter Dick and his wife, Mary, live. They are hoping to sell one of Dick's songs in order to keep the bank from foreclosing on their home. A check from a music publisher comes in the mail, but Beetle, Swat, and Smack steal it and hide it. The bank takes the house and it is torn down to make room for a new skyscraper. Hoppity overhears Dick and Mary say they want to build a house and garden on the top of the building if his songs make them rich. Hoppity finds the lost letter and gets it into a mailbox, and it is delivered to Dick. In addition to the check, the song is a huge hit and the money pours in. Dick and Mary build their house and garden in the sky and Hoppity leads all the insects to their new home.

After the Fleischer brothers' success with *Gulliver's Travels* (1939), Paramount ordered another animated feature from the cartoon studio. The new movie was set to open for Christmas of 1941, which put time and money restraints on producer Max Fleischer and director Dave Fleischer. The project was planned as a modern

The grasshopper Hoppity and his sweetheart Honey Bee are trapped inside an envelope, but greedy C. Bagley Beetle and his two henchmen Swat and Smack refuse to help them. *Paramount Pictures / Photofest. © Paramount Pictures*

version of a story by Belgian author Maurice Maeterlinck called *The Life of the Bee*, but Hollywood producer Samuel Goldwyn owned the screen rights. So an original story was concocted about a variety of insects that live in a large American city. The Fleischers and their artists had learned a great deal about animated features in making *Gulliver's Travels* and came up with a movie that surpassed it in plotting, characters, and animation. The many insect characters are kept distinct and lively, from the optimistic Hoppity to the grouchy old snail Mr. Creeper.

Voice Cast

Stan Freed	Hoppity
Pauline Loth	Honey
Tedd Pierce	C. Bagley Beetle
Jack Mercer	Mr. Bumble
Jack Mercer	Swat
Carl Meyer	Smack
Pinto Colvig	Mr. Creeper
Margie Hines	Mrs. Ladybug
Gwen Williams	Mary
Kenny Gardner	Dick
Guinn Williams	Narrator

The beetle villain is a familiar type, but he has a slyness and touch of vanity that make him amusing. More fun are his sidekicks Smack and Swat, who steal much of the attention. As in most animated films of this period, the heroine Honey is one-dimensional, but Hoppity's personality makes the relationship palatable. *Mr. Bug Goes to Town* has many of the characteristics of the better Disney movies if not the polish of that more experienced studio.

Songs

"I'll Dance at Your Wedding (Honey Dear)" (Carmichael/Loesser)
"We're the Couple in the Castle (In the Air)" (Carmichael/Loesser)
"Boy Oh Boy" (Timberg/Loesser)
"Katy Did, Katy Didn't" (Carmichael/Loesser)

The technical craftsmanship of the animators and background artists is noticeably better than that in *Gulliver's Travels*. The city and the garden are rendered in a slightly romanticized style that is soft and painterly. As in the much later films *Antz* (1998) and *A Bug's Life* (1998), the artists are ingenious in showing everyday objects enlarged and used as the houses and gathering places of the insects. This bug-eyed view of the world is both amusing and clever. The animation of the characters is also clever at times, the clothed insects taking on human characteristics while retaining their natural appendages and such. The tuxedoed Beetle, for example, believes himself quite human until he tips over on his back and needs his henchmen to get him back on his feet. The film has several impressive animation sequences. When Hoppity touches the end of a live electric wire, he lights up in a surreal manner as he dances about, creating a piece of abstract animation. At one point Hoppity is sealed inside an envelope with a transparent window and has to battle Smack and Swat from within. The animators stretch the window in various ways that also seem surreal. The coordination between setting and animation reaches its high point in the final sequence when the crawling insects climb the skyscraper among moving girders, spitting rivets, and splashing mortar.

The voice work in *Mr. Bug Goes to Town* is varied and fun. All kinds of sounds and accents are used, some simulating insect noises while others are right off the vaudeville stage. The soundtrack score by Leigh Harline, who scored Disney's *Pinocchio* the year before, is also varied, with big city jazz in between frolicsome pastoral themes. The songs by Hoagy Carmichael, Frank Loesser, and Sammy Timberg are exceptionally tuneful. The crooning ballad "We're the Couple in the Castle (In the Air)" that Dick composes and sings to Mary sounds like a hit, and the song later enjoyed some popularity on Tin Pan Alley. The sprightly "I'll Dance at Your Wedding" is a gleeful number for the ensemble and it also was a song hit. There is the happy-go-lucky march "Boy Oh Boy" and the harmonizing swing number "Katy Did, Katy Didn't," perhaps the most pleasing song in the score. It is performed by a quartet of bugs at a nightclub then is picked up by Hoppity and Honey.

Mr. Bug Goes to Town was completed on time, but it cost over $700,000. When critics and theater owners saw a preview on December 5, 1941, reaction ranged from enthusiastic to disinterest. Two days later Pearl Harbor was attacked by the

> MRS. LADYBUG: Those Human Ones! Why, the way they're taking to tramping through the lowlands, it's getting so your life ain't worth a sunflower seed anymore. One never knows who's gonna get it next.

Japanese, and Paramount pulled the film from its Christmas release. They finally released *Mr. Bug Goes to Town* two months later with little fanfare and it did poor box office, earning only $240,000. Changing the name to *Hoppity Goes to Town*, the movie was later rereleased and even later sold to television, but it never caught on. In 1989 it was put on home video, and in 2017 it found its way to Blu-ray. The film has found an audience over the years but it is still unknown to mainstream audiences.

The failure of *Mr. Bug Goes to Town* had major repercussions. The Fleischer brothers parted ways, Fleischer Studio was dissolved and turned into Famous Studios, and Paramount lost interest in animated features. In future they would bankroll cartoon shorts but not full-length animated movies. Had *Mr. Bug Goes to Town* been a major hit, the history of Hollywood animation might have been much different.

See also *Gulliver's Travels*.

Did You Know . . . ?

Throughout *Mr. Bug Goes to Town*, the faces of the humans are never seen. Only feet and other bug-eyed views of people were used.

MULAN

1998
(USA: Walt Disney Pictures)

Directed by Tony Bancroft and Barry Cook
Written by Chris Sanders, Rita Hsiao, Philip LaZebnik, Raymond Singer, and Eugenia Bostwick-Singer, based on the Chinese poem "The Song of Fa Mu Lan"
Produced by Pam Coats, Robert S. Garber, and Kendra Haaland
Score by Jerry Goldsmith
Songs by Matthew Wilder (music) and David Zippel (lyrics)
Specs: Color (Technicolor); 88 minutes; traditional and computer animation

A legendary Chinese warrior comes to life with a modern subtext in this Disney film that successfully mixes history, adventure, and comedy.

When Shan Yu and his Hun army invade China, the Emperor calls for each family to provide a warrior for the Chinese army. The invalided Fa Zhou has no sons and prepares to join the army himself, but his daughter, the headstrong and unconventional Mulan, cuts her hair and, disguised as a male soldier, joins the unit

The Chinese girl Mulan (center) disguises herself as a man and proves to be an outstanding warrior in the battle against the invading Huns. *Walt Disney Pictures / Photofest.* © *Walt Disney Pictures*

under the command of Captain Li Shang. She takes with her the wisecracking little dragon Mushu, who has been sent by her ancestors to protect her. During basic training, Mulan proves herself to be the match of any man, even though she is falling in love with Shang. An attack by the Huns destroys much of the Chinese army, but Mulan saves the day by firing a cannon into a snowy mountain and causing an avalanche that buries many of the Huns. The leader, Shan Yu, survives

Voice Cast

Ming-Na Wen	Mulan (speaking)
Lea Salonga	Mulan (singing)
B. D. Wong	Shang (speaking)
Donny Osmond	Shang (singing)
Eddie Murphy	Mushu (speaking)
Mark Moseley	Mushu (singing)
Gedde Watanabe	Ling (speaking)
Matthew Wilder	Ling (singing)
Harvey Fierstein	Yao
Jerry Tondo	Chien-Po
Soon-Tek Oh	Fa Zhou
June Foray	Grandmother Fa (speaking)
Marni Nixon	Grandmother Fa (singing)
Pat Morita	Emperor
Miguel Ferrer	Shan-Yu
James Yong	Chi Fu
Freda Foh Shen	Fa Li
Miriam Margolyes	Matchmaker
George Takei	First Ancestor
James Shigeta	General Li

and leads a party of Huns to the Imperial City, where he kidnaps the Emperor. Mulan, Shang, and some of her fellow Chinese soldiers sneak into the Imperial city and battle the Huns, Mulan engaging Shan Yu in a sword fight and defeating him. Mulan is given gifts and a royal thank you by the Emperor and, revealed as a woman, gets Shang as well.

The legend of Hua Mulan, the Chinese woman warrior, goes back to the fourth century AD and over the years has been told in stories, plays, films, and on television. The Disney version began as an animated short called *China Doll* to be made at the animation studio in Florida. As the project changed and grew in size, it ended up being the first animated feature to be made at the Florida studio. The artists spent three weeks in China making hundreds of sketches of the landscape, architecture, and people of the country. The animators also were instructed in the martial arts in order to get the fighting movements correct. The script went through many changes during development. There are so many versions of the Chinese legend that many characters and situations were considered. The decision to make Mulan's sidekick a dragon was dropped for a time, the artists fearing that the size of a dragon would distract from the heroine. It was then discovered that dragons came in all sizes in Chinese culture, and the pint-sized, very hip character of Mushu was created. *Mulan* was not only the first Disney film to have an Asian heroine and a cast of Chinese characters, it was also the first to show warfare and to feature battles. For these scenes, and the ones in the Forbidden City with large crowds of people, computer animation was used. Much of the rest of the movie is traditionally animated. Over seven hundred artists labored at the small Florida studio for four years. The result is one of the most beautiful-looking Disney films. The visuals in the film were inspired by Chinese prints, sculpture, pottery, and calligraphy. The opening credits, for example, were done with watercolor paints on rice paper. The artistic details in *Mulan*, ranging from the flowers to the weapons, are expertly done. Particular attention was paid to the architecture and clothing of the Ming and Qing dynasties. The delicate flavor of Chinese art used throughout the movie and the distinctive Asian color palette make *Mulan* look like no other film.

Songs

"Honor to Us All"
"Reflection"
"True to Your Heart"
"I'll Make a Man Out of You"
"A Girl Worth Fighting For"

Most of the voice cast for *Mulan* consists of Asian-American actors from the stage, television, and film. Ming-Na Wen was thirty-four years old when she did the speaking vocals for Mulan, but she sounds much younger, even when she uses her masculine voice to deceive her fellow soldiers. Mulan's singing was done by theater actress Lea Salonga, who had also done the singing for Jasmine in *Aladdin* (1992). B. D. Wong did the commanding vocals for Captain Shang, with pop singer Donny Osmond doing his singing. Among the other talented Asian actors heard in the film are Pat Morita (Emperor), George Takei (First Ancestor), Soon-Tek Oh (Mulan's father, Fa Zhou), James Shigeta (General Li), Gedde Watanabe (Ling),

Jerry Tondo (Chien-Po), and James Hong (Chi-Fu). Other actors giving notewor-thy performances include Harvey Fierstein as the sour soldier Yao, Miguel Ferrer as the Hun leader Shan Yu, and Miriam Margolyes as the frustrated Matchmaker. But the most dazzling vocals in Mulan are those of Eddie Murphy as the fast-talking, very modern dragon Mushu. Murphy explodes with pride, complaints, and anachronistic ad-libs, giving a raucous performance that propels the movie with energy. What Robin Williams did for *Aladdin*, Murphy does for *Mulan*.

> MULAN: My ancestors sent a little lizard to help me?
>
> MUSHU: Hey! Dragon. Dra-gon, not lizard. I don't do that tongue thing.

Mulan is a musical with five songs and a Chinese-influenced soundtrack score. Stephen Schwartz, who had contributed lyrics to *Pocahontas* (1995) and *The Hunch-back of Notre Dame* (1996), was scheduled to score *Mulan*, but when he agreed to write the songs for DreamWorks' *The Prince of Egypt* (1998), the Disney studio replaced him with Matthew Wilder (music) and David Zippel (lyrics). The tuneful song "Honor to Us All" near the beginning of the movie introduces Mulan and other characters and sets up her tomboy persona. Later Mulan reprises the num-ber as she prays to her ancestors, hoping she will not disappoint them. The merry march number "A Girl Worth Fighting For" is sung by the new recruits as they en-vision the woman of their dreams. Captain Shang sings the military number "I'll Make a Man Out of You" with an ironic lyric when it refers to Mulan. The most memorable song in the score is "Reflection," a touching lament sung by Mulan as she hopes for acceptance for who she is. For the closing credits, "True to Your Heart" is a rocking number sung by Stevie Wonder and the group 98 Degrees. As enjoyable as the songs are, it is the soundtrack score by veteran composer Jerry Goldsmith that captures the spirit of the story. A fusion of Asian music and Hol-lywood symphonics, the music in *Mulan* soars. The playful themes for the lighter moments are contrasted by the stirring passages used in the battle scenes. The soundtrack is Goldsmith at his best, which is saying a lot.

Awards

Academy Award nomination: Best Score.
Golden Globe nominations: Best Score and Best Song ("Reflection").

The final price tag for *Mulan* was $90 million, so the studio was relieved when it brought in $120 million domestically and over $300 million worldwide. The reviews for the film were mostly positive, but *Mulan* did not get the highly enthu-siastic notices that some earlier Disney animated movies had. The exotic nature of the movie was highly appealing to audiences, and girls immediately took to its self-empowered heroine. The Chinese government did not allow *Mulan* to be released in its country until 1999, when it was met with mostly dismissive reviews and disappointing business. The 1999 VHS and DVD sales were healthy, as were those for the Blu-ray edition in 2013. A 2004 direct-to-video sequel *Mulan II* followed Mulan and Captain Shang as they escorted the Emperor's three daughters across the countryside to meet their future husbands. Murphy did not reprise his Mushu but most of the voice cast from the original movie returned. A live-action screen version of the original Mulan is scheduled to be released in 2018.

Did You Know . . . ?

Singer Christina Aguilera launched her career when her recording of "Reflection" from *Mulan* was so popular it led to her first recording contract.

N

THE NIGHTMARE BEFORE CHRISTMAS

1993
(USA: Skellington Productions / Touchstone)

Directed by Henry Selick
Written by Caroline Thompson and Michael McDowell, based on the narrative poem
   by Tim Burton
Produced by Tim Burton, Denise Di Novi, Philip Lofaro, Jill Jacobs, Kathleen Gavin,
   Danny Elfman, Jim Jacobs, and Diane Minter Lewis
Score and songs by Danny Elfman
Specs: Color (Technicolor); 76 minutes; stop-motion animation

A classic stop-motion film that is a dark comedy as well as a clever fantasy, The Nightmare before Christmas *is ingenious on all levels and offers superior storytelling, characterization, animation, and music.*

Jack Skellington is the celebrated "Pumpkin King" of Halloween Town, the home of all kinds of ghoulish characters, but he is getting bored with the same scary goings-on year after year. Then he discovers Christmastown and the holiday of Christmas and gets excited once again, creating his own frightening version of

Voice Cast

Chris Sarandon	Jack Skellington (speaking)
Danny Elfman	Jack Skellington (singing)
Catherine O'Hara	Sally
Ken Page	Oogie Boogie
William Hickey	Dr. Finkelstein
Glenn Shadix	Mayor
Paul Reubens	Lock
Catherine O'Hara	Shock
Danny Elfman	Barrel
Edward Ivory	Santa

At the center of this offbeat fantasy film is an equally offbeat love story, that of the "Pumpkin King," Jack Skellington, and the put-upon servant Sally. *Touchstone Pictures / Photofest.* ©
Touchstone Pictures

the merry holiday. Calling himself "Sandy Claws," Jack acts as the new Santa while his three stooges, Lock, Shock, and Barrel, kidnap the real Santa. Jack's enthusiasm runs away with him as he rides through the sky pulled by reindeer skeletons and delivers toys that are grotesque and frightening to children and adults. Halloween Town's boogeyman, Oogie Boogie, gets his hands on the real Santa, and when Jack's admirer Sally tries to rescue Santa, Oogie captures her as well. Jack is shot down out of the sky, but he manages to return to Halloween Town to rescue Sally and Santa, declare his love for Sally, and return to being a Halloween hero.

The idea for the movie goes back to Tim Burton's childhood, when he saw a store window being changed from a Halloween display to a Christmas one. Seeing characters and images from the two holidays together was decidedly weird and he never forgot it. When Tim Burton was an animator for Disney in the 1980s, he wrote and illustrated a poem he titled *The Nightmare before Christmas*, with the idea that it might make a stop-motion television special. The Disney studio was interested in developing the poem into a feature film, but other projects postponed it until 1991, when production began in San Francisco. Most moviegoers assume that Burton wrote and directed the 1993 feature film, but he did neither. Caroline Thompson adapted his poem into a screenplay, and Henry Selick directed it. But it was Burton's original tale and designs that inspired the movie, and Burton was involved with all aspects of the production. The expensive ($18 million) and time-consuming (two years) production involved 120 animators working on some two dozen sound stages, many different settings, and hundreds of characters. In addition to creating the expressionistic world of Halloween Town, there were many locations in the so-called real world, although those were often as strange as Jack Skellington's domain. Also, both the residents of Halloween Town and those outside it are unique oddball characters that are often grotesque. The streets, houses, and interiors in Halloween Town are dark and sinister and never seem to see sunlight. There is more color outside of Halloween Town (particularly in Christmastown), but the palette for the movie is never sunny or bright. Movement throughout the film is both chaotic and poetic with some characters heavy and earthbound, others fluid and buoyant. *The Nightmare before Christmas* looked and moved like no other film before it and opened up many new possibilities for the art of stop-motion animation.

Songs

"This Is Halloween"
"Jack's Lament"
"Kidnap the Sandy Claws"
"Poor Jack"
"Sally's Song"
"What's This?"
"Jack's Obsession"
"Making Christmas"
"Town Meeting Song"
"Oogie Boogie's Song"
"Finale"

The Nightmare before Christmas is populated with bizarre and fascinating characters that are voiced with style by an exceptional cast. Jack Skellington is both a freak and an everyman. Chris Sarandon gives his lines a dreamy yet determined reading. (Composer Danny Elfman provides Jack's equally odd singing voice.) Sally is voiced by Catherine O'Hara in a similarly dreamy manner, but it is less confident. The blustering Mayor (Glenn Shadix), the creepy Dr. Finklestein (William Hickey), and the howling Oogie Boogie (Ken Page) are among the most exuberant of the voices heard. Also delightfully eccentric are the vocals by Paul Reubens, O'Hara, and Elfman as the trick-or-treaters Lock, Shock, and Barrel. *The Nightmare before Christmas* is a musical, one might even say a cockeyed opera, and long sections of the film are sung. Elfman's soundtrack score and the eleven songs he wrote have the same quirky sentiments of the story and the visuals. The ponderous march "This Is Halloween," the gleeful but dissident "Making Christmas," the reflective "Jack's Lament," the touching "Sally's Song," the explosive "What's This?," and the rollicking "Oogie Boogie's Song" were among the musical numbers, each one staged with mesmerizing style. Elfman and O'Hara both project a minor-key quality in their singing, and Page's over-the-top vocals for Oogie Boogie are both exciting and disarming. The CD soundtrack for *The Nightmare before Christmas* was understandably popular and many recording artists have done their versions of the Elfman songs.

> MAYOR: How horrible our Christmas will be!
>
> JACK: No. How jolly!
>
> MAYOR: Oh. How jolly our Christmas will be.

As postproduction was being completed, the Disney studio was rightfully nervous, wondering if there was a big enough audience for such a special, unusual film. It was also clear that this was not a movie for young children, so the studio released *The Nightmare before Christmas* under the banner of Touchstone Pictures. Because of Burton's recent success directing *Batman* (1989), *Edward Scissorhands* (1990), and *Batman Returns* (1992), the studio wanted to make it clear that the new film was a product of Burton's imagination, even though he did not write or direct it. Sometimes billed *Tim Burton's The Nightmare before Christmas*, the movie led audiences to not notice director Henry Selick. After being featured at the New York Film Festival, the movie was given a wide release around Halloween of 1993 and was met with mostly rave notices. The critics cautioned that it was not a children's film, but it was acclaimed as a dazzling adult movie. Some comparisons were made with the Dr. Seuss tale *How the Grinch Stole Christmas*, but generally the press applauded the originality of the movie. The public agreed and *The Nightmare before Christmas* made $50 million domestically on its first release.

Awards

Academy Award nomination: Best Visual Effects.
Golden Globe nomination: Best Score.

Some consider *The Nightmare before Christmas* a cult film; if so, it is a very large cult. Disney released a 3-D version in 2006 and it was a hit all over again. There were also Halloween rereleases in 2007 and 2008. The 1994 DVD and the 2011 Blu-ray editions were big sellers, and the movie has joined the list of Christmastime favorites. For a film that made no pretensions of appealing to a wide audience, it ending up doing just that. In addition to the many *Nightmare* products that remain popular, there are also video games, a card game, a party game version, and (since 2001) talk of a film sequel. *The Nightmare before Christmas* has all the markings of a classic.

See also *Corpse Bride* and *Frankenweenie.*

Did You Know . . . ?

The great horror film actor Vincent Price was contracted to do the voice of Oogie Boogie, but by the time he came to the studio the eighty-two-year-old veteran was severely ill and his vocals were too weak to use. Ken Page was hired to redo the speaking and singing vocals. Price died a week before *The Nightmare before Christmas* was released.

O

OLIVER & COMPANY

1988
(USA: Walt Disney Pictures)

Directed by George Scribner
Written by Jim Cox, Tim Disney, and James Mangold, based on Charles Dickens's
  Oliver Twist
Produced by Walt Disney Feature Animation
Songs by Barry Mann, Howard Ashman, Tom Snow, Dean Pitchford, Barry Manilow,
  Jack Feldman, Bruce Sussman, Ron Rocha, Rob Minkoff, Dan Hartman, and Char-
  lie Midnight.
Score by J. A. C. Redford
Specs: Color (Metrocolor); 74 minutes; traditional animation

Charles Dickens's classic novel Oliver Twist *is turned into an animal tale set in contemporary New York City in this freewheeling movie with a tuneful modern score.*

The orphaned kitten Oliver is left to fend for himself in New York City and falls in with a gang of street-smart dogs led by Dodger and overseen by the human

Voice Cast

Joey Lawrence	Oliver
Billy Joel	Dodger
Natalie Gregory	Jenny (speaking)
Myhanh Tran	Jenny (singing)
Dom DeLuise	Fagin
Bette Midler	Georgette
Robert Loggia	Sykes
Cheech Marin	Tito
Richard Mulligan	Einstein
Sheryl Lee Ralph	Rita (speaking)
Ruth Pointer	Rita (singing)
William Glover	Winston

Charles Dickens's orphan Oliver Twist is an abandoned kitten also named Oliver in this modern urban adaptation of the famous nineteenth-century novel. *Buena Vista Pictures / Photofest.* © *Buena Vista Pictures*

Fagin, who is very dog-like himself. While on the prowl with the gang, Oliver is rescued by the wealthy little girl Jenny, who takes the kitten to her swank Manhattan townhouse run by the pampered French poodle Georgette. The jealous pooch sees the stray as a threat and works with the gang to get rid of him. The mobster Sykes learns that Jenny is rich and kidnaps her, but Fagin and all the dogs outwit Sykes and rescue Jenny, securing a home for Oliver.

Although *Oliver & Company* was made right before the Disney studio's animation renaissance began with *The Little Mermaid* (1989), it has some of the artistry, confidence, and entertainment value of the later hits. The screenplay uses Dickens's original story effectively, finding an equivalent to Victorian London in the New York City of the 1980s. The major Dickens characters translate well into animal ones, with human counterparts for Fagin, Jenny, and Sykes. The characterization of Fagin's canine gang is excellent with such delightful critters as the terrier Dodger with his "street savoir-faire," the hipster Chihuahua Tito, the Shakespeare-spouting bulldog Winston, the dense Great Dane Einstein, and the sassy Afghan hound Rita. The villain Sykes is indeed frightening, as are his two henchmen, the twin Doberman pinschers Roscoe and DeSoto. Originally the screenplay was much darker, retaining some of the murders in Dickens's original.

Songs

"Once Upon a Time in New York City" (Mann/Ashman)
"Streets of Gold" (Snow/Pitchford)
"Why Should I Worry?" (Hartman/Midnight)
"Perfect Isn't Easy" (Manilow/Feldman/Sussman)
"Good Company" (Rocha/Minkoff)

The studio decided to soften such elements but, even with these compromises, *Oliver & Company* has one of the strongest scripts for a post-Walt animated feature.

At the time one of the few Disney animated films set in the contemporary world, *Oliver & Company* made 1980s Manhattan a major character in the tale. The movie begins with a stylized aerial view of the island and then zooms down into the streets of the city. Both the rough-and tumble districts and the upscale neighborhoods are portrayed with accuracy but still in a cartoonish manner. The up-tempo pace of New York surrounds the action, even the dogs moving to the beat of the cityscape. True to Dickens, the garbage and dark corners of the urban locale are important to the storytelling. This is nicely contrasted with the bucolic scenes in Central Park and the Manhattan that Jenny inhabits. *Oliver & Company* has a handful of sequences that use an early form of computerized animation, such as the two chase scenes. Yet the movie feels traditionally animated and feels more like the Disney features of the 1960s. Much of the contemporary flavor in the film can be credited to the expert soundtrack score by J. A. C. Redford and the vibrant songs by a variety of pop songwriters. Very contemporary sounding are Dodger's rhythmic philosophy number "Why Should I Worry?," Georgette's satirical credo "Perfect Isn't Easy," Rita's pulsating "Streets of Gold," and the bluesy "Once Upon a Time in New York City," which is sung on the soundtrack by Huey Lewis during the opening sequence. Only the sweet friendship song "Good Company," sung by Jenny to her newfound pet, has the feel of the traditional Disney songs of the past.

GEORGETTE: I, um, hope you won't think me rude, but do you happen to know out of whose bowl you're eating?

OLIVER: Yours?

GEORGETTE: Ooh! Aren't you a clever kitty? And do you have any idea whose home this is?

OLIVER: I . . . thought it was Jenny's.

GEORGETTE: Well, it may be Jenny's house, but everything from the doorknobs down is mine!

The voice cast for the film consists of popular celebrities, most of whom had never done an animated movie before. Pop singer Billy Joel is ideal as the street-smart Dodger in both his dialogue and singing. Similarly, singer-actress Bette Midler brings a very modern kind of sarcasm to the vain Georgette. Dom DeLuise's perfect cartoon voice is used effectively as the bumbling Fagin. All of Fagin's canines are expertly voiced, but the runaway performance is that by Cheech Marin as the hilarious Tito, who thinks he is the great canine Latin Lover. Young television actor Joey Lawrence gives a solid performance as Oliver, and character actor Robert Loggia drips with evil as Sykes. Director George Scribner must also be credited with keeping all the dialogue brisk and lively.

Award

Golden Globe nomination: Best Song ("Why Should I Worry?").

The Disney studio took a risk with *Oliver & Company*, spending over $31 million on an animated feature when the genre's track record of late was not encouraging. Some $15 million was also spent on the new Computer Animation Production System (CAPS), which was a wise investment for the future. When the movie was released in 1988, critical reception was mixed. Some reviewers thought it was reminiscent of the classic Disney features of the past; others compared it unfavorably to those beloved films. Moviegoers were not so divided, and *Oliver & Company* ended up earning over $74 million. The success of the movie, helped by the popularity of the stars heard on the soundtrack, encouraged the Disney studio to invest more money and talent in its neglected animation department. The result was *The Little Mermaid* (1989) and a whole new era in the studio's history. Oddly, no VHS edition of *Oliver & Company* came out until 1996 when the Disney renaissance was well underway. The DVD version was released in 2002 and the Blu-ray edition in 2013.

Did You Know . . . ?

In order to accurately capture Oliver's viewpoint, the animators took many photographs of New York City with the camera eighteen inches off the ground.

ONE HUNDRED AND ONE DALMATIANS

1961
(USA: Walt Disney Productions)

Produced by Walt Disney.
Directed by Hamilton Luske, Clyde Geronimi, and Wolfgang Reitherman.
Written by Bill Peet, based on the book *The Hundred and One Dalmatians* by Dodie Smith.
Score by George Bruns. Songs by Mel Leven.
Specs: Color (Technicolor); 79 minutes; traditional animation

A heartwarming and suspenseful tale set in contemporary England, this screen favorite introduced a new look for Disney animation. It also introduced one of Disney's most flamboyant and diabolical villains in the form of the fur-addict Cruella De Vil.

The London songwriter Roger Radcliffe is a contented bachelor, but his pet Dalmatian Pongo finds their life together dull. The canine maneuvers to get Roger to the park, where he meets Anita, who just happens to own the female Dalmatian Perdita. The human and canine couples wed, and soon Perdita gives birth to a litter of fifteen puppies. The cute pups are highly appealing to Anita's old school chum Cruella De Vil, who plans to make a fur coat out of the skins of the puppies. When Roger refuses to sell the puppies to Cruella, she arranges for her stooges, Jasper and Horace, to kidnap the pups and hide them in the old De Vil mansion in the countryside, where she has dozens of other Dalmatian pups waiting to be turned into coats. The police are unsuccessful in finding the

The London Dalmatian family in this adventure movie has many human characteristics, including watching their favorite television show starring the canine hero Thunder. *Walt Disney Pictures / Photofest.* © *Walt Disney Pictures*

kidnapped puppies, so Pongo and Perdita use a canine gossip chain called the Twilight Bark to send word out and hopefully locate the missing pups. Word soon comes back that there are dozens of Dalmatian puppies in the deserted De Vil mansion. With the help of the cat Sergeant Tibs, Pongo and Perdita rescue all the puppies and head to London. Cruella, Jasper, and Horace are hot on their trail, but the one hundred and one Dalmatians use some sly tricks to get back to London. Roger and Anita agree to adopt all of the pups and plan to build a Dalmatian plantation in the countryside.

Voice Cast

Rod Taylor	Pongo
Cate Bauer	Perdita
Ben Wright	Roger (speaking)
Bill Lee	Roger (singing)
Lisa Davis	Anita
Betty Lou Gerson	Cruella de Vil
J. Pat O'Malley	Jasper
Frederick Worlock	Horace
J. Pat O'Malley	Colonel
David Frankham	Sgt. Tibs
Martha Wentworth	Nanny
Thurl Ravenscroft	Captain
George Pelling	Danny

Walt Disney read Dodie Smith's book *The Hundred and One Dalmatians* soon after it was published in 1956 and acquired the screen rights. Unlike other authors whose work was bought by Disney, Smith was thrilled that her book was to become an animated Disney movie. Production did not begin right away because the studio was tied up with the very expensive *Sleeping Beauty,* which eventually opened in 1959 to disappointing box office. Plans for *101 Dalmatians,* as the title is often written, proceeded, but with a very limited budget. While all previous Disney features had several scriptwriters, the first draft screenplay was the work of one writer, Bill Peet. Disney thought the script so well done that production proceeded with Peet as sole author. Peet made minors alterations to the book. The name of the mother Dalmatian was changed from Missis to Perdita, some minor characters were dropped, and a chase scene was added in which Cruella and her two henchmen, Horace and Jasper, try to run the truck carrying the canines off the road. Smith thought the screenplay improved on much of the book.

Because Disney was so pleased with the script, he was not as involved in the production of *101 Dalmatians* as he had been with previous features. This might explain why the background art and animation in the film is a noticeable departure from the past. Art director Ken Anderson took his style from the British cartoonist Ronald Searle, whose sketches of London and other locales were busy line drawings with a rough, unfinished look. Color director Walter Peregoy used broad splashes of color that were not confined within the line drawings. The result was a modern and stylized look that was very 1960s in temperament. Disney, who favored an old-fashioned Victorian look, as with *Peter Pan,* or a naturalistic design, as in *Bambi,* was not happy with the new style in *101 Dalmatians,* but the project was so advanced and the budget was so tight that there was no question of redoing any of the art. Consequently, Disney was not personally pleased with the finished product. Only years later did he compliment Anderson on his work in *101 Dalmatians* and suggest that the new look was appropriate.

The use of the Xerox process in making the movie was a time saver and a money saver. The animators later totaled up all the spots on the Dalmatians throughout the finished movie and came up with over six million black spots. If each of these had to be drawn individually, the process would have taken much longer. Live-action footage was used for animating the human characters, but the most interesting movement in *101 Dalmatians* was that for the animals, particularly the Dalmatians and other canines in the movie. The animation for the dogs is not as exaggerated as in some past Disney projects. The ways they stretch, scratch themselves, run, and sit are full of variety. Near the opening of the film, the animators have fun showing how dogs often resemble their owners (and vice versa) as Pongo looks out the window at various humans and their pets walking toward the park. The animation of Cruella, on the other hand, is a masterpiece of flamboyant physical moves and gestures, her thin body whirling about with her fur coat making waves around her. She is a vibrant contrast to Roger and Anita, who are the epitome of British reserve and move in like manner.

The task of animating so many puppies on screen at the same time was daunting and could only be done by Xeroxing the images and repeating them many times over. The most difficult sequences were in the journey to London. The white-coated Dalmatians were set against backgrounds filled with snow, which caused many difficulties. It helped that the dogs were not actually white but an off-gray color that read like white on the screen. Another piece of memorable animation can be seen during the Twilight Bark as the action logically moves from inner London to a farm near the De Vil mansion. The barking of the different dogs connects the sequence, but the progression of the background art is also a unifying element.

Songs

"Cruella De Vil"
"Dalmatian Plantation"
"Kanine Krunchies"

The movie was planned as a musical, but, as the story had so much action, some of the songs were dropped and the film ended up being more an adventure than a musical. Mel Levin wrote a half dozen songs for *101 Dalmatians*, but the only one that was integrated into the plot was "Cruella De Vil," which Roger writes about Anita's outrageous school friend. It is a vampy piece of jazz and very catchy, easily recalled after one hearing. The only other song fragments to remain were a silly jingle for the dog treats Kanine Krunchies in a television ad, and the first few lines of the spirited "Dalmatian Plantation" at the end of the film. Gone were a Cockney ditty sung by Jasper and Horace and a march number sung by the canines as they escape the De Vil mansion. If *101 Dalmatians* does not have a full song score, it does have an expert soundtrack score by George Bruns that is as lively and contemporary as the art look of the film.

CRUELLA: Fifteen. Fifteen puppies! How marvelous! How marvelous! How perfectly ugh! Oh, the devil take it, they're mongrels. No spots! No spots at all! What a horrid little white rat!

NANNY: They're not mongrels! They'll get their spots. Just wait and see.

ANITA: That's right, Cruella. They'll have their spots in a few weeks.

CRUELLA: Oh, well, in that case I'll take them all. The whole litter. Just name your price, dear.

Several Disney regulars were cast for the voices, with the currently popular actor Rod Taylor voicing Pongo. All the characters, human and animal, are British, and there is a playfulness in the various accents heard throughout the film, ranging from Cockney to Scottish. Ironically, very few of the cast were British actors. The standout performance in the movie is Betty Lou Gerson's Cruella, who is as vocally exaggerated as she is physically over the top. Gerson had provided the warm narration in *Cinderella* a decade earlier, but, like the best voices actors, her versatility was such that her Cruella is a triumph of comic villainy. Gerson based her vocals on the extrovert actress Tallulah Bankhead, which might explain why Cruella is the least English-sounding member of the cast. Because the action in *101 Dalmatians* moves around quite a bit, there are more characters in the film than in many Disney features. Yet every human and animal is voiced beautifully and the sounds heard conjure up those of a British movie.

Award

British Academy of Film & Television Arts (BAFTA) Award: Best Animated Film.

One Hundred and One Dalmatians opened to enthusiastic reviews. The book was little known in the United States, so American moviegoers did not know what to expect in terms of plot. The very idea of a woman planning to kill puppies to make coats out of them was a bit severe for some audience members, but for the most part the public embraced the story and the characters. The movie did excellent box office in America, but it was even more popular in the United Kingdom and in France. It remained a hit when rereleased in theaters in 1969, 1979, 1985, and 1991. The next year the film showed up on VHS and later DVD, joining the ranks of the perennial Disney favorites. Although it cost around $4 million to make, over the years *101 Dalmatians* has earned over $215 million.

The Disney Studio made a live-action version of *101 Dalmatians* in 1996 with some changes in the plot. Also, none of the animals talked. Glenn Close's exuberant Cruella was applauded, as were the comedics of Hugh Laurie and Mark Williams as Horace and Jasper. The farcical movie lacked charm, but was popular enough that a live-action sequel, *102 Dalmatians*, was made in 2000. There was also a cartoon series on television in 1997 and 1998 and a made-for-video sequel *101 Dalmatians: Patch's London Adventure* in 2003. These sequels and spinoffs may have their merits, but none of them come close to the brilliant 1961 original, which is still an endearing work of Disney animation entertainment.

See also *Lady and the Tramp* and *The Aristocats*.

Did You Know . . . ?

One Hundred and One Dalmatians was the first animated film to make use of the Xerox process to repeat sketches that had once been copied by hand. The new process required only one hundred inkers instead of the usual 500 and helped the film come in way under budget.

P

PARANORMAN

2012
(USA: Focus Features/Laika Entertainment)

Directed by Chris Butler and Sam Fell
Written by Chris Butler
Produced by Travis Knight, Arianne Sutner, Matthew Fried, and Carl Beyer
Score by Jon Brion
Specs: Color; 92 minutes; stop-motion animation

A thriller and ghost tale with a wry sense of humor, the stop-motion fantasy ParaNorman *does not take itself too seriously but has some chilling moments all the same.*

The New England town of Blithe Hollow capitalizes on its history as the site of witch burnings in Puritan days. Eleven-year-old Norman is bullied by his school-mates and scolded by his family because he claims to be able to see and talk with

Voice Cast

Kodi Smit-McPhee	Norman Babcock
Tucker Albrizzi	Neil
Jeff Garlin	Perry Babcock
Anna Kendrick	Courtney Babcock
Leslie Mann	Sandra Babcock
Casey Affleck	Mitch
Christopher Mintz-Plasse	Alvin
Elaine Stritch	Grandma
John Goodman	Mr. Prenderghast
Jodelle Ferland	Aggie
Bernard Hill	Judge
Tempestt Bledsoe	Sheriff Hooper
Alex Borstein	Mrs. Henscher
Hannah Noyes	Salma

Young Norman has the psychic ability to see and speak with dead people, but when seven Puritan bodies rise from the grave and terrorize the town, everyone sees them. *Focus Features / Photofest.* © *Focus Features*

ghosts, including his no-nonsense grandmother. Norman's visions get more vivid when his uncle Prenderghast tells him that he must stop the curse of the witches, leaving the boy a book of bedtime stories before the eccentric old guy dies. When seven Puritan corpses rise from their graves and terrorize the town, Norman tries to calm them with the book but it turns out that the curse comes not from them but from the evil spirit of the young girl Agatha, who was sentenced to death by the seven judges three hundred years ago. With the help of his rotund friend Neil, his teenage cheerleader sister Courtney, the thick-headed jock Mitch, and the bully Alvin, Norman manages to locate the grave of "Aggie" and he reasons with her, letting the girl pass on peacefully and end the curse.

   The story for *ParaNorman* is an original one by codirector Chris Butler, but it draws on and often satirizes zombie films and the Salem witch trials. It has its own kind of logic, and the special effects are usually plot motivated. The characters are also very distinct and enjoyable. Norman is an outcast in the town because of his paranormal powers, yet the audience immediately warms up to him because he is more confused and scared than malicious. The adults in the movie are slightly grotesque, yet believable, but it is the younger characters who are so much fun, from the nerdy Neil and his dense brother Mitch to the self-absorbed Courtney and the obtuse Alvin. The voices employed are as sharp and distinct as the visual characterizations, keeping *ParaNorman* from becoming more than an adventure horror thriller. In fact, the film is not all that scary because the directors maintain a sly sense of humor throughout.

> SANDRA: Norman, I know you and grandma were very close, but we all have to move on. Grandma's in a better place
>
> NORMAN: No she's not, she's in the living room.

ParaNorman was a technological breakthrough for stop-motion animation. Special color cameras were developed by Canon that allowed the movie to be shot in 3-D without slowing down the photography process with multiple shots for each pose. The sharpness and expressive facial expressions can be noticed even when *ParaNorman* is viewed without 3-D. The ghost characters are stop-motion, but, because of filters and double exposure, they often seem traditionally animated. The movie is filled with special effects that are blended in with the puppet figures very effectively. The background art is visually interesting as well. The models of the houses in town are slightly surreal, even as they are filled with many details. The color palette recalls the brash colors of a 1950s sci-fi flick. The whole film has an orange and yellowish tint (much of the story takes place one night during an endless sunset) including the interiors, which are cluttered with props. The soundtrack score by Jon Brion is rich with variety and drama. The music often has a lighthearted flavor, even when used for the zombies. There are a few lyrical passages, but mostly the score echoes the tongue-in-cheek attitude of the film. Some song standards are also heard, such as the Donovan ditty "Season of the Witch" sung by the children during a ludicrous school play about the history of witchcraft in the town.

Awards

Academy Award nomination: Best Animated Feature.
British Academy of Film & Television Arts (BAFTA) nomination: Best Animated Film.

The budget for *ParaNorman* was roughly $60 million, a high price tag for a Laika Entertainment project, but the movie ended up making $107 million during its first release in 2012. The DVD and Blu-ray versions were released at the end of the same year and sold well. The reviews were generally supportive, and audiences responded favorably to the movie, finding it more engaging than Laika's darker *Coraline* (2009). *ParaNorman* is arguably the most family-friendly Laika movie, even though it concerns dark themes and handles death flippantly.

See also *Coraline*.

Did You Know . . . ?

The character of Mitch is a stereotypical dumb jock. At the end of the movie, it is revealed that Mitch is also gay, which is perhaps a first in a PG animated feature film.

PETER PAN

1953
(USA: Walt Disney Productions)

Directed by Clyde Geronimi, Wilfred Jackson, Jack Kinney, and Hamilton Luske
Written by Ted Sears, Milt Banta, Ralph Wright, Erdman Penner, Winston Hibler,
     William Cottrell, Bill Peet, and Joe Rinaldi, based on the play by James M. Barrie
Produced by Walt Disney
Score by Oliver Wallace
Songs by Sammy Fain, Sammy Cahn, Oliver Wallace, Erdman Penner, Ted Sears,
     Winston Hibler, and Frank Churchill
Specs: Color (Technicolor); 77 minutes; traditional animation

Of the countless stage, screen, and television adaptations of James M. Barrie's fantasy Peter Pan, *this Disney animated classic remains a favorite for many.*

Peter Pan, a mischievous boy who can fly and never grows up, often flies from Neverland to the London home of the Darling family to listen to Mrs. Darling read bedtime stories to her children Wendy, Michael, and John. One night Peter and his fairy, Tinker Bell, teach the three children to fly and they all set off for Neverland for adventures with the Lost Boys, the mermaids, and the pirates under the command of the one-handed Captain Hook. Peter rescues the princess Tiger Lily and returns her to her tribe, who have captured the Lost Boys. Hook then captures Wendy and the boys and tries to destroy Peter with a time bomb. But Tinker Bell catches on to the plot and saves Peter, who then goes and confronts Hook and the pirates. The battle is a victory for Peter and the boys and Hook is left running away from the crocodile that hungers after the pirate's other hand. The Darling children fly home to London and Peter returns to Neverland to live a life of eternal youth with the Lost Boys.

   Unlike most children's classic tales, *Peter Pan* started as a play then later was turned by James M. Barrie into a book. The original stage version opened in London in 1904 and was a resounding success. Various stage conventions of the time were used, such as having Peter played by a woman and having actors in animal costumes as the dog Nana and the crocodile. These continued not only in theater productions but also in early silent film adaptations. Walt Disney, as a boy, saw *Peter Pan* on the stage and had long wanted to make an animated feature out of the story. Early sketches and songs go back to the late 1930s, but other projects and World War II delayed the project for years. Some of the early storyboards took a dark and sinister approach to the material. The original play, after all, had

Despite all their dastardly efforts, Captain Hook and his bumbling sidekick Smee (on the floor) never seem to outwit the forever-young flying boy Peter Pan. *RKO Radio Pictures / Photofest.* © *RKO Radio Pictures*

some very adult subtexts. But by the time the studio got around to making the film, much of this darkness was replaced by a sunny comic adventure. Disney and his artists realized that with animation there was no limit to the flying, locales, and characterizations in the tale. Even the fairy Tinker Bell, usually portrayed by a beam of light, could become a fully realized creation. The screenplay is more interested in action than talk, so much of Barrie's dialogue was cut or simplified, yet there was room for some delicious physical and vocal characters and scenes.

Voice Cast

Bobby Driscoll	Peter Pan
Hans Conried	Captain Hook
Kathryn Beaumont	Wendy
Bill Thompson	Mr. Smee
Paul Collins	John
Tommy Luske	Michael
Heather Angel	Mrs. Darling
Hans Conried	Mr. Darling
Candy Candido	Indian Chief

As in the tradition of the theater, the voice actor playing Captain Hook also voices Mr. Darling. The biggest departure from the past was having Peter voiced by a boy. Another departure was the sensual, very temperamental characterization of the fairy Tinker Bell. Hook was more comic than frightening, and the sailors, led by the bumbling Mr. Smee, are farcical and far from dangerous. The portrayal of Neverland's "Indians" has not dated well and can prove embarrassing to modern audiences. Nevertheless, Disney's *Peter Pan* is perhaps the most magical version of Barrie's beloved story.

The animation in *Peter Pan* is exquisite. Both the character animation and the background art are comparable to the best Disney products. Peter is not only a very physical person when on the ground, he is even more exciting when he flies. The animators quickly learned that conveying weightlessness on paper was not as easy as it seemed. All the rules of human movement are changed when characters fly and the artists used live models on wires to help meet the challenges of gravity-free motion. Captain Hook is also rendered very physical even though he remains on solid ground. With his exaggerated facial movements and twisting body, he is a human cyclone of sorts, his hooked-arm leading the way. Other impressive characterizations include the tossing and tumbling Lost Boys and the very human-like canine nanny Nana. The background art in *Peter Pan* evoked two very different worlds. London and the Victorian house of the Darling family are portrayed in somber colors with a slightly romanticized touch, particularly the spectacular aerial view of the city when Peter and the children take flight. The color palette in Neverland is more colorful with simplified shapes and forms for the magical landscape. Even the pirate ship has a playground-like look to it, more interested in a child's idea of adventure than historic accuracy.

Songs

"The Second Star to the Right" (Fain/Cahn)
"You Can Fly, You Can Fly, You Can Fly!" (Fain/Cahn)
"Following the Leader" (Wallace/Sears/Hibbler)
"What Makes the Red Man Red?" (Fain/Cahn)
"A Pirate's Life" (Wallace/Penner)
"Your Mother and Mine" (Fain/Cahn)
"The Elegant Captain Hook" (Fain/Cahn)
"Never Smile at a Crocodile" (Churchill)

The superb voice cast included some Disney regulars. Bobby Driscoll, featured in *Song of the South* (1946) and *Treasure Island* (1950), provided the spirited vocals for Peter. Kathryn Beaumont, who did the vocals for the title character in *Alice in Wonderland* (1951), again used her very crisp but warm British voice for Wendy. Yet the outstanding vocal performance in *Peter Pan* is that by Hans Conried as Hook. He climbs up and the down the vocal scale as he barks, croons, snivels, and howls his way through the film. Disney favorite Bill Thompson and his distinctive voice give Mr. Smee a fine comic quality, both a foil and a contrast to Conried's theatrics. All of these actors also served as live models for the animators, creating certain scenes in a studio and being filmed for reference and creative ideas. Much of Hook's physical shenanigans on screen came from Conried's studio performance.

Various songwriters contributed to the score for *Peter Pan*. Frank Churchill, who had died in 1942, wrote the music for two songs with lyricist Jack Lawrence during the early development process in the late 1930s. Neither number was used in the final movie, but the music for "Never Smile at a Crocodile" can be heard as the theme for the crocodile. The lyrical "The Second Star to the Right" captures the magic and the whimsy of Barrie's story, just as the lullaby "Your Mother and Mine" conveys the pathos in the tale. The exuberant "You Can Fly" is perhaps the film's most famous song, and the way it soars on the musical scale makes it feel like flying. Both "A Pirate's Life" and "The Elegant Captain Hook" are farcical numbers that undercut any villainy in the pirates. The happy march "Following the Leader" for the Lost Boys is the very essence of adventure. Only the unintentionally offensive "What Made the Red Man Red?" fails to please. Oliver Wallace's soundtrack utilizes several of these songs but has much original music that gives *Peter Pan* a special kind of bombast. The three-note fanfare theme for Peter is used effectively throughout the movie and lets the moviegoer know that this is going to be a high-energy adventure.

PETER PAN: Tinker Bell! I hereby banish you forever.

WENDY: Please, not forever.

PETER PAN: Well, for a week then.

When *Peter Pan* was released in 1953, the reviews were complimentary. A few critics thought Barrie's somber subtext was lost, but most praised the tuneful and colorful version of the famous tale. The movie was also a hit with the public, earning over $7 million on its first release, the top-grossing film of 1953. (The film cost about $4 million.) The studio rereleased *Peter Pan* in 1958, 1969, 1976, 1982, and 1989. The VHS edition appeared in 1990 with the DVD version in 1999 and Blu-ray in 2013. Many stage, movie, and television adaptations of *Peter Pan* have come out since Disney's 1953 version. The studio itself offered the animated film sequel *Return to Neverland* in 2002. It was about Wendy's daughter Jane, who, during the London blitz of World War II, is kidnapped by Captain Hook and in Neverland meets up with Peter and other characters from the original. The movie met with mixed notices but did very well at the box office.

Did You Know . . . ?

In one of the early drafts of the movie, the whole story was told from the point of view of the dog Nana. The idea was dropped, but eight years later the idea was resurrected when the canine Pongo narrates the beginning scenes of *One Hundred and One Dalmatians* (1961).

PINOCCHIO

1940
(USA: Walt Disney Productions)

Directed by Ben Sharpsteen, T. Hee, Wilfred Jackson, Norman Ferguson, Jack Kinney, Bill Roberts, and Hamilton Luske
Written by Ted Sears, William Cottrell, Joseph Sabo, Otto Englander, Erdman Penner, Aurelius Battaglia, and Webb Smith, based on the book *The Adventures of Pinocchio* by Carlo Collodi
Produced by Walt Disney
Score by Leigh Harline and Paul J. Smith
Songs by Leigh Harline (music) and Ned Washington (lyrics)
Specs: Color (Technicolor); 88 minutes; traditional animation

---

In the opinion of many, this second animated feature musical from Walt Disney is the high point for the studio's Golden Age of animation. The gripping story, unforgettable characters, catchy songs, and superb animation have rarely been equaled by Disney or anyone else.

The tale is narrated by Jiminy Cricket, who is also in the plot as Pinocchio's conscience. The good-hearted toymaker Geppetto carves the marionette Pinocchio and prays on the wishing star that he might become a real boy. The Blue Fairy arrives that night and magically brings the puppet to life but says he must prove himself before becoming human. Pinocchio heads off to school the next day but is sidetracked by the conniving J. Worthington Foulfellow (aka Honest John), who convinces the wooden boy to go on the stage. Honest John sells Pinocchio to the greedy puppeteer Stromboli, who keeps him locked in a cage when not performing in the traveling puppet show. Pinocchio and Jiminy escape from Stromboli, but Honest John again hoodwinks the boy into going to Pleasure Island for a rest. The place is a young boy's dream of reckless fun, and Pinocchio enjoys it until he realizes that all the boys there are being turned into donkeys to work in the mines. Jiminy and Pinocchio escape again, but Pinocchio is partially transformed with a tail and donkey ears. They return home only to

---

Voice Cast

Dickie Jones	Pinocchio
Cliff Edwards	Jiminy Cricket
Christian Rub	Geppetto
Walter Catlett	J. Worthington Foulfellow
Charles Judels	Stromboli
Evelyn Venable	Blue Fairy
Frankie Darro	Lampwick
Charles Judels	Coachman
Mel Blanc	Gideon

Jiminy Cricket serves as the film's narrator and as the puppet Pinocchio's conscience, but he also provides most of the humor in the Disney classic. *Walt Disney Productions / Photofest.* © *Walt Disney Productions*

learn from the Blue Fairy that Geppetto has gone in search of Pinocchio and has been swallowed up by Monstro the whale. Pinocchio and Jiminy manage to find Monstro, get inside the whale, and rescue Geppetto. The trials prove Pinocchio to be worthy and he becomes a real boy.

In the famous children's story by Carlo Collodi, Pinocchio is a mischievous boy who learns some lessons about life only after causing a lot of trouble. He is not a terribly likable fellow, so the Disney artists tried softening him and expanded the role of the cricket by making Jiminy his guide, sidekick, and conscience. Disney's *Pinocchio* retains the innocence of a little boy, his lies and mistakes being the natural actions of an exuberant youth. It took several attempts before the character solidified visually and character-wise and the screenplay was ready for production. Like the book, *Pinocchio* on screen is an episodic tale and has more action and less singing than *Snow White and the Seven Dwarfs*. Because of the many locations and the wider scope of the plot, *Pinocchio* was even more demanding than the earlier movie and costs skyrocketed. After two years of production, the finished product had a price tag of $2.3 million, nearly twice the cost of *Snow White and the Seven Dwarfs*. Yet the result was a cinema classic. The efficient screenplay is a marvelous blending of comedy, suspense, and warmth, with both the villainous and lovable characters vividly coming to life. Certain scenes, once viewed, can never be forgotten, such as the stringless Pinocchio dancing with marionettes in Stromboli's theater, the frantic chase escaping from the whale, and the horrifying transition of the boy Lampwick into a donkey at Pleasure Island. This last scene is brilliantly done, showing the beginning of the transition then letting the moviegoer see its completion in silhouette. The animation is outstanding throughout the film and the masterly background art captures the cozy, continental European village as effectively as the garish, almost surreal Pleasure Island. The detail work by the Disney artists surpasses even that in *Snow White and the Seven Dwarfs*. Geppetto's workshop, for example, is a wonderland of toys and clocks. The scenes underwater have a look influenced by the impressionist artists while the waves and splashes recall those old celebrated Japanese etchings of the sea.

Songs

"When You Wish upon a Star"
"I've Got No Strings"
"Give a Little Whistle"
"Little Wooden Head"
"Hi-Diddle-Dee-Dee"

Disney used some recognizable voices for *Pinocchio*, most memorably the stage and screen comedian Cliff Edwards, also known as Ukulele Ike because he often accompanied himself on the little string instrument. His vocals for Jiminy are funny and contemporary sounding, and his singing of "When You Wish upon a Star" is warm and very accessible. Several actresses were tested for the voice of Pinocchio until Disney insisted a boy actor be used. Young but experienced movie actor Dickie Jones captures the innocence and sense of wonder of the character beautifully. Walter Catlett's Honest John is sly and comic, just as Charles Judels's Stromboli is blustering and intimidating. Familiar screen actress Evelyn Venable provided the warm voice of the Blue Fairy and Christian Rub's vocals for Geppetto are gentle and loving. In the small but unforgettable role of Lampwick, teen film actor Frankie Darro delights with his sarcasm then chills with his panic when turning into a donkey. *Pinocchio* also features some memorable characters who do not speak, such as the idiotic cat sidekick Gideon, the expressive cat Figaro, and even the goldfish Cleo. The characterizations in *Pinocchio* are so vivid and the acting so accomplished that, in the opinion of many, the film is able to evoke even greater emotional response than *Snow White and the Seven Dwarfs*.

JIMINY CRICKET: Well . . . guess he won't need me anymore. What does an actor want with a conscience, anyway?

The songs by Leigh Harline (music) and Ned Washington (lyrics) are not only memorable in themselves but also fit nicely into the narrative. The Oscar-winning "When You Wish upon a Star" sets the mood and theme of the movie and foreshadows Geppetto's wish, which sets the action in motion. Honest John's tuneful ditty "Hi Diddle Dee Dee" is a merry persuasion song that is so tuneful that there's no question of its working on Pinocchio. Jiminy's jaunty "Give a Little Whistle" is a contagious song that cements the friendship between the "conscience" and his young charge. "I've Got No Strings" is a merry number for the marionette show, complete with different sections pastiching various international music. *Pinocchio* has no love songs or wistful ballads, though "When You Wish upon a Star" is a lullaby-ballad that remains one of Hollywood's greatest songs. It has become the unofficial theme song for everything Disney, from films and television to theme parks and cruise liners. Its lyric has been imitated so often that the song's sentiment may seem like a cliché to some. But like the movie, "When You Wish upon a Star" is a timeless expression of optimism. Jiminy Cricket, who introduced the song, was immediately embraced by moviegoers and the studio used him for decades in other features and on television, the spry little fellow becoming an unofficial host for the world of Disney.

Awards

Academy Awards: Best Song ("When You Wish upon a Star") and Best Score.

Pinocchio was greeted in 1940 with rousing acclaim by the critics yet did not do as well at the box office as *Snow White and the Seven Dwarfs*. Its initial release brought in only $1 million and the studio went into debt. Subsequent releases eventually made *Pinocchio* a hit but it took years. The studio rereleased the movie in 1945, 1954, 1962, 1971, 1978, 1984, and 1992. The first home video edition appeared in 1985, the DVD in 2000, and on Blu-ray in 2009. The film shows up on most "best films" lists, and appreciation for it has only grown over the decades. *Pinocchio* has dated perhaps less than any other animated film; what was frightening then still is, and what was once joyous still soars.

See also *Snow White and the Seven Dwarfs*.

Did You Know . . . ?

There is no Jiminy Cricket in Carlo Collodi's original story. There is a Talking Cricket but Pinocchio kills him with a mallet.

POCAHONTAS

1995
(USA: Walt Disney Pictures)

Directed by Mike Gabriel and Eric Goldberg
Written by Carl Binder, Philip LeZebnik, and Susannah Grant
Produced by James Pentecost and Baker Bloodworth
Score by Alan Menken
Songs by Alan Menken (Music) and Stephen Schwartz (lyrics)
Specs: Color (Technicolor); 81 minutes; traditional animation

Although it is loosely based on history and not a fairy tale, the movie still has a strong love story involving the Native American Pocahontas and the British Captain John Smith. *Walt Disney Productions / Photofest. © Walt Disney Productions*

A rare Disney animated feature taken from history, this version of the early settlers of Jamestown was more romantically potent than historically accurate but was a popular and very satisfying movie all the same.

The greedy Governor Ratcliffe sets out from England in 1607 to sail to the New World and find gold, making him rich and famous. On board is Captain John Smith, who is more interested in adventure and seeing a whole new land. When

Voice Cast

Irene Bedard	Pocahontas (speaking)
Judy Kuhn	Pocahontas (singing)
Mel Gibson	John Smith
David Ogden Stiers	Governor Ratcliffe
Russell Means	Powhatan (speaking)
Jim Cummings	Powhatan (singing)
Linda Hunt	Grandmother Willow
James Apaumut Fall	Kocoum
Michelle St. John	Nakoma
Gordon Tootoosis	Keketa
Christian Bale	Thomas
Billy Connolly	Ben

the Englishmen arrive in Virginia territory and start building Fort Jamestown, the local natives, called the Powhatan, are suspicious of the foreigners and their Chief orders his people to keep away from them. The Chief's daughter, Pocahontas, engaged to wed the warrior Kocoum, is not surprised by the arrival of the English because her ancestor, Grandmother Willow, foretold it all to her. Pocahontas changes her views on the foreigners when she meets John Smith and the two fall in love. The two vow to try and bring the two peoples together, but when Kocoum is shot trying to kill Smith, the Chief declares war on the Englishmen and Smith is taken prisoner. When Smith is about to be executed, Pocahontas pleads with her father to spare him. Ratcliffe leads an attack on the tribe and in the furor Smith is shot and wounded. Pocahontas reveals that Ratcliffe is the enemy and not the Englishmen. The crew arrest Ratcliffe and prepare to return to England, where he will stand trial. Smith is so severely wounded that only medical care in Europe can save him, so the lovers must part but he promises to return for Pocahontas someday.

The historical Pocahontas has been portrayed on stage and screen many times, rarely accurately. The same is true with the Disney version. Since the movie is a love story, the scriptwriters made Pocahontas a full-grown woman rather than the young preteen she actually was when the British arrived in Virginia. In history, she wed her Native fiancée, Kocoum, after the wounded John Smith returned to England. Pocahontas later went to England with her second husband, Englishman John Rolfe, and converted to Christianity. She died there at the age of twenty-two. The famous episode, in which Pocahontas saves John Smith's life by putting herself between Smith and his executioner, has never been verified. Smith himself wrote about Pocahontas's bravery, but there is no historical proof that it happened as legend has it. The idea that Pocahontas and Smith were in love with each other is also suspect, but the Disney writers built the whole movie around this possibility. The screenplay is intelligently written and purposely breaks away from the stereotypes of both the Native Americans and the English explorers. The Powhatans are portrayed as a peaceful tribe who are in harmony with nature. Any hostility shown comes from the infringement of the Europeans. Some of the English explorers, such as John Smith, have lofty ideas about a new world, but Governor Ratcliffe is only interested in finding gold. Although some felt the Disney version bent over backwards to reverse the clichéd portrayals of Indians from the past, the script is actually very balanced with good and evil characters on both sides.

Songs

"Colors of the Wind"
"Just Around the Riverbend"
"Steady as the Beating Drum"
"The Virginia Company"
"If I Never Knew You"
"Listen with Your Heart"
"Mine, Mine, Mine"
"Savages"

The love story in *Pocahontas* is beautifully told, but it ended up rather too low-key for a children's movie. In fact, many children were bored. None of the animals talked, there was no fantasy or magic save a little conjuring by Grandmother Willow, the issues were mature ones (ecological awareness, racial intolerance, the evils of imperialism), and at the end the lovers are separated. During test screenings, kids got so restless during the love duet "If I Never Knew You" that the studio cut the scene and played the song during the end credits. (It was later restored in the rereleased version and on DVD.) With so much out of the reach of children, it is no wonder adults found more to savor in *Pocahontas* than kids. And savor it they did. Many consider *Pocahontas* the most mature, thought-provoking, and moving of the later Disney animated features. Even without plenty of kids in the theater seats, the movie had healthy box office returns. Ironically, the studio thought *Pocahontas* would be the blockbuster and *The Lion King*, in production at the same time, would be a modest success. They could not have been more wrong. Yet *Pocahontas* was a labor of love, a desire to do things in an animated movie that were usually left to live-action movies. Every aspect of the film, from the script and score to the movement and background art, was coordinated to create a poignant and meaningful drama. Mike Gabriel and Eric Goldberg directed with care, and all the elements in *Pocahontas* are balanced and effective.

> JOHN SMITH: Pocahontas, that tree is talking to me.
>
> POCAHONTAS: Then you should talk back.
>
> GRANDMOTHER WILLOW: Don't be frightened, young man. My bark is worse than my bite.
>
> POCAHONTAS: Say something.
>
> JOHN SMITH: What do you say to a tree?
>
> POCAHONTAS: Anything you want.

The production team for *Pocahontas* approached the project with thoroughness and dedication. The background artists studied the landscape near Jamestown and created a verdant depiction of nature. The primeval forests have a dreamy, romantic flavor that contrasts with the angular and rigid portrayal of the fort and the Englishmen who fortify it. Because there were no exaggerated, cartoonish characters (except perhaps Ratcliffe), the animators took special pains to make human movement both natural and flowing. Native American actors were hired to voice the tribesmen so that the vocals would not slip into stereotype. The only animal characters—Flit the hummingbird, Pocahontas's raccoon pet Meeko, and Ratcliffe's lap dog Percy—were originally given dialogue, but during production it was decided to make them more realistic. (In the early stages, there was also a talking turkey to be voiced by comic John Candy; the idea was scrapped when Candy died in 1994). Flit and Meeko still have lively personalities, but their movements and sounds are those of animals. Irene Bedard gives a warm but strong performance as Pocahontas, with her singing done by Broadway actress Judy Kuhn. Mel Gibson as John Smith does his own singing and is very moving as a man torn between two worlds. David Ogden Stiers's Governor Ratcliffe is perhaps too caricatured, but his vocals match the oversized visuals of the character. The supporting cast is solid, the standout being Linda Hunt as the wise and quixotic Grandmother Willow.

The songs by Alan Menken (music) and Stephen Schwartz (lyrics) are tuneful but restrained, closer to operetta than musical comedy. Some of the numbers take an inspirational tone, especially the Oscar-winning "Colors of the Wind." Yet equally impressive are the reflective "Just around the Riverbend," the rhythmic "Mine, Mine, Mine," and the lovely duet "If I Never Knew You." Menken's soundtrack score is also impressive. Native drums and other tribal musical clichés are kept to a minimum yet still conjure up what modern audiences sense as authentic. The lush Virginia landscape inspired some of the richest passages in the score, just as the sea-faring scenes were scored with appropriate vitality. *Pocahontas* is one of Disney's better movies when it comes to the music.

Awards

Academy Awards: Best Song ("Colors of the Wind") and Best Score.
Golden Globe Award: Best Song ("Colors of the Wind") and Golden Globe nomination: Best Score.

Believing that they had another *Beauty and the Beast* (1991) with a timeless love story, the Disney studio promoted *Pocahontas* with a television special, ads in all media, and multiple showings of the "Colors of the Wind" sequence in theaters. The film premiered in 1995 in Manhattan's Central Park before a crowd of 100,000 spectators. The reviews for *Pocahontas* were mixed, some critics complimenting the beautiful look of the film but others disparaging the historical inaccuracy of the story. The public was not so divided, and the movie earned over $346 million internationally. The cost of making *Pocahontas* was $55 million, so it was considered a major success. The VHS version was released in 1996, the DVD in 2000, and the Blu-ray edition in 2012. The direct-to-video sequel *Pocahontas II: Journey to a New World* (1998) continued the story with John Rolfe bringing Pocahontas to London and trying to plead for peace between the settlers and the native tribes. The sequel was poorly received by the press and the public.

Did You Know . . . ?

Early in the development of the screenplay, there was a spirit of a wise old man of the river who was to be voiced by Gregory Peck. But Peck thought the role needed to be more maternal so the character was reworked into Grandmother Willow with Linda Hunt providing the voice.

THE PRINCESS AND THE FROG

2009
(USA: Walt Disney Pictures)

Directed by Ron Clements and John Musker
Written by Rob Edwards, Ron Clements, and John Musker, based on *The Frog Princess*
  by E. D. Baker
Produced by John Lasseter, Aghi D. Koh, Peter Del Vecho, and Craig Sost
Score and songs by Randy Newman
Specs: Color; 97 minutes; traditional animation

With its evocative re-creation of the look and sound of Old New Orleans, The Princess and
the Frog *is a tuneful, funny, and ultimately touching movie in the old Disney tradition.*

In 1926 New Orleans, the African American waitress Tiana works hard to save
her money with the dream of opening her own restaurant someday. Arriving in
town is the loose-living spendthrift Prince Naveen, looking for a rich wife but not
willing to settle down to married life. He and his valet, Lawrence, are conned by
the voodoo man Dr. Facilier into accepting an evil charm that turns the Prince
into a frog. The only cure is to get a princess to kiss him, so when the Prince sees
Tiana dressed as a princess for Mardi Gras, he pleads with her to let him kiss her.
Because Tiana is not a real princess, the charm turns her into a frog as well. Taking
refuge in the bayou, the angry couple are told by the trumpet-playing alligator
Louis and the Cajun firefly Ray that the aged, blind Mama Odie might be able to
help them. The priestess is able to "see" into their souls and tells them to return

The working girl Tiana dresses as a princess for a masquerade party, so Prince Naveen, turned into
a frog by a spell, mistakenly thinks that kissing her will break the curse. *Walt Disney Pictures /
Photofest. © Walt Disney Pictures*

Voice Cast

Elizabeth Dampier	Tiana (young)
Anika Noni Rose	Tiana (adult)
Bruno Campos	Prince Naveen
Keith David	Dr. Facilier
Michael-Leon Wooley	Louis
Jim Cummings	Ray
Peter Bartlett	Lawrence
Breanna Brooks	Charlotte La Bouff (young)
Jennifer Cody	Charlotte La Bouff (adult)
John Goodman	Big Daddy La Bouff
Jenifer Lewis	Mama Odie
Oprah Winfrey	Eudora

to New Orleans and find a legitimate princess for the Prince to kiss. The wealthy, spoiled Charlotte LaBouff is crowned Princess of the Mardi Gras, so they seek her out while Facilier unleashes various demons from "the other side" to stop the kiss. The firefly Ray dies trying to stop the demons and his spirit joins his sweetheart Angeline, a star in the sky. Midnight arrives before Charlotte can kiss the Prince, so it looks like he and Tiana are doomed to be frogs forever. But the two have fallen in love and when they are married by Mama Odie, he kisses his bride and the spell is broken because his wife Tiana is now a real princess.

Animator-directors Ron Clements and John Musker, who had made *The Little Mermaid* (1989) and other traditionally animated movies for Disney, left the studio in 2004 when the decision was made to use more computer animation and less traditional methods. Then in 2005 the new studio head, John Lasseter, reversed that decision and invited Clements and Musker back to the studio to make a film of E. D. Baker's *The Frog Princess*, which was loosely based on the Brothers Grimm tale. The codirectors decided to move the European locale, used in most fairy tales, to America and chose New Orleans because of the mystical aspects of the story. The city would dictate the kind of songs to be used: blues, gospel, and jazz. The New Orleans setting also inspired another major change in presenting a fairy tale: an African American leading character. The time period of 1926 was chosen because that was during the city's renowned jazz age.

Songs

"Down in New Orleans"
"Friends on the Other Side"
"Ma Belle Evangeline"
"Almost There"
"Dig a Little Deeper"
"When We're Human"
"Gonna Take You There"
"Never Knew I Needed (Ne-Yo)"

The Princess and the Frog was a return to the animation style of Disney's golden age. Everything was hand drawn rather than computer generated and the movie was given a nostalgic look reminiscent of that of *Lady and the Tramp* (1955). The artists' sketches were then scanned into the computer to save the hours of copying and repeating images. The animation in *The Princess and the Frog* has the look of the Disney classics but was more efficiently executed. The depiction of both the wealthy and working-class neighborhoods is accurate but slightly romanticized. The scenes in the bayou are also good examples of stylized nature, the kind that had been seen in *Bambi* (1942). The characters were not drawn as exaggerated or oversized as in some animation though the villain Dr. Facilier is depicted as a very unhuman-like figure. Some of the animals were given very human movements, particularly the trumpet-playing alligator Louis. When Tiana and Naveen are turned into frogs, their animation is a clever mix of human and animal movement. *The Princess and the Frog* is considered a retro Disney film for the way it returns to tradition in many ways.

PRINCE NAVEEN: Excuse me, but your accent, it is funny.

RAY: I'm a Cajun, bro. Born and bred in the bayou! Y'all not from 'round here, are ya?

PRINCE NAVEEN: Actually, we are from a place far, far away from this world.

RAY: Go to bed! Y'all from Shreveport?

The Princess and the Frog was also a return to a full-scale musical with seven songs worked into the story. Randy Newman, who lived in New Orleans as a child, knew the sounds of the city well and wrote what many consider his finest film score. The blues number "Down in New Orleans" beautifully sets the scene, showing the aristocratic side of town, then the working-class neighborhoods. The vocals by Dr. John are intoxicating, and the sounds of New Orleans are bewitching. "When We're Human," Louis's tribute to namesake Louis Armstrong, is a vibrant Dixieland jazz number with wonderful trumpet work by Terence Blanchard. Mama Odie's "Dig a Little Deeper" is a rousing gospel hymn, "Friends on the Other Side" is a sinister character song for Dr. Facilier with a Cajun drumbeat rhythm, "Almost There" is Tiana's slightly swinging jazz song of determination, and "Gonna Take You There" is a raucous hillbilly song delivered with rustic panache by the firefly Ray. In a different mood is the French-flavored Cajun ballad "Ma Belle Evangeline," sung by Ray to his beloved, a star in the heavens. The voice cast of *The Princess and the Frog* all did their own singing, and it is a glorious set of voices. Theater actress-singer Anika Noni Rose shines as Tiana, and her splendid vocals hold the movie together. The deep-voiced Keith David has fun as the conniving Dr. Facilier, Jenifer Lewis brings down the house as Mama Odie, Michael-Leon Wooley's vocals as Louis match the vivacious trumpet playing, Bruno Campos is a sly and funny Prince Naveen, and Disney voice veteran Jim Cummings delivers perhaps the finest performance of his long career as Ray. Newman not only wrote the songs but also composed the soundtrack score, which is rich in jazz, Cajun folk, and mystical themes.

Awards

Academy Award nominations: Best Animated Feature, Best Score, and Best Song ("Down in New Orleans").
Golden Globe nomination: Best Animated Feature.

The Princess and the Frog met with mostly favorable reviews when it opened in 2009. Most critics lauded the traditional look of the movie and its vibrant score. Although the film cost $105 million to make, it managed to more than double that in its first release. Yet, by Disney standards, the film did not perform as well as expected. Some studio heads blamed the title. They felt the word "princess" indicated that the movie was something most appreciated by young girls. So convinced of this was the studio that it changed the title of its next project from *Rapunzel* to *Tangled*. The DVD and Blu-ray editions of *The Princess and the Frog* were released in 2010 and were bestsellers. The film is still finding a wide audience and is likely to become a moviegoers' favorite and perhaps a classic.

Did You Know . . . ?

The character of Mama Odie was based on a real New Orleans storyteller named Coleen Salley, who told children tall tales about the region. The directors of the movie consulted with Salley several times and even copied some of her familiar phrases into the script. Sadly, before the film was released, Salley passed away at the age of seventy-nine.

R

RANGO

2011
(USA: Nickelodeon Movies/Paramount)

Directed by Gore Verbinski
Written by John Logan
Produced by Tim Headington, Gore Verbinski, John B. Carls, Graham King, David
  Shannon, Adam Cramer, and Shari Hanson
Score by Hans Zimmer
Songs by John and David Thum, Rick Garcia, Kenneth Karman, Gore Verbinski, and
  James Ward Byrkit, and song standards by various artists
Specs: Color; 107 minutes; computer animation

A western spoof that also satirizes many other Hollywood films, Rango *is an accurate pastiche of the Wild West movie with an offbeat and very modern sense of humor.*

The pet chameleon Rango enjoys staging amateur theatrics in his terrarium, but when his glass home is accidentally tossed into the desert he takes on the persona of a Wild West legendary hero in order to survive. He is given some mysterious advice about the Spirit of the West from the aged armadillo Roadkill and avoids being eaten by a hawk before he meets the sassy desert iguana Beans, who takes Rango to the desperate town of Dirt, where all the animal townspeople are desperate for water. Rango accidentally kills the hawk and is made sheriff by the elderly Tortoise John, who is mayor. When the town's water supply is stolen from the bank, Rango leads a posse to find the culprits. But after chasing after the mole prospector Balthazar and his gang, the posse finds the large water bottle empty. Rango suspects the mayor is behind the theft because the crafty tortoise is buying up all the land to develop a city for humans. Tortoise John calls on Rattlesnake Jake to kick Rango out of town, but in the desert the chameleon finds the Spirit of the West, a human resembling Clint Eastwood, who encourages him to return to Dirt and face his enemies. With Roadkill's help, Rango finds where the water pipes are and learns that the mayor has purposely shut off the valve in order to create a drought. Rango returns to Dirt, outwits Tortoise John and Rattlesnake Jake, and the water comes gushing into the town.

The household pet chameleon Rango is accidentally abandoned in the desert, so he remakes himself into a legendary Wild West figure and saves the town of Dirt. *Paramount Pictures / Photofest.*
© *Paramount Pictures*

Voice Cast

Johnny Depp	Rango
Isla Fisher	Beans
Ned Beatty	Mayor
Bill Nighy	Rattlesnake Jack
Alfred Molina	Roadkill
Abigail Breslin	Priscilla
Harry Dean Stanton	Balthazar
Stephen Root	Doc
Ray Winstone	Bad Bill
Ian Abercrombie	Ambrose
Claudia Black	Angelique
James Ward Byrkit	Waffles
Blake Clark	Buford
Alex Manugian	Spoons
Joe Nunez	Rock-Eye
Timothy Olyphant	Spirit of the West

George Lucas's Industrial Light & Magic had provided the computerized special effects for several live-action movies, but *Rango* was its first involvement with an animated film. It was also the first animated project for director Gore Verbinski, who was hired by Paramount and Nickelodeon Films for his talent for action and quirky humor. The screenplay by John Logan was original, although the script drew from many westerns, such as *High Noon* (1952) and *The Good, the Bad and the Ugly* (1966), and other movies, including *Chinatown* (1974), *Star Wars* (1977), and *Raising Arizona* (1987). There is indeed plenty of action in *Rango*, but it is also filled with dialogue, mostly one-line jokes. There is a flippant tone to the film, parodying western clichés and characters. Much of this works because the voice cast has a keen sense of mockery in their delivery, particularly Johnny Depp with his energetic performance as Rango, who shifts attitudes and voice textures as quickly as the character changes his various personas. Isla Fisher's Beans is a combination of many western heroines, while Ned Beatty's oily mayor seems to ooze with greed. Among the many other memorable performances are Alfred Molina's Hispanic mole Roadkill, Bill Nighy's spooky rattlesnake, and Timothy Olyphant, whose Spirit of the West is a smooth and steady Clint Eastwood imitation. Because there are so many action sequences and so many characters in *Rango*, the dialogue

Songs

"Rango" (Thum/Thum)
"Welcome Amigo" (Garcia/Karman/Verbinski/Byrkit)
"Rango Theme Song" (Thum/Thum)
"Walk Don't Rango" (Thum/Thum)
"La Muerte a Llegado" (Garcia/Karman/Verbinski/Byrkit)
"The Bank's Been Robbed" (Garcia/Karman/Verbinski/Byrkit)

is sometimes lost in the shuffle and few of the characters are developed beyond familiar stereotypes. Yet there is so much vitality in the voices that the audience can enjoy the chaos without worrying about details.

The large number of speaking characters in *Rango* was an animation challenge. While all of the characters are desert animals—including a toad, gila monster, rabbit, mole, mouse, fox, owl, raccoon, iguana, bats, and a raven—they are dressed in human western attire with realistic props and accessories. The animal features are exaggerated to the point that it is not easy to identify exactly which desert critter it is. Yet there is no trouble in recognizing the western type and one is able to quickly place the character in the western genre. The computer animation is expert in giving each character human moves even as the animal is suggested in the motions and facial expression. Rango himself is a thin, flexible creature who appears tiny among all the larger animals, yet the animators have given the chameleon the most expressive eyes, which move independently like a real chameleon's but still have a human quality. The wrinkled face of Tortoise John is very human in its animation, yet it still resembles a tortoise. One of the most complicated pieces of animation in the movie is that for Rattlesnake Jake, who slithers like a reptile yet exudes a sense of human villainy even with his snake eyes. The background art in *Rango* continues the western satirizing with its accurate depiction of Monument Valley, stark sunsets, shifting sand, and burning sun. The town of Dirt resembles an Old West ghost town, and each structure seems to be defying gravity by the way it stands in a semi-collapsed state. *Rango* looks like a classic western, but with a flavor of farce in its settings and its characters.

RANGO: Us reptiles gotta stick together. Right, my brother?

BUFORD: I'm an amphibian.

RANGO: Ain't no shame in that.

The soundtrack score by Hans Zimmer is also full of western clichés, sometimes slipping into actual melodies from old westerns. The sounds of the spaghetti westerns from Italy are evoked often in the soundtrack, particularly Ennio Morricone's famous theme from *The Good, the Bad and the Ugly*. The harmonica, another western cliché, is often featured, as is the trumpet playing a Spanish theme. The film features a handful of original songs by various artists, most played and sung by a quartet of owls as a mariachi band. Again, the silly lyrics and the south-of-the-border music both have a satiric tone. The "Rango Theme Song," sung over the end credits by Los Lobos, is equally silly, yet accurate enough to recall a Gene Autry ditty from the 1950s.

Awards

Academy Award: Best Animated Feature.
Golden Globe nomination: Best Animated Feature.
British Academy of Film & Television Arts (BAFTA) Award: Best Animated Film.

With its complex animation and big-name cast, *Rango* was a very expensive film, costing close to $135 million. But the reviews in 2011 were mostly exemplary and the public response strong enough that *Rango* earned over $245 million. This is impressive for an animated movie that was not aimed at young children but rather at adults with an understanding of the Hollywood western. The movie is filmed with so much smoking, drinking, and gun violence that some groups protested that *Rango* should have been given a rating of PG-13 instead of PG. Both the DVD and Blu-ray editions were released later in 2011. There has also been a popular video game based on *Rango*.

See also *Home on the Range*.

Did You Know . . . ?

The animators were inspired by actor Don Knotts as Deputy Barney Fife in the television series *The Andy Griffith Show* for the look of Sheriff Rango.

RATATOUILLE

2007
(USA: Pixar Animation Studios/Disney)

Directed by Brad Bird and Jan Pinkava
Written by Brad Bird
Produced by John Lasseter, Brad Lewis, Andrew Stanton, and Galyn Susman
Score by Michael Giacchino
Song "Le Festin" by Michael Giacchino
Specs: Color; 111 minutes; computer animation

Pixar's eighth computer-animated feature, Ratatouille *took several risks, one of them being the use of a rat as the lovable hero. Yet most audience members overcame their predisposed feelings about rats and the film was a critical and popular success.*

While his father, Django; brother, Emil; and the rest of the rat colony are content eating garbage, Remy has more sophisticated tastes. He yearns to be a French chef like the late Auguste Gusteau, who opened an acclaimed restaurant in Paris and authored a series of cookbooks. Remy steals one of the cookbooks from a country cottage and escapes to Paris, where he sneaks into the kitchen of Gusteau's. The restaurant is now run by the greedy Skinner, who is using the Gusteau name to manufacture a line of frozen foods. The young Alfredo Linguini gets a job as garbage boy in the kitchen and manages to save Remy's life when Skinner orders the rat killed. Linguini learns that Remy, whom he calls "Little Chef," is an expert cook and uses Remy's help to get a job as cook-in-training in the restaurant. Linguini is smitten by the female chef Colette, but she sees Linguini and all other men

The gourmet rat Remy helps pass off the fumbling Linguini (right) as a celebrated chef but the greedy restauranteur Skinner (center) catches on to their deception. *Buena Vista Pictures / Photofest.* © *Buena Vista Pictures*

in the kitchen as a threat to her ambitions to become a first-class chef. With Remy secretly guiding Linguini, the boy soon becomes popular for his exquisite dishes. Word reaches the waspish food critic Anton Ego, who arrives at Gusteau's planning a vicious attack in his newspaper review. But Remy prepares a delectable ratatouille dish that has Ego raving and insisting that he meet the chef. After the restaurant is closed for the night, Linguini reveals to Ego that a simple rat is the chef extraordinaire. Skinner finds out that Linguini is the son of Gusteau and an heir to the Gusteau enterprise. To get even, Skinner reports to the health department that Gusteau's is infested with rats. The restaurant goes out of business, but Linguini and Colette open a small bistro called Ratatouille, where Remy continues to prepare great dishes for Ego and the public, as well as for his rat colony, which no longer has to eat garbage.

Voice Cast

Patton Oswalt	Remy
Lou Romano	Linguini
Janeane Garofalo	Colette
Ian Holm	Skinner
Peter O'Toole	Anton Ego
Brian Dennehy	Django
Peter Sohn	Emile
Brad Garrett	Gusteau
Will Arnett	Horst
John Ratzenberger	Mustafa
James Remar	Larousse

The idea of a French rat wanting to be a chef was developed by Jan Pinkava, who created a storyline and did preliminary designs for the characters and settings. The Pixar staff had their doubts about such an odd concept and tabled it. After Pinkava departed Pixar, the project was resurrected by Brad Bird, who rewrote the script. It was his idea that the great chef Gusteau should be dead and appear to Remy as a figment of his imagination. Bird also changed the design of the rats, removing some of their human characteristics and making them look more like actual rats. The animators not only studied pet rats in the studio, they toured Paris to make notes on the settings. They also brought in food experts to make sure the workings of the French restaurant's kitchen and the food created there were accurate. Michel Gagné and the other animators used the work of German painter Oskar Fischinger and Canadian animation pioneer Norman McLaren to come up with the look and movement in *Ratatouille*. The Parisian settings are very romantic, while the actions of the characters are often frantic. The character of Linguini is the most physical of the characters, his body bending and twisting through much of the movie. Remy's initial visit to the kitchen of Gusteau's Restaurant is a hyperactive sequence with rolling carts, bubbling pots, and the rat racing about trying not to be seen. The animators often took Remy's visual point of view in telling the story, most effectively when Remy is looking at the world from inside Linguini's chef hat. The scenes in which dozens of rats are moving were made ossible with computer animation. The hundreds of hairs on each of the major rat characters were unique to each creature. Animating the humans in the film was also challenging. Linguini moves more like a spastic machine than a person. The various chefs in the kitchen have few lines but are physically very distinct. The critic Anton Ego is drawn with a vulture-like posture while Colette moves in an aggressive masculine manner. The ghost of Gusteau moves more like a dolphin, floating about in the air and making somersaults as he speaks. For a film that is basically about cooking, *Ratatouille* is one of the most frenetic of the Pixar features.

LINGUINI: You're . . . Anton Ego.

ANTON EGO: You're slow for someone in the fast lane.

LINGUINI: And you're . . . thin, for someone who likes food.

ANTON EGO: I don't *like* food, I LOVE it. If I don't love it, I don't swallow.

Stand-up comic Patton Oswalt was hired to voice Remy after director Bird heard him do a routine about food. His performance captures the joke-filled side of Remy, but also his passion for food. Lou Romano voices Linguini, his vocals sometimes echoing his crazed movements. Actors Janeane Garofalo (Colette), Ian Holm (Skinner), John Ratzenberger (Mustafa), and others have such thick French accents that their voices are not easily recognized. The finest voice performance in the film is by Peter O'Toole, whose Anton Ego is a slow, smoldering piece of evil. The voices for the rat characters are American sounding rather than French. Their colloquial dialogue and personable voices help the audience get over their distaste for rats and hopefully accept them as likable characters. Yet the problem remains that these are indeed rats and not cuddly anthropomorphic critters. Individual rats have little difficulty in appearing likable, but when one sees dozens of these rodents in action, they become depersonalized and more than a little off-putting. The fact that *Ratatouille* is appealing to most moviegoers is a credit to the animators and the voice actors.

Awards

Academy Award: Best Animated Feature. Oscar nominations: Best Original Screenplay, Sound Mixing, Music, and Sound Editing.
Golden Globe Award: Best Animated Film.
British Academy of Film & Television Arts (BAFTA) Award: Best Animated Feature.

Ratatouille is not a musical with songs but it is filled with French-flavored music that moves back and forth between the romantic and the frantic. Michael Giacchino, who had previously scored *The Incredibles* for Pixar, created a lush score that is almost continuous throughout the movie. The only song heard on the soundtrack, "Le Festin," is sung in French by the Parisian singer Camille. It is an entrancing piece and adds greatly to the film's glowing depiction of Paris. Matching such music is the superb background art in *Ratatouille*. The Eiffel Tower is used often as a point of perspective, and it defines the Paris setting. Just as potent are the streets, squares, and rooftops of the city as portrayed in the backgrounds. Even Linguini's humble garret apartment has a kind of charm. The elegance of Gusteau's Restaurant is echoed in the establishment's sterling kitchen, which still manages to have a warmth of its own. From the country cottage at the beginning of the film to the sewers of Paris, the background art in the movie is exceptional.

Ratatouille opened to very commendatory reviews and strong box office. This must have come as a relief to Pixar executives because they had found resistance to the movie when they approached different companies about doing tie-ins. No food company wanted its products to be associated with rats. A new brand of Chardonnay titled Ratatouille was developed with Costco, and Remy appeared on the label with a wine glass. But the fear that children would want to drink wine because there was an animated character on the label forced the company to pull the product from the shelves. Another risk was the very title of the movie, a word Americans were not very familiar with. *Ratatouille* was very popular in America, but it was even more successful in France. The depictions of Paris and its fine cuisine were widely applauded by the French critics and public. The movie is among Pixar's most critically acclaimed productions. How a film about cooking with a rat as the main character became so beloved is as wondrous as it is mystifying.

Did You Know . . . ?

Because the word *ratatouille* was not well known to Americans, Pixar and Disney insisted that the movie title be spelled out phonetically on all advertising so patrons could pronounce the word at the box office.

THE RESCUERS

1977
(USA: Walt Disney Productions)

Directed by John Lounsbery, Wolfgang Reitherman, and Art Stevens
Written by Larry Clemmons, Ken Anderson, David Michener, Fred Lucky, Vance
  Gerry, Dick Sebast, Frank Thomas, Ted Berman, and Burny Mattinson, based on
  the books *The Rescuers* and *Miss Bianca* by Margery Sharp
Produced by Ron Miller and Wolfgang Reitherman
Score by Artie Butler
Songs by Carol Connors, Ayn Robbins, and Sammy Fain
Specs: Color (Technicolor); 78 minutes; traditional animation

The first Disney animated feature to inspire a sequel, The Rescuers *is a sparkling musical adventure with some sprightly characters and clever animation.*

The orphan girl Penny has been abducted from the Morningside Orphanage in New York City by the greedy pawnshop proprietor Madame Medusa and brought to the swampy Devil's Bayou in Florida. A valuable diamond called the Devil's Eye has been hidden in a watery cave by pirates and Medusa needs a small child to crawl into the cave opening and get it. Imprisoned on a decaying riverboat with Medusa's stooge, Mr. Snoops, and her pet alligators, Brutus and Nero, Penny manages to write a pleading letter asking to be rescued and puts it in a bottle that drifts out to sea. The bottle is washed up in New York City, where it comes to the attention of the Rescue Aid Society, an international organization of mice located

Voice Cast

Bob Newhart	Bernard
Eva Gabor	Miss Bianca (speaking)
Robie Lester	Miss Bianca (singing)
Michelle Stacy	Penny
Geraldine Page	Madame Medusa
Joe Flynn	Mr. Snoops
Jim Jordan	Orville
John McIntire	Rufua
Jeanette Nolan	Ellie Mae
Pat Buttram	Luke
George Lindsey	Rabbit
Larry Clemmons	Gramps
Dub Taylor	Digger
John Fiedler	Owl
James MacDonald	Evinrude
Bernard Fox	Chairman

The albatross Orville provides unconventional transportation to the Florida Everglades for the "rescuers" Miss Bianca and Bernard on a mission to find a kidnapped little girl. *Walt Disney Pictures / Photofest. © Walt Disney Pictures*

in the basement of the United Nations Building. The hesitant American Bernard and a fashionable Hungarian agent, Miss Bianca, are selected to rescue Penny. After interviewing the old cat Rufus at the orphanage and learning the whereabouts of Medusa, the two mice fly to Florida on the back of the albatross Orville and find Penny. In order to rescue her, they recruit the help of various animals in the bayou. When Penny is forced once again to crawl into the cave, she discovers the Devil's Eye and turns it over to Medusa, who double-crosses Snoops and tries to get away by airboat. Bernard, Bianca, and the swamp creatures manage to stop Medusa and rescue Penny. The Devil's Eye goes to the Smithsonian Institution, and Penny is adopted by a loving couple.

Plans to make a Disney film based on Margery Sharp's books about mice rescuers went back to 1962, but early developments were very sociopolitical in orientation and not to Walt Disney's liking, so the project was shelved. A decade later, a treatment in which the rescuers go to Antarctica to rescue a polar bear surfaced and a film was developed around the singer-musician Louis Prima as the bear. But the swing artist suffered a heart attack in 1973 and had to retire from show business. Drawing from the books *The Rescuers* and *Miss Bianca*, the new screenplay was developed with many characters and episodes not in the original stories. The storytelling is solid, many of the characters are masterfully done, and the use of songs on the soundtrack rather than sung by characters works very well. Animator Don Bluth joined with some veteran Disney artists to give *The Rescuers* a distinct look and movement. Instead of animating the opening credits, a series of paintings by Mel Shaw were used to show how Penny's distress message in a bottle travels from the Florida swamps to New York City. The look of the swamp is creepy and rather subjective as seen through young Penny's eyes. The animation of the many characters is first-rate, the villainess Madame Medusa getting the most physical and farcical moves. The heroes—Penny, Bernard, and Bianca—are animated in a realistic manner (although the mice walk like humans), and there are some playful movements for the other animals, in particular the alligators Brutus and Nero, the short-winded dragonfly Evinrude, and the daffy albatross Orville. One of the most sportive pieces of animation in *The Rescuers* is the alligators' attempts to drive the mice out of a pipe organ by hitting various keys and blowing them out of the pipes. Disney veteran Wolfgang Reitherman produced and codirected the movie with Art Stevens and John Lounsbery, who brought a style and craftsmanship to the film that recalled Disney's Golden Age.

Songs

"The Journey"
"Rescue Aid Society"
"Tomorrow Is Another Day"
"Someone's Waiting for You"

While *The Rescuers* is not a traditional musical, it has some excellent songs that are used as commentary rather than expressions of emotions by the characters. The opening number, "The Journey," is a wistful lullaby that accompanies the SOS bottle as it is tossed upon the seas and ends in New York harbor. A chorus sings the rhythmic anthem "Rescue Aid Society" during a meeting under the United Nations Building. While Bianca and Bernard fly on the back of Orville, the sweeping number "Tomorrow Is Another Day" is heard on the soundtrack. The plaintive ballad "Someone's Waiting for You" is the film's finest song, heard during a moment of despair by the kidnapped Penny. The female vocalist for all the songs is Shelby Flint and her voice is as caressing as it is clear and engaging.

The voice cast for *The Rescuers* was drawn mostly from American television. Some were Disney alumni, most noticeably Eva Gabor from *The Aristocats* (1970);

PENNY: Hi. Where'd you come from?

BERNARD: We found the bottle with—with your message, and we've come to rescue you.

PENNY: Did you hear that, Teddy? Our bottle worked! (looks confused) Didn't you bring somebody big with you? Like the police?

BERNARD: Uh, no. There's just, uh—the two of us.

MISS BIANCA: But if the three of us work together and we have a little faith . . .

PENNY: That's what Rufus said: "Faith makes things turn out right."

others were new to the studio, as with comic Bob Newhart as Bernard and renowned theater-film actress Geraldine Page as Madame Medusa. Her outrageous performance, alternating between curdling sweetness and bombastic outrage, supported the character's twisting and propulsive physical moves, letting Medusa join the ranks of the most notable Disney villainesses. Newhart's hesitant Bernard and Gabor's lyrical Miss Bianca hold the film together, but there are marvelous supporting characters that were voiced with panache, such as the hapless albatross Orville (voiced by Jim Jordan), the out-of-breath dragonfly Evinrude (James MacDonald), the bumbling Mr. Snoops (Joe Flynn), and various swamp dwellers played by Jeanette Nolan, Pat Buttram, George Lindsey, Dub Taylor, John McIntire, Bernard Fox, and John Fiedler. Michelle Stacy's Penny is pure innocence and naiveté, a sharp contrast to the melodramatic hysterics of Medusa.

Award

Academy Award nomination: Best Song ("Someone's Waiting for You").

Opening in 1977, *The Rescuers* received the most appreciative reviews since the studio's *Mary Poppins* in 1964. Critics thought the movie was the best animated feature to come from Disney since *The Jungle Book* (1967) and favorably compared the animation to that of the classics of the past. The box office was equally encouraging. The film cost about $7.5 million to make and on its first release earned over $48 million. *The Rescuers* was rereleased in theaters in 1983 and 1989, eventually earning over $70 million. The VHS version was released in 1992, the DVD in 2003, and the Blu-ray edition in 2012.

The movie was the Disney studio's first animated feature to spawn a sequel, *The Rescuers Down Under* (1990). Newhart and Gabor returned as Bernard and Bianca, but the rest of the characters were new. When the boy Cody in rural Australia is kidnapped by the vicious poacher MacLeish (voiced by George C. Scott), the Rescue Aid Society is contacted and Bernard and Bianca set off for the "down under" continent. Because actor Jim Jordan had died, the albatross who takes them there was named Wilbur and was hilariously portrayed by actor John Candy. *The Rescuers Down Under* has a distinctive look, both the landscape and the various animal characters inspired by the Australian setting. There are no songs in the film, making it purely an adventure movie with some pointed comic relief. When the film performed below expectations on its opening weekend, the studio foolishly pulled all advertising and wrote the movie off as a loss. Yet it eventually earned over $47 million thanks to its home video versions.

Did You Know . . . ?

After the success of *The Rescuers*, the studio planned a television cartoon series featuring Bernard and Miss Bianca. When a feature sequel was announced, the cartoon show was altered with Chip and Dale as the heroes and the series was titled *Chip 'n' Dale Rescue Rangers*.

RIO

2011
(USA: Blue Sky Studio/20th Century Fox)

Produced by Chris Wedge, Bruce Anderson, and John C. Donkin
Directed by Carlos Saldanha
Written by Don Rhymer, Jennifer Ventimilia, Joshua Sternin, and Sam Harper
Score by John Powell
Songs by John Powell, Sergio Mendez, Jemaine Clement, William Adams, and various artists
Specs: Color; 96 minutes; computer animation

Like Disney's South American films of the 1940s, Rio *reveals a colorful new world south of the border. But there is a darker side to this travel adventure.*

The blue macaw hatchling named Blu is taken from the forests of Brazil by poachers, who sell him to a pet store in the United States. In Minnesota, Blu's crate falls from the truck and he is rescued by the little girl Linda. Fifteen years later, Linda runs a bookstore and Blu is her constant companion. But when the Brazilian ornithologist Tulio comes into the store and sees Blu, he informs Linda that the bird is one of only two surviving members of that species. He insists that Linda bring Blu to Rio de Janeiro so he can mate with the female Jewel, who is the other remaining blue macaw. Despite her apprehensions, Linda agrees, and trouble begins when they arrive in Brazil during the annual Rio Carnival. The two birds do not get along at first, and that night the orphan Fernando steals Blu to sell him to the smuggler Marcela and his nitwit henchmen. All the exotic birds waiting to be shipped over-

The only two surviving blue macaws left in the world are Jewel (left) in Brazil and Blu in Minnesota, so they are brought together in Rio where they have a rather rocky romance. *20th Century Fox Film Corporation / Photofest. © 20th Century Fox Film Corporation*

Voice Cast

Jesse Eisenberg	Blu
Anne Hathaway	Jewel
Sofia Scarpa Saldanha	Linda (young)
Leslie Mann	Linda (adult)
Rodrigo Santoro	Tulio
Jemaine Clement	Nigel
Jamie Foxx	Nico
George Lopez	Rafael
Carlos Ponce	Marcel
Wanda Sykes	Chloe
Jane Lynch	Alice
Tracey Morgan	Luiz
Will.i.am Adams	Pedro
Jake T. Austin	Fernando

seas are guarded by the fiendish cockatoo Nigel. The two blue macaws escape and get help from the friendly toucan Raphael and his friends: the canary Nico, the cardinal Pedro, and the bulldog Luiz. Both Nigel and Linda search for Blu and Jewel during the confusion and chaos of Carnival, but eventually Linda is reunited with Blu, Jewel realizes she loves Blu, and Tulio confesses his love for Linda.

Director Carlos Saldanha, who emigrated from Brazil to New York City, came up with the original story for *Rio*, about a penguin from Antarctica who is washed up on the shores of Rio de Janeiro. But after the animated penguin movies *Happy Feet* (2006) and *Surf's Up* (2007) were released, Saldanha decided to make the hero a macaw. His story suggested specific locations in Rio de Janeiro to be used in the screenplay. The animators and background artists visited the Brazilian city in preparation for making the movie, and they also studied various exotic birds at the Bronx Zoo. Consequently, the look of *Rio* is more impressive than the plot, which is a series of escapes and chases. The many characters are well defined and, as voiced by an expert cast, are very enjoyable. Jesse Eisenberg's Blu is a mass of neuroses and reminds one of the hapless characters Bob Hope and Woody Allen played in their comedies. Blu's inability to fly (until the final scene) adds some intensity to the plot, but his disability is more fun as a self-deprecating character trait. Anne Hathaway's Jewel is a free spirit and a very liberated female with few surprises. Yet the various friends and villains are delightful, each distinct and memorable. Jemaine Clement's nasty Nigel is one of the more gruesome of modern villains and the smuggler Marcel also drips with malice. The comic friends of the hero are farcical without being one-dimensional stereotypes. The slobbering bulldog Luiz, voiced by Tracey Morgan, is particularly endearing, even as he is sometimes repulsive to look at, and George Lopez as the fun-loving toucan Rafael is a font of optimism and energy. The audience may be forced to run all over in Rio, but at least they are in good company.

Songs

"Real in Rio"
"Copacabana Dreams"
"Pretty Bird"
"Sapo Cai"
"Let Me Take You to Rio"
"Whoomp! There It Is"
"The Girl from Ipanema"

The city of Rio de Janeiro is portrayed in the film as a colorful and exciting metropolis at first, the Carnival sometimes resembling a Las Vegas show. But when the orphan Fernando enters the story a very different side of the city is seen. The dark and claustrophobic slums of Rio have a very somber feel. The character animators continue this mood in the way Marcel and his stooges are portrayed. They move in clumsy patterns, while all the animals, especially the birds, have very fluid motions. Particularly effective is the way the feathers on the evil Nigel give him a decrepit appearance. The city of Rio, its famous landmarks, and the beaches and ocean, are presented poetically, often using various sunlight and moonlight effects on the panorama. It is a beautiful-looking movie, and one immediately responds to its splendor. Both the festive and somber aspects of the city (and the film) are supported by the soundtrack score by John Powell. The background music suggests Latin American themes at times, but most of the scoring is either romantic or freewheeling, especially in the flying sequences. The authentic sound of Brazil comes from the songs supervised by Sergio Mendes, the Rio native who was among the first to bring bossa nova and other Latin music to the United States in the 1960s. Various artists wrote and performed the vibrant musical numbers that contribute so much to the vitality of the film. The soundtrack album for the film was a best seller and there was also a popular music video of "Telling the World" featuring songwriter Taio Cruz. Other highlights in the *Rio* score were the romantic "Fly Love" and the vigorous "Real in Rio."

Wisely, 20th Century Fox premiered *Rio* in Rio de Janeiro in March of 2011 and then in the United States a month after. The movie did strong box office

BLU: So, how far is it to this Luiz?

RAFAEL: Not far! Thirty minutes, as the crow flies.

BLU: I see . . . and how far as the macaw walks?

JEWEL: Bo-Bo here can't fly.

RAFAEL: But, he's a bird!

BLU: Not all birds fly! There are ostriches . . .

JEWEL: You are NOT an ostrich!

BLU: Well . . . not technically.

in both countries and found similar success around the world. Reviews were mostly approving, and audiences embraced the film and its music, allowing *Rio* to earn over $480 million in its first year. There were a number of marketing tie-ins for *Rio*, including an Oreo cookie with blue cream instead of white; contests with trips to Rio as prizes; character figures distributed at McDonalds; and the video game "Angry Birds Rio," which was put on the market to coincide with the movie's release. Also available was a video game of the film itself. Both the DVD and Blu-ray editions of *Rio* were released later in 2011 and sold over ten million copies worldwide.

Award

Academy Award nomination: Best Song ("Real in Rio").

Director Saldanha and most of the original cast were involved with the 2014 sequel *Rio 2*. The plot centered on Blu, Jewel, and their three children setting off into the Brazilian jungle to see if they could get back to their natural habitat. Along the way Jewel is reunited with her long-lost father and discovers that the Amazon jungle is threatened by developers. Again reviews were mixed, but international earnings surpassed those for *Rio*. The film was a plea to save the Amazon forest, but it was also light entertainment. In keeping with the spirit of the movie, 20th Century Fox donated $100,000 to the World Wildlife Fund to aid the conservation of Brazil's forests.

See also *Madagascar*.

Did You Know . . . ?

When Fox's *Rio* was such a hit at the box office, Pixar decided to scrap a film project titled *Newt* because its plot was too similar to that of *Rio*.

THE ROAD TO EL DORADO

2000
(USA: DreamWorks)

Directed by Bibo Bergeron and Don Paul
Written by Terry Rossio and Ted Elliott
Produced by Jeffrey Katzenberg, Bill Damaschke, Brooke Breton, Bonne Radford, and Dino Athanassiou
Score by John Powell and Hans Zimmer
Songs by Elton John and Tim Rice
Specs: Color (Technicolor); 89 minutes; traditional animation

The sixteenth-century con men Miguel (left) and Tulio find themselves as stowaways in a Spanish ship heading to the New World and the fabled city of El Dorado. *DreamWorks / Photofest. © DreamWorks*

A merry variation of the buddy film as well as the popular "road" movies starring Bing Crosby and Bob Hope in the 1940s, this comic adventure failed to find wide success but remains a funny and beautifully rendered animated feature.

The freewheeling con men Miguel and Tulio win a map to the legendary city of El Dorado in a crap game in Spain in 1519. Accidentally stowing away on one of Hernán Cortés's ships going to the New World in search of gold, Miguel and Tulio jump ship with Cortés's horse Altivo and make it to the shore of Mexico. Miguel recognizes some landmarks from the map and convinces Tulio to search for the famed city of gold. When they find it, the two men are mistaken for gods. With the help of the clever native girl Chel, the twosome manage to pull off the ruse of being deities and collect gold until the evil high priest Tzekel-Kan discovers the

Voice Cast

Kevin Kline	Tulio
Kenneth Branagh	Miguel
Rosie Perez	Chel
Armand Assante	Tzekel-Kan
Edward James Olmos	Chief
Jim Cummings	Cortez
Frank Welker	Altivo
Tobin Bell	Zaragoza
Duncan Marjoribanks	Acolyte

truth. The sorcerer conjures up a giant jaguar made of stone to destroy Miguel and Tulio so he can take control of El Dorado. But the con men outwit Tzekel-Kan and cast the high priest and his monster into a whirlpool that pushes them outside of the city. Cortés and his troops arrive and Tzekel-Kan promises to show the Spaniards the secret entrance to El Dorado. Learning that Cortés is on his way, Tulio devises a plan to cause a cave-in and block the only entrance to the city. In the process Miguel and Tulio lose all the gold but look forward to new adventures with Chel joining the team.

Producer Jeffrey Katzenberg was a fan of the series of Crosby-Hope "road" movies that began with *Road to Singapore* in 1940 and wanted to make an animated film that used the same elements as those in the very popular Paramount films. During the five-year development and production period, *The Road to El Dorado* went through many script changes including different versions of the story and the characters and even major changes in staff. The one consistent aspect of the project was the sixteenth-century setting in the New World and the search for gold. The plot that was finally used was similar to that of Rudyard Kipling's story *The Man Who Would Be King*, which was filmed in 1975. Two British ex-soldiers are thought to be gods by a tribe in the mountains of Asia and are worshipped and honored until the tribesmen discover the truth. Just as the heroes in the Kipling tale are friends, Miguel and Tulio in *The Road to El Dorado* are rough-and-tumble buddies who crack jokes and use friendly satire to belittle each other. The practical Tulio and the dreamer Miguel are the core of the movie and they are endlessly entertaining. It certainly helped that the two con men were played by British stage-screen actor Kenneth Branagh and American stage-screen actor Kevin Kline with spot-on comic performances, the two of them playing off each other's rhythms and freely ad-libbing. The result is a comedy treat that distinguishes the movie. Also providing effective voice work are Rosie Perez as the sexy, matter-of-fact Chel, Armand Assante as the devious Tzekel-Kan, and Edward James Olmos as the convivial chief of the tribe.

Songs

"Someday Out of the Blue (Theme from El Dorado)"
"Without Question"
"El Dorado"
"Friends Never Say Goodbye"
"The Trail We Blaze"
"It's Tough to Be a God"

The Road to El Dorado is historically inaccurate and often anachronistic. It was Spanish explorer Gonzalo Pizarro who went looking for El Dorado, not Cortés. The DreamWorks artists studied the Mayan ruins in Mexico, but the settings in the movie include distinctive features from the Aztecs and the Incas as well. Even the costumes and face painting of the tribesmen in *The Road to El Dorado* are a mixture of different cultures. Some historians also pointed out many inaccuracies in the culture of the Mayans, and the present-day organization called Mexica Movement urged members to boycott the film. Regardless, the settings for the comedy are appropriately lush and colorful. The depiction of the jungle is highly poetic and El Dorado itself shines with bright colors even before the audience is shown the golden objects. There is no attempt made in the dialogue to re-create the sound of the period or the people. The script is filled with modern humor and even the citizens of El Dorado crack a joke on occasion. This is consistent with the formula for the old Crosby-Hope "road" movies in which characters in Zanzibar, Rio, Morocco, and other exotic locales sounded like comics. Since *The Road to El Dorado* does not take itself seriously, one has to accept its carefree approach to reality.

> TULIO: Get back mortal!
>
> MIGUEL: Beware the wrath of the Gods! Be gone! Kkh kkh!
>
> TULIO: Back mortal, before we strike you with a lightning bolt!
>
> CHEL: Save it for the High Priest, honey, you're gonna need it.

Katzenberg hired composer Elton John and lyricist Tim Rice to write a musical score for the movie, hoping for the kind of success they had with his Disney production of *The Lion King* (1994). The team wrote ten songs for the movie, but so many changes had been made during production that only six were used in the final film. *The Road to El Dorado* changed from a musical comedy to a comedy adventure, and the action did not stop for songs. Miguel and Tulio sing the silly duet "It's Tough to Be a God"; the rest of the songs are performed by John on the soundtrack. All the numbers are catchy in the pop-rock mode but are relegated to the background. The opening number "El Dorado" sets the modern tone of the film, "The Trail We Blaze" is a rhythmic travel song, and "Friends Never Say Goodbye" is propulsive yet heartfelt. The finest song in the score, the memorable "Someday Out of the Blue," is the theme song for the movie, but it is only heard during the final credits. The soundtrack score by Hans Zimmer and John Powell has touches of the native sound, but most of the music is either bouncy and carefree or imposing and grand. Interestingly, the CD of the film's soundtrack includes all the songs written for *The Road to El Dorado*, not just the ones heard in the movie.

The Road to El Dorado opened in 2000 to mixed reviews. Some commentators thought the humor and the story lacking, others enjoyed the film for the unpretentious romp that it was. Few critics picked up on the homage to the "road" films of the 1940s. Like much of the moviegoing public, the critics failed to see what *The Road to El Dorado* was trying to do. Business was modest, grossing just over $76 million. But the movie's final price tag was $95 million so the venture was a financial failure. Originally, DreamWorks foresaw a series of "road" sequels starring the same characters and stars, just as in the Paramount series. But after the disappointing box office receipts for *The Road to El Dorado*, any plans for another "road" film were dropped. The movie has since developed an audience because of the 2000 DVD edition. The film has also inspired a video game, "Gold and Glory: The Road to El Dorado."

See also *The Emperor's New Groove*.

Did You Know . . . ?

Differently than the usual way of making animated movies, Kenneth Branagh and Kevin Kline did all their vocal recording together in the studio in order to come up with a comic rhythm that allowed them to play off each other.

ROBIN HOOD

1973
(USA: Walt Disney Productions)

Produced and directed by Wolfgang Reitherman
Written by Larry Clemmons, Ken Anderson, Vance Gerry, David Michener, Eric Cleworth, Frank Thomas, and Julius Svendsen
Score by George Bruns
Songs by Roger Miller, Floyd Huddleston, George Bruns, and Johnny Mercer
Specs: Color (Technicolor); 83 minutes; traditional animation

The enduring legend of Robin Hood is given an animated and animal-filled treatment in this sportive Disney version with a sprightly score.

While the evil lion Prince John overtaxes the people of England, the wolf Sheriff of Nottingham tries to capture the fox Robin Hood and his companions in the Sherwood Forest. When Robin and his faithful companions the badger Friar Tuck and the bear Little John rob a shipment of gold from the prince, the angry John puts a price on Robin Hood's head. This doesn't keep the bandit from taking on various disguises to rob from the rich and give to the poor. He is also in love with his childhood sweetheart, the vixen Maid Marian, and manages to woo her despite the

Voice Cast

Brian Bedford	Robin Hood
Peter Ustinov	Prince John
Phil Harris	Little John
Andy Devine	Friar Tuck
Roger Miller	Allan-a-Dale
Pat Buttram	Sheriff of Nottingham
Monica Evans	Maid Marian
Carole Shelley	Lady Cluck
Terry-Thomas	Sir Hiss
George Lindsey	Trigger
Ken Curtis	Nutsy
Peter Ustinov	King Richard

All of the characters in this Disney version of the legendary Old English tale are played by animals, including the Fox bandit Robin Hood and his bear companion Little John. *Walt Disney Pictures / Photofest. © Walt Disney Pictures*

prince's watchful eye. When an archery tournament is announced by John, Robin again dons a disguise and wins the competition. Knowing Robin could not resist the tournament, the sheriff has set a trap to capture the bandit, but the various animal citizens of Nottingham aid Robin's men in outwitting the prince and the sheriff. The lion King Richard returns to England from crusading, arrests his brother John and the sheriff, and gives Robin permission to wed the king's niece Marian.

Decades before his death, Walt Disney wanted to make an animated feature about the medieval legend of Reynard the Fox, but all attempts failed and the studio lost interest in the project. In the 1960s, writer Ken Anderson suggested a version of the Robin Hood legend using some of the Reynard ideas and drawings, including the concept of Robin played by a fox. At one point the story was going to be set in the American South and then in the Old West. Director Wolfgang Reitherman argued for the conventional setting of medieval England and including Prince John and King Richard in the plot. The decision to have all the characters played by various animals came from the original Reynard idea. Certain animals were tried, such as Friar Tuck as a pig and the sheriff as a goat, but were rejected. Most of the story comes from the original version of the legend, but the studio added many comic and touching bits inspired by the animals being animated. To save money and time, some action sequences are taken from previous Disney films and adapted for *Robin Hood*, such as some dancing from *The Jungle Book* (1967) and the frolicking in the woods from *Snow White and the Seven Dwarfs* (1937). Although

Songs

"Whistle-Stop" (Miller)
"The Phony King of England" (Mercer)
"Love" (Huddleston/Bruns)
"Oo-de-lally" (Miller)
"Not in Nottingham" (Miller)

Walt Disney was involved in the early development of *Robin Hood*, this is the first animated movie by the studio in which he had no input on characters or story.

The voice cast for *Robin Hood* includes some Disney regulars and some distinguished newcomers, such as British actors Peter Ustinov, Terry-Thomas, and Brian Bedford. Most of the cast was American and no effort was made to have all the characters speak with English accents. Bedford's Robin is sly but very aristocratic-sounding, while his cohorts Friar Tuck and Little John are voiced by the very American-sounding Andy Devine and Phil Harris. American country singer-songwriter Roger Miller wrote most of the songs and voiced the rooster narrator Alan-a-Dale, giving the movie the feel of an American folk legend rather than a British one. Having character actor Pat Buttram voice the sheriff was also a very American sound. But Ustinov is delightfully English as Prince John and King Richard, Terry-Thomas is the ultimate silly-ass Englishman as the snake Sir Hiss, and London actresses Monica Evans and Carole Shelley have authentic British tones. It is a varied, perhaps uneven, cast, but there are superb performances throughout.

SIR HISS: How nobly King Richard's crown sits on your royal brow.

PRINCE JOHN: Doesn't it? King Richard? I told you never to mention my brother's name!

SIR HISS: A mere slip of the forked tongue, Sire.

The look and sound of *Robin Hood* may not rival the Disney classics of the past but both are quite accomplished. The background art is reminiscent of the English landscape of the *Winnie the Pooh* shorts. The colors are broad and the black ink detailing is very fine. The character animation is very physical for many of the characters, as with the ingenious ways the snake Sir Hiss moves as if he had appendages. Hiss resembles the comic Terry-Thomas, particularly with his gap-toothed mouth, which provides a space for the snake's tongue to flicker. Ustinov's diverse vocals as Prince John and his ability to descend into baby talk at times allow for a variety of ideas in physicalizing the character. Robin moves in an almost weightless manner, while the sheriff, Friar Tuck, and Little John are heavy and plodding in their animation. *Robin Hood* calls for no magic or special effects, so the animation is rarely spectacular yet it is a noteworthy piece of thoughtful filmmaking. For example, the opening credits are a clever homage to the art in the famed Bayou Tapestry depicting the Norman Conquest.

George Bruns provided the tuneful soundtrack score, which does echo English music at times but is mostly spirited and bubbly. Miller's numbers range from the catchy and breezy "Whistle-Stop" during the opening titles to the easy-going "Oo-de-lally," which blends the sound of an English ballad with a cowboy song. Renowned songwriter Johnny Mercer, in one of his last film assignments, wrote the jocular "The Phony King of England," and Bruns and Floyd Huddleston provided the film's romantic number, "Love." None of these became popular outside of the film, though years later a speeded up version of "Whistle-Stop" found fame as the Hamster Dance on the internet.

Award

Academy Award nomination: Best Song ("Love").

Robin Hood opened in 1973 to modestly favorable reviews. Critics were not enthusiastic, yet they complimented the movie for its entertainment values. The public responded favorably, and *Robin Hood* earned over $9 million on its $6 million investment. The film was only rereleased in theaters once, in 1982, then found a whole new audience on VHS in 1984, on DVD in 2000, and on Blu-ray in 2013.

See also *The Sword in the Stone*.

Did You Know . . . ?

In an early development stage, the legend of Robin Hood was to be reset in the Wild West. That is perhaps why such Western character actors as George Lindsey, Ken Curtis, and Andy Devine were cast and why country music singer-songwriter Roger Miller was hired to work on the songs.

S

THE SECRET OF NIMH

1982

(USA: Don Bluth Productions/United Artists)

Directed by Don Bluth
Written by Don Bluth, Ken Anderson, John Pomeroy, Gary Goldman, and Will Finn,
    based on the book *Mrs. Frisby and the Rats of NIMH* by Robert C. O'Brien
Produced by James L. Stewart, Rich Irvine, Don Bluth, Gary Goldman, and John
    Pomeroy
Score by Jerry Goldsmith
Song "Flying Dreams" by Jerry Goldsmith and Paul Williams
Specs: Color; 82 minutes; traditional animation

The first non-Disney feature to successfully challenge the older company in its animation techniques and effects, The Secret of NIMH *is a mystical tale that goes beyond traditional animated filmmaking and was a triumphant directing debut for Don Bluth.*

The field mouse Mrs. Brisby, raising her four children in a cement block near the Fitzgibbon farm, cannot abandon the field as spring plowing begins because her son Timothy is ill with pneumonia and cannot be moved. She consults the Great Owl, who tells her to get help from the smart rats who live in a rose thorn bush near the farmhouse. Nicodemus, the wise old leader of the rats, is willing to help her because her late husband, Jonathan, once helped the rats escape from NIMH. Several kinds of animals were used by the National Institute of Mental Health (NIMH) to experiment on, and a serum given to the rats made then unusually intelligent and even able to read human writing. Nicodemus and the rats have used their superior knowledge to harness electricity and create a highly mechanized world. But NIMH has learned from the Fitzgibbons where the experimental rats are, and Nicodemus urges the rat community to move. He is opposed by the power-hungry rat Jenner, who arranges for Nicodemus to be killed while the rats are helping Mrs. Brisby move her house away from the tractor plow. Using the power of the magic amulet that Nicodemus gave her, Mrs. Brisby is able to save her house and her children from sinking into the mud. The rat Justin defeats Jen-

The mouse widow Mrs. Brisby (right) must move her family from the burrow before the farmers plow up the land for spring planting, but the aged mouse Auntie Shrew (left) doesn't believe her. *United Artists / Photofest. © United Artists*

ner in a sword fight to the death and the rats move to a safer location when NIMH comes looking for them.

Robert C. O'Brien's 1971 book *Mrs. Frisby and the Rats of NIMH* had been considered by the Disney studio for an animated feature when animator Don Bluth still worked there. But the studio thought the story too dark and passed on the project. When Bluth and other animators left Disney and founded Don Bluth Productions,

Voice Cast

Derek Jacobi	Nicodemus
Elizabeth Hartman	Mrs. Brisby
John Carradine	Great Owl
Dom DeLuise	Jeremy
Hermione Baddeley	Auntie Shrew
Arthur Malet	Mr. Ages
Peter Strauss	Justin
Paul Shenar	Jenner
Aldo Ray	Sullivan
Shannen Doherty	Teresa
Wil Wheaton	Martin
Jodi Hicks	Cynthia
Ian Fried	Timothy

they made some shorts on a tight budget then sought funding for a feature-length version of O'Brien's book. United Artists agreed but limited the budget to $5.7 million and the production time to two and a half years, roughly half the money and time used for a Disney animated feature. Bluth cowrote the screenplay, which added magical powers to the characters of the Great Owl and Nicodemus, and took liberties with the plotting. The title was also changed because of possible legal problems with the toy company that manufactured the Frisbee. Bluth and company secured a top-notch voice cast for *The Secret of NIMH* consisting of well-known British actors, such as Derek Jacobi (Nicodemus) and Hermione Baddeley (Auntie Shrew), and American performers, as with Elizabeth Hartman (Mrs. Brisby), Peter Strauss (Justin), and John Carradine (Great Owl). For the daffy crow Jeremy, comic actor Dom DeLuise was cast. Bluth also managed to recruit veteran Hollywood composer Jerry Goldsmith to write the soundtrack score, the first time the renowned artist had worked on an animated movie. Because of the innovative animation experiments and the complexity of the film, production went over budget and the producers had to mortgage their homes in order to complete the movie, the final cost of which was $6.4 million. *The Secret of NIMH* ended up earning $14.6 million domestically on its first release and much more on video and foreign sales.

NICODEMUS: We can no longer live as rats. We know too much.

Devotees of O'Brien's book may have been disappointed in the film because of the many changes made to the characters, but those changes helped turn a somewhat realistic tale into a mystical one. Both Nicodemus and the Great Owl are aged and wise characters who offer sound advice in the book. On screen, they are given the status of wizards with magical powers. Also added to the screenplay was the enchanted amulet that Nicodemus gives Mrs. Brisby, helping her find the strength to save her children. The book's minor character of Jenner was turned into the villain of the piece, and he becomes important during the climax of the movie. Even though this sense of mysticism was added, *The Secret of NIMH* still has human interest and comic relief. It is a tight screenplay with no dull stretches or overworked bits. Similarly, the voice cast is uniformly excellent, from the haunting vocals by John Carradine and Derek Jacobi to the comic ad-libs of Dom DeLuise. Elizabeth Hartman's Mrs. Brisby is gentle without being cloying, and there are fine character voices by Arthur Malet as the grouchy Mr. Ages and by Hermione Baddeley as the domineering Aunty Shrew. Goldsmith's soundtrack score is majestic when necessary, simple and evocative at other times. His music for the magic sections of the movie is also commendable. Songwriter Paul Williams provided the lyric for Goldsmith's lullaby "Flying Dreams" sung on the soundtrack by Sally Stevens and reprised by Williams over the end credits.

Perhaps the greatest accomplishment of the film is the striking animation and background art. Bluth was an experienced Disney animator and he longed to experiment with the form in his first feature away from Disney. But the limited budget was restrictive and much of the artistry in *The Secret of NIMH* was achieved by the animators working overtime without pay. Bluth used rotoscoping and a color Xerox process at times to save time and money but also employed some recent techniques, such as backlighting certain scenes so that light filtered through the cels. This was most noticeable in the ways the eyes of Nicodemus and the Great

Owl were unusually bright. The artists also used color gels to change the look from day to night without having to repaint the cels. In fact, lighting was used as on the stage, the color lights allowing the mood of the scene to shift quickly or gradually. Bluth experimented with video, using instant replay as a way to determine the effectiveness of a scene, and utilized double exposure to create some of the unrealistic effects. The background art is in a naturalistic tone, but the special effects use vibrant colors. It is estimated that over six hundred different colors were used in making the movie. There are also over one thousand different backgrounds in the film, nearly three times the amount in a traditional animated feature. The look of *The Secret of NIMH* was striking in 1982 and much of it is still impressive today.

United Artists gave the movie a limited release, opening in only one hundred theaters the first weekend, so it took time for *The Secret of NIMH* to catch on. Critical response was highly complimentary, especially for the animation, and the film was compared favorably to a Disney product. Most Americans discovered the film on VHS in 1983 and then later on DVD in 1998. A made-for-video sequel, *The Secret of NIMH 2: Timmy to the Rescue*, was released in 1998. A computerized reboot of the tale was begun in 2016.

See also *Watership Down*.

Did You Know . . . ?

The Secret of NIMH was the most complex and challenging animated feature film made up to that time that was not a Disney project.

SHAUN THE SHEEP MOVIE

2015
(UK/France: StudioCanal/Aardman Animations)

Directed and written by Mark Burton and Richard Starzak, based on characters created by Nick Park
Produced by Nick Park, Peter Lord, Ron Halpern, David Sproxton, Oliver Courson, Kerry Lock, Carla Shelley, Sean Clarke, Alicia Gold, Paul Kewley, and Julie Lockhart
Score by Ilan Eshkeri
Songs by Mark Thomas, Ilan Eshkeri, Tim Wheeler, and Nick Hodgson, and song standards by various artists
Specs: Color; 85 minutes; stop-motion animation

Playfully eccentric in both its characters and look, this stop-motion comedy manages to develop character and tell its story without any decipherable dialogue.

The daily routine at Mossy Bottom Farm is so predictable that the clever sheep Shaun tricks the foolish Farmer into falling asleep in his caravan (trailer) so that all the sheep can have a holiday. The farm dog, Bitzer, is onto their plan but is

The Farmer happily poses for a photo with some of his sheep and his dog Bitzer after they rescue him from the Big City and save the farm. *Lionsgate / Photofest. © Lionsgate*

helpless to stop things when the caravan accidentally starts to roll down a hill and races all the way into the Big City. The wild ride gives the Farmer such a knock on the head that he loses his memory yet he can still recall how to shear sheep. He wanders into a hair salon, where he gives a movie star a sheep-like haircut that becomes all the rage in town. Bitzer, Shaun, and the other sheep go to the Big City, where they encounter a series of misadventures, in particular running from the evil animal-control worker Trumper. Shaun concocts an elaborate plan in which the animals disguise themselves as a horse, kidnap the Farmer, and return to the farm. Regaining his memory, the Farmer is thrilled to be back home, and he breaks the daily routine with a holiday for all.

Voice Cast

Justin Fletcher	Shaun
John Sparkes	Farmer
Omid Djalili	Trumper
John Sparkes	Bitzer
Richard Webber	Shirley
Justin Fletcher	Timmy
Kate Harbour	Timmy's Mum
Tim Hands	Slip
Andy Nyman	Nuts
Simon Greenall	Twins
Emma Tate	Hazel

Animator Nick Park started animating Shaun in his 2007 animated series *Shaun the Sheep* on British television and later produced this film version, which was directed by Richard Starzak and Christopher Sadler. The movie has the look and feel of Parks's shorts and features, such as *Chicken Run* (2000) and *Wallace & Gromit: The Curse of the Were-Rabbit* (2005). Both animal and human characters are exaggerated into grotesque caricatures without hiding the texture of clay. The stop-motion animation is broad with buffoonish facial gestures and nimble body movements. The settings are more realistic, though still jocular. The screenplay for *Shaun the Sheep Movie* is filled with a variety of characters (both human and animal) and a lot of action. The farce is built on a series of comic complications that are as contrived as they are funny.

Songs

"Shaun the Sheep (Life's a Treat)" (Thomas)
"Feels Like Summer" (Eshkeri/Hodgson/Wheeler)
"Big City" (Eshkeri/Hodgson)

The most unusual aspect of the film is the absence of dialogue. Characters grunt, grumble, sigh, and make other diverse sounds but none of it could be recognized as conversation. Park had used this technique in some of his animated shorts (the dog Gromit, for example, never spoke or even barked) but to make an entire feature film with no dialogue was risky. StudioCanal, the financier and distributor of the movie, urged the filmmakers to put traditional dialogue into the feature but Starzek and Sadler remained firm. *Shaun the Sheep Movie* is not diminished by the lack of talk. In fact, it often adds to the comedy and it certainly makes the movie distinctive. A complete voice cast was hired, one actor for each character, so that the sound coming out of each animal or human was individual. And they are clownish sounds indeed. The challenge of communicating with gibberish without slipping into actual words must have been formidable, but all of the different voices succeed effectively. There are a handful of songs heard on the soundtrack (obviously none of the characters sing) and they have very clear lyrics. This makes for an unorthodox sound, like a silent movie with a pop song soundtrack. Ilan Eshkeri, who cowrote the catchy "Feels Like Summer," also composed the musical soundtrack, which is filled with homages to famous movie scores of the past. Often the ridiculous action on screen is made more farcical by Eshkeri's score, particularly in the chase scenes.

Awards

Academy Award nomination: Best Animated Feature.
Golden Globe nomination: Best Motion Picture—Animated.
British Academy of Film & Television Arts (BAFTA) nomination: Best Animated Film.

Shaun the Sheep Movie was a time and talent-consuming project that took two years and ended up costing about $25 million. When it was released in Britain and the United States in 2015, the reviews were mostly propitious, some critics comparing the film to some silent movie comedy classics. The public was equally receptive, particularly in Great Britain, where the movie earned $22 million. Internationally, *Shaun the Sheep Movie* brought in over $106 million, so the inevitable sequel is already on the books.

See also *Chicken Run.*

Did You Know . . . ?

Like other Aardman Animations features, this one is filled with visual references to all kinds of movies. *Shaun the Sheep Movie* has comic nods to *Taxi Driver, The Silence of the Lambs, The Great Escape, The Wolverine, Cape Fear, The Shawshank Redemption*, and others.

SHREK

2001
(USA: DreamWorks Animation)

Directed by Andrew Adamson and Vicky Jenson
Written by Ted Elliott, Terry Rossio, Joe Stillman, and Roger S. H. Schulman, based
   on the picture book *Shrek!* by William Steig
Produced by Stephen Spielberg, David Lipman, Sandra Rabins, Penny Finkelman
   Cox, Jeffrey Katzenberg, Aron Warner, John H. Williams, Ted Elliott, Jane Hartwell,
   Terry Rossio, and Linda Olszewski
Score by Harry Gregson-Williams and John Powell
Song standards by various artists
Specs: Color (Technicolor); 90 minutes; computer animation

A cockeyed fairy tale based on an offbeat children's book, Shrek *introduced a lovable ogre who has since become an audience favorite.*

In the kingdom of Duloc, the evil Lord Farquaad hates fairy-tale creatures in the woods and hunts them down. The Magic Mirror tells him he can only be king if he marries the Princess Fiona. The fleeing fairy-tale characters take refuge in a swamp, where the green ogre Shrek is content living in isolation from the world. In order to regain his peace and quiet, Shrek and his wisecracking Donkey set off for the castle of Duloc to convince Farquaad to let the fairy-tale characters return to the kingdom. On the way, Shrek and Donkey rescue Fiona from the clutches of a dragon and she and Shrek start to have feelings for each other, even though Fiona is beautiful and he is ugly. Donkey finds out there is a curse on Fiona and

A romance between the beautiful Princess Fiona and the ugly green ogre Shrek seems unlikely until a secret about the princess is discovered in time for a happy ending. *DreamWorks / Photofest.* © *DreamWorks*

she is only beautiful in daylight; at night she is as ugly as Shrek. When Fiona is returned to the castle, Farquaad immediately calls for a wedding. But during the ceremony, the sun sets and Fiona turns into an ogre. Shrek is thrilled, and he and Fiona wed and go back to the swamp while Farquaad is devoured by the dragon.

In 1990, the American cartoonist William Steig wrote *Shrek!* as a children's story with simple illustrations and an irreverent approach to fairy-tale heroes. Making the ogre Shrek the central character allowed Steig to playfully puncture myths and clichés about fairy tales. Producer-director Steven Spielberg bought the screen rights to the book in 1991 with the idea that the story was ideal for animation. When DreamWorks was founded in 1994, producer Jeffrey Katzenberg secured the rights from Spielberg and production began in 1995. The screenwriters altered the tale somewhat, including fantasy movies as well as fairy tales in the wry spoof. Disney films and characters were particularly chosen, though legally they could not resemble the Disney icons accurately. Steig's illustrations from the book

Voice Cast

Mike Myers	Shrek
Cameron Diaz	Princess Fiona
Eddie Murphy	Donkey
John Lithgow	Lord Farquaad
Vincent Cassel	Monsieur Hood
Jim Cummings	Captain of the Guards

were not replicated in the film, but they served as an inspiration for the animators. The character design and animation in *Shrek* is a witty mix of realistic details and outrageous exaggeration. Shrek has a green body with facial features that are somewhat human but with thin funnel ears that move back and forth to express his temperament. Fiona is traditionally beautiful until her face is enlarged and distorted to turn her into an ogre with similar ears. Donkey is anatomically correct, but certain features, such as his head and mouth, are oversized. The pint-sized Lord Farquaad is also out of proportion, with an angular head, giving the sense of a bobble-head toy. The many fairy-tale characters are rendered in similarly offbeat ways, from stick figures to bloated dolls. The background art in *Shrek* is a romanticized fairy-tale world with a pristine castle and a dramatically dense forest. The special effects are also overblown, such as Fiona's swirling transition from princess to ogre. The computer animation gives the whole movie a three-dimensional feel, making it all the more artificial and silly.

SHREK: For your information, there's a lot more to ogres than people think.

DONKEY: Example?

SHREK: Example . . . uh . . . ogres are like onions!

DONKEY: They stink?

SHREK: Yes . . . No!

DONKEY: Oh, they make you cry?

SHREK: No!

DONKEY: Oh, you leave 'em out in the sun, they get all brown, start sproutin' little white hairs . . .

SHREK: (peels an onion) NO! Layers. Onions have layers. Ogres have layers . . . You get it? We both have layers.

Comedian Chris Farley was hired to voice the character Shrek and he had nearly finished all of the recording sessions when he suddenly died in 1997. Comic actor Mike Myers was then hired, and the recording sessions began all over again. The Scottish accent adds greatly to the vocals of Shrek, and Myers's comic timing makes the character funny and endearing. In contrast to Shrek's low musical voice is Eddie Murphy's hyperactive, high-pitched vocals for Donkey. It is a high-flying performance filled with anachronisms and ad-libs similar to Murphy's Mushu in *Mulan* (1998). Cameron Diaz is a lively Fiona, her voice never changing even when her physical look does. John Lithgow gives a deliciously sleazy performance as Farquaad, difficult to take seriously but right in line with the movie's satirical sense of humor. All of the fairy-tale characters are voiced with variety and farcical glee. Adding to the anachronistic flavor of *Shrek* are a series of modern song standards heard on the soundtrack, often slyly commenting on the action. In a few cases, Donkey sang the old favorites. Among the musical numbers heard are "I'm a Believer," "On the Road Again," "Try a Little Tenderness," and "I'm on My Way." Harry Gregson-Williams and John Powell composed the soundtrack score that includes some lovely lyrical passages for the love story, dissonant magical themes, pompous fanfares and marches, and overly dramatic action music. There is also a facetious ditty, "Welcome to Duloc," by Mike Himelstein and Eric Darnell that is sung by the citizens of Duloc in a pastiche of the Munchkin sequence in *The Wizard of Oz* (1939).

Awards

Academy Award: Best Animated Feature. Oscar nomination: Best Screenplay. Golden Globe nomination for Best Motion Picture—Comedy or Musical. British Academy of Film & Television Arts (BAFTA) Awards: Best Screenplay and the Children's AWARD: Best Feature Film. BAFTA nominations: Best Film, Best Score, Best Sound, Best Visual Effects, and Best Performance in a Supporting Role (Eddie Murphy).

Being a new company with limited experience with computer animation, DreamWorks ended up spending $60 million on *Shrek*, but the film soon was a box office blockbuster, eventually earning over $484 million. The critical reaction was just as triumphant. The reviews praised the wicked humor, the buffoonish voice performances, and the appealing look of the movie. The VHS and DVD editions were released in 2001 with the Blu-ray version in 2010. In addition to video games and a 2010 Broadway musical adaptation, *Shrek* spawned three film sequels: *Shrek 2* (2004), *Shrek the Third* (2007), and *Shrek Forever After* (2010). The plotting in these films is sometimes tired, but the jokes and the characters remain fresh and all of the movies were box office hits. A fifth sequel is expected in 2019. There have also been two holiday TV specials, *Shrek the Halls* (2007) and *Scared Shrekless* (2010), plus a spin-off movie *Puss in Boots* (2011).

Did You Know . . . ?

Canadian actor Mike Myers voiced Shrek using his own natural voice. He was so dissatisfied with the result that he rerecorded all his lines with a Scottish dialect. His mother was Scottish and he was very familiar with the sound.

SLEEPING BEAUTY

1959
(USA: Walt Disney Productions)

Directed by Clyde Geronimi
Written by Erdman Penner, based on the story by Charles Perrault
Produced by Walt Disney
Score by George Bruns
Songs by George Bruns, Tom Adair, Erdman Penner, Winston Hibbler, Sammy Fain, and Jack Lawrence
Specs: Color (Technirama); 75 minutes; traditional animation

Despite the king's decree that all spinning wheels in the kingdom be burned, the evil Maleficent lures the Princess Aurora into a tower where she pricks her finger on the needle. *Walt Disney Pictures / Photofest. © Walt Disney Pictures*

The last of the Disney classics from the 1950s, this popular version of the beloved fairy tale is filled out with bubbly characters, sublime music, and first-rate animation, but it is perhaps most admired for its stunning art work.

King Stefan and Queen Leah invite all the important people in the kingdom to the christening of their baby daughter, the Princess Aurora, including the neighboring King Hubert and his young son Philip, who is betrothed to wed Aurora when she grows up. Not invited to the festivities is the evil sorceress Maleficent, who arrives unexpectedly and puts a curse on the child: before her sixteenth birthday, Aurora will prick her finger on a spinning wheel needle and die. The good fairy

Voice Cast

Mary Costa	Princess Aurora
Bill Shirley	Prince Phillip
Eleanor Audley	Maleficent
Verna Felton	Flora
Barbara Jo Allen	Fauna
Barbara Luddy	Merryweather
Taylor Holmes	King Stefan
Bill Thompson	King Hubert
Marvin Miller	Narrator

Merryweather cannot break the curse, but she has the power to change it to a one-hundred-year sleep rather than death, a sleep that can be broken by a true love's kiss. The king orders every spinning wheel in the kingdom to be burned and, in order to protect Aurora from further harm from Maleficent, the child is raised in a forest cottage by Merryweather and her fellow fairies, Flora and Fauna. Growing up with the name Briar Rose, she is collecting berries one day and meets the adult Prince Philip, both of them unaware of the true identity of the other, and falling in love. Maleficent discovers the whereabouts of Aurora, and when the girl is brought to the castle on her sixteenth birthday, the evil fairy hypnotizes her into climbing into a tower where a spinning wheel is hidden. There Aurora pricks her finger and falls asleep. The three good fairies put the entire kingdom under a sleeping spell as Aurora sleeps in the tower. Philip, after finding out that Briar Rose and Aurora are the same person, travels to the kingdom, where he is captured by Maleficent, who threatens to keep him locked in a dungeon until he is an old man. The three good fairies rescue Philip and arm him with a magic sword and shield with which he battles Maleficent, who has turned herself into a fire-breathing dragon. Philip destroys Maleficent, finds the sleeping Aurora, kisses her, and she and all the kingdom awake for a happy ending.

The idea of a Disney animated version of the fabled Sleeping Beauty legend began in the early 1950s and went through many subplots and variations until a final shooting script was decided on. The writers took much of the tale from the version by the French author Charles Perrault, but they were also influenced by the ballet version composed by Pyotr Tchaikovsky, such as naming the title princess Aurora. Perhaps the most notable aspect of the Disney script is the development of the three good fairies into major characters. They not only add humor to the dark tale but humanize the film in a way that the lovers and villain cannot. Very early on it was decided by Disney that the look of the movie would resemble the medieval illustrated manuscripts and colorful tapestries. This elongated style that emphasized vertical lines was used not only in the background art but in the characters as well. Only the three good fairies are noticeably round; the rest of the characters are taller and statuesque. The trees, mountains, cliffs, and other natural features were rendered in box-like configurations, also a technique of the late Middle Ages and early Renaissance. Yet there is also a touch of 1950s art in *Sleeping Beauty*, particularly in the faces of some of the characters. Just as Snow White captured the 1930s' idea of beauty and Cinderella the 1940s look, Aurora has the classic lines of the 1950s fashion model. The animation throughout is among the finest in the Disney catalog. The movement of Maleficent is formal and stately while Aurora's flowing motions are in time with Tchaikovsky's wonderful ballet music. The animation of Flora, Fauna, and Merryweather is the most fanciful, the three of them barely touching the ground until they decide to give up magic and live as mortals in a cottage in the forest. There they continue to bounce and cavort in lighter-than-air ways, even their bumbling turning into a dance as well. *Sleeping Beauty* contains some of Disney's most beautiful pieces of background art, and the characterizations often match it.

Mary Costa, with her opera-quality soprano singing, voices Aurora in a warm yet crisp manner. She sounds more "modern" than the previous Disney princesses, and her singing is more in the popular mode of the 1950s than an operatic

Songs

"Once Upon a Dream" (Fain/Lawrence)
"Sleeping Beauty" (Bruns/Adair)
"I Wonder" (Bruns/Hibbler/Sears)
"One Gift" (Bruns/Adair)
"Hail the Princess Aurora" (Bruns/Adair)
"The Skumps Song" (Bruns/Adair/Penner)
"Sing a Smiling Song" (Bruns/Adair)

one. Costa gives a splendid speaking performance as well, particularly when one learns that her native speech had a thick Southern accent. Three beloved Disney character actresses—Verna Felton, Barbara Luddy, and Barbara Jo Allen—voiced the three fairies with a twinkle in their vocals that is very endearing. Eleanor Audley has a touch of the melodic in her penetrating performance as Maleficent. Her vocals are among the most chilling of all Disney villainesses. Singer-actor Bill Shirley is solid as Prince Philip, both his singing and speaking vocals filled with a lyrical but weighty flavor. Bill Thompson and Taylor Holmes provide some levity as the two kings, though the latter also has some very heavy scenes to deal with.

MERRYWEATHER: I'd like to turn her into a fat ol'—hop toad.

FAUNA: Now, dear, that isn't a very nice thing to say.

FLORA: Besides, we can't. You know our magic doesn't work that way.

FAUNA: It can only do good, dear, to bring joy and happiness.

MERRYWEATHER: Well, that would make me happy.

Sammy Fain and other studio songwriters wrote several songs for *Sleeping Beauty*, but the more the project developed the more it was clear that such a Broadway sound did not fit with the symphonic music by Tchaikovsky. George Bruns adapted the famous Russian ballet music into a first-rate movie soundtrack, and most of the songs in the film are choral pieces based on Tchaikovsky's themes. The love song, "Once Upon a Dream," was sung by Aurora and the prince to the melody of the ballet's "Garland Waltz," a felicitous piece of music that was already familiar to audiences. The song version would enjoy a life of its own, recorded by such diverse artists as Barbra Streisand, Steve Tyrell, and Lana Del Ray.

Although *Sleeping Beauty* was filmed in the new wide-screen process called Technirama, the studio released both wide-screen and standard-sized prints to

Award

Academy Award nomination: Best Score.

theaters in 1959. With a price tag of over $6 million, the movie was the studio's most expensive to date. The mostly favorable notices and strong public approval resulted in decent box office earnings, but the film did not earn enough on its first release to make a profit. Only after rereleases in 1970, 1979, and 1986 did *Sleeping Beauty* become a hit, with total earnings of over $51 million. The VHS version came out in 1986, the DVD in 2003, and the Blu-ray in 2008. The Disney studio made a live-action film titled *Maleficent* in 2014, which retold the same story but in much darker form and mostly from the perspective of the evil fairy.

Sleeping Beauty is seen as the end of an era in the history of the Disney studio. The movie cost so much that Disney knew the possibility of making financially practical animated features was growing slim. Never again could the studio spend so much time and money on one movie. Also, it was clear that new methods of producing such movies had to be developed in order to survive. These innovations would come in the 1960s. But the studio would not return to the classic fairy-tale animated feature for thirty years, until the making of *The Little Mermaid* (1989).

See also *Cinderella*.

Did You Know . . . ?

Walt Disney had wanted *Snow White and the Seven Dwarfs* (1937) to end with the romantic couple dancing in the clouds. It didn't work out, and years later the same idea was tried in *Cinderella* (1950) but without success. It was finally used in *Sleeping Beauty*.

SNOW WHITE AND THE SEVEN DWARFS

1937
(USA: Walt Disney Productions)

Directed by David Hand, Ben Sharpsteen, Larry Morey, William Cottrell, Wilfred Jackson, and Perce Pearce
Written by Ted Sears, Otto Englander, Webb Smith, Earl Hurd, Dorothy Ann Blany, Richard Creedon, Dick Richard, and Merrill De Maris, based on the story by Jacob and Wilhelm Grimm
Produced by Walt Disney
Score by Paul J. Smith, Leigh Harline, and Frank Churchill
Songs by Frank Churchill (music) and Larry Morey (lyrics)
Specs: Color (Technicolor); 83 minutes; traditional animation

The first American animated feature, this Disney "experiment" is not only historically important, it is still considered one of the greatest achievements in American cinema.

Every time the Queen asks her Magic Mirror who is the fairest in the land, it replies that she is. But when Snow White grows up and the mirror tells the Queen that the young orphan is the fairest, the jealous monarch orders the Huntsman to

Running for her life from the evil Queen, Snow White takes refuge in an empty forest cottage and falls asleep only to awake later and discover seven new little friends. *Walt Disney Pictures / Photofest. © Walt Disney Pictures*

take the girl deep into the forest and kill her. Unable to carry out her wishes, the Huntsman tells Snow White to flee and never return to the castle. The lost Snow White stumbles upon the cottage of the seven dwarfs, whom she befriends. When the Queen learns from the mirror that Snow White lives, she swallows a potion turning her into an aged old crone and goes to the cottage offering Snow White a poisoned apple. One bite and Snow White falls into a coma before the dwarfs return and chase the Queen/crone to the edge of a ravine, where she falls and dies while trying to destroy the dwarfs with a boulder. The dwarfs do not have

Voice Cast

Adriana Caselotti	Snow White
Lucille La Verne	Queen/Witch
Harry Stockwell	Prince
Roy Atwell	Doc
Pinto Colvig	Grumpy
Billy Gilbert	Sneezy
Scotty Mattraw	Bashful
Otis Harlan	Happy
Pinto Colvig	Sleepy
Stuart Buchanan	Huntsman
Moroni Olsen	Magic Mirror

the heart to bury the still-lovely Snow White and are kneeling in reverence before her body when a Prince, whom Snow White had once met and loved, comes into the forest, kisses the sleeping Snow White, and she awakens for a happy ending.

Among the many remarkable aspects of this legendary animated musical filled with "firsts" is that it is so polished and doesn't look like the primitive first of anything. It was not only the first feature-length animated movie, it was also the first cartoon to use live models to simulate human movement, the first animated feature to use a multi-plane camera to achieve depth, the first movie musical to produce (in 1944) a best-selling soundtrack, and the first Hollywood film to earn over $6 million on its initial release. Producer Walt Disney had found wide success in the late 1920s with his cartoon shorts featuring Mickey Mouse and soon was exploring different kinds of animation with his series of Silly Symphony cartoons. But Disney long had wanted to move into features, even though a full-length animated movie was unheard of in Hollywood. He and hundreds of artists spent four years working on the project, which the film community saw as a grand folly. The very idea of a cartoon lasting eighty-three minutes, of animated characters singing love songs to each other, and of artists creating a complex and detailed art decor for a kids' movie was laughable. Yet the film changed the way audiences thought about cartoons, children's movies, and Disney. The script took liberties with the original Grimm brothers' tale and created names and individual characters for the dwarfs. It also softened some of the original story's more gruesome aspects, such as the Queen's requesting Snow White's liver to prove her death and the three attempts by the Queen to murder Snow White. Yet the film is still frightening and powerful at times, just as it is warmhearted and fanciful in other spots. Disney himself plotted out every scene in the movie and was able to inspire his animators to carry out his vision of the famous fairy tale. It didn't take long for everyone to realize that the budget of $250,000 was not nearly enough, and that the labor-intensive project required over one hundred additional animators, inkers, and other staff. *Snow White and the Seven Dwarfs* ended up costing the studio nearly $1.5 million. Had the film failed at the box office, Disney and his company would have been quickly bankrupted.

Songs

"One Song"
"I'm Wishing"
"Some Day My Prince Will Come"
"Whistle While You Work"
"Heigh-Ho"
"With a Smile and a Song"
"Silly Song"
"Bluddle-uddle-um-dum (Dwarfs' Washing Song)"

Disney animation had been getting more and more accomplished during the 1930s with the various shorts but the masterful artistry in *Snow White and the Seven Dwarfs* surpassed all of them. For the first time, human characters dominate the story, and the challenge was to render them realistically, yet still in the stylized medium of animation. Scenes from the script were filmed with live actors and studied by the animators to give believability to the characters. The animals in the story did not speak and were presented as in nature as much as possible. Again the animators studied the various animals that were brought into the studio for research purposes. The multi-plane camera, developed by the studio and first used in the cartoon *The Old Mill* (1937), was utilized on a greater scale to give exterior and interior scenes depth. The background art was pastoral in a fairy-story way, but the interiors of the castle and the dwarfs' cottage were elaborately detailed. The result was an animated movie that did not look or move as in previous efforts. Character animation also went further than that shown in the cartoon shorts. Each of the seven dwarfs was visually and physically distinct and each was complex enough to make an audience laugh and cry. Snow White moved like a dancer at times, and her facial expressions were varied and believable. Her prince, whose role was severely edited in the final script, came across as stiff and lacking personality. Not so for such supporting characters as the evil Queen, the Magic Mirror, and even the Huntsman. Because most of the characters were so strong, *Snow White and the Seven Dwarfs* had an emotional impact never experienced in animation before. Such memorable sequences as Snow White's flight into the forest and the Queen's transition into an ugly old hag were indeed frightening, while the Dwarfs' party with Snow White and their washing up scene were delightful. Disney's first feature was not just a long cartoon but a whole new animated film experience.

> HAPPY: This is Dopey, he don't talk none.
>
> SNOW WHITE: You mean he can't talk?
>
> HAPPY: He don't know, he never tried.

The voice talents used in *Snow White and the Seven Dwarfs* were not much known to the public, which is the way Disney planned it. He did not want the moviegoers to recognize the voices and hoped that the vocals would be associated only with the characters in the film. Young opera singer Adriana Caselotti gives Snow White simple and pure vocals with a clean soprano singing voice. Lucille La Verne's Queen is vocally smooth and icy, while the voice of the Magic Mirror by Moroni Olsen is weary and dismal. The vocals for the dwarfs are all excellent in different ways, from Billy Gilbert's nasal Sneezy to Pinto Colvig's raspy Grumpy. The Prince rarely speaks, but Harry Stockwell's singing is a pleasing tenor without operatic flourishes.

Frank Churchill (music) and Larry Morey (lyrics) wrote the songs, several of which became hits, and just about all of them are now part of musical folklore. The songwriters turned to operetta for the romantic numbers, such as "One Song," "I'm Wishing," and "Someday My Prince Will Come," then used musical comedy for the dwarfs, as with the march "Heigh-Ho," and the very European-sounding "The Dwarfs' Yodeling Song." Also very effective was the music background score by Leigh Harline and Paul J. Smith, adding suspense and drama throughout. It is interesting that Disney saw his initial animated feature as a musical, but then he had been experimenting with music in cartoons for some time and always saw

music and action linked. *Snow White and the Seven Dwarfs* started a tradition of
animated features being musicals and very few Disney products over the decades
would offer animation without songs.

When *Snow White and the Seven Dwarfs* was released in 1937, the reception was
highly enthusiastic. The reviews in the press not only lauded the film but also
silenced all the talk of an animated feature being a ridiculous idea. The response
by moviegoers was just as auspicious. The movie was an immediate hit and broke
box office records during its initial run. By 1939 it became the highest-grossing
sound film yet seen. *Snow White and the Seven Dwarfs* was rereleased in 1944, 1952,
1958, 1967, and 1975. To celebrate the fiftieth anniversary of the film, the studio
rereleased it in 1987 with four thousand prints seen in fifty-eight countries on the
same day, the largest opening day yet in the history of the movies. The VHS version was released in 1994, the DVD in 2001, and on Blu-ray in 2016. The movie is
high on various organizations' lists of greatest films and in polls. But even more
amazing is that *Snow White and the Seven Dwarfs* does not seem to age. With each
passing decade it is still a thrilling, moving, and melodic masterpiece that continues to please new and repeat audiences.

Did You Know . . . ?

Walt Disney didn't want the voice of Snow White (Adriana Caselotti) to be heard in other
movies, so he put Caselotti under contract and kept her from working in films for several years.

SONG OF THE SOUTH

1946
(USA: Walt Disney Productions)

Directed by Wilfred Jackson (animation) and Harve Foster (live action)
Written by Dalton S. Reymond, Morton Grant, Maurice Rapf, Bill Peet, Ralph Wright,
   and Vernon Stallings, based on the *Tales of Uncle Remus* by Joel Chandler Harris
Produced by Walt Disney and Perce Pearce
Score by Daniele Amfitheatrof and Charles Wolcott
Songs by Ken Darby, Allie Wrubel, Ray Gilbert, Robert MacGimsey, Charles Wolcott,
   Foster Carling, Sam Coslow, Arthur Johnston, Eliot Daniel, Hy Heath, and Johnny
   Lange
Specs: Color (Technicolor); 94 minutes; live action and traditional animation

The Disney studio turned the once-popular Tales of Uncle Remus *into an inspired piece of filmmaking that has charmed many but has also bothered some modern sensibilities. It was not Disney's first blending of animation and live action, but the process had never been perfected and used before as effectively as it was in this folklore musical.*

Young Johnny, whose parents have separated, goes to live with his mother and grandmother on a Georgia plantation during the late nineteenth century. He is lonely and confused until he befriends the local farm girl Ginny, the African American youth Toby, and the genial old storyteller Uncle Remus. Johnny's dealings with his overprotective mother, his grandmother, and two bullies in the neighborhood are interrupted by the animated stories that Remus tells him about Brer Rabbit, Brer Fox, and Brer Bear. When Johnny skips his own birthday party to listen to one of Uncle Remus's tales, his mother is so upset she refuses to let the boy see the aged African American again. Saddened by the thought that he caused such friction, Uncle Remus decides to depart for Atlanta but is stopped by Johnny running across a field toward him. A bull attacks Johnny and the boy is so seriously injured that he is close to dying until Uncle Remus entertains him with another story. Once recovered, Johnny happily joins Ginny, Toby, and Uncle Remus for further stories.

Storyteller Uncle Remus (right) has told so many tales about the misadventures of Brer Rabbit that the little fellow seems to come to life, but in an animated form. *Walt Disney Productions / Photofest.* © *Walt Disney Productions*

Voice Cast

James Baskett	Br'er Fox
Johnny Lee	Br' er Rabbit
Nick Stewart	Br' er Bear
Roy Glenn	Bullfrog

Live-Action Cast

James Baskett	Uncle Remus
Bobby Driscoll	Johnny
Luana Patten	Ginny
Ruth Warrick	Sally
Hattie McDaniel	Aunt Tempy
Glenn Leedy	Toby
Erik Rolf	John
Lucile Watson	Grandmother
Gene Holland	Joe Favers
Georgie Nokes	Jake Favers
Mary Field	Mrs. Favers

Walt Disney had read and loved Joel Chandler Harris's Uncle Remus stories as a child and for years considered making cartoons from them. In 1939 he bought the rights from the Harris family, but by then Disney had rethought the project as a live-action feature film with animation for the Uncle Remus stories. Production began in 1942 with the construction of a Southern plantation in Arizona and the first of many drawings for the animated sequences. Filming did not begin until 1944 with a proposed budget of $1,350,000, but costs escalated and *Song of the South* ended up costing over $2 million. While Harve Foster directed the live-action sequences on location in Arizona and later in Hollywood, Wilfred Jackson supervised the animation at the Disney studio. Disney had done several cartoons in the 1920s mixing live actors with animation, most memorably in his "Alice" shorts. But the fusion of animation and live actors in *Song of the South* was much more sophisticated, with the actors interacting more with the cartoon characters. The "Zip-a-Dee-Doo-Dah" scene ended up being the most accomplished live-action-animation sequences yet seen. The animated sequences in *Song of the South* are much more satisfying than the melodrama involving the humans, but the whole movie has a lazy charm about it that is often winning.

Casting the live actors and the voice actors for the movie was problematic. The studio had no "live-action" actors under contract, so child performer Bobby Driscoll was the first performer given a long-running contract by Disney. He played Johnny in *Song of the South* and later other roles, most memorably the title character in *Peter Pan* (1953). Child actress Luana Patten was cast as Ginny before going on to appear in other Disney movies. Character actress Hattie McDaniel,

Songs

"Zip-a-Dee-Doo-Dah" (Wrubel/Gilbert)
"Everybody's Got a Laughing Place" (Wrubel/Gilbert)
"Sooner or Later" (Wolcott/Gilbert)
"How Do You Do?" (MacGimsey)
"Who Wants to Live Like That?" (Darby/Carling)
"Let the Rain Pour Down" (Darby/Carling)
"All I Want" (Darby)
"Uncle Remus Said" (Daniel/Heath/Lange)
"Song of the South" (Coslow/Johnston)

who had won an Oscar playing Mammy in *Gone with the Wind* (1939), was hired to play Aunt Tempy. The difficulty was in finding an African American actor who would exude the warmth of Uncle Remus and effectively narrate the stories. The little-known forty-one-year-old actor James Baskett auditioned for the role of the talking butterfly, and Walt Disney was so impressed with his voice that he cast him as Remus, the butterfly, and Br'er Fox. (Baskett went on to win an honorary Oscar for his performance, but his subsequent career was cut short when he died of a heart attack in 1948.) The African American character actors Nick Stewart and Johnny Lee were cast as Br'er Bear and Br'er Rabbit, and they did their own singing, as did Baskett and McDaniel. *Song of the South* has some of the finest African American performances to be found in the 1940s.

JOHNNY: I wish I had a Laughing Place.

GINNY: Me, too.

UNCLE REMUS: What makes you think you ain't? Course you got a Laughing Place.

JOHNNY: Really, Uncle Remus?

GINNY: Really?

UNCLE REMUS: Everybody's got one. The trouble is, most folks won't take time to go look for it.

JOHNNY & GINNY: Where's mine?

UNCLE REMUS: Well, now, that I can't exactly say. Cause where 'tis for one mightn't be where 'tis for another.

JOHNNY: Come on, Ginny. Let's start looking.

True to its title, *Song of the South* is filled with music. Various tunesmiths wrote the songs, and they are all first-rate. "Zip-a-Dee-Doo-Dah" by Ray Gilbert and Allie Wrubel is the signature song for the film and is the most known. The catchy number has a lazy Southern feel to it, yet it moves along at a good pace. "Sooner or Later," the warm song of affection that Aunt Tempy sings to Remus, also has a languid Southern flavor. There are two exceptional songs written for the animated sequences and sung by Br'er Rabbit. "Everybody's Got a Laughing Place" is a bouncy song Rabbit uses to trick Br'er Bear and Br'er Fox, and "How Do You Do?" is a slaphappy ditty in which Rabbit greets everyone he comes across, including the Tar Baby. Other notable songs in the movie are the evocative title number that conjures up visions of the Old South, the spiritual "All I Want," the harmonic chorale "Let the Rain Come Down," and the sly philosophical song "Who Wants to Live Like That?" Daniele Amfitheatrof and Charles Wolcott wrote the soundtrack score for *Song of the South*, and it too evokes the Old South. There is also bright and playful background music for the stories. This movie overflows with splendid music.

Awards

Academy Awards: Best Song ("Zip-a-Dee-Doo-Dah") and Honorary Award to James Baskett. Oscar nomination: Best Score.

The critical reaction to *Song of the South* was mostly positive. The reviews applauded the animated stories more than the live-action scenes, but generally the notices were favorable. The National Association for the Advancement of Colored People (NAACP) thought the film perpetuated Negro stereotypes and African American newspapers were similarly critical. Yet the movie was popular in the South and across the United States in its first release, earning $2.6 million for a modest profit of $226,000. It was rereleased in theaters in 1956, 1973, 1980, and 1986. But the controversy about its depiction of African Americans continued, particularly during the civil rights movement in the 1960s. For this reason, Disney has never officially released a VHS or DVD edition of *Song of the South* in the United States. It is available in Great Britain and many other countries around the world, so there are plenty of unauthorized home videos of the film in America. Many critics and moviegoers today disagree that *Song of the South* is detrimental and offensive and maintain that the Uncle Remus stories are an important part of Southern folklore. Perhaps the controversy will never be resolved, but *Song of the South* remains a significant piece of filmmaking and an essential film in the history of animation.

Did You Know . . . ?

Because of segregation laws in Atlanta at the time, African American actor James Baskett was not allowed to attend the opening ceremony for *Song of the South* in that city. Baskett later won an Honorary Academy Award for his performance in the movie, the first time the Oscar was given to an African American male performer.

SOUTH PARK: BIGGER, LONGER & UNCUT

1999
(USA: Comedy Central Films/Paramount/Warner Brothers)

Directed by Trey Parker
Written by Trey Parker, Matt Stone, and Pam Brady
Produced by Scott Rudin, Adam Schroeder, Trey Parker, Matt Stone, Frank C. Agnone II, Mark Roybal, Deborah Liebling, Anne Garefino, and Gina Shay
Score by Marc Shaiman
Songs by Trey Parker and Marc Shaiman
Specs: Color; 81 minutes; traditional animation

Picking up where adult animation director Ralph Bakshi left off in the 1970s, this outrageous and funny satire utilizes the same talents from the popular Comedy Central television cartoon series South Park *with the addition of songs in the same comic vein.*

When preteens Stan, Kyle, Eric, and Kenny of the American town of South Park sneak into a PG-13 movie featuring the Canadian comics Terrance and Philip, they learn how to swear and are soon the envy of the other kids at school. The guidance counselor Mr. Mackey informs the boys' parents, who have the school ban any clothes featuring Terrance and Philip. After the boys continue to emulate the Canadian duo, the mothers begin a "Mothers Against Canada" (MAC) campaign. International tensions arise when Terrance and Philip appear on an American TV talk show and are arrested as criminals by the U.S. government. Canada propels a bomb across the border and President Clinton declares war on the country and threatens to have Terrance and Philip executed. In hell, Satan and his gay lover

Voice Cast

Trey Parker	Stan Marsh
Matt Stone	Kyle Broflovski
Trey Parker	Eric Cartman
Matt Stone	Kenny McCormick
Jesse Brant Howell	Ike Broflovski
Anthony Cross-Thomas	Ike Broflovski
Franchesca Clifford	Ike Broflovski
Mary Kay Bergman	Sheila
Trey Parker	Philip
Matt Stone	Terrance
Isaac Hayes	Chef
Trey Parker	Satan
Matt Stone	Saddam Hussein
Trey Parker	General
George Clooney	Dr. Gouache

South Park boys (left to right) Eric, Kyle, Stan, and Kenny are so excited after seeing a Canadian movie starring Terrance and Philip that they start imitating the foul-mouthed comics. *Paramount Pictures / Photofest. © Paramount Pictures*

Saddam Hussein threaten to rise up and destroy the world if the two Canadians are executed. Stan and his friends form a resistance movement and put the atheistic Frenchman known as The Mole in charge. Canada attacks the army base where Terrance and Philip are to be executed and in the confusion Stan and The Mole help the two Canadian comics escape. When the mothers find Terrance and Philip and shoot them, Satan and Hussein rise up and attack both the American and Canadian armies. Hussein gets power hungry and tries to take over the world so Satan has to cast him back into hell. Kenny, who has died and gone to hell, pleads with Satan to make everything go back to the way it was in South Park before all the trouble began. Satan grants his wish, the deceased ones return to life, Canada and the United States are friends again, and Kenny rises up to heaven, where he is attended to by naked angels.

The television series *South Park* was developed by Brian Graden from characters created by Trey Parker and Matt Stone, and soon after its 1997 debut the animated show had a large following on cable TV. The series was known for its far-fetched plots, eccentric characters, cookie-cutter art work, and broad spoofing of a variety of serious subjects. The large screen version retained the look, characters, and setting of the TV series but went even further in its audacity. Current world events, bad parenting, prejudice, death, religion, and celebrity worship are all lampooned in the movie, but the central theme is one of censorship. If *South Park: Bigger, Longer & Uncut* has anything serious to say, it is about the dangers of smothering self-expression. The film's very title, an obvious phallic reference, challenges conventional guidelines for what is and is not acceptable. There is a naughty-boy "try and stop me" attitude in both the TV series and the movie (which is rated R) that has been accepted and even embraced by a sizable portion of the public. The *South Park* franchise is built on seeing how far one can go, then surprising everyone by going further. Such an attitude gave screenwriters Parker, Stone, and Pam Brady a sense of new freedom, even as they had to battle Paramount and other establishment organizations. The resulting film is not a compromise. It is blatantly offensive and obstinate; it is also very funny.

Songs

"Mountain Town"
"Hell Isn't Good"
"Blame Canada"
"Wendy's Song"
"Uncle Fucka"
"It's Easy, Mmmkay"
"Kyle's Mom's a Bitch"
"Up There"
"La Resistance"
"I Can Change"
"The Mole's Reprise"
"I'm Super"
"Eyes of a Child"
"What Would Brian Boitano Do?"

Like the TV series, the background art and the animation are primitive, as if a child's drawing had come to life but not very realistically. The artistic palette is mostly primary colors, and the facial expressions are minimal. It is the voices that keep the South Park characters lively. As in the series, Parker and Stone voice most of the male characters. Other regulars from the TV program also contributed to the vocals in the film. No attempt is made to come up with deeply layered characters. Each voice, whether for an adult or a child character, is a phony "cartoon" voice, keeping the movie far from reality and allowing the scatological dialogue to be even more incongruous. The distinctive sound of *South Park: Bigger, Longer & Uncut* somehow makes the movie more potent. Childish voices spewing out four-letter words is obviously funny, but it is also disconcerting. As with the cardboard cut-out look of the movie, the primitive vocals seem to mock the genre itself.

South Park: Bigger, Longer & Uncut is a full-scale musical, and the songs by Parker and Marc Shaiman continue the facetious tone of the plot. Most of the numbers are pastiches of Broadway and movie songs, in particular Disney films.

CHEF: Haven't you heard of the Emancipation Proclamation?

GENERAL: I don't listen to hip-hop.

The most memorable number, "Blame Canada," is a driving march in which the neighbor to the North is blamed for everything that is wrong in the world. Sung by the mothers and other adults in town, it is a rapid piece that is surprisingly catchy. Another notable song is the opening "Mountain Town," which parodies the "Belle" number from *Beauty and the Beast* (1991) in which location and characters are musically introduced. There is a hyperactive square dance number "Kyle's Mom's a Bitch," sung by the children; a heavy metal rock tirade titled "Hell Isn't Good"; Satan's "Up There," a mocking inspirational number with celestial backup singers; a spoof of a heart-wrenching blues number called "Eyes of a Child"; "I Can Change," a Greek-flavored duet for Stan and Saddam Hussein; and "I'm Super," an exuberant song of selfishness for Big Gay Al. In all, there are sixteen musical numbers, yet none interrupts the movie's break-neck tempo.

Awards

Academy Award nomination: Best Song ("Blame Canada").

South Park: Bigger, Longer & Uncut was given a wide release in 1999 despite fears by Paramount of a backlash by conservative groups. In its efforts to do marketing tie-ins, such as T-shirts and fast-food meals, Paramount met with some resistance, even though the television show already had significant merchandising. The final cost of the movie was around $21 million, so there was some concern when *South Park: Bigger, Longer & Uncut* was rated R and a sizable portion of the *South Park* TV fans were denied access to the film. The reviews were mostly positive and, despite boycotts from conservative groups, the movie ended up earning over $83 million internationally. The 1999 DVD sold well and, a decade later, the Blu-ray edition was also successful.

Did You Know . . . ?

Because of its R rating, many teenagers below the legal age got to see the movie by buying tickets to the Will Smith film *Wild Wild West* (1999), which was rated PG-13, then sneaking into the theater showing *South Park: Bigger, Longer & Uncut*.

THE SWORD IN THE STONE

1963
(USA: Walt Disney Productions)

Directed by Wolfgang Reitherman
Written by Bill Peet, based on the book by T. H. White
Produced by Walt Disney
Score by George Bruns
Songs by Richard M. and Robert B. Sherman
Specs: Color (Technicolor); 79 minutes; traditional animation

When the scrawny youth Wart pulls the sword Excalibur from the stone and is declared King of England, only the far-sighted magician Merlin is not at all surprised. *Walt Disney Productions / Photofest. © Walt Disney Productions*

The legendary tale of King Arthur is partially explored in this Disney animated favorite about the early years of the great king.

During the Dark Ages, England is without a king until some worthy knight can pull the sword Excalibur out of a stone that it is imbedded in. No one has succeeded, so the land is left without a ruler. The twelve-year-old orphan Arthur, called Wart because of his small size, meets the wizard Merlin, who instructs him about life in unconventional ways. The wizard turns Wart into a fish, a squirrel, and then a sparrow in order to observe life with a fresh viewpoint. While in bird

Voice Cast

Rickie Sorenson	Wart (Arthur)
Richard Reitherman	Wart (Arthur)
Robert Reitherman	Wart (Arthur)
Karl Swenson	Merlin
Junius Matthews	Archimedes
Martha Wentworth	Madame Mim
Sebastian Cabot	Sir Ector
Norman Alden	Sir Kay
Alan Napier	Sir Pellinore
Thurl Ravenscroft	Black Bart
Sebastian Cabot	Narrator

form, Wart is captured by the witch Madam Mim. In order to rescue him, Merlin engages in a battle of magic with the old woman and defeats her. Wart becomes the squire of the brawny but brainless knight Sir Kay and accompanies him and Sir Ector to a jousting tournament in London. On the day of the contest, Wart forgets Kay's sword back at the inn and on the way there to retrieve it he spots a sword sticking out of a stone. He is able to pull it out, and when he presents it to Ector and Kay, they recognize it as Excalibur. The crowd quickly sees the significance of Wart's feat and proclaims him the King of England. After being crowned king, Wart is overwhelmed by his new position and he panics. But Merlin reassures him that he will do great things in his life. The wizard even suggests the Knights of the Round Table to Wart and then departs for the twentieth century.

T. H. White's *The Sword in the Stone* was published in 1938 and Walt Disney bought the film rights the next year, but the project lay dormant for over two decades. In 1958 White's book was republished with two other books about the Arthurian legend as the trilogy titled *The Once and Future King*. It became a best seller and the latter two books served as the inspiration for the Broadway musical *Camelot*, which opened in 1960. When Disney saw the musical his interest in *The Sword in the Stone* was rekindled. White's books are not children's fare but complex narratives filled with history, satire, and magic. Bill Peet adapted the book with an eye on entertaining children and their parents, but moviegoers looking for White's intricate storytelling were disappointed. On the other hand, the screenplay is concise and playful, with no subplots and only a handful of characters. Young Arthur, called Wart, enjoys a series of life experiences through the magic of Merlin, and the audience sees everything from the boy's point of view. Merlin is depicted as a very modern teacher with a 1960s sentimentality. Because he knows the future, Merlin makes references and jokes about things that make no sense to Wart but are enjoyed by the audience. Merlin's owl, Archimedes, provides a more sour commentary, which is often delicious. Sir Ector, Wart's foster father, and the blockheaded Sir Kay are presented as farcical characters who deride the boy at every turn. The plot's villain, Madame Mim, is also farcical, a sorceress more interested in outwitting Merlin than in doing actual harm. *The Sword in the Stone* is well structured, from the prologue that explains the legend of the sword, to the hopeful ending where Wart begins his journey toward adulthood.

Songs

"The Legend of the Sword in the Stone"
"That's What Makes the World Go Round"
"Higitus Figitus"
"A Most Befuddling Thing"
"The Marvelous Mad Madame Mim"

The Sword in the Stone takes place in the Dark Ages and the background art supports the idea of a time with little sunshine and primitive living conditions. The castle is seen as uncomfortable rather than romantic, and the forest is scary and forbidding instead of verdant and poetic. Yet there is a light touch in some of the settings, such as Merlin's cottage filled with objects out of place in the medieval world. The animation is first-rate with Wart's preadolescent awkwardness very accurate and even endearing. Ector, Kay, and the other knights are heavy and plodding in their movements, even when they are not wearing armor. Merlin moves lightly, practically ignoring gravity at times. Similarly, the daffy Madame Mim is a bouncing mass of rubber that never comes to rest. The magic duel between her and Merlin is the outstanding piece of animation in the movie, if not one of the most clever sequences in all the Disney canon.

ARCHIMEDES: If the boy goes about saying the world is round, they'll take him for a lunatic.

ARTHUR: The world is round?

MERLIN: Yes. Yes, that's right, and it also, uh, goes A-round.

ARTHUR: You mean it'll be round *someday*.

MERLIN: No, no, no, it's round now. Man will discover this in centuries to come. And he will also find that the world is merely a tiny speck in the universe.

ARTHUR: Universe?

ARCHIMEDES: Ah! You're only confusing the boy. Before you're through, he'll be so mixed up, he'll . . . he'll be wearing his shoes on his head!

Oddly, the voice cast is very proficient in various British dialects but the voice of Wart is very American. Ricky Sorenson's voice broke into an adolescent squeak during production so director Wolfgang Reitherman had his two sons, Richard and Robert, complete Wart's vocals. The fact that none of the three voices match each other is obvious and detracts from the characterization. Karl Swenson is alternately grouchy and enthusiastic as Merlin, a character based on Disney himself, and Martha Wentworth gives a lively and prankish performance as Madame Mim. Sebastian Cabot serves as narrator as well as the voice for the blustering Sir Ector, excellent in both cases. George Bruns composed the soundtrack score, which includes some medieval touches here and there but is mostly contemporary, especially the lighthearted music for each of Wart's adventures as different animals. The songwriting brothers Richard M. and Robert B. Sherman wrote the songs, which are clever but not nearly as memorable as the team's later work. "That's What Makes the World Go Round" has a catchy melody and "Higitus Figitus" is a sprightly number with a nonsense lyric. But *The Sword in the Stone* doesn't feel like a musical. Bruns's soundtrack music does the job so well that the songs sometimes seem unnecessary.

The critics were not very kind to *The Sword in the Stone*. Several objected to the great Arthurian legend being reduced to a children's cartoon. Yet some reviews

Award

Academy Award nomination: Best Score.

complimented the movie for its playful touch and strong animation. The public was not so divided. The film cost about $3 million and easily earned five times that much during its first release in 1963. Although *The Sword in the Stone* was not rereleased in theaters, its 1986 VHS version sold very well and new generations of children and adults discovered it for the first time. The DVD in 2001 and the Blu-ray edition in 2013 continued to introduce audience to this modest but thoroughly enjoyable Disney feature.

See also *Robin Hood*.

Did You Know . . . ?

This film was the first animated Disney movie scored by the brothers Richard M. and Robert B. Sherman. They would soon become the most famous of Disney songwriters.

T

TANGLED

2010
(USA: Walt Disney Pictures)

Directed by Nathan Greno and Byron Howard
Written by Dan Fogelman, based on the story "Rapunzel" by Wilhelm and Jacob Grimm
Produced by John Lasseter, Glen Keane, Roy Conli, and Aimee Scribner
Score by Alan Menken
Songs by Alan Menken (music) and Glenn Slater (lyrics)
Specs: Color; 100 minutes; computer and traditional animation

A classic story reimagined as an action adventure, Tangled *looks and sounds very different from any Rapunzel movie that might have been made in the Golden Age of Disney. Yet underneath the glossy computer rendering and the pop music there is a traditional fairy tale with romance and a happily-ever-after ending.*

The vain sorceress Mother Gothel has learned how to stay eternally young by using a magic flower she stole hundreds of years ago, but it has now been stolen from her. When the King and Queen of Corona give birth to a baby with golden hair with the same special magical powers, Gothel steals the baby and raises her as her own child, keeping her in a tall tower and not letting her cut her hair. Named Rapunzel, the girl is almost eighteen years old and doesn't know she is a princess. She yearns to see the outside world, but Gothel teaches her that there is nothing but evil and heartache outside her tower. The small-time thief Flynn Rider, running from the law, discovers Rapunzel's tower and offers to accompany her to see the world. Rapunzel agrees and the twosome encounter colorful ruffians and imperial soldiers who try to capture them, suffer temporary imprisonment, and manage clever escapes. The kingdom is preparing for the annual ceremony of the lanterns, which the King and Queen hold on the birthday of their long-lost daughter. With the help of the deadly Stabbington brothers, Gothel finds Rapunzel and returns her to the tower, where she is chained up. Flynn discovers the power of Rapunzel's hair and climbs the tower, where he cuts her hair. With her source of

Rapunzel may have spent her life locked in a tower, but she is worldly wise enough to tie up the intruding bandit Flynn Rider with her golden hair. *Walt Disney Pictures / Photofest.* © *Walt Disney Pictures*

eternal youth gone, Gothel disintegrates into dust. Rapunzel is returned to her joyous parents, and Flynn is pardoned, allowing the couple to wed.

Disney artist-animator Glen Keane had begun developing a Rapunzel film back in 1996 and over the next fourteen years the project went through many changes in plot, character, and personnel. Under the working title *Rapunzel Unbraided*, the movie was planned as a comic spoof of the classic Brothers Grimm fairy tale. At one point the setting was changed to present-day San Francisco, while in other versions the whole movie had Rapunzel stuck in the tower until the happy ending. In 2008, when Keane suffered a heart attack, he stepped down from the project and the direction was taken over by Nathan Greno and Byron Howard, though Keane remained a producer and supervisor for *Tangled*. The final script was a combination of many ideas but written by Dan Fogelman. The

Voice Cast

Delaney Rose Stein	Rapunzel (young)
Mandy Moore	Rapunzel (adult)
Zachary Levi	Flynn Rider
Donna Murphy	Mother Gothel
Jeffrey Tambor	Big Nose Thug
Brad Garrett	Hook Hand Thug
Paul F. Tompkins	Short Thug
Richard Kiel	Vlad
M. C. Gainey	Captain of the Guard
Ron Perlman	Stabbington Brother
John DiMaggio	Stabbington Brother
Frank Welker	Pascal

character of the charming bandit Flynn Rider was enlarged until he was just as important as the princess Rapunzel. The villainess was turned into the slyly subtle Mother Gothel, who can be so sweet that Rapunzel thinks she is her loving mother. The new script gets Rapunzel out of the tower early on in the story so she and Flynn can have a series of adventures and fall in love. The dialogue in *Tangled* is often hip and anachronistic, Rapunzel sounding and behaving like a contemporary teenager and Flynn playing at mock heroics in his vocal and physical bravado. The movie has a slick computerized look and was filmed to be shown in 3-D, but watching the film with conventional projection there is still a lot of depth in the visuals. The characters have smooth, almost plastic faces, and the hair (particularly in the case of Rapunzel) is ultra-realistic with the computer revealing every strand. Yet the background art is very traditional and romanticized. The artists were inspired by the Rococo paintings of French artist Jean-Honoré Fragonard, in which nature and humans are idealized with soft edges and lush color. The tower, the forests, the castle, and other locations are filled with details that only a computer could manage. There are bigger crowd scenes and more objects in *Tangled* than in just about any previous Disney movie. For the festival of lights, over 45,000 lanterns are seen. Because of its many challenges and the number of technical experiments undertaken during the production, *Tangled* ended up being the most expensive animated feature yet produced by Disney, the final price tag totaling around $270 million.

Songs

"When Will My Life Begin"
"Incantation Song"
"Mother Knows Best"
"I've Got a Dream"
"I See the Light"
"The Tear Heals"
"Something That I Want" (Grace Potter)

Singer-turned-actress Mandy Moore was selected to do the speaking and singing vocals for Rapunzel early in the development process. Since the songs in *Tangled* were contemporary sounding, the studio wanted a popular star known for her singing. Film and theater actor Zachary Levi had sung on Broadway and was also cast for his modern style of singing. The much-awarded Broadway actress Donna Murphy had little film or television experience but was more than capable of giving the complex and seething performance that the role of Mother Gothel required. Gothel is perhaps the most deceptive of Disney villainesses, her caressing voice able to both seduce and frighten. Because everything she does is under the guise of a warm and nurturing mother, her evil is all the more insidious. Murphy is superb in conveying this duality. There are not many speaking characters in *Tangled*, but the voices throughout are commendable. Jeffrey Tambor, Brad Garrett, Paul F. Tompkins, and Richard Kiel were particularly enjoyable as the thugs that Rapunzel and Flynn encounter on their adventures.

RAPUNZEL: I've been looking out of a window for eighteen years, dreaming about what it might feel like when those lights rise in the sky. What if it's not everything I dreamed it would be?

FLYNN RIDER: It will be.

RAPUNZEL: And what if it is? What do I do then?

FLYNN RIDER: Well, that's the good part I guess. You get to go find a new dream.

Alan Menken, Disney's most successful composer, returned to the studio to score *Tangled* with Glenn Slater providing the lyrics for several songs, only six being used in the final cut. The musical numbers are in the pop-rock mode, yet Menken sneaks in a few medieval flourishes here and there. The only song that got widely noticed is the dreamy ballad "I See the Light." Rapunzel and Flynn sing the enticing number sitting in a small boat as thousands of floating lanterns surround them, surely one of the most romantic scenes in the Disney canon. Mother Gothel's persuasive "Mother Knows Best" is a triumph of two-faced villainy, the lyrics expressing love and devotion but the subtext sending chills to those not blinded by Gothel's hypnotic influence. "I Got a Dream" is a silly list song sung by the thugs in a tavern that is full of giddy surprises. Perhaps the most accomplished song in the score is Rapunzel's yearning number "When Will My Life Begin," which is heard three times in the film. It is an up-tempo number used to introduce Rapunzel as she looks forward to seeing the world. Later the song is reprised as a lament about her situation and then heard again as she and Flynn enjoy her newfound freedom. The driving rock song "Something That I Want" was written and sung by Grace Potter over the closing credits. If the songs in *Tangled* are modern, Menken's soundtrack score is in the classical Hollywood mode, with rousing action music played on percussion, lyrical folk tunes on pipes, pseudo-medieval dance music, and mystical passages with a choral background.

Awards

Academy Award nomination: Best Song ("I See the Light").
Golden Globe nominations: Best Animated Film and Best Song ("I See the Light").

Not long before the movie was released in 2010, the studio changed the title from *Rapunzel* to *Tangled* for marketing reasons. Disappointed at the modest success of *The Princess and the Frog* (2009) and blaming the use of the word "princess" for failing to find a wider audience, the Disney executives wanted a less feminine title for the new movie. The change was heavily criticized by those in the business, mockingly imagining past Disney classics retitled *The Glass Slipper, Seven Little Men, The Spinning Wheel*, and *Under the Sea*. It is not possible to gauge how effective the title change was. *Tangled* did good business but was not a runaway hit. It earned over $200 million in North America, not enough to cover the film's high cost; but internationally *Tangled* grossed nearly $600 million. The reviews were positive but not overly enthusiastic. Some critics did not like the glossy look of the movie, but most admired the storytelling, the characters, and the songs. *Tangled* was a best-selling home video when the DVD and Blu-ray editions were released in 2011. There has since been an animated short titled *Tangled Ever After* (2012), video games, the TV-movie *Tangled: Before Ever After* (2017), and the television cartoon program, *Tangled: The Series* (2017).

See also *Sleeping Beauty*.

Did You Know . . . ?

When Zachary Levi auditioned for the role of Flynn Rider, he used an Errol Flynn–like British accent and the directors liked it and cast him. Yet during the development of the movie the British accent was dropped and Levi ended up using his own American speech instead.

TARZAN

1999
(USA: Walt Disney Pictures)

Directed by Kevin Lima and Chris Buck
Written by Tab Murphy, Bob Tzudiker, and Noni White, based on the book *Tarzan of the Apes* by Edgar Rice Burroughs
Produced by Bonnie Arnold and Christopher Chase
Score by Mark Mancina
Songs by Phil Collins
Specs: Color (Technicolor); 88 minutes; traditional animation with some computer effects

---

Disney's version of the familiar jungle tale becomes an engrossing animated musical that is not only exciting to watch but is filled with reflections on prejudice and family.

As the only survivors of a shipwreck off the coast of Africa, a British couple and their baby try to make a home in the jungle but the leopard Sabor kills the parents. The gorilla Kala, who has recently lost her baby to the same leopard, finds the orphaned human and raises him with the name Tarzan. Kerchak, the leader of the gorilla tribe, does not trust Tarzan because he knows too well how dangerous humans can be. Tarzan grows up happy and contented in the jungle until one day he comes across the English zoologist Professor Archimedes Q. Porter and his daughter Jane, who are on expedition with their guide Clayton. Tarzan rescues Jane from a troop of baboons and the two fall in love. The professor has come to Africa to study gorillas, but Clayton plans to capture the apes and ship them to zoos in England. When Tarzan leads Jane and the professor to where the gorillas live, Clayton and his men attack, killing Kerchak and putting the rest of the apes in cages. With Kerchak's dying words he asks Tarzan to take over leadership of

Raised in the jungle, the "ape man" Tarzan is confused, mystified, and smitten when he first meets the strange creature Jane, who, in some ways, is very much like him. *Walt Disney Pictures / Photofest.* © *Walt Disney Pictures*

the gorilla family. Tarzan fights Clayton, who is strangled when caught in some vines, and frees the apes from the cages. Jane and the professor decide to remain in Africa with Tarzan and the apes.

Considering the many adaptations of Edgar Rice Burroughs's *Tarzan of the Apes* (1912) for various media over the years, it is surprising that the idea of a Disney animated version did not arise until 1994. Kevin Lima was assigned to work on a treatment of the familiar story and his early drafts of the screenplay concentrated on the idea of family. Two parallel worlds are presented, the human one and a community of gorillas living in Africa. The orphaned boy Tarzan is caught between these worlds, loved by his foster mother, the ape Kala, and seen as a threat by Kerchak, the leader of the gorilla family. The appearance of Jane and her father reveals to Tarzan the world of humans, just as the devious hunter Clayton represents the evils of that world. Chris Buck was brought on as codirector and the final

Voice Cast

Alex D. Linz	Tarzan (boy)
Tony Goldwyn	Tarzan (adult)
Minnie Driver	Jane
Glenn Close	Kala
Lance Henrikson	Kerchak
Brian Blessed	Clayton
Rosie O'Donnell	Terk
Nigel Hawthorne	Professor Porter
Wayne Knight	Tantor

script was written by Tab Murphy, Noni White, and Bob Tzudiker. The animation for *Tarzan* was done in studios in Paris, Orlando, and Burbank, with different aspects of the film assigned to different groups. The background art was painted in a traditional manner but then filtered through a computer program. The new technique, named Deep Canvas, later won a special Academy Award. The character animators studied footage of athletes to bring the character of Tarzan to life. They also took anatomy lessons in order to understand the way Tarzan's muscles work. Often Tarzan's moves in the movie resemble those of a surfer, skateboarder, or a gymnast. The team of animators working on the gorilla characters traveled to Kenya and Uganda to observe the great apes in the wild rather than in zoos. Although the gorillas speak and even sing in the movie, their movements are very accurate. The making of *Tarzan* turned out to be a much more complicated project than originally thought, and the film ended up costing $130 million. Yet the visual look of the film, with an eye on the beauty of nature and the expressive faces of both human and ape characters, is priceless.

Songs

"You'll Be in My Heart"
"Two Worlds"
"Son of Man"
"Trashin' the Camp"
"Strangers Like Me"

Brendan Fraser, a beefy actor who resembles the Tarzan type, was the first choice to play the Ape Man, but after auditioning twice he was thought too modern sounding and actor Tony Goldwyn was cast. Minnie Driver, a London-born actress working mostly in America, was cast as the very-British Jane. The two other English characters, the professor and the deceiving guide Clayton, were cast with distinguished British actors Nigel Hawthorne and Brian Blessed. Ironically, the famous Tarzan yell heard in the movie was provided by Blessed, not Goldwyn. When TV celebrity Rosie O'Donnell auditioned for the film, the directors wanted her to play the sassy Terk, so the role was changed from a male ape to a female one. Woody Allen was originally cast to play the neurotic elephant Tantor, but he was replaced by Wayne Knight when Allen left the project to do the leading role in *Antz* (1998). Actress-singer Glenn Close is ideal as the nurturing ape Kala, the only character who sings in *Tarzan*. The deep-voiced American actor Lance Henrikson brings dignity and authority to his vocals for the tribal leader Kerchak.

TARZAN: Kerchak, forgive me.

KERCHAK: No. Forgive me, for not understanding that you have always been one of us. Our family will look to you now.

TARZAN: No. Kerchak.

KERCHAK: Take care of them, my son. Take care of them.

Tarzan is not a full-scale musical because most of the songs are heard on the soundtrack rather than sung by the characters. British composer-performer Phil Collins wrote the five songs, and each one is top-notch. Kala sings the enticing lullaby "You'll Be in My Heart" to the infant Tarzan, then Collins picks up the number and sings it over the action that follows. The rest of the songs are also commentary numbers sung by Collins, and each one is effective. "Two Worlds," the theme song for the movie, has a pulsating rhythm and tells of the strong family ties in both the human and animal world. The rocking "Strangers Like Me" expresses Tarzan's amazement when he discovers the human world and wants to be part of it. Another pulsating number is "Son of Man," heard while Tarzan grows from a boy to an adult. The most unusual (and fun) song in *Tarzan* is the scat number "Trashing the Camp," in which Terk and some of the other apes discover the humans' empty camp and start striking various objects to make music. There is nothing particularly African sounding in Collins's songs, but Mark Mancina's soundtrack score is filled with tribal drumming, the hypnotic sounds of the jungle, and full orchestral passages that give *Tarzan* an epic sense of majesty.

Awards

Academy Award: Best Song ("You'll Be in My Heart").
Golden Globe Award: Best Song ("You'll Be in My Heart").

Tarzan opened to very favorable reviews in 1999, most critics noticing and applauding the distinctive new look of the film. There was also praise for the characterization, voices, storytelling, and songs. The movie earned over $31 million its first weekend, the biggest Disney opening since *The Lion King* (1994). By the time the first release had played worldwide, *Tarzan* had grossed over $448 million. The VHS and DVD editions were released in 2000, the Blu-ray version in 2012. The film inspired two direct-to-video sequels, *Tarzan and Jane* (2002) and *Tarzan II* (2005). There have also been video games, the television series *The Legend of Tarzan* (2002), and a Broadway musical adaptation (2006).

Did You Know . . . ?

The fictional character of Tarzan has appeared in more films than any other character. Second most popular is Dracula followed by Sherlock Holmes. Tarzan has appeared in over two hundred movies, television programs, and video games.

THE THREE CABALLEROS

1945
(USA: Walt Disney Pictures)

Directed by Norman Ferguson, Clyde Geronimi, Jack Kinney, Bill Roberts (animation sequences), and Harold Young (live-action sequences)
Written by Ted Sears, Bill Peet, Roy Williams, James Bodrero, Elmer Plummer, Homer Brightman, Ernest Terrazas, William Cottrell, Del Connell, and Ralph Wright
Produced by Walt Disney
Score by Edward H. Plumb, Paul J. Smith, and Charles Wolcott
Songs by Ned Washington, Charles Wolcott, Ary Barroso, Ray Gilbert, Manuel Esperón, Ernesto Cortázar, Agustín Lara, Edmundo Santos, Dorival Caymmi, Joáo de Barro, and Felipe Gil
Specs: Color (Technicolor); 71 minutes; traditional animation and live action

A one-of-a-kind experience that still pleases audiences, The Three Caballeros *is an anthology program, a musical celebration of Latin America, a rare Donald Duck feature, and a travelogue all wrapped up with dizzying visuals and expert animation.*

For his birthday, Donald Duck receives three packages in the mail, each a gift leading into a live-action or animated sequence. The first gift is a movie projector that shows two short films. A young gaucho in Argentina lassos a wild rhea (a form of ostrich) and the penguin Pablo in Antarctica attempts to move to a warm climate. The sequence also introduced the silly Aracuan bird, who pops up here and there throughout the rest of the movie. The second gift, a pop-up book about Brazil, leads to a sequence in which José Carioca and Donald tour the beautiful city of Bahia and dance the samba with some beautiful women. The third gift, a piñata, introduces the rooster Panchito Pistoles and the three caballeros take off on a flying serape to see the sights of Mexico.

During World War II, President Roosevelt instituted a program called the Good Neighbor Policy to reach out to Latin America. Since trade with Europe and Asia was greatly reduced because of the war, the US government paid Hollywood to make films promoting Central and South America. Disney and a team of studio em-

Voice Cast

Clarence Nash	Donald Duck
Joaquin Garay	Panchito
José Oliveira	José Carioca
Pinto Colvig	Aracuan Bird
Leo Carillo	Old Gaucho
Sterling Holloway	Professor
Fred Shields	Narrator
Frank Graham	Narrator

The parrot José Carioca (center) and the rooster Panchito Pistoles (right) welcome the American Donald Duck to South America, the three birds becoming "feathered friends." *Walt Disney Pictures / Photofest. © Walt Disney Pictures*

ployees toured Latin America and shot live footage of cities, towns, carnivals, bull-fights, festivals, and other positive images of life "south of the border." The result was the documentary *Saludos Amigos* in 1942, in which the Disney team was seen touring and filming life in Latin America. The film also featured four animated segments with appearances by Donald Duck, Goofy, and some new characters, notably the parrot José Carioca. *Saludos Amigos* also included some Latin songs, particularly "Aquarela do Brasil," which became a hit in the United States as "Brazil."

Songs

"The Three Caballeros" (Esperón/Cortázar/Gilbert)
"Have You Ever Been to Baía?" (Caymmi)
"Mexico" (Wolcott/Santos/Gilbert)
"Baía" (Barroso/Gilbert)
"Saludos Amigos" (Wolcott/Washington)
"Jesusita en Chihuahua (The Cactus Polka)" (Esperón/Cortázar)
"Pregoes Carioca" (de Barro)
"Lilongo" (Gil)
"You Belong to My Heart" (Lara/Gilbert)

The short (forty-two minutes) *Saludos Amigos* was so successful in both North and South America that Disney followed it up with *The Three Caballeros* in 1944. Once again, the anthology film is a travelogue, and the live-action footage is very appealing. But it is the animation, particularly during the title song, that is outstanding. The bright colors of Latin America are utilized in the animated sequences, and they blend effectively with the travelogue footage. The character animation for the three feathered friends is vibrant and expressive, even if a bit frenetic at times. *Caballero* is Spanish for "gentleman" or may even refer to a knight, but these three birds are far from gentlemanly. Dressed like banditos, they fire their pistols as if they were animated firecrackers. The movie made both José Carioca and Panchito Pistoles popular animated figures, and they remained favorites in Latin American countries for many years.

DONALD DUCK: What's this?

PANCHITO: What's this? This is your gift from Mexico, Donald: a piñata!

DONALD DUCK: Oh, boy, oh, boy, a piñata! . . . What's a piñata?

PANCHITO: A piñata is full of surprises. Presents. It's the very spirit of Christmas.

DONALD DUCK: Christmas! (singing) Jingle bells, jingle bells, jingle all the way . . .

PANCHITO: Oh, no, no, Donald! For goodness sake, not "Jingle Bells." In Mexico, they sing "Las Posadas."

One of the treats in both *Saludos Amigos* and *The Three Caballeros* is the fusion of animation and live-action footage. Not since the 1920s, when the young Disney made a series of "Alice" cartoons, had the studio put the two media together. With the new technology, the mixing of live and animated filmmaking was as exciting as it was impressive. Disney would polish the process and feature it in such movies as *Song of the South* (1946) and *Mary Poppins* (1964), as well as in the studio's television programs. The songs in *The Three Caballeros* are sung in Portuguese, Spanish, and English. The hit song "You Belong to My Heart" was a well-known Mexican ballad and here was given an English lyric by Ray Gilbert. The dreamy "Baía" was a Brazilian ballad; again Gilbert provided an English lyric, and it too enjoyed some popularity in the United States. Even the raucous title number was a preexisting song, a festive Mexican song that was given a snappy new lyric by Gilbert. The only totally original song in *The Three Caballeros* was the atmospheric "Mexico," by Gilbert and Charles Wolcott. Like the musical numbers heard in Hollywood's live-action musicals of the 1940s, the songs in the two Disney films encouraged a new popularity for Latin American music in the United States.

Awards

Academy Award nominations: Best Score and Best Sound.

The finished print of *The Three Caballeros* sat on the shelves for a year while Disney waited for Technicolor film stock to become available during the wartime shortage. The movie premiered in Mexico City in 1944, then in the United States in 1945. The reviews were mixed. Some critics enjoyed the colorful spree, but others thought *The Three Caballeros* too wild and out of control. There were complaints by some reviewers over Donald's lusting after the shapely human females, a few even finding the cactuses in the sequence to be rather phallic. Audiences around the world were not so fussy and made the movie a hit, although actual box office figures are hard to pin down. The anthology film was rereleased in theaters in 1958, 1966, 1973, 1977, and 1981. Thereafter it found a new audience on video in 1982 and on DVD in 2008. Sequences from *The Three Caballeros* have also appeared on Disney's television shows over the years.

See also *Melody Time*.

Did You Know . . . ?

Donald Duck was already world famous, but after *The Three Caballeros* was released, the characters of Jose Carioca and Panchito also became internationally known and inspired a series of comic books in various languages.

TOY STORY

1995
(USA: Pixar Animation Studios/Disney)

Directed by John Lasseter
Written by Joss Whedon, Joel Cohen, Alec Sokolow, and Andrew Stanton
Produced by Ed Catmull, Steve Jobs, Bonnie Arnold, and Ralph Guggenheim
Score and songs by Randy Newman.
Specs: Color (Technicolor); 81 minutes; computer animation

Both nostalgic and state of the art, Toy Story *is a landmark in the history of American animation. It is not only the first computer-animated feature film, it remains one of the best in the new genre.*

The toys belonging to six-year-old Andy Davis come to life when the humans aren't around. An old-fashioned cowboy doll named Woody is Andy's favorite toy until he receives the space ranger toy Buzz Lightyear for his birthday. The rivalry between the two toys grows and when Woody accidentally knocks Buzz out of Andy's window the other toys think it was done on purpose. Woody does everything to get Buzz back, including hitching a ride on the Pizza Planet delivery truck to return him to Andy. Both toys are in trouble when they are captured by the sadistic boy Sid next door, who likes to destroy toys. Andy and his mother and

The toy cowboy Woody cannot believe that the newcomer Buzz Lightyear thinks he is a real flying space man and not just a toy like the rest of them. *Walt Disney Pictures / Photofest.* © *Walt Disney Pictures*

his baby sister move to a new house, but Woody and Buzz manage to escape the clutches of Sid and chase after the moving van, joining the other toys, who now see Woody as a hero.

Animator-director John Lasseter first saw the possibilities of computer animation when he studied Disney's *Tron* (1982), an early and unsuccessful effort in the field. As a Disney animator, Lasseter experimented with computer animation and proposed to the studio a completely computer-animated approach to the upcom-

Voice Cast

Tom Hanks	Woody
Tim Allen	Buzz Lightyear
Don Rickles	Mr. Potato Head
Wallace Shawn	Rex
Jim Varney	Slinky Dog
Annie Potts	Bo Peep
John Ratzenberger	Hamm
Erik von Detten	Sid
John Morris	Andy Davis
Laurie Metcalf	Mrs. Davis
Sarah Freeman	Hannah

ing project *The Brave Little Toaster*. The Disney executives dismissed both the idea and Lasseter, giving him the freedom to continue his experiments elsewhere. He cofounded Pixar Studios with like-minded artists, and in 1988 Pixar released the computer-animated cartoon *Tin Toy*, which received the Academy Award for best animated short. The Disney studio, now under new management, was so impressed with *Tin Toy* and the possibilities of computer animation that CEO Michael Eisner invited Lasseter to return to Disney and make a feature-length version of *Tin Toy*. Although Lasseter was tempted by the offer, he wanted to retain control over his work and hoped to develop Pixar into a major studio. For the first time in its history, the Disney studio made a deal to finance and distribute an outside studio's work and the Disney-Pixar team was born.

Tin Toy is a five-minute computer cartoon about the toy Tinny, a one-man band that walks and plays musical instruments. He is played with, slobbered over, and ignored by the chubby baby Billy. The short movie shows other toys as well and suggests a whole new world of toy characters that come to life when there are no humans around. Developing this simple premise into a full-length screenplay was filled with problems, including financial restraints placed on the experimental project. The Billy character was changed to the six-year-old Andy, and a variety of his toys came to life. Tinny was retained in the early drafts of the screenplay but was now a space cadet. A ventriloquist's dummy was created to explain how a toy could talk, but the film's whole concept changed when it was decided that *Toy Story* would be a buddy story in which an odd pair of toys do not get along until a crisis in the playroom comes up. The story was set in the past, and Lasseter wanted to animate several of the beloved toys he grew up with. Some toy companies were not willing to give permission to use their products, but others were, such as Playskool, which supplied Mr. Potato Head, James Industries for the Slinky, and Beton Toy and Novelty Company for the green plastic Army Men. The animators created several new toys, including the two central characters: Woody, the pull-string speaking cowboy, and Buzz Lightyear, the battery-powered spaceman. Story problems continued throughout production and, even after famous actors recorded voices for the film, significant character changes occurred. For example, Woody was written as the con man of the comic duo. He outwitted, deceived, and even acted mean to the other characters. The early completed scenes with Tom Hanks's vocals, when viewed by the creators and Disney executives, made it clear that the movie's central character was not at all likable. The script was rewritten, Hanks was brought back to the recording studio, and the *Toy Story* everyone knows and loves today was gradually made.

The computer animation in *Toy Story* required many artists familiar with the rapidly changing computer programs, and Pixar was hard pressed to find enough qualified staff. Each of the characters was made in model form and polished

Songs

"You've Got a Friend in Me"
"Strange Things"
"I Will Go Sailing No More"

before it was transferred to a computer screen. Then various moves and facial expressions were created and put into the computer's memory so that the animators could bring the toy or human to life. It was a time-consuming process but the artists and the studio were so pleased with the results that it was soon clear something special was happening. The studio also allotted more money for the movie since it was quite clear it could not be made for the original budget of $17 million. (*Toy Story* ended up costing $30 million.) The computerized background art was also unique, the computer allowing for the replication on wallpaper patterns, printed curtains, and the wooden or tile floors. The computer was also able to produce scenes with multiple characters in them, such as the dozens of alien troll dolls inside the crane box at the Pizza Planet. *Toy Story* looked like no previous movie. If the visuals seemed somewhat plastic or artificial looking, all the better for the depiction of toys. The humans come across as a little stilted and stiff, just as they were in the early Disney features in the 1930s. One can find more sophisticated and diverse computer animation in the later Pixar movies, yet there is still something exciting and unique in the splendid look and movement in *Toy Story*.

WOODY: All right, that's enough! Look, we're all very impressed with Andy's new toy.

BUZZ: Toy?

WOODY: T-O-Y, Toy!

BUZZ: Excuse me, I think the word you're searching for is "Space Ranger."

WOODY: The word I'm searching for—I can't say, because there's preschool toys present.

Because *Toy Story* was not a major project from an established studio, Pixar had difficulty finding name actors who would be willing to work for below-normal wages on such an experimental film. Paul Newman, Billy Crystal, Jim Carrey, Bill Murray, and Chevy Chase were among the stars to turn down jobs voicing *Toy Story*. Tom Hanks was one of the highest-paid actors in Hollywood at the time and had been Lasseter's first choice for Woody from the start. When Hanks was approached, the actor admitted that as a child he had always wondered what his toys did when he went off to school. He gladly signed on to the project. Tim Allen, then starring in the TV sitcom *Home Improvement*, was cast as Buzz after several other actors turned it down. The rest of the cast consisted of seasoned character actors, stand-up comics, and some newcomers. The entire voice cast is excellent, but the standouts include Don Rickles's complaining Mr. Potato Head, Wallace Shawn's worry-wart dinosaur Rex, Jim Varney's down-home Slinky Dog, Annie Potts's sensual Bo Peep, and Erik von Detten's creepy Sid. While most animated movies give the hero a comic sidekick or two, *Toy Story* was filled with sparkling supporting characters that immediately charmed audiences.

Disney wanted *Toy Story* to be a musical, but Lasseter did not want the action stopped for songs. Instead, Randy Newman wrote three songs, which he sang on the soundtrack while the action continued on screen. During the opening credits, the genial song "You've Got a Friend in Me" is sung by Newman over a montage establishing the close relationship between Andy and his cowboy friend Woody.

When Andy loses interest in Woody and starts to favor Buzz, the song "Strange Things (Are Happening)" is heard. In contrast, when Buzz realizes that he is not a real space ranger but only a toy, Newman sings the lament "I Will Go Sailing No More." For the closing credits, the catchy buddy song "You've Got a Friend in Me" was reprised as a duet by Newman and Lyle Lovett. Newman also composed the film's lively soundtrack score that ranged from silly childlike tunes to dark and dramatic passages for when the toys are in danger.

Awards

Special Academy Award to John Lasseter for making the first computer-animated feature film. Oscar nominations: Best Screenplay, Best Score, and Best Song ("You've Got a Friend in Me").

Golden Globe nominations: Best Motion Picture—Comedy or Musical and Best Song ("You've Got a Friend in Me").

British Academy of Film & Television Arts (BAFTA) Award: Best Special Visual Effects.

Although Pixar and Disney knew they had a special product in *Toy Story*, neither studio was expecting the movie's huge success. It more than earned its production cost the first weekend and went on to make over $373 million internationally. *Toy Story* also received nearly unanimous cheers from the press, the critics applauding the story, the computerized look, and the delightful set of characters. The 1996 VHS version was one of the fastest-selling products in animation history. *Toy Story* was released on DVD in 2000 and on Blu-ray in 2010, and they also were giant sellers. The merchandizing for the movie went through the roof. Children wanted to own the toys featured in the film, both the old established ones and those new figures created for *Toy Story*. Sales for the old toy Mr. Potato Head, for example, skyrocketed. The direct-to-video movie *Buzz Lightyear of Star Command: The Adventure Begins* was released in 2000, the same year the television cartoon series *Buzz Lightyear of Star Command* appeared. The original *Toy Story* was rereleased in theaters in a 3-D format in 2008.

There have been two extremely popular sequels to *Toy Story*, with a third entry slated for a 2019 release. *Toy Story 2* (1999) reunited most of the characters from the original, all of them living in Andy's new home. With Sid gone and the rivalry between Woody and Buzz resolved, the sequel created a new conflict in the form of the greedy toy store owner Al McWhiggin (voice of Wayne Knight). He recognizes Woody as a valuable vintage toy and steals the cowboy to sell to a wealthy collector in Japan. The story's other villain is the toy prospector Stinky Pete (Kelsey Grammer), who seems quite friendly until he turns on Woody near the end of the movie. Buzz and the other toys rescue Woody from the Japan-bound plane just in time. Of the other new characters introduced in the sequel, the most memorable are the cowgirl Jessie (Joan Cusack), Mrs. Potato Head (Estelle Harris), and fashion icon Barbie (Jodi Benson). The critics, who usually looked unkindly on sequels, were enthusiastic in their compliments for *Toy Story 2*. Because of the tremendous success of *Toy Story*, the budget for *Toy Story 2* was upped to $90 million; the film ended up earning nearly $500 million internationally.

While *Toy Story 3* (2010) sounded more like a financial ploy than an artistic endeavor, the second sequel ended up being the most emotional and moving of the three movies and a favorite of many. Andy, now seventeen years old and getting ready to go away to college, plans to put his old favorite toys in storage, but his mother mistakenly thinks the bag of toys is trash and puts it out with the garbage. The toys escape and have a series of adventures, notably a stint in a day care center where toys are mistreated by children by day and tormented by Lotso Bear (Ned Beatty) and his gang by night. Woody and the toys manage to escape the center only to end up nearly buried in a landfill. In the tender final scene, Andy gives the rescued toys to the little neighbor girl Bonnie and asks her to love them as he always has. Over two dozen new characters are introduced in *Toy Story 3*, but the core characters from the original movie continue to hold the plot and the film together. Costs for animated films had risen so quickly that *Toy Story 3* cost $200 million but with more critical praise and popular approval, it ended up earning over $1 billion.

See also *The Brave Little Toaster*.

Did You Know . . . ?

Actor-comedian Billy Crystal was offered the role of Buzz Lightyear but declined it. He later stated is was the worst decision of his career. Crystal later got to voice Mike Wazowski in *Monsters, Inc.* (2001) and *Monsters University* (2013) for Pixar.

TRON

1982
(USA: Lisbergert/Kushner/Disney)

Directed by Steven Lisberger
Written by Steven Lisberger and Bonnie MacBird
Produced by Ron Miller, Donald Kushner, and Harrison Ellenshaw
Score by Wendy Carlos
Songs by Journey
Specs: Color; 96 minutes; live action, traditional, and early computer animation

---

Far ahead of its time, Tron *used computers not only as its subject matter but also as a means to illustrate its sci-fi story, mostly set inside a computer. Sometimes uneven, always visually exciting,* Tron *took years to become a hit.*

The brilliant computer game programmer Kevin Flynn was fired from ENCOM by the greedy Ed Dillinger, who stole Flynn's programs and made a fortune from them. He also created the Master Control Program that has gotten so powerful that it is moving away from computer games and hacking the Pentagon and other

Yori (left) and Tron (right) were once human but now live inside a computer where they are continually subjected to playing computer games run by Master Control. *Walt Disney Pictures / Photofest.* © *Walt Disney Pictures*

world systems. The programmer Alan Bradley and his girlfriend, Lora, help Flynn break into the ENCOM computer system, but Master Control uses a laser to digitalize Flynn and trap him inside the nightmarish computer world. Turned into a computer program called Clu, Flynn meets up with Alan and Lora's computer versions of themselves, Tron and Yori, and they set out to deactivate Master Control with the help of the aged programmer Dumont. Master Control's henchman, Sark, attempts to destroy Flynn and Tron, but after several deadly confrontations, some in the form of computer games, Master Control is dissolved. With the proof that Dillinger stole his programs, Flynn becomes the top executive at ENCOM.

Animator Steven Lisberger began working on the concept for *Tron* in 1976 when he discovered the early computer game Pong and saw the possibility of a feature film taking place inside a computer. Starting his own company, Lisberger made a thirty-second test introducing Tron and the computer game look of his proposed

Live-Action Cast (some used in voicing animated characters)

Jeff Bridges	Kevin Flynn/Clu
Bruce Boxleitner	Alan Bradley/Tron
David Warner	Ed Dillinger/Sark
Cindy Morgan	Lora/Yori
David Warner	Master Control Program
Barnard Hughes	Dr. Walter Hughes/Dumont
Dan Shore	Ram
Peter Jurasik	Crom
Tony Stephano	Peter/Sark's Lieutenant

film. The Disney Studio was impressed enough to finance the animated film, which had some live-action sequences and human actors who were also seen and heard as the animated characters. The project went through many changes before production began in 1980. Since computer animation was in its infancy, Lisberger could not figure out how to do the whole film with only computers. Live action and traditional animation were used, but with some unique innovations, such as highlighting live film footage with "backlit animation," using computer graphics for the backgrounds, and shooting in black and white and adding color touches in postproduction. The result is a movie that fascinates one visually if not emotionally. Lisberger and Bonnie MacBird wrote the screenplay, which was basically the tired story of a few stout individuals toppling a megapower. The characters are either likable or starkly despicable without much depth or human interest. The plot is a series of adventures that do not disappoint with their visual and audio pyrotechnics. The racing vehicles that travel in parallel or perpendicular lines have the excitement of a high-tech computer game. Also dazzling are the geometric shapes and lines that twist and turn only as a computer can manage. *Tron* may be overpowering for some spectators' eyes and brains; much the same could be said for video games themselves.

> RAM: You really think the Users are still there?
>
> TRON: They better be. I don't wanna bust out of here and find nothing but a lot of cold circuits waiting for me.

With so much going on visually, it is easy to overlook the outstanding sound and music in *Tron*. The sound effects in the movie are wide ranging, from the clunking noise of early pinball machines to high-frequency sounds that were not heard until computers introduced them. When in the computer world, even the human voices sound different, as they echo in a weird synthesized manner. The soundtrack score by Wendy Carlos is equally as effective. Carlos was a pioneer in the field of synthesized and electronic music and scored only three movies in her long career. The music for *Tron* moves from traditional pipe organ and orchestra to fully electronic sounds. The theme for the racing vehicles is fluid and intoxicating. There are also grandiose fanfares and high-energy cyber-marches that add to the vivacious nature of the film. Carlos was able to find the audio equivalent to what Lisberger was doing on the screen. Also heard on the soundtrack are two songs, "1990s Theme" and "Only Solutions," by the American band Journey.

While character development in *Tron* is nil, some of the acting is quite compelling. Jeff Bridges's scrappy renegade Flynn is the central character of the film, and he is endlessly animated without being drawn by artists. Much of the movie

Awards

Academy Award nominations: Best Sound and Best Costumes.
British Academy of Film & Television Arts (BAFTA) nomination: Best Special Visual Effects.

calls for Bridges to play against Bruce Boxleitner (Alan/Tron) and Cindy Morgan (Lora/Yori), who come across as less than interesting, but his scenes with Dan Shor as the cockeyed program Ram are better. David Warner gets to voice three villains in the film: the human Dillinger, the computerized Sark, and the ominous Master Control, whose deep and cold computer voice is chilling. Also bringing a touch of humanity to *Tron* is character actor Barnard Hughes as the worried human programmer Dr. Gibbs and the burnt-out computer "guardian" Dumont.

Tron was an expensive film to make—approximately $17 million—so when its first release in 1982 brought in only $4 million in the United States, the Disney studio was disappointed and cooled on computer filmmaking. They would not get involved in computer animation again until they funded Pixar's *Toy Story* in 1995. Reviews for *Tron* were mixed, with critics praising the visuals and disparaging the story. Moviegoers either loved it or loathed it. The home video version was released in 1983 and the DVD in 1998. Yet after a few years, *Tron* started to get a cult following. By the new century, interest in the film encouraged the sequel *Tron: Legacy* (2010). Both Bridges and Boxleitner reprised their roles of Flynn and Bradley in the new film, which takes place in a virtual reality called the Grid. This time the movie was an immediate success. There has also been a sizable franchise based on the two *Tron* films, including comic books, videos, a television series, and video games.

To fully appreciate *Tron*, one has to consider that it was made in the early 1980s and was quite a pioneer in its use of computers. *Tron* inspired John Lasseter to venture into computerized animation, resulting years later in the Pixar films. Viewing the movie today, one notices how dated some aspects of *Tron* are, but, for the most part, it is still a propulsive and fascinating film.

Did You Know . . . ?

Some Disney animators refused to work on the animation for *Tron*. They were afraid that the use of computers would make hand-drawn animation obsolete.

U

UP

2009
(USA: Pixar Animation Studios/Disney)

Directed and written by Pete Docter and Bob Peterson
Produced by John Lasseter, Andrew Staton, Jonas Rivera, Denise Ream, and Kori Rae
Score by Michael Giacchino
Specs: Color; 96 minutes; computer animation

An adventure film with a heart of gold, Pixar's Up *is so accomplished in so many ways that it was the first animated feature to be nominated for an Oscar for Best Picture since* Beauty and the Beast (1991).

Nine-year-old Carl Fredricksen idolizes the explorer Charles F. Muntz, whose 1940 adventures in South America are featured in the newsreels at the local movie theater. The tomboy Ellie also worships Muntz and dreams of going to South America to Paradise Falls where Muntz is searching for a rare exotic bird. Carl and Ellie grow up together, marry, and continue to dream about going to Paradise Falls, but it never happens. When Ellie dies, the elderly Carl becomes a recluse in his old house and refuses to move when the neighborhood is to be razed for skyscraper construction. Threatened with having to go into a retirement home, Carl ties thousands of helium balloons to his house, allowing it to rise off its foundations and float southward to South America. The young wilderness explorer Russell accidentally stows away on the flying house and accompanies Carl on the trip. The house lands on a cliff overlooking Paradise Falls, and in exploring the area the two find an elusive giant bird, which they call Kevin. They also find Muntz, now old but still seeking the rare bird that has eluded him all these years. A pack of speaking dogs works for Muntz, who rides in a dirigible as he searches for Kevin. Muntz turns vicious when he learns that Carl and Russell know the whereabouts of the bird. He finally finds Kevin and imprisons the bird and Russell in the dirigible, but with the help of the kindly dog Dug, Carl rescues them, and Muntz falls to his death. Carl and Russell return home in the dirigible and remain close friends. The balloons deflate, and Carl's air-bound house finally lands near Paradise Falls.

Rather than be sent to a home for senior citizens, Carl Fredricksen (in the window) attaches thousands of helium balloons to his house and flies away to South America. *Buena Vista Pictures / Photofest. © Buena Vista Pictures*

Like many Pixar films, *Up* has an original story based on personal experiences rather than a book or play. Writer-director Pete Docter had experienced the urge to fly away from all his troubles during times of stress and knew many others felt the same way at times. *Up* is a fantasy-adventure about a man who actually does fly away from his troubles. Against tradition, the hero is an old man, Carl Fredricksen, who is alone, grumpy, and even bitter. His whole life is told in the film's opening montage, showing his childhood dreams, his like-minded

Voice Cast

Jeremy Leary	Carl Fredricksen (young)
Ed Asner	Carl Fredricksen (adult)
Jordan Nagai	Russell
Sebastian Warholm	Russell
Christopher Plummer	Charles Muntz
Elie Docter	Ellie
Bob Peterson	Dug and Alpha
Delroy Lindo	Beta
Jerome Ranft	Gamma
Josh Cooley	Omega
John Ratzenberger	Construction Foreman
Mickie McGowan	Police Officer Edith
David Kaye	Newsreel Announcer

wife, their inability to have children, and her eventual death. It is one of the most powerful sequences in all animated movies. The aging Carl is contrasted by the scout Russell, who is young, eager, and optimistic. *Up* is essentially a buddy movie starring this odd couple. It is not a realistic film, as it defies the rules of gravity and probability. Instead it is a lyrical movie with the flavor of a romanticized dream. The script for *Up* went through many variations during development. In one draft, it was a castle and not a house that took to the air, and in another version Carl and Russell landed on a Soviet spy ship. Eventually the final story materialized along with the South American setting. The concept of knowing what a dog is thinking led to the hilarious character Dug. The explorer Muntz was based on eccentric flyer Howard Hughes. The energetic youth Russell was drawn from Docter's own childhood and resembles Carl himself when he was young. Several writers contributed ideas to the screenplay, but in the end it was the work of Docter and codirector Bob Peterson.

CARL: Hey, let's play a game. It's called "See Who Can Be Quiet the Longest."

RUSSELL: Cool! My mom loves that game!

The Pixar artists visited Venezuela and drew hundreds of sketches of the landscape as well as several high waterfalls. The unique vegetation, wildlife, and rock formations in the country inspired the artists to avoid rendering a clichéd jungle and to make the locale for *Up* new and unusual. The character animation is slightly exaggerated, but often not far from reality. The aged face of Carl with its perpetual frown was based on the elderly Spencer Tracy, though one can detect some of Ed Asner, who provided the voice for Carl. Russell is very round and bouncy, much like one of the many balloons seen in the film. The young Muntz is a dashing figure inspired by movie swashbuckler Errol Flynn. The most difficult piece of animation in the movie was the many balloons. In order to pick up a house the size of Carl's, over twenty million helium balloons would be needed. A computer could actually create the image of that many balloons, but each balloon would be so small that they would just look like colored dots. So the artists made about 20,000 balloons for the first lift off and then reduced the number to half that for the flying sequences showing the journey to South America. Using dozens of different colors for the balloons added to the magic of the flight, making something very improbable into something poetic and romantic.

Veteran TV actor Ed Asner plays Carl with the same kind of gruff persona he exuded as the television character Lou Grant. Yet there is something ultimately sad in Carl's personality that goes beyond grouchy. Carl is difficult to warm up to, but because we know his background the audience stays with him. The eight-year-old Asian-American Jordan Nagai had never acted professionally before, but Docter and the staff were impressed by his rapid word delivery and endless enthusiasm. Russell is refreshingly different, being lovable without being too cute. Renowned stage and screen actor Christopher Plummer is very effective as Charles Muntz, his rich and golden voice sounding dashing and heroic when needed or deep and sinister when his obsession gets the better of him. Bob Peterson voices the goofy, friendly canine Dug as well as the vicious, conniving Doberman Alpha, giving an expert performance in both roles. The small but important roles of Young Carl and Young Ellie are played to perfection by Jeremy Leary and Elizabeth Docter, the codirector's daughter.

The masterful soundtrack score by Michael Giacchino is character driven. Most of the major characters have a musical motif, much as in an opera. The musical motif for Ellie is a delicate piano passage that can be as happy as a merry-go-round ride but then as sad as a weeping lament. The theme for Muntz is a bold march that signifies victory, but it also can turn sinister when Muntz gets desperate and evil. Russell's music is dissident and funny, while the theme for the bird Kevin is scattered and silly. Carl has no music in him until the house takes to the skies and then an old-fashioned dance band is heard. There are no songs in *Up*, but the film remains one of the most musically pleasing of any Pixar movie.

Awards

Academy Awards: Best Animated Feature and Best Score. Oscar nominations: Best Picture, Best Screenplay, and Best Sound Editing.
Golden Globe Awards: Best Animated Feature and Best Score.
British Academy of Film & Television Arts (BAFTA) Awards: Best Animated Film and Best Score. BAFTA nominations: Best Animated Film, Best Screenplay, and Best Sound.

Because of Pixar's reputation for superior animated movies, there was a great deal of anticipation for *Up* when it opened in 2009. Neither the press nor the public was disappointed. The critics raved about all aspects of the film and stated that moviegoers could enjoy *Up* on several levels. The movie, which cost $175 million to make, earned over $293 million in North America and $735 million internationally. The DVD and Blu-ray editions were released late in 2009 and sold millions of copies. For the home video, special animated shorts were made. *Up* also inspired some video games and a children's book titled *My Name Is Dug*.

Did You Know . . . ?

The young Asian-American actor Jordan Nagai was cast as the voice for the Boy Scout Russell because at the audition he never stopped talking. Russell is Disney's first Japanese-American character.

W

WALL-E

2008
(USA: Pixar Animation Studios/Disney)

Produced by John Lasseter, Jim Morris, Lindsey Collins, Thomas Porter, and Gillian Libbert
Directed by Andrew Stanton
Written by Andrew Stanton and Jim Reardon
Score by Thomas Newman
Song "Down to Earth" by Thomas Newman and Peter Gabriel, and song standards by various artists
Specs: Color; 98 minutes; computer animation with some live-action footage

A fascinating and sobering Pixar film about the future, WALL-E *is science fiction with some emotional pull. In this apocalyptic tale, machines are humankind's curse but also its salvation.*

Eight centuries in the future, planet Earth is a wasteland filled with crumbling cities and mountains of trash. Humans had abandoned the planet in the 2100s and now live in space on a megacorporation's luxury "starliner," *Axiom*. Back on Earth, a robot trash collector and compactor called WALL-E is still operational and daily continues to collect trash and place the compacted cubes into huge piles. WALL-E is lonely but finds some comfort in his private collection of interesting objects, including a surviving VHS tape of the 1968 movie musical *Hello, Dolly!* Watching scenes from the film, WALL-E learns about dancing and human love. When the robot EVE is sent to search for any signs of plant life on Earth, WALL-E falls in love with her and shares his special collection of objects. EVE slowly develops feelings for WALL-E, but when he shows her a seedling growing in an old boot, she recognizes it as plant life, and her mother ship returns to take her and the plant to *Axiom*. WALL-E attaches himself to the ship and follows EVE to *Axiom*, where he tries to find her in the complex artificial world of machines and humans. The Captain of the *Axiom* is McCrea, bloated and idle like all of the pampered humans on the starliner. Learning that there is life on Earth, he activates the ship's "recolonization" process for everyone to return to Earth. But the devious control

The trash-collecting robot WALL-E attaches himself to the spaceship that is taking his sweetheart EVE from planet Earth to the "starliner" *Walt Disney Pictures / Photofest. © Walt Disney Pictures*

robot AUTO tries to destroy the plant and keep the humans in space. WALL-E and EVE help the Captain save the plant, dismantle AUTO, and return to Earth, where the humans start to cultivate the land and the two robots are united forever.

Director and cowriter Andrew Stanton first proposed the idea for *WALL-E* to producer John Lasseter in 1994, but it took several years, different treatments and titles, and various endings before a shooting script was agreed on. The first forty minutes of the movie, with hardly any dialogue, fell into place easily with the concept of a Robinson Crusoe–like character stranded on the dead planet Earth. The rest of the film was more difficult and, consequently, very different. In fact, *WALL-E* feels like two different movies. The opening scenes showing WALL-E's everyday life, and how it changes once he meets EVE, is casually paced and quiet with many delicate touches. The later scenes aboard the *Axiom* are fast-paced and noisy. Much of the second half of the movie is a frantic chase with characters

Voice Cast

Ben Burtt	WALL-E
Elissa Knight	EVE
Jeff Garlin	Captain McCrea
Ben Burtt	M-O
Angus MacLane	BURN-E
John Ratzenberger	John
Kathy Najimy	Mary
Sigourney Weaver	Ship's Computer
Teddy Newton	Steward Bots
MacInTalk	AUTO

Live Actor

Fred Willard	Shelby Forthright

running, being captured, escaping, and then more running. The entire film is tied together with its ecological themes as well as the unifying power of love. While *WALL-E* is critical of human consumerism and waste, it is also nostalgic about the products of the past, such as those that WALL-E collects and treasures. It is also ironic that the only deeply felt emotions in the movie are those encountered in the two machines, WALL-E and EVE. They serve as a springboard for a new creation, acting like a futuristic Adam and Eve. The humans on *Axiom* are presented as selfish and lacking curiosity of any kind. Only the discovery of a plant from Earth prompts them to start behaving in a more human manner. The screenplay for *WALL-E* may be uneven, but it is filled with wonderful ideas and represents a high point in Pixar's storytelling.

> SHIP'S COMPUTER: Voice confirmation required.
>
> CAPTAIN: Uhhh . . .
>
> SHIP'S COMPUTER: Accepted.

The design for *WALL-E* can also be divided into two different movies. The apocalyptic rendering of a trash-filled Earth is both fascinating and disturbing. One sees a civilization in ruins and, even more sobering, it is recognizable as our contemporary world. The background artists studied photos of postwar devastation and applied them to a modern metropolis. The piles of trash so closely resemble the dilapidated skyscrapers that they blend together in one nightmarish landscape. The animation of WALL-E himself is not only clever, with his ability to maneuver so efficiently in such a desolate world, but also filled with character warmth. His binocular eyes are as expressive as the most fully rendered human, and he immediately engages the audience's affection. The smooth and simple design of EVE is less revealing, and it takes the moviegoer some time to warm up to her. The first forty minutes of the movie are just about these two characters, and they hold our attention impressively. The design for the *Axiom* is as sleek and clean as Earth is jumbled and dirty. The bloated humans on board also look shiny and new, as do the various robots that run the space city. While the look of the film's second half is meticulously done, the interior of the *Axiom* seems too familiar from other science fiction movies. The furious action that dominates this long portion of *WALL-E* does not allow the viewer to take in all the details of the design. Even the computerized crowds fail to interest us as much as WALL-E and EVE as they struggle through all the chaos to the hopeful ending.

Awards

Academy Award: Best Animated Film. Oscar nominations: Best Screenplay, Best Score, Best Song ("Down to Earth"), Best Sound Mixing, and Best Sound Editing.

Golden Globe Award: Best Animated Film. Golden Globe nomination: Best Song ("Down to Earth").

British Academy of Film & Television Arts (BAFTA) Award: Best Animated Film and Children's Award: Best Feature Film. BAFTA nominations: Best Score and Best Sound.

The voice work in the movie is unique since little of the dialogue is spoken by humans. The mechanical sounds and occasional words that come out of the machines dominate the soundtrack. The sound effects are particularly skillful, creating new and unusual sounds that range from mechanized chatter to soothing white noise. The compelling musical score by Thomas Newman adds considerably to this unconventional soundtrack. Some musical passages are sweeping as in a sci-fi epic, others are delicate and intimate. The use of two Jerry Herman songs from *Hello, Dolly!* is quite ingenious, juxtaposing a period film musical with a dark future. The effect is more than ironic, it is revealing. Some other song standards are heard during the film and Newman wrote an original number, "Down to Earth," with Peter Gabriel for the end credits.

WALL-E opened in 2005 to mostly rapturous reviews and immediate box office success. Although the movie ended up costing $180 million, it earned more than that in six weeks. By the time international receipts were in, *WALL-E* had grossed over $530 million. The DVD and Blu-ray versions were both released in 2008 and were also extremely popular.

Did You Know . . . ?

The shape of the robot EVE may look familiar to many viewers. It was designed by Jonathan Ive, Senior Vice-President of Industrial Design at Apple, who also designed the first iPod.

WALLACE & GROMIT: THE CURSE OF THE WERE-RABBIT

2005

(UK/USA: Aardman/DreamWorks)

Directed by Steve Box and Nick Park
Written by Steve Box, Nick Park, Mark Burton, and Bob Baker
Produced by Cecil Kramer, Michael Rose, Peter Lord, Nick Park, Carla Shelley, Claire Jennings, and David Sproxton
Score by Julian Nott
Specs: Color; 86 minutes; stop-motion and some computer animation

The oddball couple of inventor and cheese enthusiast Wallace and his silent but smart dog, Gromit, had found international fame through a series of stop-motion shorts by Nick Park, so it was probably only a matter of time before the silly duo was starred in a feature film.

British cheese lover Wallace and his dog, Gromit, run a security agency that protects the local vegetable gardens from rabbits while the village is in preparation for the annual Tottington Hall's Giant Vegetable Competition. They have captured so many rabbits that Wallace decides to invent a device that brainwashes the rabbits into losing their appetites for vegetables. Soon the countryside is being tormented by a giant Were-Rabbit who attacks the gardens at night. The hunting enthusiast Lord Victor Quartermaine vows to shoot and kill the Were-Rabbit, but he is shocked when he sees the mild-mannered Wallace turn into the giant creature in the moonlight. The next day, Victor is armed with golden bullets and hunts for the Were-Rabbit, hoping to impress Lady "Totty" Tottington and marry her for her money. The chase causes havoc at the fair, and soon Gromit is involved in an aerial dogfight with Victor's dog, Philip. Wallace, in the form of the Were-Rabbit, kidnaps Totty and climbs the tower of Tottington Hall, where Victor tries to shoot him. Gromit in his plane stops Victor as Wallace falls from the tower and is saved by landing on the cheese tent. Gromit disguises Victor as the Were-Rabbit and the hunter is chased away by the townspeople. Wallace returns to his human form and is given the top prize by Totty, who turns her estate into a sanctuary for rabbits.

Voice Cast

Peter Sallis	Wallace
Ralph Fiennes	Victor Quartermaine
Helena Bonham Carter	Lady Tottington
Peter Kay	PC Mackintosh
Nicholas Smith	Rev. Clement Hedges
Peter Sallis	Hutch

Wallace (right) and his silent but wise dog Gromit, who run a business capturing rabbits who invade the local vegetable gardens, face big trouble when a Were-Rabbit appears. *DreamWorks / Photofest.* © *DreamWorks*

Moviegoers were familiar with Wallace and Gromit from such popular shorts as *A Grand Day Out* (1989), *The Wrong Trousers* (1993), and *A Close Shave* (1995). After the success of Nick Park's stop-motion feature *Chicken Run* (2000), DreamWorks wanted to coproduce a Wallace and Gromit movie with Aardman Animation, but it was not a happy alliance. The American studio kept requesting changes from Park and Aardman to make the film more accessible for American children. DreamWorks even wanted a recognized movie star to voice Wallace instead of British character actor Peter Sallis, who had played Wallace in all the shorts and whose distinctive voice was internationally known. Disagreements about the movie resulted in two different versions of the film, one released in the United States and another for other countries.

WALLACE: Burrowing bounders! They must be breeding like . . . well, rabbits.

Wallace and Gromit: The Curse of the Were-Rabbit required many more characters, settings, and special effects than *Chicken Run* and production took five years, the team of animators averaging three seconds of footage each working day. In addition to the many interiors and exteriors, the film involves hundreds of props, including all kinds of vegetables and flowers. Some scenes utilized dozens of moving characters and others involved complicated effects, such as amusement park planes that fly, rapidly burrowing animals, and Wallace's hilariously complex inventions. The characters were as exaggerated and unrealistic as in the earlier shorts. Interestingly, the animals (including dozens of rabbits) are closer to reality than the human characters, which have outrageously oversized heads, hair, mouths, and ears. The streets and countryside are rendered in a playful but fairly accurate style; even Wallace and Gromit's mechanized house comes across as somewhat believable. The visual humor is matched by the vocals. Peter Sallis's Wallace is as dry and naive as ever. Helena Bonham Carter is a daffy Lady Tottington, and Ralph Fiennes pulls out all the stops as the bullying Victor. Yet the character who most intrigues is Gromit, who never speaks (or even barks) yet conveys attitude and ingenuity with the simplest of facial expressions. Some computer animation was used in the filming, but just about all of *The Curse of the Were-Rabbit* is the result of hands-on stop-motion animation.

Awards

Academy Award: Best Animated Feature Film.
British Academy of Film & Television Arts (BAFTA) Award: Best British Film and the BAFTA Children's Award.

Although the movie cost around $30 million, *Wallace and Gromit: The Curse of the Were-Rabbit* was an immediate hit in Great Britain, Australia, and the United States and ended up grossing $192 million internationally. It was also a hit on DVD in 2006. The film remains one of the most successful of all stop-motion features.

See also *Chicken Run* and *Shaun the Sheep Movie*.

Did You Know . . . ?

The actor Peter Sallis, who voiced Wallace, was in the cast of the British thriller *The Curse of the Werewolf* in 1961.

WATERSHIP DOWN

1978
(UK: Nepenthe Productions)

Produced, directed, and written by Martin Rosen, based on the novel by Richard Adams
Score by Angela Morley
Song "Bright Eyes" by Mike Batt
Specs: Color (Technicolor); 91 minutes; traditional animation

A British animated feature that is far from children's fare, Watership Down *tells a dark story with no compromising in the depiction of violence and the struggle to survive.*

The rabbits living in a warren in the British countryside are careful to avoid their many predators and are thriving under the leadership of their Chief. But the rabbit Fiver has prophetic powers and warns the Chief that the warren will soon be destroyed by man. Few believe Fiver, but he and his brother Hazel lead a group of rabbits out of the warren before it is turned into a new housing development. Hazel and his group follow Fiver's directions to an ideal warren on top of a hill, where they can best protect themselves. They name it Watership Down. But with no females in the group, the community will die out eventually. Hazel leads a party to rescue some females from the Fascist warren run by General Woundwort, and, with the help of the German seagull Kehaar, they succeed, but with some tragic losses. The General and his henchmen follow the rescue party's trail back to Watership Down to take revenge on Hazel and his community. Hazel taunts a dog from a local farm to follow him to Watership Down, where the canine drives away the General's cohorts. The warren prospers and, years later, the aged Hazel dies one day and joins the godlike spirit El-Ahrairah in the sky.

When a housing development threatens to destroy the warren where a colony of rabbits live, some of them head for higher ground only to encounter new dangers. *AVCO Embassy Pictures / Photofest. © AVCO Embassy Pictures*

Voice Cast

John Hurt	Hazel
Richard Briers	Fiver
Ralph Richardson	Chief Rabbit
Michael Graham Cox	Bigwig
John Bennett	Captain Holly
Simon Caddell	Blackberry
Harry Andrews	Gen. Woundwort
Terence Rigby	Silver
Roy Kinnear	Pipkin
Richard O'Callaghan	Dandelion
Lynn Farleigh	Cat
Mary Maddox	Clover
Zero Mostel	Kehaar
Hannah Gordon	Hyzenthlay
Nigel Hawthorne	Captain Campion
Joss Ackland	Black Rabbit
Michael Hordern	Frith

Richard Adams's 1972 novel *Watership Down* was a surprise success, both in Great Britain and internationally. An animated film version was begun by director John Hubley, but after his death in 1977 the project was completed by Martin Rosen, who directed and produced the final film. Some of Hubley's work remains in the prologue, which tells the mythic story of how rabbits were cursed with many predators but blessed with speed. Adams's book was illustrated, and efforts were made to re-create the pastoral look of those pictures in the movie. While the prologue has simple animation with colorful symbols and stylized animals, the rest of the film is rendered in watercolors with a bucolic flavor. The animation of the rabbits is not very detailed and, except for their mouths moving when they speak, there is very little human-like movement. Adams's book is very complex, with many parallels to human civilization. The movie simplifies the story somewhat and rearranges certain events for the sake of a dramatic plot. There is a great deal of violence in the book, and the screen version does not shirk from it. The wounds and blood are not portrayed realistically but are graphic and disturbing all the same. To this day, some parents who unknowingly show the movie to young children are outraged that an animated film about rabbits could be so upsetting.

A sterling cast of mostly British actors was recruited for the voicing of the many characters in *Watership Down*. John Hurt (Hazel), Richard Briars (Fiver), and Harry Andrews (General Woundwort) lead the cast, but even secondary roles are

FIVER: Look. Look. That's the place for us. High, lonely hills, where the wind and the sound carry, and the ground's as dry as straw in a barn. That's where we ought to be. That's where we have to get to.

voiced by such distinguished actors as Ralph Richardson, Denholm Elliott, Nigel Hawthorne, Michael Hordern, Michael Graham Cox, Terence Rigby, and Richard O'Callaghan. The movie's only humor comes from Zero Mostel, who, in his last screen role, voices the cockeyed seagull Kehaar. Angela Morley's soundtrack score for *Watership Down* is a low-key and rather quiet series of tracks that might serve for a nature ballet. Morley's score is subtle, suggesting fear and terror without overtly dramatic music. Among the more peaceful passages is a delicate theme on flute and harp. There is also a mystical section with harp and strings and a slightly swinging theme for the seagull Kehaar. The prologue and main theme, a melancholy yet lyrical piece, was written by Malcolm Williamson. There is also a folk-like ballad, "Bright Eyes" by Mike Batt, that is sung on the soundtrack by Art Garfunkel.

Watership Down opened in England to laudatory reviews, although some complained about the violence in the movie. The box office was very healthy in Great Britain but disappointing in the United States. Over time, the movie has brought in enough money to repay its initial investors a 5,000 percent profit. A picture book of Adams's original story illustrated with scenes from the film was a best seller, there was a television series in 1997, and a BBC mini-series is in development. The fact that an animated film could be so dark and still find a wide audience in 1978 makes *Watership Down* some kind of landmark in movie animation.

See also *The Secret of NIMH.*

Did You Know . . . ?

Although it is rated PG, *Watership Down* is considered one of the most violent animated films ever made.

WHO FRAMED ROGER RABBIT

1988
(USA: Touchstone / Amblin Entertainment)

Directed by Robert Zemeckis (live-action sequences) and Richard Williams (animated sequences)
Written by Jeffrey Price and Peter S. Seaman, based on the book *Who Censored Roger Rabbit?* by Gary K. Wolf
Produced by Steven Spielberg, Kathleen Kennedy, Frank Marshall, Robert Watts, Don Hahn, Steve Starkey, and Alan Dewhurst
Score by Alan Silvestri
Song standards by various artists
Specs: Color; 104 minutes; traditional animation and live action

An ingenious private eye spoof involving humans and animated cartoon characters, the film is outstanding for its highly advanced blending of live-action and hand-drawn animation.

Humans and Toons do not always get along in Hollywood, but private eye Eddie Valiant gets involved with Roger Rabbit when he tries to clear him of a murder charge. *Touchstone Pictures / Photofest. © Touchstone Pictures*

In 1947 Los Angeles, animated characters called toons act in all the Hollywood cartoons and live in a wacky section of town named Toontown. The toon Roger Rabbit suspects that his sexy wife Jessica Rabbit might be unfaithful and is so upset he keeps ruining every shot while making a Baby Herman cartoon. Producer R. K. Maroon hires the washed-up, alcoholic private eye Eddie Valiant to follow Jessica and get photos of her infidelity. Eddie has hated toons and Toontown ever since his brother was killed by a toon, but he accepts the job because he is desperate for money. He takes photos of Jessica playing patty-cake with Marvin Acme, the human jokester who owns the Acme Corporation, which supplies all the gimmick props for cartoons. When Maroon and Eddie show Roger the photos, he explodes and runs off. The next morning Acme is found dead and the powerful Judge Doom is sure Roger is the murderer. Eddie realizes Roger is innocent and hides him from Doom's weasel toons while he searches for the real killer. With the help of his girlfriend, Dolores, Eddie learns that Acme's missing will leaves all of Toontown to the toons and that he was murdered for the valuable real estate. After Maroon is also killed, Eddie and Jessica determine that Doom is the culprit. They and Roger are captured by Doom, who plans to melt the toons and all of Toontown so that he can build a freeway on the site. In the scuffle in the Acme warehouse, Doom is revealed to be a toon in disguise, and the murderer of not only Acme and Maroon but also Eddie's brother. Doom is disintegrated in his own deadly "dip" and the toons rejoice to learn that they own Toontown.

Voice Cast

Charles Fleischer	Roger Rabbit
Kathleen Turner	Jessica Rabbit (speaking)
Amy Irving	Jessica Rabbit (singing)
Lou Hirsch	Baby Herman
David L. Lander	Smart Ass
Fred Newman	Stupid
Richard Williams	Droopy
June Foray	Wheezy
Mel Blanc	Daffy Duck
Mae Questel	Betty Boop
Wayne Allwine	Mickey Mouse
Tony Anselmo	Donald Duck
April Winchell	Mrs. Herman

Live-Action Cast

Bob Hoskins	Eddie Valiant
Christopher Lloyd	Judge Doom
Joanna Cassidy	Dolores
Stubby Kaye	Marvin Acme
Alan Tilvern	R. K. Maroon
Richard LeParmentier	Lieutenant Santino
Joel Silver	Raoul

The Disney studio purchased the film rights to Gary K. Wolf's novel *Who Censored Roger Rabbit?* soon after it was published in 1982, but the project was stalled several times until production began in 1985. Robert Zemeckis directed the live-action footage and Richard Williams directed the animation, but the two tasks overlapped so much that the movie's costs quickly rose. Models and puppets were used to represent the cartoon characters when the live-action scenes were filmed. The animated characters were later added to the film stock, but with such meticulous artistry that the fusion of the two media was innovative and dazzling. Never before had actors had so much physical contact with animated characters on screen. Also, details such as eye contact between the two, shadows of toons on humans and real objects, and the use of actual and animated props were so masterfully done that *Who Framed Roger Rabbit* looked like no other movie. The plot follows the pattern of private eye melodramas of the 1940s but with the added enjoyment of presenting two worlds: the somewhat realistic Hollywood of the time and the chaotic, surreal Toontown. Toons move about the live-action world frequently, and at one point Eddie enters Toontown. The villain, Judge Doom, is a toon disguised as a human, thematically unifying the clever screenplay. While Roger, Jessica, and a few other toons were original for the film, the screen was filled with dozens of familiar Disney and Warner Brothers animated characters. Never before had such famous cartoon characters as Mickey Mouse, Daffy Duck,

Donald Duck, and Bugs Bunny been seen together in one movie. Warner Brothers agreed to the arrangement as long as Disney promised to give equal time to the famous faces from each studio. It is impossible to take in all these notable cartoon stars in one viewing of *Who Framed Roger Rabbit*, but just the presence of so many toons gives the movie a nostalgic glow.

> JESSICA RABBIT: You don't know how hard it is being a woman looking the way I do.
>
> EDDIE VALIANT: You don't know how hard it is being a man looking at a woman looking the way you do.
>
> JESSICA RABBIT: I'm not bad. I'm just drawn that way.

The live-action cast is headed by character actors Bob Hoskins and Christopher Lloyd as Eddie and Judge Doom, both capturing the flavor of a 1940s melodrama even as they satirize it. Also commendable are veteran actors Stubby Kaye and Alan Tilvern as Acme and Maroon. The voice cast gives some delicious performances as well. Charles Fleischer's manic vocals are as exuberant as Roger Rabbit's high-flying movements. Kathleen Turner's deep, sexy voice matches the slithering body language of Jessica. Also splendid is Lou Hirsch's hoarse adult voice for child toon star Baby Herman. Just as the live actors sounded like they were in a 1940s film, the voice actors re-created the brash sound of that decade's cartoons. Similarly, Alan Silvestri's soundtrack music is accurate to the Hollywood scores of 1940s melodramas. There is a haunting main theme for Eddie that aches with loneliness, bluesy and sultry music for Jessica, and prankish melodies for some of the toon sequences. A highlight of the movie is Jessica's lusty rendition of "Why Don't You Do Right?" with Amy Irving singing on the soundtrack.

Awards

Academy Awards: Best Visual Effects, Best Film Editing, and Best Sound Effects, as well as a special Oscar to Richard Williams: the animation characters. Oscar nominations: Best Cinematography, Best Art Direction, and Best Sound.
Golden Globe Award: Best Special Effects. Golden Globe nominations: Best Screenplay, Best Cinematography, Best Editing, and Best Production Design.
British Academy of Film & Television Arts (BAFTA) Awards: Best Special Effects. BAFTA nominations: Best Screenplay, Best Cinematography, Best Editing, and Best Production Design.

When it came time to release *Who Framed Roger Rabbit* in 1988, it became clear that there was too much sex and violence to sell it under the Disney name, so the film opened as a Touchstone Picture, Disney's banner for more adult movies. The $30 million budget had risen to over $50 million, so the studio was very nervous about its critical and popular acceptance. The reviews praised both the film's extraordinary technical aspects and its entertainment value and *Who Framed Roger Rabbit* collected many awards and citations. The public was equally pleased, making the box office strong from the start. By the time the movie was shown internationally, it had earned over \$329 million. The VHS version in 1989 and the DVD edition ten years later both sold well. The Blu-ray version, released in 2013, was the result of a restored print in which the original was digitally enhanced frame by frame. A sequel has been in discussion since 1989, and the possibility of *Who Framed Roger Rabbit 2* is still very real.

Did You Know . . . ?

An old Hollywood superstition says that film titles that end with a question mark are jinxed. So the producers left the question mark out when they titled *Who Framed Roger Rabbit*.

WIZARDS

1977
(USA: Bakshi Productions/20th Century Fox)

Produced, directed, and written by Ralph Bakshi
Score by Andrew Belling
Specs: Color; 80 minutes; traditional animation and live-action footage

---

A highly imaginative sci-fi movie with unusual graphics and backgrounds, Wizards *may be uneven but it was ahead of its time and today is a cult favorite.*

Millions of years after an atomic war has destroyed Earth, the surviving inhabitants of the planet are either mutants, under the leadership of Blackwolf in the land of Scortch, or magical elves and fairies under the protection of the wizard Avatar, Blackwolf's brother, who reigns in Montagar. When Blackwolf rouses the mutants to war by showing ancient film footage of Hitler and the Nazis, Avatar sets out with the fairy Elinor and the elf Weehawk to destroy the movie projector and stop the pro-war propaganda. With them on the journey to Scortch is the robot Necron 99, an assassin for Blackwolf that was converted by Avatar and renamed Peace. Blackhawk launches his mutant attack on the magical creatures, but when Avatar kills Blackwolf and the projector is disabled, the mutant army collapses and there is peace once again.

After finding notoriety with his controversial adult cartoon features such as *Fritz the Cat* (1972) and *Heavy Traffic* (1973), director-animator Ralph Bakshi embarked on an elaborate fantasy project based on folklore and science fiction. Because funding for the movie from 20th Century Fox was limited, Bakshi was not able to develop many of the ideas he had for the film. When he ran out of money and additional funds were refused, he completed some battle scenes by taking old war movies and rotoscoping them. This process of tracing live-action footage onto frames was normally used to save money. Bakshi went further by not tracing the new images but coloring the negatives to create a surreal look that was neither

The robot Necron 99 used to be an assassin for the diabolical wizard Blackwolf, but the good wizard Avatar reformed him and renamed him Peace. *20th Century Fox / Photofest. © 20th Century Fox*

Voice Cast

Bob Holt	Avatar
Steve Gravers	Blackwolf
Jesse Welles	Elinor (speaking)
Susan Anton	Elinor (singing)
Richard Romanus	Weehawk
David Proval	Peace
Christopher Tayback	Peewhittle
Angelo Grisanti	Frog
Jim Connell	President
Hyman Wien	Priest
Barbara Sloane	Fairy
Mark Hamill	Sean
Peter Hobbs	General
Tina Romanus	Prostitute
Ralph Bakshi	Fritz
Susan Tyrrell	Narrator

animation nor live action. Also, actual film footage of Nazi propaganda was used intact as part of Blackwolf's own propaganda scheme. While Bakshi supervised the animation of the characters, he hired such creative artists as Mike Ploog and Ian Miller to provide the background art. The budget did not allow for name actors to supply the voices though narrator Susan Tyrrell and voice actor Mark Hamill later became very famous. The $1.2 million budget nearly doubled by the time postproduction was finished.

AVATAR: I'm too old for this sort of thing. Just wake me up when the planet's destroyed.

There are so many kinds of animation and styles of background art in *Wizards* that the film is always visually interesting even when the plot lags or the characters start to run out of steam. Most impressive are the stunning backgrounds for the different locales. The prologue and bits of narration are accompanied by stills with expressive sketches and muted colors. The land of Scortch is rendered with intricate line drawings filled with grim details. Montagar is illustrated with colorful and simple landscapes of fauna and flora. Often live-action footage of smoke or fire is set behind the animated images, again creating a very unique mix of media. The animation of the characters is not particularly impressive though the design of the creatures and the way they are costumed is highly original. There is also some fine voice work in *Wizards*, such as Bob Holt's Avatar, a fun impersonation of Peter Falk, and Tyrrell's somber but effective narration.

Fox did not give *Wizards* a wide release in 1977, so it took a while for the unusual film to find an audience. Once it did, the box office was very strong, earning $9 million on a $2 million investment. The reviews were mostly approving, applauding the originality of the visuals over the story or the characters. Over the years, *Wizards* has gathered a faithful following and was often seen in art houses before it was available on DVD in 2004. A Blu-ray edition was released in 2012, the thirty-fifth anniversary of the film. Bakshi planned a sequel to *Wizards*, but it has yet to materialize. He used many of this movie's techniques for his 1978 animated adaptation of *Lord of the Rings*, which was a disappointment and a box office failure.

See also *Fritz the Cat*.

Did You Know . . . ?

The film was originally titled *War Wizards*, but George Lucas, who was making the first *Star Wars* movie, asked Bakshi to change the title to *Wizards* so there would be no confusion between the two films. Interestingly, Mark Hamill was in both movies.

Y

YELLOW SUBMARINE

1968
(UK/USA: Apple Films/King Features/United Artists)

Produced by Alan Kozlowski, Al Brodax, and Mary Ellen Stewart
Directed by George Dunning
Written by Lee Minoff, Al Brodax, Erich Segal, and Jack Mendelssohn
Songs written and performed by John Lennon, Paul McCartney, George Harrison, and Ringo Starr
Specs: Color; 90 minutes; traditional animation and some live-action footage

One of the most imaginative animated films of the 1960s, this surreal fantasy featuring cartoon images of the Beatles and their songs remains both a visual and musical treat.

The peaceful, music-loving kingdom of Pepperland, under the wise supervision of Sergeant Pepper and his Lonely Hearts Club Band, is attacked by the Blue Meanies and placed under a frozen spell. The Pepperland citizen Old Fred escapes and seeks the help of the Beatles, Paul, John, George, and Ringo. The Beatles leave their British homeland and travel in a yellow submarine through exotic, fantastical places—such as the Sea of Time, the Sea of Monsters, the Sea of Holes, the Foothills of the Headlands, and the Sea of Nothing—before arriving at the desolate and lifeless Pepperland. Using music and love, the Beatles defeat the Meanies and restore music to the land.

The Beatles (John Lennon, Paul McCartney, George Harrison, and Ringo Starr) were contracted to make three films for United Artists. *A Hard Day's Night* (1964) and *Help!* (1965) were both very popular, but the foursome did not enjoy making *Help!* and wished to somehow get out of their movie commitment. When the Canadian-born producer-director George Dunning suggested an animated film using existing Beatles songs, the Fab Four thought it an ideal way to get out of the movies and concentrate again on studio recordings. Several writers contributed to the screenplay, a good-versus-evil tale set in London and in imaginary worlds. The plot is an episodic journey with many tangents along the way, most inspired by a Beatles song. The dialogue is casual and droll with plenty of in-jokes not likely to be understood by the American public. Even so, some of the lines became fashion-

On their journey to Pepperland to defeat the Blue Meanies, the four Beatles have to travel through the Sea of Holes with the Nowhere Man (far right). *United Artists / Photofest.* © *United Artists*

able catchphrases in pop culture. It was decided early on that the four principal characters would be the four Beatles, as in the two previous Fab Four films. But professional actors were hired to imitate the quartet's speaking voices. The only authentic Beatles' voices heard in the movie are those in the songs, all taken from existing Beatles recordings. There was some disagreement with United Artists over *Yellow Submarine* fulfilling the contract or not. It was indeed a Beatles film,

Voice Cast

John Clive	John (speaking)
John Lennon	John (singing)
Geoffrey Hughes	Paul (speaking)
Paul McCartney	Paul (singing)
Paul Angelis	George (speaking)
Peter Batten	George (speaking)
George Harrison	George (singing)
Paul Angelis	Ringo (speaking)
Ringo Starr	Ringo (singing)
Lance Percival	Old Fred
Dick Emery	Max
Paul Angelis	Chief Blue Meanie
Dick Emery	Nowhere Man
Dick Emery	Lord Mayor
Paul Angelis	Narrator

even though the only contribution by the foursome was to give permission to use their recordings. The Beatles do appear on screen for the brief epilogue, thereby making it indeed a Beatles movie and fulfilling the contract with United Artists. The actors doing the Beatles' speaking voices—John Clive, Geoffrey Hughes, Peter Batten, and Paul Angelis—are more than clever imitators. They have excellent comic timing and deliver their lines in a quietly jovial manner. Director Dunning and the animators used plenty of psychedelic and pop-art design and there was nothing subtle about the drug-induced kind of imagination at work. Yet the movie is primarily a simple, wholesome fable with a childlike view of good and evil.

Songs

"Yellow Submarine"
"Lucy in the Sky with Diamonds"
"All Together Now"
"Eleanor Rigby"
"Hey Bulldog"
"Think for Yourself"
"With a Little Help from My Friends"
"Baby, You're a Rich Man"
"Sgt. Pepper's Lonely Hearts Club Band"
"When I'm Sixty-Four"
"All You Need Is Love"
"Nowhere Man"
"It's All Too Much"
"Only a Northern Song"
"A Day in the Life"

Dunning selected which of the many Beatles songs to use in the film, only a few of them having much to do with the plot. Most of the songs were already hits from the group's albums, so it is arguably the finest collection of Beatles songs ever heard in one film. Aside from the quality of the numbers, the songs revealed the remarkable versatility of the Beatles' work. "Sgt. Pepper's Lonely Hearts Club Band" is an old-time march with a rapid section in the rock mode. "All You Need Is Love" and "All Together Now" are slaphappy sing-along songs, "When I'm Sixty-Four" is an Edwardian music hall turn, "Nowhere Man" is a lazy number sung at half-speed, "Baby, You're a Rich Man" is early rock and roll in the vein of Buddy Holly, "Lucy in the Sky with Diamonds" is a driving number with two very different sections, "With a Little Help from My Friends" is a jovial drinking song, "Eleanor Rigby" is a somber dirge, and the title number is like a 1950s novelty song. With some original background music by George Martin, the soundtrack for *Yellow Submarine* is one of the musical glories of its era.

Artist Peter Max had popularized the Pop Art Movement in the 1960s and the look of *Yellow Submarine* is clearly influenced by it. The art director for the film was the Czech-born illustrator Heinz Edelmann, who adapted some of Max's ideas into three-dimensional images and movie movement. The stills from *Yellow Submarine* are dazzling, but one has to see them in motion in order to fully

GEORGE: Maybe we're both part of a vast yellow submarine fleet.

RINGO: There's only two of us.

JOHN: Well, then, I would suggest that yonder yellow submarine is none other than ourselves . . .

OLD FRED: Going backwards.

JOHN: In time.

appreciate Edelmann's important contribution to the movie. The bright colors of Pop Art are there, but so is the ingenious use of black-and-white photographs in the background. Edelmann also used optical illusions, colored negatives, and a number of other artistic tricks in bringing *Yellow Submarine* to life. The characters themselves are simply drawn with minimal facial expressions. The four Beatles were easily recognized, of course, but each figure was more like a cut-out in a spectacular field of color images. No other film before or since has looked quite like *Yellow Submarine.*

When the movie was released in Great Britain and the United States in 1968, it was greeted with laudatory reviews and vigorous box office. *Yellow Submarine* had cost 250,000 pounds, but by the end of its first release the film grossed four times that much. Because of legal complications over the songs, the movie was not released on VHS until 1987. Restored DVD and Blu-ray versions were not available until 2012, the same year *Yellow Submarine* was rereleased in selected theaters. The movie soundtrack album was a best seller in the 1960s and 1970s and, like the film, continues to be a favorite of Beatles fans.

Did You Know . . . ?

The use of black-and-white photos mixed with colorful cartoon images in *Yellow Submarine* inspired the animator Terry Gilliam, who later did the art work for the *Monty Python's Flying Circus* television programs.

Z

ZOOTOPIA

2016
(USA: Walt Disney Pictures)

Directed by Byron Howard, Rich Moore, and Jared Bush
Written by Jared Bush and Phil Johnston
Produced by John Lasseter and Clark Spencer
Score by Michael Giacchino
The song "Try Everything" by Sia Furler, Tor Erik Hermansen, and Mikkel Storleer
   Eriksen
Specs: Color; 108 minutes; computer and traditional animation

A clever spoof of an urban crime drama, Zootopia *not only has animals playing the usual human types but the film also creates a whole new anthropomorphic world that is as fascinating as it is clever.*

In a world of anthropomorphic mammals, natural instincts have been replaced with a very human-like civilization. The rabbit Judy Hopps grew up on her parents' carrot farm in Bunnyburrow but goes to the big city of Zootropolis, where she wants to be a police officer. Graduating from the Police Academy, Judy finds that few animals take a bunny cop very seriously, and she is assigned to parking duty. Disappointed, she works hard collecting a record number of parking fees. Judy also runs up against the fox Nick Wilde, who is a con man and a thief who slips away before she can arrest him. When she learns of the unsolved police case of the missing otter Emmitt Otterton, Judy volunteers to take on the job. Her investigation brings her back in contact with Nick and, because she believes he has some useful information about the case, Judy gets the sarcastic fox to work with her. The complicated case brings Judy and Nick into the presence of Mr. Big, a tiny shrew who is the crime boss of Zootropolis's underworld. The case also implicates high officials in the city government who are covering up the knowledge that some wolves are reverting to their animal instincts and are preying on other mammals. Judy finds out that Mayor Lionheart's assistant, the sheep Bellweather, is behind a plot to let the predators take over the city. Judy exposes Bellweather

Bureaucracy in the city of Zootropolis can slow things down, as the rabbit Judy Hopps and the fox Nick Wilde discover when trying to get information from the sloth Flash. *Walt Disney Pictures / Photofest. © Walt Disney Pictures*

and is duly decorated. Nick gives up his life of petty crime and joins the police force, where he will work on other cases with Judy.

Zootopia had been conceived as a detective tale with a fox as the antihero. It wasn't until the film was completed and screened with test audiences that the creators realized that they were in trouble. Moviegoers did not identify with or even like the fox Nick Wilde, so the whole film suffered. The Disney artists rethought the entire project, creating the optimistic and hopeful rabbit Judy and making her the center of the story. Nick's wisecracking now had a foil and the relationship

Voice Cast

Della Saba	Judy Hopps (young)
Ginnifer Goodwin	Judy Hopps (adult)
Kath Soucie	Nick Wilde (young)
Jason Bateman	Nick Wilde (adult)
Idris Elba	Chief Bogo
J. K. Simmons	Mayor Lionheart
Maurice LaMarche	Mr. Big
Alan Tudyk	Duke Weaselton
Jenny Slate	Bellweather
Nate Torrence	Clawhauser
Bonnie Hunt	Bonnie Hopps
Don Lake	Stu Hopps
Tommy "Tiny" Lister	Finnick
Tommy Chong	Yax
Leah Latham	Fru Fru
Octavia Spencer	Mrs. Otterton
Shakira	Gazelle
Raymond S. Persi	Flash
Peter Mansbridge	Peter Moosebridge

(as well as the movie) finally worked. Phil Johnston and Jared Bush's screenplay is an accurate homage to the crime melodramas of the past, filled with familiar character types and terse dialogue. The fact that all the characters are mammals is not only refreshing but it provides a wry commentary on the human condition. In one of the movie's most celebrated scenes, Judy and Nick are confronted with the slow-paced bureaucracy of the big city by having to deal with a sloth clerk to get information. The story's underworld is portrayed with hard-nosed satire, culminating in the Godfather-like mobster being played by a diminutive shrew. The script includes many clues, suspects, revelations, and red herrings, making the tale complicated to the point of ridiculousness. Yet the whole movie holds together beautifully and never seems to run out of steam.

> STU: You want to talk about making the world a better place, no better way to do it than becoming a carrot farmer.
>
> BONNIE: Yes! Your dad, me, your 275 brothers and sisters, we're changing the world.
>
> STU: Yeah.
>
> BONNIE: One carrot at a time.
>
> STU: Amen to that.

The look of *Zootopia* is its crowning achievement. The animal characters dress, walk, and talk like humans but each personality is suggested by the species of the mammal. The sly fox Nick—the animators patterned his physical look after the fox hero of Disney's *Robin Hood* (1973)—is an obvious example, as are the buffalo police chief Bono and the lion mayor. Sometimes the animal image works against type. Judy looks like a fluffy bunny in a kids' cartoon, but she has a determined look and a scrappy personality. The mild sheep Bellweather seems timid and forlorn but ends up being the calculating villain. The way each character is costumed is very revealing as well. These animals not only walk on two feet but dress like contemporary humans. As fascinating as the characters is the background art. Zootropolis is a marvelous combination of various neighborhoods each with a distinct character: Tundratown, Rainforest District, Sahara Square, and so on. The city resembles a modern urban center yet has a cockeyed sense of animalia about it. The moviegoer not only sees this bustling metropolis but is immersed in a world as fanciful as Oz.

The contrasting characters of Judy and Nick are voiced well by Ginnifer Goodwin and Jason Bateman. Her rapid delivery is cheerful to the point of annoying, while his lazy, insulting manner helps cut through all the talk of achieving your

Awards

Academy Award: Best Animated Film.
Golden Globe Award: Best Picture—Animated.
British Academy of Film & Television Arts (BAFTA) nomination: Best Animated Feature.

goals and having your dreams come true. *Zootopia* has many characters, and the voice cast is first-class right down to the smallest role. An obvious standout is Maurice LaMarche's Marlon Brando-like Mr. Big, exaggerated just enough to be silly. Michael Giacchino's soundtrack score is a slaphappy combination of different moods and styles. One hears jazz, suspense music, funky dance numbers, jaunty travel music, an Italianate folk theme (for Mr. Big), and even some delicate romantic music. There are a few familiar songs heard on the soundtrack, but none of the characters sing except for the pop star Gazelle (vocal by Shakira), who sings "Try Everything" in a lively concert scene. Because of its intricate plotting and complex visuals, *Zootopia* is a film that can be better appreciated on subsequent viewing. It is more ambitious than most animated movies and is likely to intrigue moviegoers for generations to come.

Zootopia was released in 2016 and was an immediate hit. The movie cost about $140 million but, including the home video versions quickly put on the market, it has already grossed over $1 billion. The notices in the press were almost unanimously positive, many of the reviews applauding its self-motivated heroine and its imaginative world of human-like animals.

Did You Know . . . ?

All of the dozens of different animals in *Zootopia* are mammals. No birds, fish, amphibians, or reptiles were included, although a few insects are seen.

Bibliography

Amidi, Amid. *The Art of Pixar*. San Francisco: Chronicle Books, 2011.

Anderson, Wes. *The Making of "Fantastic Mr. Fox."* New York: Rizzoli, 2009.

Arnold, Gordon B. *Animation and the American Imagination: A Brief History*. Santa Barbara, CA: Praeger Press, 2016.

Bacher, Hans. *Dream Worlds: Production Design for Animation*. Burlington, MA: Focal Press, 2007.

Bailey, Adrian. *Walt Disney's World of Fantasy*. New York: Everest House, 1982.

Bain, David, and Bruce Harris. *Mickey Mouse: Fifty Happy Years*. New York: Harmony Books, 1977.

Bakshi, Ralph. *The Animated Art of Ralph Bakshi*. Atglen, PA: Whitford Press, 1990.

Barrier, Michael. *Hollywood Cartoons: American Animation in Its Golden Age*. New York: Oxford University Press, 2003.

Beck, Jerry. *The Animated Movie Guide*. Chicago: Chicago Review Press, 2005.

Beckman, Karen. *Animating Film Theory*. Durham, NC: Duke University Press, 2014.

Bendazzi, Giannalberto. *Animation: A World History*. Burlington, MA: Focal Press, 2015.

Bennett, Tara. *The Art of "Ice Age."* London: Titan Books, 2016.

———. *The Art of "Rio."* London: Titan Books, 2014.

Brodax, Al. *Up Periscope Yellow: The Making of the Beatles' "The Yellow Submarine."* Pompton Plains, NJ: Limelight Editions, 2004.

Brotherton, Phil. *The Art of "The Boxtrolls."* San Francisco: Chronicle Books, 2014.

Buchan, Suzanne. *Pervasive Animation*. New York: Routledge, 2013.

Cabarga, Leslie. *The Fleischer Story*. Boston: Da Capo Press, 1988.

Canemaker, John. *Magic Color Flair: The World of Mary Blair*. San Francisco: Walt Disney Family Foundation Press, 2014.

———. *Two Guys Named Joe: Master Animation Storytellers Joe Grant and Joe Ranft*. New York: Disney Editions, 2010.

———. *Walt Disney's Nine Old Men and the Art of Animation*. New York: Disney Editions, 2001.

Cavalier, Stephen. *The World History of Animation*. Oakland: University of California Press, 2011.

Cawley, John. *The Animated Films of Don Bluth*. New York: Image Publishers, 1991.

Clarke, James. *Animated Films*. London: Virgin Books, 2010.

———. *The Films of Pixar Animation Studio*. Harpenden, UK: Oldcastle Books, 2013.

Cohen, David S. *The Ballad of "Rango": The Art and Making of an Outlaw Film*. San Rafael, CA: Insight Editions, 2011.

Coyle, Rebecca (ed.). *Drawn to Sound: Animation Film Music and Sonicity*. Sheffield, UK: Equinox Publishing, 2010.

Culhane, John. *Disney's Aladdin: The Making of an Animated Film*. New York: Disney Editions, 1992.

———. *Walt Disney's Fantasia.* New York: Harry N. Abrams, 1999.

Deja, Andreas. *The Nine Old Men: Lessons, Techniques and Inspiration from Disney's Great Animators.* Burlington, MA: Focal Press, 2015.

Deneroff, Harvey. *The Art of "Anastasia."* New York: HarperCollins, 1997.

Docter, Pete. *The Art of "Inside Out."* San Francisco: Chronicle Books, 2015.

Edera, Bruno. *Full Length Animated Feature Films.* Winter Park, FL: Hastings House, 1984.

Finch, Christopher. *The Art of "The Lion King."* New York: Hyperion Books, 1994.

———. *The Art of Walt Disney.* New York: Harry N. Abrams, 1973.

Fleischer, Richard. *Out of the Inkwell: Max Fleischer and the Animation Revolution.* Lexington: University Press of Kentucky, 2005.

Friedman, Jake S. *The Art of Blue Sky Studios.* San Rafael, CA: Insight Editions, 2014.

Furniss, Maureen. *Animation: Art and Industry.* Bloomington, IN: John Libbey Publishing, 2009.

———. *A New History of Animation.* London: Thames & Hudson, 2016.

Gibson, Jon M. *Unfiltered: The Complete Ralph Bakshi.* Bloomington, IN: Universe Press, 2008.

Gilland, Joseph. *Elemental Magic: The Classical Art of Hand-Drawn Special Effects Animation.* Burlington, MA: Focal Press, 2009.

Grant, John. *Encyclopedia of Walt Disney Animated Characters.* New York: Hyperion, 1998.

———. *Masters of Animation.* New York: Watson-Guptil, 2001.

Hahn, Don. *Animation Magic Book: Behind the Scenes Look at How an Animated Film Is Made.* New York: Disney Editions, 1996.

Hansen, Erik. *The Influence of CG Rendering on Animation.* New York: WBP, 2016.

Harryhausen, Ray, and Tony Dalton. *A Century of Stop-Motion Animation.* New York: Watson-Guptil, 2008.

Hauser, Tim. *The Art of "Up."* San Francisco: Chronicle Books, 2009.

———. *The Art of "WALL-E."* San Francisco: Chronicle Books, 2008.

Hieronimus, Robert R. *Inside "The Yellow Submarine."* Iola, WI: Krause Publications, 2002.

Hilty, Greg. *Watch Me Move: The Animation Show.* London: Merrell Publishers, 2011.

Hischak, Thomas. *Disney Voice Actors: A Biographical Dictionary.* Jefferson, NC: McFarland, 2011.

———. *The Oxford Companion to the American Musical: Theatre, Film and Television.* New York: Oxford University Press, 2008.

Holliss, Richard, and Brian Sibley. *The Disney Studio Story.* New York: Crown, 1988.

———. *Walt Disney's Mickey Mouse: His Life and Times.* New York: Harper & Row, 1986.

———. *Walt Disney's "Snow White and the Seven Dwarfs" and the Making of a Classic Film.* New York: Simon and Schuster, 1987.

Hopkins, John. *"Shrek": From the Swamp to the Screen.* New York: Harry N. Abrams, 2004.

Johnston, Ollie, and Frank Thomas. *The Disney Villain.* New York: Hyperion, 1993.

———. *The Illusion of Life: Disney Animation.* New York: Disney Editions, 1995.

———. *Walt Disney's "Bambi": The Story and the Film.* New York: Stewart Tabori & Chang, 1990.

Jones, Chuck. *Chuck Amuck: The Life and Times of an Animated Cartoonist.* New York: Farrar, Straus and Giroux, 1989.

Jones, Kathleen. *"Shrek": The Art of the Quest.* San Rafael, CA: Insight Editions, 2007.

Jones, Stephen. *"Coraline": A Visual Companion.* New York: It Books, Mti Edition, 2009.

Julius, Jessica. *The Art of "Moana."* San Francisco: Chronicle Books, 2016.

———. *The Art of "Zootopia."* San Francisco: Chronicle Books, 2016.

Kallay, William. *The Making of "TRON": How "TRON" Changed Visual Effects and Disney Forever.* Seattle: William Kallay, 2011.

Kaufman, J. B. *"Pinocchio": The Making of the Disney Epic.* San Francisco: Walt Disney Family Foundation Press, 2015.

———. *"Snow White and the Seven Dwarfs": The Art and Creation of Walt Disney's Classic Animated Film*. San Francisco: Walt Disney Family Foundation Press, 2012.

Kemper, Tom. *"Toy Story": A Critical Reading*. London: British Film Institute, 2015.

Kothenschulte, Daniel, and John Lasseter. *The Walt Disney Film Archives: The Animated Movies 1921–1968*. New York: Taschen America, 2016.

Kurtti, Jeff. *The Art of "The Little Mermaid."* New York: Hyperion Books, 1997.

———. *The Art of "Mulan."* New York: Hyperion Books, 1998.

———. *The Art of "The Princess and the Frog."* San Francisco: Chronicle Books, 2009.

———. *The Art of "Tangled."* San Francisco: Chronicle Books, 2010.

———. *"A Bug's Life": The Art and Making of an Epic of Miniature Proportions*. New York: Disney Editions, 1998.

Lasseter, John, and Pete Docter. *The Art of "Monsters, Inc."* San Francisco: Chronicle Books, 2001.

———, and Steve Saly. *"Toy Story": The Art and Making of the Animated Film*. New York: Disney Editions, 1995.

Lawson, Tim, and Alisa Pearsons. *The Magic Behind the Voices: A Who's Who of Cartoon Voice Actors*. Jackson: University Press of Mississippi, 2004.

Lenburg, Jeff. *The Encyclopedia of Animated Cartoons*. New York: Facts on File, 1991.

———. *Who's Who in Animated Cartoons*. New York: Applause Books, 2006.

Levy, Lawrence. *To Pixar and Beyond*. Boston: Houghton Mifflin Harcourt, 2016.

MacLean, Fraser. *Setting the Scene: The Art and Evolution of Animation Layout*. San Francisco: Chronicle Books, 2011.

Maltin, Leonard. *The Disney Films*. Fourth edition. New York: Disney Editions, 2000.

———. *Of Mice and Magic: A History of American Animated Cartoons*. New York: McGraw-Hill, 1980.

March, Julia, and Victoria Taylor (eds.). *Pixarpedia*. New York: DK Publishers, 2009.

Meinel, Dietmar. *Pixar's America: The Re-Animation of American Myths and Symbols*. New York: Palgrave Macmillan, 2016.

Miller-Zarneke, Tracey, and Cressida Cowell. *The Art of "How to Train Your Dragon."* New York: Newmarket Press, 2010.

———. *The Art of "Meet the Robinsons."* New York: Disney Editions, 2007.

Osmond, Andrew. *100 Animated Feature Films*. London: British Film Institute, 2011.

Paik, Karen. *The Art of "Monsters University."* San Francisco: Chronicle Books, 2013.

———. *The Art of "Ratatouille."* San Francisco: Chronicle Books, 2007.

———. *To Infinity and Beyond: The Story of Pixar Animation Studios*. San Francisco: Chronicle Books, 2007.

Pallant, Chris. *Demystifying Disney: A History of Disney Feature Animation*. London: Bloomsbury Academic, 2013.

Pilcher, Steve. *The Art of "Finding Dory."* San Francisco: Chronicle Books, 2016.

Pointer, Ray. *The Art and Inventions of Max Fleischer: American Animation Pioneer*. Jefferson, NC: McFarland, 2016.

Price, David A. *The Pixar Touch: The Making of a Company*. New York: Vintage, 2009.

Priebe, Ken A. *The Advanced Art of Stop-Motion Animation*. Boston: Cengage Learning PTR, 2010.

Rebello, Stephen. *The Art of "Hercules": The Chaos of Creation*. New York: Hyperion Books, 1997.

———. *The Art of "The Hunchback of Notre Dame."* New York: Hyperion Books, 1996.

———. *The Art of "Pocahontas."* New York: Hyperion Books, 1995.

Salisbury, Mark. *"Frankenweenie": The Visual Companion*. New York: Disney Editions, 2013.

Schickel, Richard. *The Disney Version: The Life, Times, Art and Commerce of Walt Disney*. Revised edition. New York: Touchstone, 1986.

Sibley, Brian. *"Chicken Run": Hatching the Movie.* New York: Harry N. Abrams, 2000.

Smith, Dave. *Disney A to Z: The Official Encyclopedia.* Third edition. New York: Disney Editions, 2006.

Smoodin, Eric. *Snow White and the Seven Dwarfs.* London: British Film Institute, 2012.

Solomon, Charles. *The Art of "Frozen."* San Francisco: Chronicle Books, 2013.

———. *Enchanted Drawings: The History of Animation.* New York: Random House, 1994.

———. *Tale as Old as Time: The Art and Making of "Beauty and the Beast."* New York: Disney Editions, 2017.

———. *The "Toy Story" Films: An Animated Journey.* New York: Disney Editions, 2012.

Thomas, Bob. *Disney's Art of Animation: From Mickey Mouse to "Hercules."* New York: Hyperion Books, 1997.

Thomas, Frank, and Ollie Johnson. *Disney Animation: The Illusion of Life.* New York: Abbeville Press, 1981.

Vaz, Mark Cotta. *The Art of "Bolt."* San Francisco: Chronicle Books, 2008.

———. *The Art of "Finding Nemo."* San Francisco: Chronicle Books, 2003.

———. *The Art of "The Incredibles."* San Francisco: Chronicle Books, 2004.

Webb, Graham. *The Animated Film Encyclopedia.* Jefferson, N.C.: McFarland, 2011.

Weber, Francis. *Mickey's Golden Jubilee.* Los Angeles: Junipero Serra Press, 1979.

Weishar, Peter. *Blue Sky: The Art of Computer Animation.* New York: Harry N. Abrams, 2002.

Wells, Paul. *Understanding Animation.* New York: Routledge, 1998.

Wiedermann, Julius. *Animation Now!* Cologne, Germany: Taschen, 2007.

Wright, Jean Ann. *Voice-Over for Animation.* Burlington, MA: Focal Press, 2009.

Zahed, Ramin. *The Art of DreamWorks Animation.* New York: Harry N. Abrams, 2014.

Index

Note: Page numbers in bold indicate the main entry for a film.

Gibson, Mel, 70, 253
Gilbert, Billy, 297
Gilbert, Ray, 211, 301, 321
Gilkyson, Terry, 30, 165
Gilliam, Terry, 355
Glasser, Paul, 14
Glover, Danny, 27
Glover, Savion, 133
Goldberg, Eric, 252
Goldberg, Whoopie, 189
Goldman, Gary, 17
Goldsmith, Jerry, 224, 283
Goldthwait, Bobcat, 137
Goldwyn, Sam, 219
Goldwyn, Tony, 317
Gone with the Wind, 301
The Good, the Bad and the Ugly, 260–61
Gooding, Cuba, Jr., 140
Goodman, Benny, 198–200
Goodman, John, 94, 217
Goodwin, Ginnifer, 358
The Goof Troop, 120
A Goofy Movie, **120–23**
Gottfried, Gilbert, 6–7
Gould, Alexander, 104
Graden, Brian, 304
Grahame, Kenneth, 3–4, 117
Grammer, Kelsey, 18, 326
A Grand Day Out, 340
Grant, Campbell, 4
Grant, Joe, 172–73
Grant, Richard E., 80
The Great Escape, 69, 287
The Great Mouse Detective, 15, **123–26**
Greene, Ward, 173
Gregson-Williams, Harry, 27, 71, 289
Greno, Nathan, 312
Grimes, Tammy, 180
Grimm, Jacob and Wilhelm, 255, 296, 312
Groff, Jonathan, 114
Guaraldi, Vince, 52
Guillaume, Robert, 189
Gulliver's Travels, **126–30**, 218–20

Hackman, Gene, 27
Haimes, Marc, 167
Halas, John, 21–22
Hall, Ellis, 71
Hall, Ron, 212
Hamill, Mark, 350–51
Hamlet, 188

Handling Ships, 22
Hanks, Tom, 63, 324–25
Hanna, William, 66
Hannah, Daryl, 194
Hansen, Daniel, 206
Happy Feet, **131–34**, 271
Happy Feet Two, 134
A Hard Day's Night, 352
Harline, Leigh, 220, 248, 297
Harris, Estelle, 326
Harris, Jared, 49
Harris, Joel Chandler, 300
Harris, Phil, 30, 164, 279
Harrison, George, 168, 352
Hartman, Elizabeth, 283
Hartman, Phil, 55
Hatcher, Teri, 77
Hathaway, Anne, 271
Hawthorne, Nigel, 317, 344
Head, Edith, 154
Heath, Gordon, 22
Heavy Traffic, 111, 348
Hello, Dolly!, 335, 338
Help!, 352
Henney, Daniel, 42
Henrikson, Lance, 317
Hercules, 94, **134–38**, 212
Hercules: The Animated Series, 138
Hercules: Zero to Hero, 138
Here Be Monsters!, 48
Herman, Jerry, 338
Herrmann, Bernard, 105
Hickey, William, 229
High Noon, 260
Himelstein, Mike, 290
Hingle, Pat, 177
Hinnant, Skip, 110
Hirsch, Lou, 347
Hirschfeld, Al, 6, 99
Hoffman, Al, 74
Hoffman, Dustin, 171
Holloway, Sterling, 11, 164, 199, 203
Holly, Buddy, 354
Holm, Ian, 264
Holmes, Taylor, 293
Holt, Bob, 350
Home Improvement, 325
Home on the Range, **138–42**
Hong, James, 171, 224
Ho'omalu, Mark Keali'i, 186
Hope, Bob, 271, 274–76

About the Author

Thomas S. Hischak is an internationally recognized author and teacher in the performing arts. He is the author of twenty-eight nonfiction books about film, theatre, and popular music, including *1939: Hollywood's Greatest Year, The Oxford Companion to the American Musical, The Encyclopedia of Film Composers, The Rodgers and Hammerstein Encyclopedia, Broadway Plays and Musicals, Through the Screen Door, The Tin Pan Alley Encyclopedia, Disney Voice Actors, The Disney Song Encyclopedia, Word Crazy: Broadway Lyricists, American Literature on Stage and Screen, Theatre as Human Action*, and *The Oxford Companion to American Theatre*.

He is also the author of forty published plays that are performed in the United States, Canada, Great Britain, and Australia. Hischak is a Fulbright scholar who has taught and directed theatre in Greece, Lithuania, and Turkey.

Hischak is emeritus professor of theatre at the State University of New York at Cortland, where he has received such honors as the 2004 SUNY Chancellor's Award for Excellence in Scholarship and Creative Activity and the 2010 SUNY Outstanding Achievement in Research Award.